William Bernard Brownlow

A short History of the Catholic Church in England

William Bernard Brownlow

A short History of the Catholic Church in England

ISBN/EAN: 9783743329300

Manufactured in Europe, USA, Canada, Australia, Japa

Cover: Foto ©ninafisch / pixelio.de

William Bernard Brownlow

A short History of the Catholic Church in England

A SHORT HISTORY OF THE CATHOLIC CHURCH IN ENGLAND.

A SHORT HISTORY

OF THE

CATHOLIC CHURCH IN ENGLAND

SECOND AND REVISED EDITION

LONDON
CATHOLIC TRUTH SOCIETY
21 WESTMINSTER BRIDGE ROAD S.E.

1897.

PREFACE TO FIRST EDITION

THE Father of English History, in his preface to *The Ecclesiastical History of the English Nation*, commends the earnest study of the actions of men of renown, especially of our own nation. "For if history relates good things of good men, the attentive hearer is excited to imitate that which is good; or, if it mentions evil things of wicked persons, nevertheless the religious and pious hearer or reader, shunning that which is hurtful and perverse, is the more earnestly excited to perform those things which he knows to be good and worthy of God." The history of the Church is the record of a divine institution, of the fortunes of the Bride of Christ in her way through this world. There are the divine and the human elements. There are the mind and will of man, actuated by all the various passions and motives that influence man; and there is the Spirit of God ever abiding in the Church, preserving her from error, overruling evil for good, and guiding her by strange and mysterious ways to the end for which she is destined. If we had an inspired historian, like the compiler of the Paralipomenon, we should be able clearly to distinguish between the action of God and the spirit of man. As it is, we can only try to interpret history by the application of those principles of right and wrong which our holy Religion gives us, and by comparing together "things new and old." The first matter of importance is to get the facts accurately reported, and then we can proceed to draw our conclusions from them. There is, in this country, an increasing desire to know the exact truth, whether it be palatable or not. Libraries at home and abroad are being searched for MSS. that throw light on every historical detail. Ruins of ancient buildings are carefully explored, and, by the aid of descriptions and plates, the old historic edifices are made to rise again, and tell their story of what took place within their walls. That many mistakes are made in this process of imaginary reconstruction is, of course, inevitable; but they will be corrected in due time by further discoveries. The series published under the supervision of the Master of the Rolls, the Calendars of State Papers, the Reports of the Historical Parliamentary Commission, the publications of the Camden and Surtees, and (more recently) of the "Henry Bradshaw" Societies, the

Episcopal Registers of Exeter, edited by Prebendary Hingeston-Randolph, and a variety of papers printed in the transactions of different County Archæological Societies have brought together such a mass of valuable material for the History of England, that it becomes a matter of considerable difficulty to one who wishes to write a short History to select the particular materials that will be most useful, since it is impossible for him to master all.

The English Church History contained in this volume does not pretend to be full or exhaustive enough to be of much service to learned students. It claims to be a simple, but, as far as possible, an accurate, account of the History of Catholic Christianity in this country. Pains have been taken to verify the facts recorded, to relate in some detail the more salient points in the story, and to bring into prominence the important lessons that the events teach us. Attempts have been made frequently during the last fifty years to make the History of the Church a weapon wherewith to attack the Church herself. *Tales of the Ancient British Church* used to fill the imaginations of English children with the dream of a primitive Church in this country that was not only independent of Rome, but in doctrine and practice Protestant. The "continuity theory" was sedulously propagated by the late Professor Freeman in his *Norman Conquest*, and anti-Catholic prejudice has been not a little strengthened through the brilliant romance of the Tudor period by the late Mr. J. A. Froude. A number of Anglican clergy and laymen are trying diligently, by the aid of beautiful magic lantern slides, to prop up the tottering cause of the Established Church by indoctrinating the masses with very misleading ideas about even the bare facts of English Church History. It is hoped that this little volume will do something towards correcting these mistakes; and thus enable Catholics, who have not time to study larger works, to answer popular objections. It is published at the lowest possible price, so as to be within the reach of all. It is hoped that those who are charged with the education of Catholic youths in colleges, convents, and other schools, even in elementary schools, may see their way to use it as a text-book, so that their pupils may grow up with at least a good elementary knowledge of so important a branch of history. Those who have the charge of schools and lending libraries will do well to see that this History finds a place among their volumes.

I venture to call attention to a few points in our national history. Our knowledge of the ancient British Church must necessarily be very imperfect. It is by putting together what little is known, and filling up the details by a reference to contemporary history that we can alone hope to arrive at a true idea of what it was. It has been my conviction for years that, as St. Irenaeus was the contemporary of Pope Eleutherius, in or about whose time British Christianity first comes into notice, it is from that Father's works that we can gather the most authentic knowledge of the doctrine and practice of the British Church. Bishop Stubbs and Mr. Haddan, who reject the account that Bede gives of the missionaries sent by Eleutherius, ascribe British Christianity to the Church of Lyons, of which St. Irenaeus was Bishop. If the British Church learned Christianity from Lyons, it must have agreed with the celebrated *dictum* of St. Irenaeus:—

" In every Church there is, for all who may wish to see what things are true, the tradition of the Apostles made manifest throughout the whole world. And we have in our power to enumerate those who were by the Apostles instituted Bishops in the Churches, and the successors of those Bishops down to ourselves . . . But, as it would be a very long task to enumerate the successions of all the Churches, . . . we point out that tradition which the greatest, most ancient, and universally known Church—founded and constituted at Rome by the two most glorious Apostles, Peter and Paul—derives from the Apostles. For with this Church, on account of its more powerful headship, it is necessary that every Church, that is the faithful everywhere dispersed, should agree ; in which Church has always been preserved that tradition which is from the Apostles" (*Adv. Haer.* iii. 3).

In the same way, although Dr. Lingard has brought out clearly enough the conformity of the Anglo-Saxon Church with the doctrine and practice of the Catholic Church now; yet that conformity would have been made even more striking if the whole teaching of St. Gregory the Great had been treated as part of the evidence, for it is inconceivable that the Anglo-Saxon Church should have rejected any part of the teaching of its Apostle. The close and intimate union of that Church with Rome, and the glorious band of saints which it produced in its golden age, make that period of our national history most delightful to study.

The notion that submission to the Pope was brought into England by the Norman Conquest is another historical fallacy that the sober facts of history will dispel. In fact, the jealousy of Rome, and the placing of legal barriers between the English clergy and their head, the Pope, only dates from the times of the Conqueror, though it comes out again and again in various statutes which paved the way for the schism of the sixteenth century.

The part of this volume which will strike most readers as somewhat new is that dreary time from Elizabeth to the end of the last century. The writer has treated this period with great care; and, without entering into too many harrowing details, has told the

Preface.

story of the patient endurance of English Catholics through the two centuries of persecution in a way that cannot fail to touch the heart, and move our gratitude to those who handed down the torch of truth under such terrible difficulties. Their patience, not less than the heroic constancy of our recently beatified martyrs and the glories of the Saints of more ancient times, quickens our faith, stimulates our hope, and enkindles our charity. They encourage us to meet with cheerful confidence our own little trials, and to say: "We are the children of saints, and look for that life which God will give to those that never change their faith from Him" (*Tob.* ii. 18).

✠ W. R. BROWNLOW.
BISHOP OF CLIFTON.

Whitsuntide, 1895.

PREFACE TO SECOND EDITION

In this Second Edition several corrections and amendments have been made, so as to render the History more accurate in detail. The chief improvements, however, are the addition of an Index, and of a Chronological Table extending from the landing of St. Augustine to the Bull of Pope Leo XIII. on Anglican Orders. For this we are indebted to the Rev. Luke Rivington. With a view to render the work more useful as a text-book in schools, the principal events are marked by titles in Clarendon type, so as to arrest the attention and impress more strongly on the memory of the reader the more prominent facts of English Church History.

☩ W. R. B.

Clifton, January 21, 1897.

CONTENTS

CHAPTER I.

THE EARLY BRITISH CHURCH 1

Uncertainty regarding the first introduction of Christianity into Britain — Early traditions — Missioners sent by Pope Eleutherius — The hierarchy established in Britain — Persecution under Diocletian — Alban the Proto-martyr — Conversion of the Empress Helena — British bishops present at the Council of Arles — Their loyalty to the Holy See — St. Ninian and St. Palladius sent from Rome to Britain — St. Patrick converts Ireland — St. Kieran and St. Cadoc — The Pelagian heresy — It is combated by St. Germanus and St. Lupus — Defeat of the Picts in the Alleluia battle — Second visit of St. Germanus to Britain — Saxon invasion — British Christians driven into Wales — The Church lives and flourishes there.

CHAPTER II.

CONVERSION OF THE ANGLO-SAXONS . . . 17

Some British children attract the attention of Pope Gregory I. in the market-place at Rome — He determines to attempt the evangelization of Britain, and sends Augustine thither — Reception of the missionaries by Ethelbert — Conversion of the men of Kent — Augustine obtains episcopal consecration at Arles — He founds Canterbury Cathedral — He asks the Pope's decision on some questions of morals and discipline — Reason of the difference between Celtic customs and Roman use — Augustine seeks to introduce uniformity — The Britons reject his proposals, and refuse to co-operate in the conversion of the Saxons — Fulfilment of Augustine's prediction — Laurentius succeeds Augustine in the archiepiscopal see — Final establishment of conformity in Wales and Ireland—Spread of the Gospel among the East Saxons—Their return to heathenism—Misfortunes of the Church in Kent—Laurentius is arrested by a vision on the eve of departure—Paulinus, consecrated bishop, accompanies a Kentish princess to the north—The Christian religion is accepted in Northumbria—Labours of Paulinus—East Anglia converted by Felix.

CHAPTER III.

ENGLAND A CHRISTIAN COUNTRY . . . 35

Invasion of Northumbria and massacre of the Christians—Flight of Paulinus—Oswald gains a victory and ascends the throne of Northumbria—St. Aidan fixes his see at Lindisfarne—St. Birinus the Apostle of the West Saxons—Death of Oswald—Proofs of his sanctity—Penda ravages Northumbria, and invades Wessex—Missioners penetrate into the kingdom of Mercia—Second mission to the East Saxons—Cedd is consecrated bishop—Extension of Christianity in Mercia on the death of Penda—St. Chad, Bishop of Lichfield—Conversion of Sussex by Wilfrid—Temporal advantages consequent on the adoption of the true religion.

CHAPTER IV.

CONFIRMATION OF THE PAPAL AUTHORITY . . 49

Dispute in Northumbria concerning the time of celebrating Easter—All differences ended at the Whitby Council—Colman resigns his bishopric rather than adopt the Roman use—Wilfrid appointed to succeed him—Transfers the see to York—Chad supersedes Wilfrid—Theodore is sent from Rome to fill the see of Canterbury—All the English bishops are placed under his authority—He reinstates Wilfrid—Decrees of the Council of Hertford—The organization of the Church a model for the State—Wilfrid appeals to Rome against the judgement of his metropolitan, and obtains a decision in his favour—On his return he is exiled from Northumbria—Synod of Hatfield—Wilfrid is restored to the bishopric of York—Is persecuted again by the king for maintaining his right—Wilfrid again journeys to Rome to appeal to the Sovereign Pontiff against injustice—The result of this appeal

Contents.   xvii

CHAPTER V.
                                                        PAGE
SOME SAINTS OF THE ANGLO-SAXON CHURCH   66

Cuthbert the great Thaumaturgus—Eadbert, his successor at Hexham—Benedict Biscop—Civilization and learning promoted through his exertions—Hilda, Abbess of Whitby— Whitby a seminary for learned and holy priests—Cædmon, the bard-monk—Aldhelm, the minstrel-bishop—His attachment to the see of Peter—The Venerable Bede—His literary ability and industry—Alcuin, the scholar and theologian— Egwin, Bishop of Worcester—His devotion to the Blessed Mother of God—King Ina rebuilds the abbey of Glastonbury —His benefactions to the Church—Willibrord and other English monks preach the Gospel in Friesland—Boniface, the Apostle of Germany—His labours and martyrdom—Willibald and Winibald, his nephews.

CHAPTER VI.
TROUBLES OF THE ANGLO-SAXON CHURCH .   86

Relaxation of morals and discipline in the English Church— St. Boniface urges reform of the prevalent abuses—Council of Cloveshoe—Pope Adrian I. sends two Legates to England— Method of ratifying documents—Offa, king of Mercia—Payment of Peter's pence introduced—Harassing invasions of the Danes—Destruction of monasteries—King Ethelwulf journeys to Rome with his son Alfred—Payment of tithes enforced by a law of the State—Further depredations of the Danes—Fate of King Edmund—Alfred conquers the Danes, and obliges them to embrace Christianity—His devotion to the welfare of his subjects—Degeneracy of the English clergy—Canons respecting celibacy—Archbishop Odo—St. Dunstan—Reforms effected by him whilst Primate of England—Ethelwold, Bishop of Winchester—The story of Eadburga—The Abbess Edith—Council of Winchester—Dunstan's fearlessness in rebuking vice—His death.

CHAPTER VII.
RESTORATION OF TRANQUILLITY   .   .   108

Fresh incursions of the Danes—Massacre of St. Brice's Day— Martyrdom of Archbishop Elphege—Cnut the model of a wise and Christian monarch—His reverence for the See of Peter

PAGE

and the Blessed Virgin—His rebuke of flattery—Retrogression in Church matters—Edward the Confessor—His sanctity—His reasons for appointing Normans to high posts in Church and State — Flight of Archbishop Robert — Stigand usurps his place—Aldred's election to the see of York—Wulstan—Aldred defends the property of the Church—Westminster Abbey rebuilt by Edward the Confessor—Invasion of England by William of Normandy—The Rood at Waltham—William the Conqueror receives the crown.

CHAPTER VIII.

THE FAITH AND PRACTICE OF THE ANGLO-SAXON CHURCH 124

Docility of our forefathers in matters of faith—Pilgrimages a favourite devotion of the English—Distant shrines—English sanctuaries—Devotion to the Blessed Mother of God—Origin of the Feast of the Conception—Our Lady of Coventry—The Rosary—Devotion to the Holy Eucharist—Care for the service of the sanctuary—Rigorous penances of ancient times—Communion under one kind—Position and income of the clergy—Gilds—Prayers for the departed—Method of announcing deaths—The Book of Life—Story of Imma—The "month's mind."

CHAPTER IX.

CHANGES CONSEQUENT ON THE NORMAN CONQUEST 146

The Normans not an alien race—Policy of William I.—Synod of Winchester—Stigand is removed, and the see given to Lanfranc—The difficulties he encounters—His reception by the Pope—The formation of Ecclesiastical Courts—Trial by ordeal—Changes introduced by Lanfranc—Anselm, Abbot of Bec, visits England—Death of William the Conqueror—His character contrasted with that of his successor—Ralph the Firebrand—Anselm chosen Archbishop—Evil conduct and temporary repentance of Rufus—Council of Rockingham—Subservience of the prelates to the King—Rufus pillages the Church, and persecutes Anselm—Anselm retires to Lyons until the King's death.

CHAPTER X.

THE CHURCH UNDER THE NORMANS . . . 169

The reign of Henry I.—A period of struggle and dispute—The right of investiture—Ancient manner of electing bishops—Decrees of the Council of Clermont—Reasons why Anselm refused investiture at Henry's hands—The dispute is referred to the Papal Court for settlement—Enactments of the Council of Winchester—The King persists in investing bishops—Anselm refuses to consecrate those that are so invested—He journeys once more to Rome—The King seizes the archiepiscopal estates, and levies a fine on the clergy—A compromise is effected—Death of Anselm—A Papal Legate is sent to settle the respective jurisdiction of York and Canterbury—The Church in Scotland declared directly dependent on the Holy See—Rise of the Cistercian Order—The clergy support Stephen's claim to the throne—He alienates them by his injustice—Miserable condition of the country—Heroic conduct of Thurstan, Archbishop of York—The succession is secured for Henry of Anjou by Archbishop Theobald—Rise of the system of Universities.

CHAPTER XI.

ST. THOMAS OF CANTERBURY . . . 189

An English Pope—Henry II. chooses Thomas à Becket for his Chancellor—Character and conduct of Becket—He is created Archbishop, and resigns the Chancellorship—He opposes the King in the matter of taxation—First serious rupture between the Archbishop and the King—Constitutions of Clarendon—Becket refuses to subscribe them—He is forced to fly to France—Embassy to the Pope—Becket is confirmed in the primacy, and made Apostolic Legate—Insults offered to him by Henry—England is threatened with an interdict—Henry yields—A reconciliation is effected—Becket returns to England—His martyrdom—Devotion of Becket to the Blessed Virgin—Remorse of the King—Becket is canonized—His shrine becomes a place of pilgrimage—Submission of Henry to the Papal See—Shame and misery of the last years of his reign.

CHAPTER XII.

STRUGGLES BETWEEN CHURCH AND STATE . . 210

Government of the State confided to ecclesiastics during the absence of the King—Longchamp, Bishop of Ely—Hubert,

Contents.

PAGE

Bishop of Salisbury, is created Primate and Chief Justiciary of England—Rising of the populace in London—Evils ensuing on the absorption of the clergy in secular matters—Services rendered to the country by Hugh, Bishop of Lincoln—Character of King John—Differences between the cathedral chapter and the suffragan bishops concerning the election of the Primate—Choice of a successor to Archbishop Hubert—Appeal to Rome—The Pope's decision rejected by the King—England is laid under an interdict—Excommunication of John—Right of the sovereign Pontiff to depose Christian princes—John, being deposed, resigns his crown to the Papal envoy, and receives it from him as the Pope's vassal—Justification of his conduct—Attitude assumed by Langton on his elevation to the primacy—The Great Charter is annulled and Langton suspended by the Pope—Reasons for this act—On the accession of Henry III., Langton resumes the government of his diocese—Rise of the Universities of Oxford and Cambridge—Coming of the Friars—St. Edmund of Canterbury—His struggles to defend the clergy and laity against royal aggression—He retires from the contest.

CHAPTER XIII.

GRIEVANCES OF THE CHURCH IN ENGLAND . 238

Efforts of Grosseteste, Bishop of Lincoln, to effect a reform of discipline—"The Pope's militia"—Grosseteste opposes the presentation of foreign ecclesiastics to English benefices—His veneration for and obedience to the Holy See—Displeasure caused to the nation by the exercise of the papal right of supersession—Insurrection of the Barons—Limits of the spiritual and temporal jurisdiction defined in the reign of Edward I.—The clergy are summoned to Parliament—Statute of Mortmain—Excessive taxation of the clergy by the King—They resist his exactions—The Bull *Clericis laicos*—Privileges won for the nation by the exertions of Churchmen—Archbishop Winchelsey—Suppression of the Order of Templars—The Church again involved in disputes with the Crown—The Black Death—Its disastrous consequences—Non-payment of the tribute promised by John—Explanation and justification of the system of Provisions—Statutes of Provisors and of *Præmunire*—The civil government is withdrawn from the hands of churchmen.

Contents.   xxi

CHAPTER XIV.

WYCLIF AND THE LOLLARDS 266

Opposition of the Norman King to temporal jurisdiction on the part of the Pope—A spirit of insubordination to papal authority creates a predisposition to heresy in the nation—Wyclif attacks first the practice, then the doctrines of the Church—His "Poor Priests" disseminate revolutionary principles—Revolt of the Commons—Heretical teaching of Wyclif and his followers suppressed in Oxford—Wyclif retires to Lutterworth—His death—Translations of Holy Scripture—Study of the Scriptures approved by the Church—Doctrines of the Lollards subversive of social order—Religious development of Lollardism—Stringent measures passed in Parliament for the suppression of heresy—Sir John Oldcastle.

CHAPTER XV.

CONDITION OF THE CHURCH BEFORE THE REFORMATION   288

French legislation on the subject of Papal Provisions—Statute of *Præmunire* confirmed—Operation of these statutes unfavourable to the progress of learning—Interference of the Supreme Pontiff for their abolition—Disobedience not a denial of authority—Evidence of England's loyalty to the Holy See—The three Patrons of England—Devotion of Mediæval England to the Mother of God—Our Lady's Dowry—Famous shrines of our Lady—Walsingham—Offerings made by pilgrims—Religious gilds—Causes of religious discontent in England, which rendered the Reformation possible—Deterioration and demoralization of the clergy—The Great Schism of the West—The Church a promoter of learning.

CHAPTER XVI.

EVENTS IMMEDIATELY PRECEDING THE SCHISM . 310

Revival of letters in Italy—The movement assumes a religious aspect in England—Archbishop Warham—Colet—Erasmus—More—Henry VIII. a patron of the "New Learning"—Evil tendency of the movement in Germany—Luther's writings burnt at St. Paul's Cross—The King desires his marriage to be annulled—Reasons for a divorce—Title of Defender of the Faith conferred on Henry—Rise of Wolsey—He is supreme in Church and State—Opinions of theologians concerning the divorce—A Legatine Court of inquiry opened in England by order of the Pope—Queen Catherine appeals to the Holy See—Fall of Wolsey—The Chancellorship accepted by More—The King claims to be Supreme Head of the Church—The Convocation of Canterbury concedes the title, with a qualifying clause—Slow progress of the matrimonial suit—Policy of Clement VII.—Cranmer is made Archbishop—His oath at consecration—He pronounces the marriage with Catherine void, and solemnizes the marriage with Anne—Her coronation and excommunication.

CHAPTER XVII.

THE ROYAL SUPREMACY 332

The Royal authority substituted for the Papal by Act of Parliament—The bishops and others agree to this—Reasons why the new order of things was acquiesced in by the nation—Conduct of the bishops inexcusable—How the struggles of previous centuries prepared the way for the assumption of Royal Supremacy—Penal statutes to enforce conformity powerless in some instances—Execution of Carthusian monks—Martyrdom of Bishop Fisher and of Sir Thomas More—Rise of Thomas Cromwell—His activity as royal vicegerent—Suppression of monasteries in earlier times—Their wholesale spoliation and destruction by Henry's Commissioners—The Pilgrimage of Grace—Fate of the Abbot of Glastonbury—Alienation of the Church property—Miseries of the poorer folk in consequence of the dissolution of monasteries—The Headship of the Pope acknowledged as an integral part of Catholic belief in pre-Reformation times.

CHAPTER XVIII.

CHANGES IN DOCTRINE 356

Action of the Papal Court in regard to the schism of the English Church—Cardinal Pole is appointed Legate—Failure of his mission—Changes in the Form of Worship and articles of belief made by the King—Revival of Lollardry—Bishop Latimer burns the effigies of our Lady—Henry endeavours to arrest the rapid progress of innovation—Six articles of doctrine—The King's Book—Ascendency of the Protestant party on the accession of Edward VI.—Further spoliation of the Church—The First Book of Common Prayer—Revolt of the people in consequence of the abolition of Catholic practices

Contents.   xxiii

PAGE

—Introduction of foreign divines—Work of Cranmer and his Protestant Council — Testimony of modern non-Catholic writers to the social evils resulting from the change of religion—Reversal in the position of ecclesiastical parties on the accession of Queen Mary.

CHAPTER XIX.

REUNION WITH ROME 373

Caution with which the Queen acted in regard to religious changes—The Reformers prohibited from preaching in public —Obstacles in the way of the re-introduction of Catholic worship—Recognition of the Queen's legitimacy by Parliament, and repeal of the religious acts of the preceding reign— Cardinal Pole is again appointed Papal Legate—The Spanish alliance—Negotiations with Rome concerning the holders of Church property—Public reconciliation of England with Rome —Submission of the clergy to the Holy See, and re-establishment of the ancient system of religious polity—Violent invectives of reformed preachers—Three propositions as a test of heresy—Conviction and punishment of obdurate heretics— Ridley and Latimer are burnt at Oxford—Cranmer's vacillation and death at the stake—Labours of Cardinal Pole to reinstate the true Faith—Charge of unorthodoxy brought against him—Restitution of ecclesiastical revenues by the Queen—Her death a misfortune for the country—Her character and virtues—Religious toleration unknown in the sixteenth century—Persecution inculcated by the Reformers.

CHAPTER XX.

RELAPSE INTO SCHISM 393

Accession of Elizabeth—Her religious sentiments—Innovations introduced by the Queen's command—The bishops refuse to officiate at her coronation, with the exception of Bishop Oglethorpe, who performs the ceremony—The Act of Supremacy and Act of Conformity passed in Parliament— England is again severed from the unity of Christendom— Conduct of prelates and ecclesiastical dignitaries in regard to the Oath of Supremacy—The Queen's views concerning ecclesiastical authority—Alterations in the form of worship—Effect of the religious changes on the people—Cruelty of Elizabeth towards the Catholics who refuse to conform—A Bull is issued by Pius V. deposing Elizabeth—Fidelity of the Marian priests —Tyrannical enactments against recusants.

CHAPTER XXI.

PERSECUTIONS . . 415

A large proportion of the Catholic laity remain faithful under persecution—Seminaries founded abroad for the education of English aspirants to the priesthood—The landing of Catholic priests in England is declared to be treason—The first victims—Fate of Jesuit missionaries—Penalties inflicted with unrelenting severity on laymen who refuse to conform—Condition of prisons at that time—Father Southwell, S.J.—Methods of torture practised in the prisons—Barbarous manner of putting priests to death—Babington's conspiracy—Execution of the Queen of Scots—Defeat of the Spanish Armada—Multiplication of penalties against recusants—Domiciliary visits of pursuivants—Failure of Elizabeth's policy—The Faith kept alive by the unconquerable devotion of English priests—Temporary revival of the hopes of Catholics on the accession of James I.—Worse sufferings are inflicted on them—Patience of English Catholics under persecution—The Gunpowder Plot.

CHAPTER XXII.

CONDITION OF CATHOLICS UNDER THE STUARTS . 437

Revision of the Penal Code—Restrictions imposed on the liberty of Catholics—A new oath of allegiance causes dissension amongst Catholics—The Holy Father interposes to allay the severity of the persecution—Temporary respite on account of the projected Spanish alliance—Episcopal government granted to English Catholics—Marriage of the King's son to a Catholic princess—Puritan fanaticism evokes a fresh outbursts of persecution—Pope Urban VIII. sends a pastoral letter to the faithful in England—The moderation evinced by Charles I. provokes Protestant animosity—Rise of Archbishop Laud—He endeavours to remedy abuses in Anglican worship and is consequently accused of Romanist tendencies—Number of missionary priests in England in this reign—They are anew proscribed and executed as traitors—The civil war—Loyalty manifested by the Catholic nobles—Freedom of faith proclaimed under Cromwell's rule to all saving Papists and Prelatists—Acts of rapacity and sacrilege—Divine judgements on individuals and the nation at large.

Contents.

CHAPTER XXIII

CONDITION OF CATHOLICS UNDER THE STUARTS
(*continued*) 453

Tranquillity is restored and the Episcopal Church re-established on the death of Cromwell—Charles II. desires to obtain toleration for his Catholic subjects—His efforts are resisted by Parliament—Revival of the cry of "No Popery"—The Test Act obliges Catholics to resign offices held under the State—The false depositions of Titus Oates inflame Protestant hatred—Outbreak of another terrible persecution—The victims who suffer are the last of a long line of martyrs—Charles II. is reconciled to the Church in his last hours—A Catholic king ascends the throne in the person of James II.—He attempts to re-establish the Catholic religion in his dominions—The Vicar Apostolic endeavours to check his precipitance—The emancipation of Catholics provokes the Protestant clergy to rebel—The landing of William of Orange gives the signal for a revolution—James II. takes flight—The Catholic Church in England is involved in fresh calamities.

CHAPTER XXIV.

TROUBLES OF THE EIGHTEENTH CENTURY . . 465

Religious toleration for all except Catholics—Revival of the Oath introduced by James I.—Disabilities and liabilities of Catholics—Results of this legislation—Division of England into four districts—The rising in Scotland—Further oppression of Catholics—Bishop Challoner—First Relaxation of the penal laws—The Gordon Riots—Political status of Catholics—The Toleration Act.

CHAPTER XXV.

CATHOLIC EMANCIPATION . . . 481

Mr. Pitt desires to secure for Catholics equality of civil rights—Opposition of George III. to this measure—The Bill is ultimately passed by Parliament—Proposal to place the Catholic clergy under control of the State—Determined resistance of Dr. Milner and the Irish prelates—Decision of the Holy See—Daniel O'Connell—Abolition of the Oath of Supremacy and abjuration—Catholic education—Catholic marriages—Exceptions in the offices of State open to Catholics—English colleges on the continent destroyed by the French Revolution, are transferred to England—Return of religious orders of women from convents of English origin abroad—Hospitality shown to exiled French clergy.—Test imposed against Gallican principles—Beneficial effect of the presence of the *émigrés* on religion in this country—Precautions observed by Catholics at the close of the last century—Testimony of Cardinal Newman —Virtue of Catholics in past times.

CHAPTER XXVI.

THE CATHOLIC REVIVAL. . . . 496

Increase in the number of Catholics in England on the restoration of religious liberty—The Oxford Movement—Numerous conversions amongst the Anglican clergy—Newman—Manning —Augmentation of the number of vicariates in England—Re-establishment of the hierarchy—Dr. Wiseman, first Cardinal Archbishop of Westminster—Immigration of the Irish—Rapid extension of Catholicism in recent years—Seminaries and colleges—Religious congregations of men and of women— Beatification of the English Martyrs—Reparation needed for the national apostasy—Words of Pope Leo XIII. addressed to the English pilgrims on the occasion of his episcopal jubilee— Re-dedication of England to the Holy Mother of God and St. Peter by Cardinal Vaughan—Condemnation of Anglican Orders.

INDEX . 513

CHRONOLOGICAL TABLE.

[N.B.—*The third column, containing the events, is the backbone of the Table. The list of Popes is not complete: it only gives the Popes in whose reigns the several events occurred. The same applies to the list of Kings. The date in the second column applies only to the event, not to the accession of the Pope or King, which is sometimes given in brackets. The names in italics are those of the Archbishops of Canterbury.*]

POPES.	A.D.	EVENTS.	KINGS.
Gregory I.	597	*Augustine* lands in Kent.	Ethelbert
	603	Conference with British Bishops	(Kent).
Sabinianus	605	*Laurence*, Abp.	Eadbald
Boniface V.	619	*Mellitus*, Abp.	(Kent).
	624	*Justus*, Abp.	
Honorius	626	Paulinus converts Edwin and occupies York.	Edwin (Northumbria)
	627	*Honorius*, Abp.	
	631	Felix converts East Anglia.	
	633	Pagan invasion of Northumbria.	
	635	Battle of Heavenfield.	Oswald
		Aidan in Northumbria.	(Northumbria)
		Birinus in Wessex.	Cynegils
			(Wessex)
Theodore I.	642	Oswald killed—Penda's ravages.	Penda (Mercia)
			Oswy
			(Northumbria)
Martin I.	650	Peada, Penda's son, baptized.	Peada (Mercia)
	654	Cedd in East Saxony.	
	655	*Deusdedit*, Abp.	
Eugene I.	656	Dimma, Bp. of Mercia.	
	659	Christianity restored in Essex.	Sigebert
Vitalian	664	Council of Whitby.	(Essex).
	665	Wilfrid, Bp. of York.	
	668	*Theodore*, Abp., consecrated at Rome. First Primate.	Oswy (Northumbria)
	673	Council of Hertford.	
Agatho	678	Wilfrid appeals to Rome.	Egfrid
	680	Council of Hatfield.	(Northumbria)

xxviii *Chronological Table.*

POPES.	A.D.	EVENTS.	KINGS.
	681	Wilfrid converts Sussex.	Aldfrid (Northumbria)
Sergius I.	693	*Brihtwald*, Abp.	Ina (Wessex).
John VI.	703	Wilfrid's second appeal to Rome.	
	705	Wilfrid, Bp. of Hexham.	
	709	Wilfrid's death.	
	721	King Ina at Rome.	
	724	Boniface, Bishop in Germany.	
	731	*Tatwin*, Abp.	
Gregory III.	734	Death of Ven. Bede.	Ethelbald
	735	*Nothelm*, Abp.	(Mercia).
	741	*Cuthbert*, Abp.	
Zachary	747	Council of Cloveshoe.	
	759	*Bregwin*, Abp.	
	766	*Jaenbert*, Abp.	
Adrian I.	785	Papal Legates in England.	Offa (Mercia).
	787	Lichfield an Archbishopric.	
	793	*Ethelhard*, Abp.	
Leo III.	795	Danish invasion.	
	805	*Wulfred*, Abp.	
Gregory IV.	832	*Theologild*, Abp.	
	833	*Ceolnoth*, Abp.	
	836		Ethelwulf.
Leo IV.	853	Alfred goes to Rome.	
	870	*Ethelred*, Abp.	
Adrian II.	871	Alfred becomes King.	Alfred.
Stephen VI.	890	*Plegmund*, Abp.	
Landus	914	*Athelm*, Abp.	Edward I.
	923	*Wulfhelm*, Abp.	
John XI.	934	*Odo*, Abp.—reforms.	Athelstan.
John XII.	959	*Alfsin*, Abp.	Edwy.
	960	*Dunstan*, Abp.	Edgar.
Benedict VI.	972	Ethelwold, Abp. of York.	
John XV.	988	*Ethelgar*, Abp.	Edward II.
	990	*Siric*, Abp.	
	995	*Elfric*, Abp.	
John XVIII.	1005	*Elphege*, Abp.	
Benedict VIII.	1012	Martyrdom of Elphege.	Edmund
	1013	*Elfstan*, Abp.	(Ironside).
	1016	Cnut, King of England.	Cnut.
	1020	*Agelnoth*, Abp.	
John XIX.	1027	Cnut's pilgrimage to Rome.	
	1038	*Eadsine*, Abp.	
Benedict IX.	1042	Edward the Confessor crowned.	Edward
	1051	*Robert of Jumièges*, Abp.	(Confessor).
Leo IX.	1052	Stigand elected Abp.	
Alexander II.	1066	William the Conqueror.	William I.
	1070	*Lanfranc*, Abp.	
		Synod of Winchester under Papal Legates.	

Chronological Table.   xxix

POPES.	A.D.	EVENTS.	KINGS.
	1071	Lanfranc goes to Rome for the pall	
Urban II.	1093	*Anselm*, Abp.	William II.
	1094	Council of Rockingham.	(Rufus, 1087).
	1098	Anselm at Rome.	
Paschal II.	1100	Quarrel about investiture.	Henry I.
	1102	Council at Westminster (Celibacy).	
	1103	Anselm goes again to Rome.	
	1109	Death of Anselm.	
	1114	*R. d'Escures* (Rudolph), Abp.	
Callistus II.	1122	*William de Corbeuil*, Abp.	
	1125	Canterbury invested with Legatine authority.	
Honorius II.	1128	The Cistercians at Waverley.	
Innocent II.	1139	*Theobald*, Abp.	Stephen
		Bishops imprisoned.	(1135).
		Archbishop Thurstan, of York (1114–1144).	
Eugene III.	1148	England under interdict.	
		St. William of York (1144–1147).	
Adrian IV.	1154	Archbishop Theobald, Regent.	Henry II.
(Nicolas Breakspear).	1162	*Thomas à Becket*, Abp.	
Alexander III.	1164	Constitutions of Clarendon.	
	1170	Murder of St. Thomas.	
	1174	The King's penance.	
		Richard, Abp.	
		Hubert, Bp. of Salisbury.	
Lucius III.	1181	Carthusians at Witham.	
	1185	*Baldwin*, Abp.	
Urban III.	1186	Hugh, Bishop of Lincoln.	
Celestine III.	1193	*Hubert Fitz Walter*, Abp.	Richard I.
		Quarrel about election of Abp.	(1189).
Innocent III.	1207	*Stephen Langton*, Abp.	John (1199).
	1208	England under interdict.	
	1213	John becomes Pope's vassal.	
	1215	Magna Charta.	
Honorius III.	1220	Arrival of Dominicans.	Henry III.
	1222	Arrival of Franciscans.	(1216).
	1229	*Richard Grant*, Abp.	
Gregory IX.	1234	*Edmund Rich* (St.), Abp.	
	1235	Grosseteste, Bp. of Lincoln.	
Innocent IV.	1250	Council of Lyons.	
Clement IV.	1265	Simon de Montfort and the Barons.	
Gregory X.	1272	*Kilwardby*, Abp.	Edward I.
	1279	*Peckham*, Abp.	
Boniface VIII.	1294	*Winchelsey*, Abp.	
	1296	Bull "Clericis Laicos."	[(1307).
Clement V.	1308	Suppression of Knight Templars	Edward II.

Chronological Table.

POPES.	A.D.	EVENTS.	KINGS.
	1313	Reynolds, Abp.	
	1328	Mepeham, Abp.	
John XXII.	1333	Stratford, Abp.	Edward III.
Clement VI.	1349	The Black Death. *Bradwardine*, Abp.	(1327).
	1349	Islip, Abp.	
	1351	First Statute of Provisors.	
Innocent VI.	1353	Statute of *Præmunire*.	
Urban V.	1366	Langham, Abp.	
Gregory XI.	1368	Wittlesey, Abp.	
	1374	Wyclif made Rector of Lutterworth.	
	1375	Sudbury, Abp.	
	1377	Wyclif summoned for heresy.	Richard II.
Urban VI.	1381	Courtenay, Abp., Wyclif's attack on the Eucharist.	
	1384	Death of Wyclif.	
Boniface IX.	1397	Arundel, Abp.	
	1401	Statute against Lollardism.	Henry IV.
John XXIII.	1414	Chichely, Abp.	(1399).
Martin V.	1417	Sir John Oldcastle executed.	Henry V. (1413).
	1426	Martin V. condemns the Statute of Provisors.	Henry VI. (1422).
Eugenius IV.	1443	John Stafford, Abp.	
Nicolas V.	1452	John Kemp, Abp.	
	1454	Thomas Bouchier, Abp.	
Callistus III.	1455	Wars of the Roses.	
			Edward IV. (1461).
			Edward V. (1485).
			Richard III. (1485).
Innocent VIII.	1485	Wars of the Roses end.	Henry VII.
	1486	John Morton, Abp.	(1485).
Alexander VI.	1501	Henry Dean, Abp.	
	1503	William Warham, Abp.	
Leo X.	1517	Wolsey made Legate.	Henry VIII.
Clement VII.	1527	Henry's marriage with Catharine questioned before Wolsey and Warham.	(1509).
	1529	Henry's marriage before Legatine Court.	
	1530	Death of Wolsey.	
	1531	Henry's title "Head of the Church."	
	1532	Thomas Cranmer, Abp.	
	1533	Secret marriage with Anne Boleyn.	

Chronological Table. xxxi

POPES.	A.D.	EVENTS.	KINGS.
		Cranmer condemns Catherine's marriage.	
	1534	Pope condemns Henry. Establishment of Royal Supremacy.	
	1535	Martyrdom of Bishop Fisher. Martyrdom of Sir Thomas More. Thomas Cromwell, Vicar General.	
Paul III.	1536	Lesser Monasteries dissolved. Pilgrimage of Grace.	
Paul III.	1539	Greater Monasteries dissolved.	
	1549	New Prayer Book—First.	Edward VI.
Julius III.	1552	Second Prayer Book.	(1547).
	1554	Reunion with Rome.	Mary (1553).
	1556	*Cardinal Pole*, Abp.	
Paul IV.	1558	Death of Pole, last Abp. of Canterbury.	
Pius IV.	1559	Royal Supremacy restored. Act of Uniformity.	Elizabeth (1558).
	1568	Seminary at Douay founded.	
	1570	Pius V. excommunicates Elizabeth.	
Sixtus V.	1586	The Babington Conspiracy.	
	1588	The Spanish Armada.	
Innocent IX.	1592	Penal Statutes enforced.	
Leo XI.	1605	Gunpowder Plot.	James I.
Paul V.	1606	Revision of the Penal Code against Catholics.	(1603).
Urban VIII.	1623	*William Bishop* (Bp. of Chalcedon).	
	1628	Fresh martyrdoms.	Charles I.
	1640	Persecution of priests.	(1625).
Innocent X.	1645	Execution of Laud.	
	1649	Execution of Charles I.	
Clement X.	1673	The Test Act.	Charles II.
Innocent XI.	1678	Severities against Catholics.	(1660).
	1681	Oliver Plunket, last martyr in England.	
	1687	Religious Toleration proclaimed. England divided into four Vicariates.	James II. (1685).
	1688	Trial of the seven bishops.	
Alexander VIII.	1689	Toleration for all but Catholics.	William and Mary (1688).
		Bps. *Giffard* and *Petre*, Vicars Apostolic (1687-1758).	George I. (1714).
Clement XII.	1730	Challoner arrives in England.	George II. (1727).

Chronological Table.

POPES.	A.D.	EVENTS.	KINGS.
Pius VI.	1778	Catholic Relief Bill.	George III.
	1780	Gordon Riots.	(1760).
	1791	The Toleration Act.	
Pius VII.	1808	Oscott founded by Bp. Milner.	
Pius VIII.	1829	Removal of Catholic disabilities.	George IV.
			(1820).
Gregory XVI.	1840	Eight Vicariates created.	William IV.
			(1830).
	1845	Submission of John Henry Newman.	VICTORIA (1837).
Pius IX.	1850	Restoration of the Hierarchy.	
	1851	Ecclesiastical Titles Act.	
Leo XIII.	1886	Beatification of English Martyrs.	
	1893	England dedicated anew to the Mother of God and to St. Peter.	
	1895	Letter of Leo XIII. *ad Anglos*.	
	1896	Encyclical *Satis Cognitum* on the Unity of the Church. Bull *Apostolicæ Curæ* declaring Anglican Orders null and void.	

A Short History of the Catholic Church in England.

CHAPTER I.

THE EARLY BRITISH CHURCH.

Introduction of Christianity.—By whom and at what exact epoch Christianity was first introduced into Britain is a question respecting which no historic certainty exists. "We see," says the historian Fuller, "that the light shined there at a very early period, but we see not who kindled it." Almost all ancient traditions of the past concur in asserting that the Gospel was preached in these islands during the Apostolic ages. Some writers are of opinion that the Prince of the Apostles himself took occasion to visit Britain in the year when the Emperor Claudius banished all the Jews from Rome; others say that the missionary journeys of St. Paul were extended to our shores, but these statements are destitute of any foundation. Gildas, the earliest native historian, writing in the sixth century, alleges positively that the faith was implanted among our forefathers by the apostles, or by their disciples; yet he avowedly knew nothing of the early history of the Church in his own country beyond what he found in foreign writers, for the simple reason that all native records were destroyed in the troublous time of the Saxon invasion. Where historic evidence is so scanty, and uncertified legend abounds, it is difficult to draw the line of demarcation between truth and fiction.

St. Joseph of Arimathæa.—The story of the coming of St. Joseph of Arimathæa in the first century is perhaps hardly credible, but should be recorded, as it has in its favour a generally-accepted tradition. He is supposed to have been sent with twelve companions by St. Philip to Britain, and, landing on the south-west coast, to have reached Glastonbury, then called Avalon, an island surrounded by marshes and streams. On the ground allotted to him by the British king Arviragus he erected a chapel, or rather a little oratory, formed of branches woven together, which was afterwards replaced by a more substantial structure—the first sanctuary dedicated to our Lady in England. It is, at all events, by no means improbable that the Christian faith was spread to some extent in Britain during the first century by certain members of the family of Caradoc (called by the Romans Caractacus), who were taken as prisoners to Rome. Bran the Blessed, the father of Caractacus, who was detained seven years in Rome as a hostage for his son, is stated by the Triads, and other Welsh records of a later date, to have been converted by the preaching of St. Paul, and on his return to have evangelized his fellow-countrymen, the Cymri. A thirteenth-century collection of early British traditions, which cannot all be imaginary, gives full

particulars of these hostages. Claudia, the wife of
Pudens the senator, spoken of by St. Paul in his
epistle to St. Timothy (2 Tim. iv. 24), is said to have
been another distinguished British convert. She was
the daughter of Cogidumnus, the native king of
Sussex, who is mentioned by Tacitus as possessing
independent authority. The inscription upon a slab
of grey marble, discovered at Chichester in 1713,
confirms this statement. The marriage of Claudia to
Pudens, and the fact of the descent of this princess
from the "blue-eyed Britons," are mentioned by the
poet Martial in his epigrams.[1] Pomponia Græcina
also, the wife of an ex-governor of Britain, accused and
acquitted A.D. 57 before her husband, Aulus Plautius,
"qui ovans se de Britannis retulit," of practising an
"externa superstitio" (Tacitus, *Annales*, xiii. 32), is
assumed to have been both a Christian and a Briton.
Thus by means of communication with Rome, and
perhaps the presence of Christian soldiers in the
invading armies, the new doctrines were, it may be
believed, disseminated early in the British Isles.

Pope Eleutherius.—About the year 170, when
M. Antoninus Verus and Commodus were emperors,
Ven. Bede states (*Eccles. History*, bk. i. ch. 4) that
messengers were sent by a local chieftain, named
Lucius, to Pope Eleutherius, with the request that
teachers might be sent to instruct his subjects in
the Christian religion, and that he himself might be
admitted into its pale. This demand was gladly
acceded to; missionaries were ordained and dispatched
to Britain; Lucius was baptized, and the faith was
freely propagated in his dominions. The temples

---

[1] "Claudia, Rufe, meo nubit Peregrina Pudenti."—*Epig.* iv. 13.
"Claudia, cœruleis cum sit Rufina Britannis edita."—*Ibid.*, xi. 54.

wherein the flamens had burnt incense and offered sacrifices to the heathen deities were demolished, and Christian churches raised on their sites. The early British Church was organized, and the hierarchy established, by the missionaries Fugatius and Damianus, the first episcopal sees that were erected being apparently those of London, York, and Caerleon-on-Usk. So successful was the preaching of the envoys that Tertullian was able to boast, at the close of the second century, that places in Britain where the Roman arms could not penetrate were subject to Christ, that His name was honoured there, and His kingdom established.[1] Origen, too, though he states that a great part of the inhabitants had not yet heard the word of God, still says that the power of the Saviour was as manifest in Britain as in Mauritania; and Arnobius speaks with admiration of the rapidity wherewith the word of God had reached the Indians in the east and the Britons in the west.

The faith was kept "in quiet peace, inviolate and entire," Bede tells us, in these islands until the outbreak, in the commencement of the fourth century, of the persecution under the Emperor Diocletian. At that time the British Church counted its members by thousands, and they, like other Christian communities, had to attest the reality of their faith by shedding their blood. Abandoned to the mercy of the pagan priests and magistrates, they were hunted into caverns and forests, where numbers perished

[1] These words of Tertullian form the first trustworthy testimony to the existence of a British Church. They are sufficiently precise to show the writer's belief, as in a well-known fact, that there were Christians in Britain. The passage was probably written A.D. 208, when the Emperor Severus was engaged in quelling a revolt in Britain.

The Early British Church. 5

from want; while those who fell into the hands of their persecutors had no other alternative than to abjure their religion or to suffer death. Out of all these, the names of three only have been handed down to posterity—Julius and Aaron, inhabitants of the city of Caerleon; and Alban, a citizen of Verulam, who, on account of his sufferings and courage, has been honoured with the title of Britain's protomartyr.

St. Alban.—History tells us that Alban, although himself a pagan, gave shelter to a Christian priest flying from pursuit. He watched his guest's habits, admired his virtue and his perseverance in prayer, listened to his instructions, and received from him the sacrament of baptism. The retreat of the fugitive was discovered, and soldiers were sent to arrest him. Alban, having assumed the attire of the priest, gave himself into the soldiers' hands in his stead. He was at once carried before the magistrate, when he fearlessly owned himself a Christian, and refused to offer sacrifice to the gods. The judge, being much incensed, ordered him to be scourged, believing he might by stripes shake that constancy on which he could not prevail by words. But when he perceived that Alban was not to be overcome by tortures, he sentenced him to death, and he was led away to execution, beyond the river which ran by the city. A vast crowd of persons accompanied the prisoner and his guards, so that the bridge over the river was thronged to such an extent as to render it impossible for Alban to pass over it. Desirous to obtain the crown of martyrdom as speedily as possible, on approaching the stream he lifted up his heart in prayer, and immediately a dry passage was made for him in the bed of the river. On observing this, the executioner, touched by grace, flung away his sword, and casting himself at Alban's feet, declared himself ready to suffer with, or if possible for, him. Meanwhile the prisoner ascended the eminence where he was to be beheaded; and here another miracle occurred, for at his prayer a spring of water suddenly burst forth to quench his thirst. Nor was this all; Bede tells us the executioner who dealt the death-stroke lost his sight at the same moment that the martyr expired, his eyes falling from his head to the ground.

The constancy of St. Alban, and the wonders attending his execution, caused the conversion of so many that the Roman governor ordered the persecution to be suspended. At that time Britain was governed by Constantius Chlorus, a tolerant and humane man, who did not encourage, though he could not prevent, the enforcement of the imperial edicts against the Christians. It is related of him that when certain Christians of his court offered to conform to the idolatrous worship, he dismissed them from his service, saying that men who were faithless to their God would not be faithful to their prince. Before he had assumed the title of Cæsar, while commanding one of the Roman legions quartered at Colchester, Constantius had married Helena, the only daughter of Coël, the local king of what is now Essex, a beautiful and accomplished princess. She was the mother of his son Constantine, who became emperor on Constantius's death, and shortly after gave his support to the Christian faith. Then the Christians came forth from the places where they had been compelled to hide, and appeared again in public;

they rebuilt the churches that had been laid low, founded shrines in honour of the holy martyrs, kept the festivals and performed all the rites and ceremonies of the Church. In this they were encouraged by the favour of the emperor, and that of his mother, the British-born Empress Helena, who, as is well known, was herself converted late in life, and journeyed to Jerusalem, whence she brought the true Cross, the Holy Coat, and many relics of the sacred Passion.

British Bishops at Councils.—Constantine on his conversion ordered the assembly of a council at Arles in 314, at which Eborius, Bishop of York, Restitutus, Bishop of London, and Adelphius, Bishop of Caerleon-on-Usk were present. The fact that the British Church was invited to send representatives to take part in the deliberations of this council affords proof of the unquestionable orthodoxy of that Church, and of its communion in faith and discipline with the rest of Christendom. At this council the Donatists were compelled to submit to the Church or forfeit the Emperor's protection. That of Nicæa, in 325, was called to denounce the heresy of Arius, who denied "that the Son was consubstantial with the Father;" there also a deputation of bishops from Britain attended, and accepted all the decrees. At two other councils besides, held in the fourth century, British prelates sat and voted, although the poverty of the Church in their country was such as to compel them to accept the offer made by the Emperor to defray their expenses out of the imperial exchequer. They gave in their adhesion to all the decisions of the synod of Arles, and concurred in laying a report of the proceedings at the feet of the Supreme Pontiff, as their head and spiritual sovereign. Then these bishops, returning to their several sees, sought to knit the minds of their flocks more closely to the truth, so that the British Church was not only recognized as an integral part of the Universal Church, but noted for its loyalty to the faith of Christ and the see of Rome. St. Hilary of Poitiers, about the year 358, congratulates the bishops of Britain on their freedom from all contagion of the detestable Arian heresy. St. Chrysostom says that in the British Isles, as in the East and South, or beside the Euxine, men may be heard discussing points of Scripture with differing voices, but not with differing belief. St. Jerome, too, before the close of the fourth century, affirms that Britain worships the same Christ, and observes the same rule of faith, as other nations.

Papal Care for Britain.—Meanwhile, the Supreme Pontiff had not been unmindful of the needs of these remote islanders. Fearing lest, in consequence of its insular position and distance from the fount of Catholicity, divergences in government and discipline, doctrine and worship, should creep into the British Church, he from time to time sent missionaries, who, while they strove to extend the limits of the Church by the conversion of tribes that were yet pagan, should also enforce uniformity of faith and practice amongst the Christian portion of the population. These missionaries were mostly natives of Britain, who had been educated abroad. One of the most notable of them was Ninian, a noble Cumbrian youth, who, having gone on a pilgrimage to the tomb of the Apostles, "had been regularly instructed in Rome in the faith and mysteries of the truth" (Bede, iii. 4). He was consecrated Bishop by Siricius, the successor of St. Damasus, and returned to Britain to preach the Gospel to the Picts of the Lowlands, a rough and barbarous race, whose conversion was the result of his apostolic labours. St. Ninian was a friend of St. Martin, the Bishop of Tours; he is noteworthy for having maintained the Catholic faith when the teaching of Pelagius, his contemporary and countryman, was spreading in Britain, and for having written a commentary on the Psalms. The extent of his diocese is a matter of question; but we know that he erected in Galloway a church of stone, a thing most unusual at that time, which was known as the *Candida Casa* of Whithorn. The deacon Palladius was another missioner, sent by Pope Celestine to the Irish, then called Scots. Being unsuccessful in his work, he withdrew to Cornwall, and was succeeded by St. Patrick.

St. Patrick.—The birthplace of this saint is not positively known. When a youth he was seized by pirates and carried to Ireland, where he was kept in slavery for six years. On effecting his escape, he entered a monastery in the north of Gaul to study, with the view of devoting his life to the evangelization of the land of his captivity. For sixty years he laboured amongst the Irish: the success of his apostolate is well known. Three times he is said to have journeyed to Rome: first, to obtain the blessing of the Holy Father on his mission; secondly, to report the result of his exertions; thirdly, to receive the pallium, with the title of Apostolic Legate for the see of Armagh. Another missionary in the early part of the fifth century was, it is said, St.

Kieran, the Apostle of Cornwall, who was trained and sent out to this country by Pope Damasus; and we may also here mention St. Cadoc, the son of a Welsh prince, who, renouncing the possessions that would be his on his father's death, entered religion, and became abbot of a monastery at Chepstow. Seven times, tradition says, he visited Rome, and twice he made a pilgrimage to the Holy Sepulchre, whence he brought back altar-stones, as was then customary, whereon to offer the adorable sacrifice. These penitential journeys were undertaken for the repose of the souls of his departed relatives. The early Christians of Britain seem to have had a great devotion to pilgrimages; and, despite the difficulties and perils of travelling in those days, a great number of palmers visited Jerusalem and Rome.

Mission of St. Germanus.—When, in 411, the Roman legions were withdrawn from Britain for the defence of Italy, almost the whole nation had been converted to the religion of Christ, and possessed a regularly constituted hierarchy of archbishops and bishops throughout the entire island. It had, as we have said, been remarkably free from visitations of noxious heresy; the only one that obtained any footing there being that of Pelagius. The sweep of this moral pestilence through the land may in a great measure be attributed to the nationality of its propounder. The Celtic Christians of these northern climes recognized in Pelagius their countryman, known to them under his baptismal name of Morgan. A man of great originality of thought, he had early gone to seek his fortunes in Rome. His thirst for notoriety led him into heterodoxy; he denied original sin, and asserted the power of man to

save his soul without the aid of divine grace. Some
of his disciples, Britons like himself, returning to the
land of their birth, propagated there his erroneous
doctrines. Alarmed at the manner in which these
doctrines spread, the clergy, finding themselves in-
competent to refute the heresy, solicited theological
assistance from the bishops of Gaul assembled in
synod at Troyes. Meanwhile Pope Celestine, having
heard from the deacon Palladius of the danger that
threatened the faith in Britain, commanded St. Germanus, Bishop of Auxerre,[1] to proceed thither and
combat the heresy. He was accompanied by Lupus,
Bishop of Troyes; by their preaching they most
effectually established the true doctrine, to the great
encouragement of the faithful. We learn from the
Ven. Bede that a public meeting was convened at
Verulam, where the representatives of Pelagianism
were called upon to defend their tenets. On the one
side, says the historian (bk. i. ch. 17), was divine
faith, on the other human presumption; on the one
side piety, on the other pride. The holy priests

[1] That the mission of Germanus was derived direct from Rome we
know on the testimony of Prosper, a Gaul by birth, who lived at the
time, and from his office of secretary to Pope Celestine, is certain to
have possessed correct information. In his Chronicle he states that, in
the year 429, Celestine, at the application of the deacon Palladius, sent
Germanus in his own place, that is, as his legate, that he might drive
out the heretics, and guide the Britons to the Catholic faith: "Ad
actionem Palladii diaconi Papa Celestinus Germanum Antisiodor-
ensem episcopum *vice sua* mittit, ut deturbatis haereticis, Britannos
ad Catholicam fidem dirigat" (Prosp. in Chron. post ann. 455).
Prosper does not make this statement once only, but repeats it in
his controversial work against Cassian (*Contr. Cassian.* c. 41, c. an.
432). Lupus, the bishop of the city where the council of prelates was
sitting when the petition for spiritual aid arrived, was chosen as the
companion of Germanus, probably by the Gallican bishops (see Lingard,
Anglo-Saxon Church, ch. i.).

refuted every assertion of their adversaries in the hearing of the people; the triumph of orthodoxy was complete.

After witnessing this defeat of their spiritual foes, the Christian inhabitants of Britain entreated Germanus to defend them against their temporal adversaries. Since the departure of the Romans, they had been much harassed by the incursions of the wild tribes of the north—the fierce Picts. These marauders had been especially troublesome during the Lent of 430, while the Gallican bishops were preparing catechumens for the great annual baptism at Easter. As soon as the festival was over, Germanus consented to lead the people against the Picts. He had been a soldier in early life, and had commanded the imperial troops in Gaul. With the instinct of a general he laid his plans. He placed them in bands in ambush among the hills, and on the appearance of the enemy, he shouted, "Alleluia!" This word was repeated loudly three times by his followers, whose voices reverberated amongst the hills. The unwonted sound struck terror into the barbarians, who, thinking themselves outnumbered, fled in dismay. The influence gained by Germanus through this bloodless victory was further enhanced by the many miracles he wrought; amongst these is recorded that of healing a man lame from his youth, and of restoring sight to a girl who was blind, by means of a reliquary which he habitually wore suspended around his neck.

Before leaving the island, the two prelates paid a visit to St. Alban's tomb, to return thanks to Almighty God for the success of their ministry. By the orders of St. Germanus the grave was opened, and a box containing the relics of some saints laid therein, to express the union of the souls of the just in heaven. He also took from the spot a handful of dust, still reddened with the holy martyr's blood, to be deposited in a new church at Auxerre, which he intended to dedicate to St. Alban.

St. Germanus made a second journey to Britain in 447, to complete the overthrow of heresy. This time he was attended by Severus, Bishop of Troyes, a disciple of his former companion. A few who had relapsed into Pelagianism were reclaimed, and the teachers of heresy were expelled from the island. The testimony of Bede is that for a long time afterwards the faith was held pure and uncorrupt in Britain. This was, perhaps, owing to the important monastic foundations made by Germanus during his second visit. St. Germanus was no less zealous for purity of morals than for integrity in the faith. He solemnly excommunicated Vortigern, the British king, for incest, and incurred the hatred of that dissolute prince. Mementoes of his mission may be found in the ruins of St. German's Cathedral, Isle of Man, in the church of St. Germans in Cornwall, and in Llanarmon—Llan (church of) Garmon—in North Wales.

Saxon invasions.—The Church in Britain was not destined to enjoy a long period of tranquillity. A year had hardly elapsed since the Gallic bishops had departed, before the Teuton tribes began their work of conquest. Engaged by Vortigern, the chief king of Britain, to aid in repulsing the Picts and Scots, these mercenaries turned their arms against their employers, and the land was swept with fire and sword. They did not come all at once, nor overspread the country from one centre, but landed at different places, at intervals of greater or less length, pillaging the surrounding regions, and putting all the defenceless inhabitants to the sword. Thus they gradually made good their footing in the island, and eventually obtained undisputed possession of the land they conquered. The Britons did not surrender their right to the soil without a determined struggle; the fact that more than a century was required by the Saxons to subdue the country districts of the east and south proves that the land was stubbornly fought for and hardly won. Their principal opponent in the west was the famous King Arthur, the hero of early legend, represented as the flower of chivalry and Christian courage. Tradition says of him that when mortally wounded in his last battle, he bade his followers carry him to Glastonbury, the "island valley of Avilion," in order that he might more perfectly prepare to depart out of this world to life eternal.

The enthusiastic love of Christianity, aroused by Germanus shortly before the first Teutonic invasion, inspired the Britons with the resolution to die in defence of their churches rather than leave them to be desecrated and destroyed by the Anglians and Saxons. Nothing could exceed the fury wherewith these merciless invaders, worshippers of Woden and Thor, set about destroying the Christian sanctuaries of the land. The priests' blood was spilled upon the altars and the churches burned to the ground, many of the people perishing in their ruins. For a long time Theon, Bishop of London, and Thadioc, Bishop of York, held to their sees, but at last they were compelled to retire, taking with them their reliquaries and the sacred vessels, to the Cambrian mountains, where a vast number of their fellow-

The Early British Church.

Christians had sought refuge from their relentless foes. Thus the idolatry and ignorance of the Teutonic barbarians was transplanted into the most flourishing provinces of Britain; the refinements of civilization disappeared, the light of the Gospel was quenched, or rather carried into the hilly district of Wales, the most inaccessible parts of Cornwall, and the rocky fastnesses of the northern isles. Some of the inhabitants sought shelter across the sea, sailing in frail coracles to the coast of Gaul, where in Armorica, the Brittany of to-day, they formed a settlement, and spread the knowledge of the faith. The firm Catholicity of the Bretons at all times is doubtless due to this band of missionaries, amongst whom were many saints—Sampson of Dol, Maglorius, Illtyd, Dubric, Malo, and others.

The Church in Wales.—Even during these disastrous times, when pagan darkness once more overspread the greater part of the island, the ancient British Church lived and flourished in Wales. Four bishoprics were established, with a cathedral church and a monastic college attached to each. These religious houses, the most important of which was that of Bangor, founded for the observance of monastic discipline, prayer, manual labour, and study, served as training schools for the clergy and depositories of literature. This period is also not without many illustrious saints, whose names will never be forgotten. There was St. Finian, who went to preach in Ireland; St. David, of Menevia, who soon after his ordination journeyed with two companions to Jerusalem, and received as a gift from the Patriarch the splendid jewel afterwards known as the Glastonbury sapphire; St. Kentigern, who founded the see which took its name from St. Asaph, the second bishop who filled it; St. Columba, the great Irish saint, who founded the monastery of Hii, or Iona, which became a centre of missionary activity to all the adjacent districts, and later on sent apostles to Friesland, and other parts of Germany; St. Columban, also a native of Ireland, who founded monasteries in Burgundy and the Apennines; St. Winifred, who, flying from the Saxon prince, her suitor, was beheaded by him, and restored to life by St. Beuno, the great Welsh saint, her friend and teacher; besides many others, of whom record is made in the pages of hagiology.

Although the British Christians did not neglect the duty of speading the truth in other lands, they appear to have made no attempt to convert their Teutonic conquerors. As far as possible they held aloof from them; no amalgamation of the races took place. From the English Channel to the Firth of Forth, from Essex to the river Severn, the laws, language, and religion of the Saxons and Angles held undisputed sway; the original inhabitants were almost exterminated, and the few who remained, demoralized by years of incessant warfare, were reduced to a state of slavery. The Christian teachers who were to evangelize the new kingdom of England were to come, not from Wales or Ireland, but from Italy.

CHAPTER II.

CONVERSION OF THE ANGLO-SAXONS.

Augustine sent by Pope Gregory.—In consequence of an incident which happened at an earlier period of his life, Pope Gregory I. had become much interested in the welfare of the Anglo-Saxons. It chanced that one day, while he was still a simple monk, as he was passing through the market-place at Rome, where traders from foreign lands were exhibiting for sale various kinds of merchandise, he paused to look at some slaves, prisoners taken in war, brought thither by a Jewish slave-dealer in expectation of finding a purchaser for them. Gregory could not help pitying the captives. He was particularly struck by the appearance of some little boys, beautiful children, with ruddy cheeks and blue eyes, and fine golden hair falling in tresses on their shoulders. In those days long hair was a token of exalted birth, only kings and nobles being accustomed to allow its growth, persons of inferior rank or servile condition having their heads closely cropped. Gregory saw that these poor children who stood there trembling, dreading the fate in store for them, must have suffered some reverse of fortune; their parents had probably been killed in war, and the boys, brought up in care and comfort, were now exposed to the hardships of slavery in a foreign land. He asked from what country they came? "From Britain," the dealer replied; whereupon Gregory inquired whether they were Christians. On hearing they were heathens: "Alas!" he exclaimed, "that faces so bright and comely should be in the power of the Prince of Darkness! To what nation do they belong?" When told that they were Angles, he added, "Well may they be so called, for they are fair as the angels, and it were meet that they should be fellow-heirs with angels in heaven. From which of the provinces of Britain do they come?" "From Deira," was the reply. "Indeed," continued Gregory, "the name is of good omen, *de irâ Dei eruti sunt* (they are delivered from the wrath of God)." And hearing that the name of their king was Ella, or Alla, he said that Alleluia ought to be sung in his dominions.

This incident, trifling as it may appear, was destined to produce important results. Gregory determined to make every effort in his power for the evangelization of Britain. He desired to proceed thither himself in the character of a missionary, but circumstances prevented him from executing his design. He did not, however, relinquish it, and when elevated to the Chair of Peter, he commissioned Augustine, the prior of a Benedictine monastery in Rome, to undertake the task he so ardently desired to see accomplished. With him he sent forty monks. This band of missionaries had not got very far on their way before misgivings arose in their minds. In Gaul, where they wintered, they heard reports of the fierce and barbarous character of the people to whom they were going; they realized the perils and difficulties that they would encounter, and the obstacle involved in their ignorance of the Saxon tongue. Their courage faltered; they sent back Augustine to beseech Gregory to permit them to return to their quiet monastery on the Cœlian hill. The Pope furnished them with interpreters and bade them go on their way in reliance on the divine assistance. They obeyed, and in the early part of 597 reached the English shores, landing in the Isle of Thanet, on the very spot where Hengist, the Saxon invader, had landed rather more than a century before.

At that time Ethelbert, a monarch of power and ability, reigned in Kent. He had married a princess named Bertha, sister to Charibert, King of Paris. She was a Christian, and had been accompanied to England by a Frankish bishop, Liudhard by name: with her husband's permission she had caused the ruined church of St. Martin, near Canterbury, the royal residence, to be fitted up for divine service. Ethelbert was consequently not wholly unacquainted with the ecclesiastical character and functions of Augustine, when the band of missionaries entered his dominions and solicited an interview with him. Still he had a strange fear lest they should exercise a magical influence over him, and would only consent to meet them in the open air, where their enchantments, should they employ any, would have less power than within the walls of his palace. Augustine, who was a man of tall stature and majestic deportment, attended by his companions, proceeded to the appointed spot with imposing ceremony, with cross and banner and chanted litanies. Ethelbert received them kindly; he assured them of his protection, promised to supply their wants, and gave them liberty to preach to his subjects. At first he paid little heed to their instructions, but a year later he was baptized, and with him ten thousand, it is said, of the men of Kent. Pope Gregory, in a letter addressed to the Patriarch of Alexandria, speaks with joy of the success attending the labours of the missionaries who toiled in "the most remote part of the world," as Britain was then accounted to be.

Consecration of Augustine.—The next step was for Augustine to obtain episcopal consecration. For this purpose he repaired, in accordance with the commands received from Rome, to Arles, where he was consecrated by Bishop Vergilius assisted by other Frankish bishops. If it be asked why it was Augustine went to Arles for consecration, instead of to Rome, the reason is not far to seek. It must be remembered that the journey from Britain to Rome was in those days a lengthy and tedious affair, beset with perils of all kinds for the traveller, and subject to vexatious delays. Under the most favourable circumstances it could not be accomplished in less than several months, and it was most important that Augustine should be absent from the scene of his missionary labours for as short a period as possible. Gregory therefore desired him to go to the Bishop of Arles, who, being Vicar Apostolic of Gaul, was his representative in that country. Thus this act on Augustine's part, far from showing a spirit of independence was one of strict obedience to the Holy See.

Instructions from Rome.—On his return to England, Ethelbert gave him a palace at Canterbury, with permission to build a church, and lands for the

Conversion of the Anglo-Saxons.

maintenance of the priests who were to be its ministers. Close to the palace there was an old church, erected in the time of the Romans, but since desecrated. This Augustine restored and enlarged, dedicating it to "the Holy Saviour Jesus Christ." On its site the Cathedral of Canterbury now stands: the present structure, although very ancient in parts, is of a date long subsequent to the age of Augustine; it was rebuilt by Lanfranc, in the eleventh century, after the original fabric had been destroyed by fire. Six months later, Augustine received from Pope Gregory the pallium, in token of the archiepiscopal jurisdiction conferred on him; with it were sent a supply of sacred vessels, relics of the Apostles and early martyrs, and numerous manuscripts of value.

In the following year Augustine despatched envoys to Rome, with letters asking the decision of the Holy Father on several important questions affecting morals and discipline. Amongst other things he inquired how he was to deal with the bishops of Britain and Gaul, and whether the liturgical differences which existed in the two countries were to be tolerated. To these Gregory replied that all the bishops of Britain were confided to his care, that "the unlearned might be taught, the weak strengthened, the perverse corrected:" but that with the bishops of Gaul he must not interfere, as he gave him no authority over them. In regard to variations of custom, provided the faith were one, the Pope did not esteem them harmful to the Church, but in every place those were to be chosen which were pious, religious, and upright. He added many other instructions as to the plan of ecclesiastical government, and the manner of dealing with the barbarous people. Moreover, hearing that the harvest was great and the labourers few, he sent four new missionaries, who reached England at the close of 601. They were the bearers of things necessary for the service of the Church, and of letters exhorting Augustine not to destroy the pagan temples, but to convert them from the worship of devils to the service of the true God, and to form friendly relations with the Welsh bishops, that they might co-operate with his clergy in the conversion of the Saxons.

Augustine and the British Bishops.—Hitherto Augustine had had little or no intercourse with the Celtic Christians. The result of the Anglo-Saxon invasion had been, as we have seen, not to destroy but to isolate them, and to cut them off almost entirely from intercommunion with the rest of Christendom. The consequence of this was that, although they had preserved their religion intact, they were not in harmony with the Roman missionaries on certain matters not affecting the essentials of Christianity. For one thing, they fixed the date of Easter in accordance with the antiquated rule— not that followed in the East, but one laid down in the fourth century for Western Christendom. At a subsequent period improved cycles had been adopted, but the Britons retained the old method of reckoning, probably because they were unacquainted with the new mode, possibly because no injunction to adopt it had been issued by Rome. Their manner of administering the rite of baptism, too, differed from the Roman use, for they contented themselves with a single, instead of triple, immersion. Another point of diversity was the shape of the tonsure; the

Conversion of the Anglo-Saxons. 23

Roman monks shaved the crown of the head, leaving a ring of hair around it; the Britons shaved the front part of the head, leaving the hair untouched at the back. On these and other points of detail, Augustine, aware of the desirability of external uniformity, was desirous that they should conform to the usages of the Universal Church. With this design he met them in conference; but the Britons adhered pertinaciously to their traditions, nor could they sufficiently overcome their intense hatred of the race that had massacred their forefathers and overthrown their altars, to unite with him in preaching the Gospel amongst them.

Augustine, finding they would not yield to his exhortations or be persuaded by his arguments, had recourse to miraculous evidence in support of his claims. A blind man was brought, for whom the Britons could do nothing, but who, at the touch of the archbishop, immediately recovered his sight. Although impressed by this miracle, the British Christians refused to abandon the customs of their ancestors without conferring with their brethren. A day was fixed for a second meeting, at which seven Welsh bishops, with the principal monks from the monastery of Bangor Iscoed, near Wrexham, attended. On their way thither the deputies had consulted a recluse, esteemed for his wisdom and sanctity, as to the means of ascertaining whether Augustine were a man of God, whose counsels should be followed. The reply of the hermit shows that long seclusion from the world had rendered him unable to distinguish between official dignity and personal pride. "If he rise at your approach," he said, "you may think him to have learned of Christ who is meek and lowly of heart, and listen to him submissively; if he receive you sitting, who are more in number, despise him as he despises you, and maintain your ancient usages." The bishops came to the synod after the archbishop had taken his seat; he did not rise, and this they considered as an insult.

He only asked three things of them: (1) That they should celebrate Easter at the same time with other Christians; (2) that they should administer baptism according to the Roman ritual; (3) that they should join with him in preaching the Gospel to the Saxons. These demands are deserving of attention, because they prove that there was no divergence between him and them on any point of doctrine, or in regard to the supremacy of the see of Rome; for otherwise he would not have solicited them to become his fellow-labourers, or at least would have made a fourth stipulation. The Britons refused to acknowledge him as their archbishop; they rejected his proposals, and would not abandon their cherished customs at his bidding. "If you will not accept peace with brethren," Augustine replied, in sorrow and disappointment, "you will have to accept war with enemies; if you will not teach the way of life to the English, you will be punished with death at their hands." The bishops withdrew: their rejection of Augustine's authority had been prompted by wounded self-love; it contained no denial of the Pope's supremacy, and must be regarded merely as disobedience to Gregory's ordinance whereby an extraordinary power of jurisdiction was conferred on Augustine with a view to the re-establishment of the Church in England. The reader will readily understand the difference between refusing to obey a command, and a denial of the right of the ruler to issue the command. Moreover, the authority wherewith Augustine was invested was more than that of an ordinary metropolitan; it was an authority of superintendence over all the bishops of Britain, personal to Augustine, and not intended to descend from him to his successors (Lingard, *Anglo-Saxon Church*, ch. ii).[1]

The prediction he uttered on this occasion was verified within eight years after Augustine's death. Ethelfrid, the pagan king of Northumbria, entered the territories of Cadvan, king of North Wales, and the two armies met in the vicinity of Chester. The monks of Bangor assembled on a neighbouring eminence, secure, as they thought, from the fight, whence they hoped, like Moses of old, to determine by their prayers the fate of the battle. Ethelfrid descried this unarmed crowd, and hearing why they were there—"If they pray for our defeat," he said, "they too are enemies and fight against us." A detachment of soldiers was ordered to put them to the sword. The number of monks slain is said to have been twelve hundred, but probably many besides monks were there. Bangor was demolished; only fifty of its ill-fated community escaped by flight.

---

[1] It may here be remarked that the condemnation by Gregory of the title of Universal Bishop, even as applied to the occupant of the Holy See, was no disavowal on his part of the universal spiritual jurisdiction which is an inherent attribute of that See. He objected to the title as implying that the person who bore it was the only rightful bishop in the world. Just as the title Bishop of Paris or Carthage implies that no one else can be the rightful Bishop of those places; so if any one is bishop of the whole world there can be no other rightful bishop of the whole world. So Gregory reasoned, but it is manifest that the reasoning does not touch the case of one who claims, not to exclude other bishops, but to hold superior authority over them.

Laurentius.—Another attempt in the direction of union and co-operation with the Celtic Church was made shortly after the death of Augustine, which occurred in 605. Immediately before his departure to his eternal reward, the archbishop, fearing lest the see should remain vacant, had conferred episcopal consecration on Laurentius, one of the monks who had accompanied him to Britain, and nominated him as his successor. Laurentius, Bede tells us (*Hist.* ii. 4), " began his archiepiscopate with strenuous efforts to extend the foundations of the Church, and took pains to raise its fabric to the due height, by the frequent utterances of holy exhortation and the continual example of pious conduct." He wrote epistles to both the Irish and the British bishops, entreating them to be at one in Catholic observance with the Church throughout the world. His overtures were rejected. The Irish clung with as much tenacity as the Welsh to the Celtic customs; in fact, an Irish prelate named Dagan, having come to Canterbury for the purpose of conferring with the bishops, was apparently so much displeased with what passed in the discussion, that he refused so much as to eat with them. The Southern Irish, however, altered their Paschal reckoning in deference to the Pope's expostulation about the year 634; the Northern Irish and the Picts did the same in the commencement of the following century; while the Welsh, with the national spirit engendered by long isolation, did not yield to the pressure put upon them until all other churches of the British communion had adopted the Roman Easter. They conformed in the latter half of the eighth century, but the last echo of this controversy did not die out until the commencement of the ninth.

Mellitus, Bishop of London. — Meanwhile, before Augustine's death, the light of the Gospel had spread from Kent to the adjoining kingdom of the East Saxons. Sebert, its ruler, was nephew to Ethelbert; thus the missionaries easily gained access to his dominions. Mellitus, one of the four sent from Rome in 601, was chosen for this mission: after the conversion of the king, he was consecrated to the bishopric of London. London, the chief city of the East Saxons, was already renowned for its opulence, and was the resort of many merchants. All around the city, which was surrounded by a wall, was open country; at a distance of some two miles to the west was an islet in the river, overgrown with thorns and brushwood. On this island stood the remains of a Roman temple dedicated to Apollo; there Sebert raised a church in honour of St. Peter, which, rebuilt by Edward the Confessor and again by Henry III., is now Westminster Abbey. The bones of Sebert were laid to rest in the structure he erected. He also founded another church in London on the ruins of another heathen temple, occupying the site of the present Cathedral of St. Paul.

The Beginning of Troubles. — But with the death of Sebert, affairs took a different turn. The East-Saxon realm was left to his three sons, who, having in some measure abandoned idolatry, now openly resumed their heathen practices, and encouraged their subjects to do the same. One day when the bishop was celebrating Mass, and administering the Holy Eucharist to the people, they came into the Church, and, as is reported, rudely asked him why he did not give them also the fine white bread which he used to give to their father Saba (a familiar abbreviation of Sebert), and which he continued to distribute to the people? Mellitus replied to them: "If you are willing to be washed in the laver of salvation in which your father was washed, you may also partake of that holy bread whereof he used to partake; but if you despise the laver of life, you cannot possibly receive the bread of life." They answered, "We will not enter into that laver, for we know not what need we have of it, yet we will eat of that bread." And when Mellitus repeatedly told them it could not be done, since no one was admitted to partake of the sacred oblation without the holy cleansing, they said in anger: "If you will not comply with us in so small a matter, you shall not remain in our province," and they commanded him and his followers to leave their kingdom. Thus Mellitus lost his bishopric and saw his work suddenly arrested, for on his departure the land went back to heathenism.

The expelled bishop rejoined his brethren in Kent, but they, too, were involved in difficulties. Ethelbert was dead, and the accession of his son Eadbald had proved very prejudicial to the faith. He had formed an illicit union with his father's widow, a young and beautiful woman, whom Ethelbert had espoused on the death of Queen Bertha. On the missionaries venturing to expostulate with the king, he had abjured the religion which forbade the gratification of his passions. A reaction had consequently taken place against the new creed; the people, just as they had before followed the example of the king and court in embracing Christianity, now imitated them in their abandonment of it. Disheartened by these misfortunes, Laurentius had summoned Justus,

Bishop of Rochester, to Canterbury. On the arrival of Mellitus, the three prelates held a sorrowful consultation. They agreed that it would be better for them to return to their own country, where they might serve God in freedom, than to remain where no good was to be done, amongst barbarians who had revolted from the faith. Accordingly Mellitus and Justus withdrew to Gaul, intending to await events. Laurentius was to follow; but on the night before his departure he caused his bed to be prepared within the monastery church of St. Peter and St. Paul, outside the wall of the city. After praying long with tears for his flock, he lay down to sleep. In the dead of the night, as Bede relates, the Prince of the Apostles appeared to him, and scourging him severely, asked him why he was about to forsake the sheep he had committed to his care, reminding him of his own example, who for the sake of the little ones entrusted to him by Christ, had undergone, at the hands of unbelievers, imprisonment, afflictions, stripes, and finally the death of the cross. Next morning Laurentius hastened to the king, and, taking off his garment, exhibited to him the marks of the castigation he had received. Eadbald, astonished, inquired who had presumed to inflict such stripes on so great a man? When Laurentius told him that he had suffered thus for his salvation, the king was deeply impressed; he renounced his unlawful marriage, cast away his idols, embraced the faith of Christ, and after receiving baptism, promoted the interests of the Church to the utmost of his power. The fugitive bishops were recalled: Justus returned to the see of Rochester, but "the Londoners would not receive Mellitus back, as they preferred to be under their idolatrous priests." On the death of Laurentius, in 619, Mellitus succeeded him in the archiepiscopal see.

Paulinus and the Conversion of Northumbria.—From the south of the island the knowledge of the Gospel passed to the most northern of the Anglo-Saxon nations. Edwin, the king of Northumbria, asked in marriage Ethelburga, the daughter of Ethelbert, and on being told a Christian princess might not wed a heathen prince, lest she should lose her faith, he promised not only that she and her attendants, and any ecclesiastics who might accompany her, should enjoy free exercise of their religion, but that he would adopt the faith she professed, if, on examination by wise persons, it should be found better than his own. His terms were accepted. Paulinus, one of the three companions of Justus when he came to Britain in 601, was by him consecrated bishop, in order that he might accompany the Kentish princess to the north, to be to her what the Frankish bishop, Liudhard, had been to her mother, in the then heathen court of Ethelbert. Paulinus laboured much, not only to prevent those Christians who went with him from being corrupted by intercourse with pagans, but, for a time, without effect, to convert some of the heathen to a state of grace.

On Easter-day of the following year (626) it chanced that Edwin had a narrow escape from death, an attempt on his life being made by an assassin in the pay of Cwichelm, king of the West Saxons. The same night the queen gave birth to a daughter, and Edwin gave thanks to his gods in the hearing of Paulinus, who assured him that those thanks were due to the God of the Christians, whose blessing he had implored on them both in the service of the day. The king listened to him with attention; he consented that his infant daughter should be brought up as a Christian, and promised that he too would embrace the faith should he succeed in his meditated vengeance on his enemy. Accordingly, before his departure, the little Eanfled was baptized, and with her eleven of the royal household. When the king returned home victorious from his expedition, he allowed himself to be instructed by Paulinus, but, probably from political motives, he was slow to resolve, and a year passed in anxious deliberation.

At length, when the Witan, or great council, was assembled, Edwin asked the advice of those present. Coifi, the high priest of Northumbria, was the first to reply. It might have been expected that prejudice and interest would have been armed with arguments against a foreign creed, but it was not so; his attachment to paganism had been weakened by disappointment, and he openly declared his contempt for deities who failed to reward faithful service. Then an aged thane spoke: his words betrayed the craving of the human mind for an explanation of the mystery of existence, and for some knowledge of the hereafter. "So seems the life of man, O king," he said, "as a sparrow's flight through the hall when you are sitting at meat in winter-tide, with a warm fire lighted on the hearth, but the icy rain-storm without. The sparrow flies in at one door, and tarries for a moment in the light and heat of the hearth-fire; then, flying forth from the other, vanishes into the wintry darkness whence it came. So the life of man tarries for a moment in our sight; but what is before it, what after it, we know not. If this new teaching tell us aught with certainty of these, let us follow it." Paulinus then addressed the assembly, with such success that the high priest himself suggested the immediate demolition of the heathen altars, and forthwith commenced the work with his own hands, by hurling a spear into the temple most venerated by the people. Thus, as by a national act, Northumbria accepted Christianity. The king erected a wooden chapel at York, on part of the ground now covered by the Minster, and having gone through the necessary course of instruction on catechumens, he and his court were baptized on Easter Eve, 628. Amongst the neophytes was his grandniece, Hilda, the future Abbess of Whitby. When the people heard that their monarch and the nobles had become Christians, they readily listened to the preachers; the result being that, like Augustine in Kent, Paulinus is said to have baptized ten thousand in one day. Pope Honorius sent the pallium to Paulinus, as the northern metropolitan. A few years ago there was a cross in Dewsbury Church with the inscription: "*Paulinus hic prædicavit et celebravit.*"

The kingdom over which Edwin ruled extended from the Humber to the Firth of Forth, and was divided into two provinces, the northern being called Bernicia, the southern one Deira. York was in the latter, therefore to Paulinus belongs the honour of being the first to proclaim the Word of Life to the tribe whose children had attracted the attention of Gregory in the market-place of Rome. The labours of this great missionary were, we are told, prodigious. For six years he worked indefatigably, travelling about catechizing and preaching, his whole mind intent on bringing the Northumbrian people to a knowledge of the truth. His royal convert was also instrumental in extending Christianity beyond his own dominions. He persuaded Eorpwald, King of East Anglia, to become a Christian; but the nobles were not disposed to follow the king's example. To prevent the establishment of the new religion among them, they inflicted on him a death which was virtually a martyrdom. But only for a time did this act have the desired effect; three years later Sigebert, the half-brother of the murdered king, who had long, on account of a family feud, been exiled in Gaul, returned to reign in East Anglia. During his sojourn among the Franks, he had been instructed in the mysteries of the faith, and being, as Bede says, "a most Christian and religious man," he was anxious that his subjects should share the privileges he enjoyed.

Felix and the Conversion of East Anglia.—At that juncture Felix, a Burgundian prelate, who had been strongly moved to go and preach the Gospel in England, arrived at Canterbury, and was sent by the archbishop to East Anglia. He settled at Dunwich, a city on the coast of Suffolk, now annihilated by the inroads of the ocean, and began, in 631, an episcopate of seventeen years, so full of happiness for the cause of Christianity, that Bede may well describe his work with an allusion to the good omen of his name. An important feature in this mission was the founding of schools by the king, such as he had seen in Gaul, for the education of youth and the training of native clergy. Felix was assisted in his labours by Fursey, a monk belonging to a noble Irish family. He was renowned for his sanctity and virtue, and did much by his preaching for the conversion of the people, besides erecting a monastery, of which Sigebert, after resigning his crown to a relative, somewhat later became an inmate. His repose was disturbed by the invasion of a foreign enemy. A band of Mercians penetrated into his dominions, and the East Anglians called for their aged monarch to lead them against the foe. With reluctance he left his peaceful cell to mix in the tumult of battle. On arms being offered him he refused to carry them, as repugnant to his monastic profession, and with a wand directed the operations of the army. But the Mercians prevailed: both the kings were slain, and the country fell a prey to the ravages of the conquerors.

Nevertheless the converts did not abandon their faith; before the death of Felix, the whole kingdom was reclaimed from the errors of paganism, and the Church, with the co-operation of the king who succeeded to the throne, established on a firm basis. The little town of Felixstowe derives its name from the memory of this bishop, who was long revered as the apostle of East Anglia.

CHAPTER III.

ENGLAND A CHRISTIAN COUNTRY.

Invasion of Northumbria: Paulinus leaves. Oswald King.—The ancient superstitions were not to fall in England without a desperate struggle for existence. Whilst Christianity was striking deep root in the eastern provinces, its progress in the north was arrested by an unexpected calamity. Cadwalla, the king of North Wales, desirous to revenge himself on Edwin for a former defeat, allied himself, although professedly a Christian, with Penda, the pagan king of Mercia, who combined the fierce energy of a Teuton warrior with the sternest hatred of the new creed. Together they entered Northumbria, and in a battle, of which the rival religions furnished the war-cries, routed the army of Edwin. The king himself was slain, and for twelve months the land was pillaged and its inhabitants ruthlessly put to death by the victors. Paulinus, seeing nothing was to be gained by remaining, and that there was no safety for the queen, who was committed to his care, except in flight, gathered together the treasures of the sanctuary—a large golden cross and a golden chalice, "hallowed for the service of the altar"—and taking with him Queen Ethelburga and her young children, put to sea and returned to Kent. Northumbria would have relapsed into idolatry but for the exertions of a deacon named James, remarkable for his skill in church music, whom Paulinus left in charge at York, and who with steadfast courage, laboured assiduously, and "by teaching and baptizing rescued much prey from the power of the old enemy of mankind." On the death of Edwin, two princes of the royal line, who had been living in exile with the Scottish monks, and had from them learnt the principles of the Gospel, returned to Northumbria and assumed the government. They thought, by repudiating their Christian belief, to conciliate the invaders; but before long they were both slain by Cadwalla, and another prince, named Oswald, nephew to Edwin, who had been educated by the Celtic missionaries in Iona and had embraced Christianity, "with a small band of followers, but fortified by the faith of Christ," took the field against the enemy. He encountered the hostile army near Hexham; a cross of wood was hastily erected by his order, and his soldiers, prostrate before it, earnestly implored the help of heaven. From prayer they arose to battle and victory at Heavenfield; Cadwalla was killed, and the conqueror ascended, without a rival, the throne of his ancestors (635). It is said that the wood of that cross, the first erected in Bernicia, had the miraculous virtue of healing the sick.

St. Aidan in Northumbria.—Oswald, who is described as "a man beloved by God," was desirous in commencing his reign to restore Christianity to the nation. It was natural that he should turn for teachers to instruct his people to the monks of Iona, who had

sheltered his youth. The first sent was, however, too
stern and unbending to make way with the people,
and he returned home in disgust at their indocility.
While he described to the assembled community the
difficulties of the mission, a voice rose in rebuke:
"Brother, did you not deal too rigidly with those
barbarians? You should have remembered the
maxim of the Apostle about milk for babes, and
stooped to their ignorance, and then raised their
minds to the sublime precepts of the Gospel." The
brethren saw in the giver of this counsel the best
man to carry it into effect; the speaker, Aidan by
name, was appointed to the mission in Northumbria,
and after receiving episcopal ordination he repaired
to Oswald's court. His see was not fixed at York,
but on the island of Lindisfarne or Holy Island,
off the coast of Northumberland, given him by
the king for this purpose, which place, Bede says
(bk. iii. ch. 3), "as the tide ebbs and flows twice
a day, is enclosed by the waves of the sea like
an island; and again, twice in the day, when the
shore is left dry, becomes contiguous to the land."

St. Aidan was a "man of singular meekness, piety,
and moderation," whose exemplary life contributed
greatly to recommend the doctrine that he taught.
At the commencement of his labours, as he was
imperfectly acquainted with the language of the
people, the king himself used to act as his interpreter when he preached a sight which the historian
calls "truly beautiful." Aidan strictly observed
the monastic rule, and rarely appeared at the king's
table. We read, however, that he was sitting at
dinner with him one Easter day, and a silver dish,
full of dainties, had just been placed before them

when a servant, whose charge it was to relieve the poor, entered and told the king that a great multitude of needy persons from all parts were assembled, begging some alms of him. Oswald immediately ordered the meat set before him to be carried to the poor, and the dish broken in pieces and divided amongst them. Thereupon Aidan, delighted with this charitable action, taking the king's right hand, exclaimed, "May this hand never decay!" This prayer was fulfilled, for Oswald's hand and arm, being severed from his body when he fell in battle, remained uncorrupt; in the time of Bede they were preserved in a silver case, as revered relics, in St. Peter's Church in the royal city of Bamborough.

Birinus in Wessex.—While Christianity was thus making rapid progress in the kingdoms of the north and east, a new apostle appeared in the south. Birinus, a monk of Gaul, animated with the desire of extending the conquests of the Gospel, had obtained from Pope Honorius the commission to sow the seeds of the faith amongst the Saxon tribes in some part of Britain where no teacher had as yet penetrated. He was consecrated missionary bishop, and in 634 landed on the south-west coast, where in the kingdom of Wessex he found a wild, untutored tribe ignorant of Christianity. Amongst these heathen he laboured earnestly, and won his way to the favour of Cynegils, the king. Birinus had not long opened his mission, when Oswald of Northumbria came to the court to ask in marriage the daughter of Cynegils. The arguments of the missionary were powerfully aided by the persuasions of the royal suitor; both the princess and her father embraced the religion of Christ. Oswald became at once the godfather and son-in-law of

Cynegils, for, as Bede quaintly observes, "the victorious king of the Northumbrians received him as he came forth from baptism, and by an alliance most pleasing and acceptable to God first adopted him, thus regenerated, for his son, and then took his daughter in marriage." This happened in 635, at Dorchester in Oxfordshire, where Birinus founded his episcopal see.

Penda's Ravages. Oswald killed.—Oswald reigned about seven years longer in Northumbria; like his predecessor, the good King Edwin, he perished in battle. He was slain at Oswestry (Oswaldestry) whilst fighting against the fierce king of Mercia, Penda. His last words, when he found himself hemmed in by his foes, were those of prayer for the souls of his soldiers, and after his death his sanctity was made manifest by miracles. Dust taken from the spot where he fell was found to possess virtue to heal the sick, and even splinters of the stake whereon his head, after the barbarous fashion of the times, was impaled and carried to York, effected numerous cures. "It is not to be wondered," says Bede in his eulogy of this Christian monarch, "that the sick should be healed in the place where he died, for whilst he lived he never ceased to provide for and help the poor and infirm." "Nor," he continues, "was the fame of the renowned Oswald confined to Britain. The rays of his healing brightness spread beyond the sea, for at a later period St. Willibrord, the missionary of Friesland, was heard to speak of the wonders wrought in that remote region by some relics of that most reverend king." The head of Oswald (who was subsequently canonized) was interred in Lindisfarne. Two centuries later it was removed and placed in the coffin of St. Cuthbert. On the tomb of that saint in Durham Cathedral being opened in 1104, it was found between his arms. Hence St. Cuthbert is represented as holding St. Oswald's head in his hands, as may be seen on the north side of the steeple of St. Mary's in Oxford.

The fall of the good King Oswald was felt as a blow to Christianity throughout the whole island. The tidings reached the Bishop Paulinus in Kent, where he had accepted the vacant see of Rochester, and Ethelburga, widow of King Edwin, in her minster at Lyminge. They commemorated the name of the martyr-king by dedicating to him the little church of Paddlesworth, of old a dependency of Lyminge, which still bears his name. The victorious Penda, continuing his ravages in Northumbria, penetrated as far as Bamborough, the royal fortress. Despairing of success in an assault, he pulled down the cottages around, piled their wooden fabric against the walls, and fired the mass of timber. St. Aidan, from his retreat on the islet of Farne, beheld the clouds of smoke and flame drifting over the city, and lifting his hands in prayer exclaimed: "See, Lord, what harm Penda is doing!" Immediately—so runs the tale—a change of wind drove the flames back on those who had kindled them, so they were forced to desist from attacking a city which they understood to be divinely protected. Penda gave up the attempt to conquer Northumbria, and turned his arms against Cenwalch, the son of Cynegils, who had succeeded to the throne of Wessex.

This prince, who was in no way favourably disposed to the new lore introduced into the kingdom by Birinus, had married Penda's sister, and on his accession to the crown, repudiated her for the sake of another woman. To avenge this insult, the king of Mercia marched into Wessex, and drove Cenwalch into exile. He fled to the court of East Anglia, where Anna, the successor of Sigebert, reigned. There he remained for three years, during which time, having seen how much Christianity had improved the land, he too accepted the faith, and on his restoration to his kingdom, became one of its zealous supporters. The men of Wessex conformed to the example of their ruler, and before long the province was a stronghold of Christianity. In 648, the Anglo-Saxon Chronicle tells us, the church at Winchester was built by the king's orders, and the episcopal see was transferred to that city, probably because Dorchester, being on the confines of Mercia, was constantly exposed to the inroads of its warlike neighbours. Hedda, who was then bishop of the diocese, caused the remains of St. Birinus, the Apostle of the West Saxons, to be translated to the cathedral of Winchester.

Conversion of Mercia begun.—Mercia, whose monarch, long a terror to the adjacent kingdoms, was regarded as the champion of paganism, was itself destined in its turn to receive the Gospel, and that through the instrumentality of the Northumbrian princes with whom hostilities had so frequently been carried on. Peada, the son of Penda, was a suitor for the hand of Alchfleda, the daughter of Oswy, who had succeeded Oswald, and had married Eanfleda, the royal infant who had been the first to receive Christian baptism in Northumbria. Oswy would not permit this marriage without some guarantee that she would be allowed to continue a worshipper of Christ; whereupon Peada, who had become acquainted with Christian teaching through intercourse with one of the sons of Oswy who had married his sister Kynburga, readily agreed not only to allow Alchfleda to follow the religion wherein she had been trained by the monks of Lindisfarne, but himself to be baptized. Moreover he allowed four priests, chosen for this purpose by Finan, the bishop who on the death of Aidan had taken his place, to accompany the princess and evangelize the kingdom over which he ruled in the lifetime of his father. The old king, though himself an irreclaimable pagan, offered no opposition to the missionaries, though he spoke with the greatest contempt of those whose Christian profession was discredited by their heathen practices.

East Saxony.—About this time a second mission to the East Saxons was inaugurated. Sigebert, their king, went on a visit to the court of Oswy, and was by him persuaded to forsake his idols and receive Christian baptism. Thirty-seven years had elapsed since Mellitus had been expelled, and now the faith was once more to be planted in his diocese, not again to be uprooted. On returning to his own land, Sigebert asked for a supply of teachers to convert and baptize his people. The rapid extension of their field of labour had caused a dearth of suitable missioners for new districts; the men trained in the college founded by St. Aidan were all at work in different provinces. Bishop Finan summoned a monk named Cedd, brother to St. Chad, afterwards Bishop of Lichfield, and sent him with another priest to preach to the East Saxons. These missionaries met with such success that, on the return of Cedd to

Lindisfarne to confer with Finan, the latter, hearing how well the work of the Gospel had prospered in East Saxony, called to him two other bishops to assist in the ordination, and consecrated Cedd bishop of the East Saxons. The newly-made prelate went back to his mission, and there, as the historian says, pursuing with more ample authority the work he had begun, he built churches in several places, ordaining priests and deacons to assist him in the work of the ministry. This is supposed to be a foreshadowing of the parochial system, which grew up very gradually in England. The centres of mission work specially named are a city called Ithancestir, of which no trace remains, and another situated on the banks of the Thames, probably the Tilbury of the present day. In each of these places he gathered a flock, we are told, of the servants of Christ, whom he taught to observe the discipline of the regular life, as far as their untrained minds could receive it.

Conversion of Mercia completed.—The peace of Northumbria was destined once more to be disturbed by the incursions of the King of Mercia. Oswy had done all in his power to conciliate this inveterate enemy of Christianity. Besides the double alliance between the royal houses, he had endeavoured to purchase peace by the offer of a large gift. All was in vain. Penda crossed the frontier to make a last attempt to subjugate Northumbria. Oswy, aware that his own forces were far inferior to those of the invader, and that he had little chance of resistance, had recourse to the divine protection : " if the pagan will not accept our gifts," he said, " let us offer them to the Lord who will." He therefore vowed if he were victorious that he would dedicate his infant daughter, Elfleda, to God in the monastic life, and give twelve pieces of land for building as many religious houses. The armies met; the terrible old pagan, who had slain five kings, was himself smitten down at last, and with him fell the Teuton divinities whose worship he had so strenuously upheld. Oswy assumed the government of the greater part of Mercia, and effectually promoted the extension of Christianity in that kingdom. Three years later the Mercian chiefs asserted their independence, threw off his sovereignty, and raised Wulfhere, a son of Penda, to the throne. He is described as a vigorous and active ruler, the first king of all Mercia who received the faith and was cleansed in the laver of regeneration. He married Ermenilda, daughter of the king of Kent; their daughter, Werburga, became the head of a nunnery, and the minster of Chester, where she was venerated as a patron saint, grew up around her shrine. It is curious to remark that nearly all the children and several grandchildren of the cruel Penda died in the odour of sanctity.

Thus the Mercians, having expelled the officers of a foreign king, recovered their liberty and their lands; and being thus set free, Bede tells us, they together with their king, rejoiced to serve Christ, the true King, that they might obtain the everlasting kingdom of heaven. The three provinces were united in one bishopric. The see was at first fixed at Repton, the capital of Mercia, and afterwards, when St. Chad was bishop, removed to Lichfield. The name Lichfield means "field of the dead"; it was given to the spot because of the traditionary martyrdom of a thousand Christians during the Diocletian persecution. The cathedral is still dedicated to St. Chad, or Ceadda, a monk of Lindisfarne, who was in 666 made bishop of York, and was translated to the Mercian bishopric somewhat later. So simple and lowly was this prelate that in his humility he always travelled on foot on his long missionary journeys, until the archbishop commanded him to ride on horseback. His episcopate was a short one, but it deserved the epithet of "most glorious," and procured for Chad a high place amongst the saints of his country. Venerable Bede records that when his death drew near, the voices of singers singing sweetly descended from heaven, and filled the little cell wherein he was praying. Then the same celestial melody ascended, and returned heavenward as it had come. The prelate confided to one of his clergy that it was the soul of his brother Cedd, come with a choir of angels to summon him to the heavenly reward he longed for, and that in seven days they would return and take him with them. He fell ill of an epidemic prevalent at that time, and on the seventh day expired. Many miracles were worked at his tomb.

Sussex converted by Wilfrid.—The inhabitants of Sussex, the most ancient and certainly the most insignificant of the kingdoms of the Saxon Heptarchy, were the last to embrace the Christian religion. They long resisted the efforts of the missioners, but finally their obstinacy was overcome by the zeal and address of a northern prelate, Wilfrid, of whom more will be said hereafter. Exiled from his diocese by the intrigues of his enemies, he was offered a refuge by Ethelwalch, king of Sussex, who, being himself a Christian, desired him to attempt the conversion of his subjects. Some years previously Ethelwalch had invited into his realm some five or six Irish monks under the abbot Dicul. They had built a very small monastery, where they served God in humility and great poverty, unregarded by the natives, who would not listen to their preaching. Wilfrid came to reap the harvest of souls for which these obscure servants of God prayed and worked. Fifteen years before, when returning from Gaul after his episcopal consecration, he had been wrecked on the Sussex coast, and narrowly escaped with his life and that of his companions from the ferocity of the inhabitants, urged on by their pagan priest. He now came under the protection of the king; and, having gained much practical experience during his foreign travels, he knew how to turn to account a temporal emergency as a spiritual opportunity. A famine had reduced the barbarous people to great distress. Wilfrid rendered them good service by teaching them how to capture the fish in which the rivers and the sea abounded, and otherwise relieving their physical misery. Gratitude and confidence in Wilfrid induced the people to listen to his instructions; they renounced their old superstitions, and within the space of five years the Christian worship was firmly established in Sussex, and a monastery founded at Selsey, then a peninsula joined to the mainland by a narrow strip of ground.

Isle of Wight.—The conquest of Sussex for the faith was followed by that of the Isle of Wight. The island had been wrested from Wessex by one of the kings of Mercia; it was reconquered by Cadwalla when he came to the throne of Wessex. On commencing the struggle, this king, fierce pagan as he then was, vowed that, should he succeed, he would surrender a fourth part of the island to the servants of Christ. He kept his word, received the faith from St. Wilfrid, and, inspired with devotion to the Prince of the Apostles, journeyed to Rome to receive baptism from the hand of the successor of St. Peter. He was baptized on Holy Saturday, 689, by Pope Sergius, who gave him the name of Peter. In this instance the saying, "See Rome and die," proved true; Cadwalla fell sick and died within the shadow of his patron's basilica, before he laid aside the white garments which it was usual for a neophyte to wear for a week after baptism, or sullied with any stain his baptismal innocence.

Thus, within a century from the coming of Augustine, the conversion of the Angles and Saxons was successfully completed. Originated by the charity of Gregory the Great, this enterprise was unremittingly pursued by the zeal of his disciples, aided by the co-operation of apostolic labourers from Gaul and Italy, of Scottish missionaries from Iona, and Celtic monks from Ireland. Into whatever realm these heralds of the Gospel penetrated, their first object was invariably to obtain on behalf of the religion they came to teach the favour of the prince. His patronage secured, no opposition prevented their success. To attempt the instruction of the ignorant barbarians without the support of the civil power was useless, but the conversion of the monarch once effected, in most cases his example was speedily followed by a large proportion of his subjects. It is noteworthy that of the saints of the early English calendar, some three hundred in number, more than half are personages of royal birth or extraction. The adoption of the true religion was, besides, the means of conferring many temporal advantages on the people. Not unfrequently those who were living as bondsmen obtained on their baptism the grant of their liberty, so that they were set free from the yoke of slavery to man at the same time that they were delivered from the bondage of the devil. When Sunday began to be observed as a day sanctified by repose from labour, the churls, or slaves, who tilled the ground for their masters, obtained one day of rest out of the seven. A tenth part of the produce of the land was appropriated for the relief of the destitute and the maintenance of the clergy. The admission of ecclesiastics to the councils of state led to improvements in the laws, and their presence at court restrained the unruly thanes, and was instrumental in the adoption of more pacific policy conducive to the tranquillity of the country and welfare of the people. Thus with the introduction of Christianity came the beginning of civilization; and doubtless the announcement of the life that is to come met with readier acceptance because it was accompanied by some promise of the life that now is, some initiation into the arts that improve its conditions. Of all the tribes that composed the German race, none was more formidable, none more savage than the Saxons. They were barbarians, robbers, idolators, thoroughly illiterate and inhumanly cruel, till Christianity came to regenerate and transform them. That it succeeded, we have seen; and to its success is attributable not only the wisdom of their customs and institutions, but their continuance in the land which their injustice had wrested from its rightful owners.

CHAPTER IV.

CONFIRMATION OF THE PAPAL AUTHORITY.

Dispute about Easter.—We have somewhat anticipated the course of events in the south of England, in order to complete, in the preceding chapter, the history of the subjugation of the kingdoms of the Saxon Heptarchy to the Christian faith. It will be necessary now to return to Northumbria; where, sixty years after the death of Augustine, the crisis foreseen by him had arrived. The Scottish monks, who had been chiefly instrumental in the conversion of this northern kingdom, all held to the British time for celebrating Easter, in opposition to the Roman custom, which was followed by the first missionaries, namely, the clergy who accompanied the queen on her coming from Kent. The dispute concerning this and some other matters of ecclesiastical discipline was again causing dissension. During the lifetime of the holy Aidan and his successor Finan, the differences of observance had been tolerated, but the next bishop, Colman, also of Irish extraction and Scottish ordination, did not possess their power of conciliation. It became necessary to enforce uniformity, lest confusion on minor points might lead to confusion on matters of greater moment. The matter in contest appears to us somewhat trivial, but the fact that it was made the subject of controversy affords convincing evidence that in regard to faith and doctrine not the slightest divergence existed; otherwise these points of external difference would have faded into insignificance. The only thing that gives them importance is that the persistent adhesion of the British bishops to the Celtic usages has by some been regarded as a tacit assertion of their independence of the supremacy committed by the Holy See to the Archbishop of Canterbury. The monks of Lindisfarne, and the religious houses whose foundation followed that of Lindisfarne, looked for their ecclesiastical traditions to Ireland; they quoted the constitution of Columba, not of Gregory, and recognized as their metropolitan the Abbot of Iona. Something like a faction, too, had grown up within the court. The king was profoundly attached to the teaching of the monks, whose sanctity and zeal gave weight to the Celtic traditions; whereas the queen, who had been brought up in Kent, held, with all her followers, to the Roman use, which she had been trained to consider as the correct one.

Council of Whitby, 664.—It so happened that one year the king's party were keeping high festival and celebrating Easter with pomp and rejoicing, while the queen and her attendants were still fasting, and about to enter upon the mournful solemnities of Holy Week. In consequence of this, the king determined that a council should be held to decide the question and put an end to the strife. The assembly was con-

Confirmation of the Papal Authority. 51

voked at the monastery of Streaneshalch, afterwards called Whitby. This religious house had been erected by the Abbess Hilda on the proud height looking towards the sea, which is now crowned by the ruined church of a monastery, founded two centuries after her minster was laid desolate. Bede gives a full account of this council, which must be summarized here. The principal subject of discussion was the observance of Easter, which had called out the strongest feeling. The Celtic churches included the fourteenth day of the equinoctial moon within the number of possible Easter Sundays; the other churches insisted on excluding it, alleging, on the authority of the Nicene Council, the duty of keeping clear of the day upon which the Jews celebrated the feast. In other words, the Paschal festival among the Scots might fall on any Sunday from the 14th to the 20th, inclusive; whereas at Rome and in all other churches, the time was fixed from the 15th to the 21st day of the moon, and to keep this rule was to observe the Catholic Easter.

At this council were present, besides the chief clergy of Northumbria, the Abbess Hilda and several royal personages, Agilbert, Bishop of Paris, and Cedd, Bishop of London, who had come on one of his periodical visits to a monastery he had founded in the north. Agilbert had been Bishop of Dorchester after St. Birinus, but had been driven away by Cenwalch because he could not speak English. He had come now to visit Wilfrid at Ripon, and had ordained him priest. The king opened the proceedings by urging the desirability of uniformity of custom amongst those who were united in faith. He observed that it behoved them to make inquiry and assure themselves which was the true tradition, before all else, in regard to the observance of Easter. Thereupon he called upon the Bishop of Lindisfarne to speak first and defend the Celtic use. Colman replied that the custom he followed in keeping Easter was that of his forefathers, and of the elders who had sent him thither, and the same that St. John the Evangelist was recorded to have observed, with all the churches over which he presided. Agilbert was then invited to speak on behalf of the Roman practice, but he desired that his friend, the young priest Wilfrid, might state the case in his stead, as he could better explain it in the English tongue than the bishop could by means of an interpreter. Thereupon Oswy ordered Wilfrid to speak.

Wilfrid was a young noble, who had been a brilliant ornament of the court of Oswy, but in the height of his popularity had renounced the world and become a monk at Lindisfarne. Afterwards he had a great desire to visit the tomb of St. Peter, and Queen Eanfleda helped him to carry out his design. In company with another young noble, Benedict Biscop, he set out for Rome, visited the tombs of the Apostles, and received the Pope's blessing. On his return, he narrowly escaped death at the hands of Ebroin, the mayor of the palace. His acquaintance with the Churches of Italy and France raised him above the insular traditions in which he had been brought up, and he returned to England a devoted son of the Pope, and a strenuous advocate of Roman customs.

He began by dilating on the wide prevalence of the Catholic Easter, which he had found in France and Italy, when he travelled through those countries, and at Rome, where Peter and Paul had taught and suffered. The same he had ascertained to be observed in Africa, Asia, Egypt, Greece—in fact, throughout Christendom, save only among the Picts and Britons in two remote islands (*extra orbem positi*). He urged that Colman was wrong about St. John, as although he, at a time when concession was requisite, had allowed the Jewish converts to keep Easter on the same day as that on which they were accustomed to celebrate the Pasch, namely, the 14th day of the month, he had not intended this custom to be permanent. Now St. Peter, when he preached at Rome, gave directions that Easter should always be kept on a Sunday, and that the Sunday chosen should be next after the evening of the 14th day. Wilfrid then proceeded to point out that the Celts did not follow the tradition of St. John, since they, too, observed Easter on a Sunday, but were in error as to their calculation, beginning a day too early and ending a day too soon, making it possible that the feast should fall on the 14th, whereas this day was to be excluded. Colman replied by appealing to Anatolius' Paschal canon, and asked whether it were credible that Columba, the father of the Scoto-British Church, and his successors, men eminent for sanctity and miracles, would have been allowed to go wrong in such a matter. Wilfrid easily disposed of these objections, winding up by asking, "Although that Columba of yours—and I may say *ours* too, if he were Christ's servant—was a saint and wonder-worker, is he to be preferred to the blessed Prince of the Apostles, to whom were given the keys of heaven?"

Then the king asked Colman whether those words were really spoken by our Lord to St. Peter? He answered, "It is true, O king!" "Can you show that any such power was given to your Columba?" Colman replied, "No." "Do you both agree," the king inquired further, "that these words were specially directed to St. Peter?" They both said, "We do assuredly." "Then," added the king, with a quiet smile, "I do not care to contradict that doorkeeper, lest when I seek admission to the kingdom of heaven, there should be none, he being my adversary, to open the portals for me." All the nobles and people present, including St. Hilda, applauded this decision, and it was agreed that throughout Northumbria the Roman reckoning for Easter should in future be adopted. Such was the close of the Whitby conference. Colman, perceiving that his traditions were rejected, and the founders of his order set aside, resigned his bishopric and retired to Iona with some of his clergy who would not comply with the observance of Easter and the shape of the tonsure (for about that there was also much controversy). Cedd, the Bishop of London, abandoned the usages of Lindisfarne, and returned to his bishopric, but only to fall a prey to a pestilential fever, which in that same year (664) carried off a great number of the inhabitants of the British Isles. Amongst other victims of this epidemic was Deusdedit, the Archbishop of Canterbury, and Tuda, the newly-consecrated prelate who was chosen as Colman's successor. Wilfrid, the disputant who had so ably defended the Roman use in the recent conference, was appointed by the king to fill the place of the latter.

Wilfrid Bishop of York.—When nominated to the see of his native province, Wilfrid stipulated that the bishopric should be transferred to York, where it was originally fixed, and that he should receive episcopal consecration from the Roman, not the Celtic bishops. As the see of Canterbury was vacant at that time, he repaired to Gaul, and was ordained in a synod of bishops at Compiègne, with unusual magnificence, by his friend Agilbert, the former Bishop of Dorchester, then Bishop of Paris.

Whilst Wilfrid lingered awhile in Gaul, the King of Northumbria, at the instigation of the Scottish monks or by the desire of the people, appointed Chad to the bishopric of his realm. Chad hastened to Canterbury for consecration. On arriving he found no archbishop had as yet been chosen; consequently he proceeded to Winchester, whose bishop, Wini, was almost the only one of the Saxon prelates spared by the pestilence. As the Council of Nicæa required the co-operation of three bishops to consecrate another bishop, Wini called to his aid two British prelates from Cornwall and Devon to perform the ceremony. Wilfrid, on his return, found Chad already in possession of his diocese, and much beloved by the people. Understanding that he had lost the favour of the Northumbrians, Wilfrid retired to his monastery at Ripon, employing himself in building abbeys and churches, and occasionally exercising his episcopal functions in Kent and Mercia, while the see of Canterbury was yet unfilled.

At this juncture Oswy, king of Northumbria, and Egbert, king of Kent, the most powerful of the English princes, consulted together concerning the state of the Church in this country. It was suffering greatly from the mortality among the English bishops, and still more from the lack of the permanent establishment of the metropolitan see. The bishops of Canterbury continued to receive the pallium from Rome, and their authority was recognized in all the Saxon dioceses founded by missionaries from the continent; while the churches founded by the Scottish clergy obeyed a succession of bishops sent from Iona by order of the abbot of the monastery established on that island. The remedy for the inconveniences arising out of this state of things was to place all the bishops of the Anglo-Saxon kingdoms under the authority of the Archbishop of Canterbury.

Theodore Archbishop of Canterbury, 669.—The two kings accordingly, with the consent of the Church, chose Wighard, one of the native clergy, described as a good man, well instructed in faith and learning, to fill the vacant see, and sent him for consecration to Rome. He carried with him royal gifts of silver and gold to the Supreme Pontiff, and a letter of request, the object of which was, that all the prelates of the Anglo-Saxon kingdom might be made subject to the successors of St. Augustine. No sooner had Wighard reached Rome than he was struck down by malaria. The task of providing a substitute devolved on Vitalian, who was then Pope. It was not until after several refusals on the part of those who objected to the distance of the country and the barbarism of the people, that the office was accepted by Theodore, a Greek monk, sixty-six years old, a scholar, a man of vast experience, and well versed in ecclesiastical discipline. As his head was shaven entirely, after the fashion of the Greeks, he waited at Rome four months till his hair was sufficiently long to allow of his receiving the coronal

Confirmation of the Papal Authority. 57

tonsure, in order that he might not be unacceptable to the Kentish clergy. His arrival in Britain in May, 669, forms an epoch in the ecclesiastical history of the Anglo-Saxons.

Theodore was a man of consummate practical ability, and sincerely determined to do the work for which he had been directly sent from Rome and consecrated by the Pope's own hands—that of making his authority felt as chief pastor of the several English churches, and welding them together in subordination to the archiepiscopal see of Canterbury. He immediately entered upon a visitation of all the dioceses—organizing monasteries, establishing schools, correcting such things as he found deficient, whether in church ministrations or monastic discipline. What was more important, he consecrated bishops for the vacant sees—all but three were unfilled at that time—added several bishoprics to those already existing, and grouped them all round Canterbury as their centre. Everywhere he was welcomed, for his coming was regarded as a public blessing by both kings and people. He visited Northumbria, condemned the intrusion of Chad on the ground of his consecration not being legitimate, and established Wilfrid in possession of the diocese to which he had been ordained. Chad, who had been ruling the Church of York in a most excellent manner, willingly withdrew; the piety and humility he displayed induced Theodore to appoint him to the bishopric of Lichfield.

Council of Hertford, 673.—In 673, when Theodore had made himself sufficiently acquainted with the needs of the people, he summoned a synod of bishops and clergy at Hertford, to confer respecting their future operations, and the observance of such things as were necessary for the unity and peace of the Church. All present were asked if they would agree to maintain the ancient canonical decrees of the Fathers. On their unanimous assent, ten articles selected from a collection of canons approved by the Council of Chalcedon, were laid before the assembly, and accepted by them as specially adapted to the needs of the country. These rules were in substance as follows :—

1. That there should be uniformity in keeping Easter. 2. That no bishop should invade another bishop's diocese. 3. That bishops should not in any matter disturb the monasteries consecrated to God, or take away any part of their property. 4. That monks should not move from one monastery to another without leave from their own abbot. 5. That no cleric should leave his diocese at his own pleasure, or be received in another without letters of recommendation from his bishop. 6. That bishops and clergy should not officiate anywhere without the permission of the bishop in whose diocese they were known to be. 7. That there should be a yearly synod held. 8. That no bishop should through ambition set himself above another, but take rank according to the time and order of consecration. 9. That additional bishops should be appointed as the number of the faithful increases. 10. That persons should not marry within the prohibited degrees, nor be wrongfully divorced, nor marry again if divorced.

All the prelates assembled in synod acknowledged the authority of the archbishop as their one primate. Theodore was the first archbishop to whom all England submitted, says Bede, adding, in reference to the commencement of his episcopate, "never were there happier times since the Angles came to Britain."

So ended the Council of Hertford, a memorable event in the annals of the English Church, hardly less so in those of the English people. For while it gave expression and consolidation to the idea of ecclesiastical unity, it was also the first of all national gatherings for general legislation; the precursor of the witenagemotes and parliaments of the one imperial realm. Moreover Theodore, in his work of organization, in his creation of parishes, his arrangement of dioceses, above all, in the way in which he grouped them all round the see of Canterbury, was unconsciously doing a political work. The regular subordination of priest to bishop, of bishop to primate, in the administration of the Church, supplied a model on which the organization of the State formed itself. The single throne of the one primate at Canterbury accustomed men's minds to the thought of a single throne for their temporal ruler; the tendency to national unity had already declared itself, and the policy of Theodore clothed that unity which was still in the future with a sacred form and divine sanctions.

Wilfrid appeals to Rome.—Wilfrid, who, as we have seen, had been reinstated in his bishopric by command of Archbishop Theodore, led in private an austere and exemplary life, while in public he was indefatigable in the discharge of his episcopal duties. For some years he enjoyed the confidence and favour of Egfrid, the son and successor of King Oswy; but an occasion arose on which he incurred the royal displeasure. It was on account of Queen Etheldreda, as we learn from the record of Eddi, Wilfrid's companion and biographer. Shortly after her marriage, into which she had been reluctantly forced, Etheldreda had extorted permission from her husband to leave the court and retire to a religious house, and when, revoking his consent, he desired her to return, she refused to do so. The king considered that Wilfrid had encouraged her to resist his insistence, and held him responsible for her refusal to leave the convent: in his resentment he sought to eject him from his bishopric. About that time Theodore visited Northumbria, and by persuasion of the king, during the temporary absence of Wilfrid, without his participation or knowledge, he used his legatine authority to divide the vast diocese into three smaller ones. For each of the new sees he consecrated a bishop, so that Wilfrid found himself excluded, not from a part only, but from the whole of his bishopric. He hastened to the court to complain of this injustice, but his remonstrances were unheeded, and Egfrid, at the instigation of the princess he had espoused in Etheldreda's place, banished him from the kingdom. Thereupon Wilfrid resolved to appeal from the judgement of his metropolitan to the superior authority of the Apostolic See.

The direct route through Gaul being beset with dangers for him, on account of the treachery of his enemies, he journeyed to Rome by way of Friesland, and, unable to restrain his zeal for the ministry of evangelization, preached the Gospel to the barbarous Friesians. This was the commencement of the apostolate carried on with marvellous success at a later period by St. Willibrord and other English monks. On arriving at Rome, Wilfrid found that Theodore had sent a representative thither to oppose him. A council of fifty prelates was appointed to examine and judge the case. A detailed account has been preserved of the proceedings by Wilfrid's friend Eddi; it is full of the most pronounced statements of the doctrine of the papal supremacy. In his petition Wilfrid does not demand that there shall be no division of the diocese, but that the new bishops shall be canonically appointed, and taken from his own clergy. The decision was entirely in his favour. After spending some months in Rome he returned to Northumbria, provided with a papal bull ordering that he should be restored to the office and privileges whereof he had been unjustly deprived. A synod was called (679), as the historian relates (Eddi, *Vita Wilfridi*, c. xxxiv.), "to hear the salutary counsels sent by the Apostolic See for the peace of the Churches. But when they read some things that were hard to them and opposed to their desires, some contumaciously refused to obey." The enmity of the king prevented him from listening to the dictates of justice; but to say that his refusal to obey the mandate was due to any rejection of papal authority is quite unfounded. On the contrary, it is clear from his conduct that he accepted it, for Wilfrid was thrown into prison, and every effort was made, not to make him renounce papal authority, but to extort from him a confession either that he had gained the verdict by corrupt practices, or that the document he brought was a fabrication. His constancy defeated every artifice; he was at length liberated through the mediation of an abbess who was related to the king, on condition that he should never again enter the kingdom. Wilfrid retired to Mercia, where, as has been related, he knew how to make his own misfortunes turn out for the furtherance of the Gospel.

Council of Hatfield, 680.—It was during the period of Wilfrid's exile from his diocese that Pope Agatho, alarmed by the spread of the Eutychian and Monothelite heresies, made inquiries concerning the state of the Church in England. For the purpose of ascertaining whether it was free from the contagion of false doctrine, he summoned the Archbishop of Canterbury and his suffragans to attend a council in Rome; but on the length of the journey, and the necessities of their dioceses, being urged as an excuse for their non-attendance, the Pope consented to accept a written proof of their orthodoxy. Accordingly, in 680, Theodore called an assembly of the bishops and the more learned of the clergy at Hatfield, in Yorkshire, to make a public profession of their faith. At this synod, from which Wilfrid was necessarily absent, the abbot John, who had accompanied St. Benedict Biscop from Rome, was present as papal deputy. The agreement of all in the sound Catholic doctrine was found to be unanimous. A document was drawn up declaring their adhesion to the decrees of the five first General Councils and to the condemnation of Monothelitism by Martin I.,[1] to which all present appended their signatures, and which was duly forwarded to Rome.

[1] The principal errors broached since the condemnation of the heresy of Arius at Nice, 325, were :—(1) That the Holy Ghost was not God, condemned in the first Council of Constantinople, A.D. 381; (2) the Nestorian heresy, that in Christ were two persons, condemned in the Council of Ephesus, 431; (3) the Eutychian, that Christ had but one nature, condemned in the Council of Chalcedon, 451; (4) the Monothelite heresy, that Christ had but one will, condemned in the Second Council of Constantinople, 680.

Theodore's Repentance.—Before his death Theodore expressed great regret for his injustice to Wilfrid. It was not in his power fully to repair the injury he had done him, but he wrote letters in his favour to the kings of Mercia and Northumbria, testifying to the innocence, patience, and merit of the exiled bishop, and adjuring Alfrid, the successor of Egfrid, "for the fear of the Lord *and on account of the commands of the Apostolic See*, to deign to become reconciled to him." The result of this was Wilfrid's restoration, first to the monastery of Hexham, then to the bishopric of York, together with his own monastery of Ripon, the first religious house in the north which followed the rule of St. Benedict. Eata, the intruder of Hexham, was at that time just dead (686), but Bosa was ejected from York and Eadhed from Ripon, quite in accordance with the papal mandate. Wilfrid did not, however, entirely recover his former jurisdiction. He retained the see of Hexham only for a year, when it was given to John of Beverley, and Cuthbert was regarded as legitimate bishop of Lindisfarne until his death in 687. It was doubtless his assent which rendered this arrangement valid.

The Result of Wilfrid's Appeal.—Only for five troubled years did he wield his episcopal authority before the quarrel broke out afresh. The king ordered Wilfrid to resign the abbey and the revenues of Ripon for the creation of a new diocese. Upon his refusal, the monarch violently deposed and ejected him. Wilfrid, his life being in danger, again withdrew to Mercia, and placed himself under the protection of the king. There he remained for nine years, until in 703 he was invited to attend a council summoned by

Bertwald, Theodore's successor in the see of Canterbury. On his arrival Wilfrid was required to promise upon oath that he would abide by the decree of the metropolitan, whatever it might be. He saw the object of his opponents; they hoped to wrest from him the weapon wherewith he had already defeated them—the right of appeal. Accordingly he replied that he would accept the decision, provided it were conformable to the canons and previous decrees of the Apostolic See. Thereupon he was ordered to relinquish the exercise of his episcopal functions in punishment of his alleged contumacy; being offered as a favour the possession of his own monastery of Ripon, on condition that he would confine himself to its precincts. Wilfrid's indignation was aroused by the terms proposed to him. "What!" he exclaimed, "after an episcopate of nearly forty years, am I to subscribe to my own degradation? If justice be denied me here, I appeal to a higher tribunal; let whosoever would depose me accompany me to Rome, and prove his charge before the Sovereign Pontiff." The king and Archbishop Bertwald were indignant. They replied, "Let him be branded and condemned by us as altogether to be blamed, because he has preferred their judgement [*i.e.*, that of the Romans] before our own." They did not disbelieve in the Holy See as the highest ecclesiastical tribunal, but they would have preferred to settle this matter themselves. They sent their representatives to Rome, whither Wilfrid now went once more. The Archbishop was ordered by the Pope to convoke a council, and then leave it to the option of the bishops of York and Hexham to settle the matter in dispute amicably with Wilfrid, or repair to Rome, and there plead their cause before a larger council.

Confirmation of the Papal Authority. 65

With this answer Wilfrid returned to England. Archbishop Bertwald did all he could for the restoration of peace, but Aldfrid, the king of Northumbria, was for a while inexorable. But on his deathbed he repented of his disobedience to the Holy See, and eventually a peaceful arrangement was effected. Wilfrid had already acquiesced in the establishment of a separate bishopric of Lindisfarne: he now consented to forego his claims to York, to which see John of Beverley, the Bishop of Hexham, was translated, contenting himself with the bishopric of Hexham and the abbey of Ripon. The three prelates promised to forget all causes of dissension, and in token of their reconciliation exchanged the kiss of peace and received the Bread of unity.

Thus ended this long and tedious controversy. The importance of the subject will excuse the somewhat lengthy manner in which it has been told. Wilfrid was the first Anglo-Saxon bishop who claimed the protection of the See of Rome, by thus invoking the papal prerogative of receiving and deciding appeals from the judgement of provincial or national councils, or individual acts of injustice on the part of the ecclesiastical or secular power. The result proved the utility of the supreme jurisdiction exercised by the Sovereign Pontiff; we read no more from the time of Wilfrid until the reign of Edward the Confessor of any arbitrary deposition of bishops at the will either of king or metropolitan.

Wilfrid was left in peaceful possession of his bishopric during four years, until the day of his death, 709. He was buried at Ripon, in the church he had built and dedicated to St. Peter the Apostle. At a later period he was canonized.

CHAPTER V.

SOME SAINTS OF THE ANGLO-SAXON CHURCH.

WE have in the foregoing pages seen the Church built up and consolidated in Britain as a regularly constituted and organized society, recognizing the supreme authority of Rome. We will now examine a few of the living stones which served to strengthen the towers and adorn the walls of this glorious edifice.

St. Cuthbert.—Cuthbert, the great wonder-worker of early English Christianity, whose name has made Lindisfarne memorable, was called to the love and service of God in an extraordinary manner while yet a child, tending sheep on the hills beyond the Tweed. On the night of St. Aidan's death, he had a vision which showed him a company of angels carrying the soul of the saint to heaven in a globe of fire. This decided him to embrace the religious life; next morning he gave over the sheep to their owner, and made his way to the log-houses which then formed the monastery of Melrose. He was attracted to this monastery, where the rule of St. Columba was at that time followed, by the fame of Boisil the abbot, who was renowned for sanctity and virtue. Cuthbert soon surpassed all the brethren in studies, prayer, and manual work; on the death of Boisil he succeeded to his office and duties, adding to the latter the work of an evangelist throughout the adjacent country. His labours while in that monastery made him famous throughout the north; so that in 664, a new prior being wanted in Lindisfarne, he was removed to that important post, that the monks might profit by his example and teaching, and by his experience of monastic discipline. There he had to encounter opposition which would have worn out one less firm, and exasperated one less loving. But Cuthbert, a man of extraordinary patience and cheerfulness, possessed the art of gradually bringing round his antagonists to concur in his wishes. His skill in speaking, says his biographer Bede, was so great, his power of persuasion so vast, and the light of his countenance so angelic, that no one in his presence concealed from him the secrets of his soul. His zeal for what was right amounted almost to sternness, but this was combined with infinite tenderness towards the sinner.

After Cuthbert had been twelve years at Lindisfarne he felt the need of seclusion, and retired to the neighbouring islet of Farne, where, after banishing the evil spirits that haunted it, he constructed for himself a cell, surrounded by a wall of stones and turf so high that he could see nothing but the heaven above. A larger hut was built upon the island for the visitors who came to seek his genial sympathy, and to profit by his salutary instructions, as well as to accommodate the monks who brought him supplies of food. Bede relates that one Christmas Day, some Lindisfarne monks came over to Farne, and begged him to leave his cell, to spend the solemn and joyful day with them in the great house. He consented; they all sat down to their Christmas dinner, in the midst of which, as if stirred by an inward impulse, he began to talk of watchfulness against trials. The monks thought there was a time for all things. "Let us spend this day in gladness," they said; "it is our Lord's birthday." "Well," he replied, "let us do so." Presently, while they were enjoying themselves with meats and stories, he was again moved to speak of preparing for trials. The poor monks became a little impatient; they thought the advice good, but inopportune: "we have enough days for fast and vigil; to-day we rejoice in the Lord in memory of the great joy for all people." But when once more the irrepressible warning broke from his lips, they felt that it meant something. On returning home, they found one of their brethren dead of a pestilence, which raged for nearly a year afterwards, and carried off the majority of the community.

When Archbishop Theodore divided the diocese of Northumbria, Cuthbert was obliged reluctantly to quit his retreat and accept the bishopric of Hexham, to which he was consecrated in St. Peter's Minster at York. He did not, however, fill that see, since he exchanged with Eata, his former abbot, who had been made bishop of Lindisfarne. After governing the diocese for two years, he resigned his bishopric, and withdrew, about Christmas 686, to Farne, to prepare for his approaching death, excessive austerities having worn out his once robust frame. Two months later Herefrid, who had succeeded him as abbot of Lindisfarne, visited him, and, finding him ill, desired to leave some monks who had accompanied him to take care of the bishop. Cuthbert would not allow it. For several days they were prevented by storms from revisiting the island; when they did so, they beheld a sad sight. Cuthbert was lying on a couch in the guest-house, his face ghastly with exhaustion. He had been there for five days and nights, unable to move, with nothing to eat but a few onions. He had, moreover, during that time suffered more than ever before from the persecutions of his spiritual foes. The monks carried him back to his cell; he addressed to them a few last words, exhorting them above all to strictness in abstaining from communion with those who swerved from Catholic unity. The night was passed in tranquil expectation of future bliss. Shortly after midnight, having received from Herefrid the Body and Blood of the Lord, he "passed away without a groan, into the life of the fathers." Many marvels are related of the saint—healing the sick, predicting future events, changing water into wine by tasting it, and so forth. He was buried at Lindisfarne, on the right hand of the altar of St. Peter's Church, there to remain until the terror of the Northmen's invasion impelled the monks to begin that series of wanderings with the body of the saint, which ended in 999 with its interment in Durham Cathedral. His shrine was regarded with great veneration, and more than four hundred years after his death his body was found to be incorrupt. The shrine was plundered and demolished by Henry VIII., in 1540, but the body was re-interred in the cathedral.

St. Eadbert.—Eadbert, the successor of Cuthbert, was a man of the same pious simplicity, remarkable for his knowledge of Scripture and observance of divine precepts, and particularly for almsgiving, insomuch that he gave to the poor a tenth part, not only of all animals, but of all fruits of the earth, and even of his own garments. He improved the cathedral church of thatched oak which Finan had erected and Theodore had dedicated to St. Paul, by removing the weeds from the roof and covering it and the walls with sheets of lead. He, too, was wont to retire for devotion during a great part of Lent, and the season of Advent, to a secluded island.

St. Benedict Biscop.—Two years after Cuthbert's death (689) there passed out of this life one whom we have seen accompanying Wilfrid on his earliest journey to Rome, to improve himself in the knowledge of divine things. Benedict Biscop was one of the highest officers at the court of Oswy, the pious king of Northumbria, who bestowed on him many fair estates and great honours. At the age of twenty-five he gave up the pleasures of the world, and made a pilgrimage of devotion to the shrine of the Apostles. This was the first of five journeys thither, undertaken, not like those of Wilfrid, in the defence of a great principle, but for the sake of piety and culture; to study the rules of the monastic profession where they were observed with the strictest exactitude, to learn at the fountain-head of Catholicity how to carry out the ceremonial of the Church with the highest perfection. Benedict was again in Rome, after having taken the religious habit, when Theodore left for England to assume the supreme ecclesiastical jurisdiction: at the command of Pope Vitalian he accompanied the archbishop as his guide and interpreter, and was entrusted by him with the government of the monastery at Canterbury. Two years later, devotion led him again to the Holy City; he returned thence with a valuable collection of books, relics, and pictures of Christ, His holy Mother, and the saints. Twice more we find him wending his way to Rome, in order to enrich the abbey dedicated to St. Peter, which he had erected on a spacious domain given to him by the king of Northumbria (Wearmouth), and another subsequently built at Jarrow, with all that was needed for the due performance of Christian worship, and the adornment of the sanctuary. Lingard says: "Bennet contributed more to the civilization of his countrymen than any person since the Roman missionaries. By the workmen whom he procured from Gaul, they were taught the arts of making glass and building with stone; the foreign paintings with which he decorated his churches excited attempts at imitation, and the many volumes which he deposited in the library of his monastery invited the industry and nourished the improvements of the monks." It is said that he caused scenes from the Gospel history to be hung on the walls of his minster, in order that all who entered, however illiterate, should have holy thoughts suggested to them, and receive instruction from the pictures that met their eye. On his last visit to Rome, whither the eyes of all Christendom turned for liturgical guidance, we learn from Venerable Bede that he obtained from Pope Agatho that "John, precentor of the Church of the holy Apostle Peter, and Abbot of the monastery of St. Martin," one of the four monasteries attached to the Basilica of St. Peter, might go with him to England to teach in his monastery at Wearmouth the manner of singing the divine office throughout the year as was done at St. Peter's. The two famous abbeys founded by St. Benedict Biscop contained at his death no less than six hundred monks. They were destroyed by the Danes, but were rebuilt in part, and were priories and dependencies of Durham until their dissolution under Henry VIII.

St. Hilda and Whitby.—The abbey of Streaneshalch, or Whitby, where the conference which decided the adoption of the Roman usages was held in 664, had been founded and was presided over by a lady of royal birth, the Abbess, afterwards St. Hilda. She was one of the earliest Northumbrian converts baptized by Bishop Paulinus, and was remarkable for wisdom and prudence, and singular administrative ability. This monastery was a double one, since a confraternity of monks as well as a sisterhood of nuns occupied buildings on the domain. These establishments were held in high esteem by our ancestors, and so edifying was the deportment of their inmates, that the breath of slander never presumed to tarnish their character. That a society of men should in any case be subject to the authority of a woman appears to us a strange reversal of positions. Yet this arrangement was not out of harmony with the ideas of the age, and grew out of its institutions. To provide for the spiritual wants of the nuns, as well as of the labourers dwelling on the monastery lands, the founder or foundress of a religious house caused a church to be erected, and, contiguous to it, a range of buildings to accommodate the priest and inferior clerks required for the performance of the daily service, and to impart instruction to both the sisters and the common people. The inmates of this second house, in which the discipline of an abbatial institution was maintained, still looked up to the abbess as their head, since her religious profession did not deprive her of her secular rights: she was the "lady," on whose property they dwelt, by whose bounty they were supported, and with whom the appointment of their superior rested.

The monastery at Whitby became a seminary for learned and holy priests: no less than five of the monks, all of them men of signal merit and sanctity, were raised to the episcopate within a short space of time. One of these was St. Wilfrid, whose career has already been traced; another was St. John of Beverley (so called from the monastery he founded in Deira), Bishop of Hexham, who is said to have been, on account of his wonderful gift of healing, an object of greater reverence than any northern saint except Cuthbert.

Besides the many illustrious ecclesiastics whose names shed glory upon Whitby, there was one monk whom his brethren venerated for a gift which was to raise him to the position of father of English poetry. Cædmon, a rustic labourer employed on the monastery lands, although a man well advanced in years, was unable to join his fellows in the alliterative versification with which the peasantry at that time were wont to amuse themselves. Hence, when he was at feasts, and it was expected that for mirth's sake each should sing in turn, no sooner did he see the harp come towards him [1] than he rose from the table and went homewards. Once when he had done this, and,

---

[1] See Lingard, *Anglo-Saxon Church*, ch. ix. "To chant the songs of gleemen to the harp was an acquirement common to the lowest classes."

leaving the festive assembly, had lain down to rest in the cattle-shed of which he had charge, there appeared to him in his sleep one who, calling him by name, bade him sing some song to him. Cædmon answered: "I cannot sing, that is why I left the feast and came hither." The other rejoined, "However that be, you must sing to me." "What shall I sing?" asked Cædmon. "Sing the beginning of created things." And so verses came to his lips, and when he woke, he retained in his memory what he had sung in his sleep. The next morning he told his master of the gift he had received, and was by him conducted to the abbess, who, in the presence of several learned men, heard his story. All agreed that heavenly grace had been conferred on him by the Lord; they translated for him a portion of Holy Writ, bidding him, if he could, turn it into poetry. On the following day Cædmon gave it to them in excellent verse; whereupon the abbess bade him lay aside his secular habit and enter the monastery. She ordered him to be instructed in the whole course of sacred history, for he was unable to read; and then his teachers became his hearers, while he sang to them of the creation of the world, of the chief events recorded in the Scriptures, of the last judgment, of the future happiness and misery of man. His language was so grand, his numbers so harmonious, that he was looked upon as one inspired; the fame he acquired led many others to compose religious poems, but "none could compare with him, for he learnt not the art of poetry from men, but of God."

St. Aldhelm.—Contemporary with this bard-monk in the north was St. Aldhelm, the minstrel-pontiff as he has been denominated, in the south. A near relative of Ina, the good king of the West Saxons, he was educated in the school of Adrian at Canterbury, and afterwards joined a small Irish community at Mailduf's burgh, or Malmesbury. Aldhelm, while a youth, used to compose ballads in the vernacular on subjects likely to interest the common people, and taking his station on a bridge, or at the junction of cross roads, would sing them to the harp. The passers-by, fascinated like all Saxons by the sound of music, stopped to listen ; and when a crowd had collected, he would glide from lighter minstrelsy into some more serious strain, and end by instructing his audience in Christian doctrine. On the death of the founder, Aldhelm became abbot of Malmesbury ; he raised its reputation, and increased its buildings and revenues. The lowly chapel was superseded by an august church in honour of the Prince of the Apostles, the most glorious structure at that time in the whole realm, besides two others, dedicated respectively to Our Lady and St. Michael. The historian William of Malmesbury fills several pages with an account of the benefactions and privileges accorded to this house by royal personages, in addition to a papal indult, to obtain which Aldhelm, by the invitation of Pope Sergius, travelled to Rome. Whilst there he was instrumental, by causing an infant of nine days old to speak, in clearing the Supreme Pontiff of a shameful accusation which the tongue of calumny had dared to bring against the Vicar of Jesus Christ. On the division of the diocese of Winchester (704), after the death of Bishop Hedda, the successor of St. Birinus, Aldhelm was compelled to quit his cell to fill the episcopal see of Sherborne, which he held for five years. He there founded the church on the site of which the present magnificent minster stands. One of the miracles recorded of him is that by a word he caused the beams brought for the roof of the church, which proved to be too short, to attain the right length.

St. Aldhelm was among the most learned of scholars: his writings are numerous. He was the first Englishman who published books in Latin, both prose and verse; his Saxon poetry was also much esteemed. Whilst abbot of Malmesbury he wrote a long letter to Geraint, king of Cornwall, respecting the adoption of the Easter rule and other Roman usages. This epistle shows his firm attachment as an Anglo-Saxon to the faith of Christ, and the foundation which He laid, the See of Peter. "We entreat you on our knees, in view of our future common country in heaven, and of the angels, our future fellow-countrymen; we adjure you not to persevere in your arrogant contempt of the decrees of St. Peter and the traditions of the Roman Church, by a proud and tyrannical adhesion to the ordinances of your ancestors. . . . To sum up everything in one word, it is vain for any of you to make an empty boast of the Catholic faith, while you follow not the dogma and rule of St. Peter."

St. Bede.—While the people of Wessex gloried in the fame of Aldhelm, another and still greater scholar was gradually rising into notice in Northumbria. Bede —who, from his eminent sanctity and learning, was called, shortly after his death, "the Venerable"—was born in 673, and at the early age of seven was placed under the care of St. Benedict Biscop, to be educated in his monastery of Wearmouth. On the completion of the buildings at Jarrow he was transferred thither under the charge of the Abbot Ceolfrid. While Bede was still little more than a boy, a dire calamity befell the monastery: a virulent pestilence carried off every one of the choir monks, excepting the abbot and himself. Amid their sorrow these two survivors continued faithfully, albeit with voices broken by tears, the daily recitation of the Divine Office, until the vacant stalls began again to be occupied.

When nineteen years old, on account of his superior merit and piety, Bede was admitted to deacon's orders by St. John of Beverley, and was ordained priest by the same bishop at the age of thirty, the discipline of the Church at that time not allowing any man to be ordained under that age. From the time of his entrance into the cloister he never left its precincts, except for brief visits on some literary errand to Bishop Egbert of York, Bishop Acca of Hexham, a great patron of learning, or to the king, Ceolwulf, at whose request he wrote his Ecclesiastical History. He says of himself: " I spent my whole life in the same monastery, and while attending to the rules of my Order and the service of the Church, my constant delight was to be learning, or teaching, or writing." From the list of the writings that posterity owes to his pen, it may be seen how varied were his talents and acquirements, how vast his erudition, how assiduous his application to study. We find among them introductions to several sciences, treatises on astronomy and chronology, homilies, lives of saints, commentaries on many of the books of Holy Scripture. By far the most celebrated of his works is his Ecclesiastical History of the Anglo-Saxons. Nearly all that we know with certainty of the century and a half that follow the landing of Augustine we derive from it. This history was completed four years before his death, which took place in 753. How this great student and scholar bore himself when his last hour drew nigh, in what a tranquil and devout frame of mind he closed his life of seclusion from the world, with what faith and fervour he received the Holy Viaticum and Extreme Unction, all this has been described by one of his disciples, an eye-witness of the final scenes, in words of simple pathos.

Two weeks before Easter he fell into a state of extreme weakness, accompanied with difficulty of breathing. He still preserved his accustomed cheerfulness, and in spite of prolonged sleeplessness continued his daily lectures to the pupils about him, spending the night in thanksgiving and prayer with outstretched hands to God. Thus the days passed until Ascensiontide, both master and scribes working diligently, for Bede was desirous of completing his version of St. John's Gospel, which he was translating into the English tongue. A few days before the Ascension his malady increased, and he bade the scribes to whom he dictated work quickly, for he knew not how long he might last. "At dawn on the Wednesday before the Ascension," his disciple writes, "he ordered us to write speedily, which we did, till the hour of tierce (nine o'clock). At that hour we walked in procession with the relics as the rubrics for the day prescribed.[1] At three o'clock in the afternoon he said to me, 'I have some valuables in my little chest, pepper, napkins, and incense. Run quickly and bring the priests to me, that I

---

[1] It was customary in Anglo-Saxon times to carry the relics of the saints in solemn procession, with clergy and people, on the three days preceding Ascension Day, now known as Rogation Days. They were on that account called "gang-days."

may make them such presents as God has given to me.' I did as he bade me. He spoke to each in turn, entreating them to celebrate masses and pray for him diligently, which all readily promised to do. 'The time of my dissolution is at hand,' he said, 'I wish to be released, and to be with Christ.' All burst into tears when they heard him say that they would see him no more in this world. He himself continued to speak cheerfully until sunset. At that hour a youth said, 'Beloved master, there is still one sentence unwritten.' 'Then write quickly,' said Bede. In a few minutes the youth spoke again: 'It is finished.' 'Thou hast spoken truly,' replied the dying monk; 'take my head between thy hands, for it is my delight to sit opposite to that holy place in which I used to pray; let me sit and invoke my Father.' Sitting thus on the pavement of his cell, he repeated for the last time, 'Glory be to the Father, and to the Son, and to the Holy Ghost'; as he pronounced the last words he breathed out his spirit, and took his departure for heaven."

Alcuin.—The loss sustained by the death of Bede was repaired by the ability and learning of Alcuin, who was born in York, and received his education in the schools founded in that city by Archbishop Egbert, to the direction of which he was subsequently appointed. Under his rule they gained a wide reputation; students from Gaul and Germany flocked to York that they might profit by the lectures of the Anglo-Saxon, and to attain distinction in his school became the surest road to ecclesiastical and civil honours. Alcuin was invited to France by Charlemagne, to assist in the foundation of the University of Paris. Besides his work as a teacher, he took part in many theological controversies on the continent; another object that engaged his attention was the correction of the liturgical books, which in most churches were disgraced with numerous errors, arising from the ignorance or negligence of the transcribers. To him belongs the honour of having drawn up the votive mass of the Blessed Virgin, and of appointing Saturday for its celebration.

St. Egwin.—Another of the great saints of the Anglo-Saxon Church was Egwin, Bishop of Worcester, 692. In the early part of his episcopate he became the victim of detraction on the part of some of his flock, whose heathenish practices he reproved with severity. He was driven from his see, and accused at Rome. For the purpose of clearing himself he repaired to the Eternal City. Before starting on his journey he vowed that if God prospered him, he would erect a church to the honour of His Blessed Mother; furthermore he bound his feet with iron shackles, the key of which he threw into the river Avon. Thus he made a penitential pilgrimage to Rome, and straightway on his arrival, cast himself on his knees in prayer before the tomb of the Apostles. The legendary account amusingly adds that a fish just caught in the Tiber was found to contain the key which the bishop had cast into the Avon, and that the fame of this wonder spread throughout Rome. What is certain is that Egwin was considered a holy man, and was reinstated in his see. On his return he founded the abbey and church of Evesham, under the invocation of the Blessed Virgin, who herself vouchsafed to appear to him, shining gloriously, to indicate the spot on which it was to be raised. The land for this purpose was granted to him by the pious Ina, king of the West Saxons, of whom mention must not be omitted, on account of the numerous religious foundations he made.

King Ina.—This king was one of the chief benefactors of the Church in the commencement of the eighth century. He it was who established on the site of the ancient British foundation the famous abbey of Glastonbury, already in his time a favourite place of pilgrimage, and the coveted resting-place of many kings. During the period of the Saxon invasion, Glastonbury had proved a suitable place for harbouring a congregation of native Christians. But in 658 "the one famous holy place of the conquered Britons which had lived through the storm of foreign conquest," as Freeman terms it (*Norman Conquest*, vol. i. p. 436), fell into Saxon hands: a Saxon community of monks took possession of the wooden basilica which had replaced the original oratory of the Blessed Virgin, associated with the memory of St. David of Menevia and many saints of the Celtic race. In 708 King Ina rebuilt the monastery and the abbey church, endowing them with rich privileges. Out of love to God and His Blessed Mother, he built the silver chapel, as it was styled; for the construction of this alone he gave 2,640 lb. of silver, besides gold and silver images, candlesticks, and other gifts of extraordinary value. The bishopric of Sherborne was also founded by Ina, and the charge of it was confided to St. Aldhelm, the first scholar of his day. The code of laws which he formed shows that he was no less solicitous for the ecclesiastical than for the civil well-being of his kingdom. Furthermore, he built and endowed schools at Rome for the training of Anglo-Saxon youths intended for the priesthood.

In 726, when the highest human felicity he was apparently enjoying, he resigned his sceptre, and went on a pilgrimage to Rome, where he shortly afterwards died.

Missionaries.—While the Church extended her spiritual conquests in England, and produced so many heroes of sanctity, her children were not unmindful of the duty of bringing foreign nations to the obedience of the faith of Christ. Long years previous to the conversion of the Saxon Heptarchy, the Celtic Church had despatched missionaries to Gaul and Switzerland, as we learn from the lives of St. Columban and other missionary monks. The Anglo-Saxons were not less strongly animated with zeal for the spread of the Gospel. St. Wilfrid had, as has been seen, more through accidental circumstances than from design, been the first to preach to the idolatrous Friesians, who occupied a large tract of country about the mouth of the Rhine. Later on twelve monks from Wilfrid's monastery at Ripon, with the Northumbrian St. Willibrord at their head, landed on the coast of Germany, and solicited the protection of King Pepin. Having obtained his permission to settle in his dominions, Willibrord left his companions and hastened to Rome, to implore the sanction and blessing of the Holy Father upon his enterprize. After some years of successful labour he was consecrated bishop of Utrecht. Two other English monks, named Ewald, who entered Friesland with the design of converting the barbarians, were put to death by them. We are told that their bodies were cast into the Rhine, and were carried up against the stream for forty miles, a long ray of light resting on them, marking their progress, until they reached the place where their fellow-countrymen and brethren in religion were encamped. By them they were interred with the honour due to martyrs.

St. Boniface.—But it is to Winfrid, a monk of Exeter, better known as St. Boniface, that the glory of being the Apostle of Germany belongs. In 715 he went with the permission of his abbot to preach in Friesland; he met, however, with no success, owing to the disturbed state of the country, and returned to England, to set out afresh four years later for Rome. Pope Gregory II. commissioned him to go forth on his task of converting the German tribes "in the Name of the Indivisible Trinity and by the inviolable authority of Blessed Peter." Boniface laboured in Thuringia, Hesse, and Saxony, converting thousands to the faith: Willibrord wished to resign to him the see of Utrecht, but the Pope recalled him to Rome and consecrated him Archbishop of Mayence. Later on he received the pallium, with powers to establish episcopal sees, and was given jurisdiction over all the lands which his zeal had evangelized. He received legatine powers to hold councils all over France and Germany. He anointed Pepin king of the Franks, and paved the way for the empire of his son Charlemagne. Having established his disciples in the three metropolitan sees of Mayence, Cologne, and Utrecht, he prepared for his last journey. When nearly seventy years of age, he resumed his apostolic labours amongst the Friesians, where paganism still lingered. He converted and baptized thousands, and on the Vigil of Pentecost prepared to confer on the neophytes the sacrament of confirmation. Instead of the Christians, a body of armed barbarians appeared on the scene. Boniface forbade his attendants to fight in his defence, saying that the long-wished-for day had come to admit him to eternal joys, and encouraging them to meet death with fortitude. The aged bishop was martyred, together with the whole company, numbering fifty-two persons.

St. Boniface, among the many apostolic services which he rendered to German Christianity, induced several of his own fellow-countrymen to follow his example and come over to help him in his labours. A special mention of four out of this number must not be omitted. Willibald and Winibald, his nephews, were the children of a West-Saxon chieftain, Richard, who is himself venerated as a saint. At the instigation of Willibald, then in his early youth, Richard and his two sons undertook a pilgrimage to Rome with the intention of going on to the Holy Land. This further journey was successfully accomplished by Willibald who remained in Palestine for some years, but Richard died at Lucca, and Winibald, whose disposition was towards solitude, retired to Monte Cassino. Later, on one of his visits to the Holy See, St. Boniface asked to have his two zealous nephews to assist him in Germany, and the desire was granted. Willibald became Bishop of Eichstedt, took a leading part in the public work of the ministry, and contributed largely to hand down to subsequent generations the spirit and the methods of St. Boniface. Winibald built and became abbot of the monastery of Heidenheim, a double monastery after the pattern of so many in England, his sister, Walburga, being invited over to take charge of the portion assigned to the nuns. Lioba was also a relative of Boniface, and, like Walburga, had been brought up in the convent at Wimborne. Desiring to follow in the steps of her relation, she too passed over into Germany, where she was made abbess of the convent at Bischoffsheim, and took a prominent part in organizing the monastic life among those newly won to the faith.

Such was the work which St. Boniface accomplished on the Continent. In the following chapter the influence he exercised over the Church in his own country will be seen.

CHAPTER VI.

TROUBLES OF THE ANGLO-SAXON CHURCH.[1]

Lax Discipline. St. Boniface urges Reform.—
In the first half of the eighth century the attention of the Holy See was again directed to England, not on account of any suspicion of unorthodoxy in matters of faith, but because of the corruption of morals and relaxation of ecclesiastical discipline which since the death of Theodore had crept in under the less vigilant rule of his successors. Tidings of the degeneracy and vices of his fellow-countrymen reached the ears of St. Boniface, who, in the foreign land where, as has been seen, he had by his intrepidity and zeal triumphed over heresy and idolatry, was still mindful of his English origin. From the heart of Germany he wrote a hortatory

---

[1] Freeman (*Norman Conquest*, App. A to vol. i.) says that the name Anglo-Saxon, though open to many objections, is a genuine description of the nation, and justified by ancient authority; but it is quite clear that it never passed into general use, and that the name by which our forefathers knew themselves was English and no other. As, however, it is employed by Lingard and other writers from whom we quote, as a convenient if somewhat inaccurate mode of designating the English of the ante-Norman period, we may be allowed to make use of it in this history.

letter to Ethelbald, the king of Mercia,[1] who had been guilty of violating the privileges of churches and monasteries, urging him to reform, and to Egbert, bishop of York, exhorting him to second his admonitions to the king. He also suggested practical means for combating the abuses he reproved. He wrote to Archbishop Cuthbert, dwelling on the great responsibilities of the pastoral office, and telling him of the synod lately held under his auspices at Mayence. In this assembly, composed mostly of prelates of English birth, the bishops, besides enacting various necessary regulations, had decreed to hold, while life should last, the Catholic faith and unity and subjection to the Roman Church; to be subject to St. Peter and his successors; that the metropolitans should apply to that See for their palliums, and should strive to follow canonically the precepts of St. Peter, in order that they might be counted amongst the sheep entrusted to his care. Boniface advised Cuthbert to summon a similar council in order to devise remedial measures for the evils that prevailed. The women who went on pilgrimages to Rome and elsewhere often fell into scandalous habits : these pilgrimages should be stopped. Kings and nobles were in the habit of violently entering religious houses, expelling the abbot or abbess, and usurping the right of command over the community and the property : this must be prevented. Monks were compelled to perform forced work for the king, a custom not to be

---

[1] Osred, the young king of Northumbria, and Ceolred, king of Mercia, were the first to venture upon the spoliation of the monasteries and the violation of the privileges granted to them. The judgements of God fell on them ; one was murdered, the other went mad, and the line of both became extinct.

tolerated; luxury in clothing and other irregularities had made their way into the cloister, an abuse which must be strongly repressed.

Council of Cloveshoe, 747.—In consequence of this expostulation on the part of St. Boniface, and in accordance with the injunctions of Pope Zachary, who, in addition to paternal exhortations to amendment of life, threatened excommunication unless the corrupt practices becoming prevalent in England were checked, Cuthbert convened a council at Cloveshoe in 747.[1] It was attended by twelve bishops, many priests and dignitaries, and by King Ethelbald and his nobles. The Pope's letters were diligently read in Latin and English as apostolic authority had ordered. Thirty-two canons were enacted for the reform of the clergy and monastic bodies, the greater uniformity and regularity of public worship, and the general encouragement of piety and devotion. An injunction was laid upon priests to follow the Roman ritual in the administration of baptism, in the solemnization of mass, in the style of singing. "*juxta ritum Romanæ Ecclesiæ*"—according to the rite of the Roman Church—occurs again and again. They were expressly forbidden to engage in secular business, and exhorted to expound to their respective flocks the ceremonies of Holy Mass, and the words in an unknown tongue employed in the administration of the sacraments; to enforce the observance of Sunday, the fasts of the ember-days, the giving of alms, the duty of prayer. It was also decreed that the feasts of

---

[1] The situation of this place is mere matter of conjecture. It was possibly Dorchester, in Oxfordshire, or, some say, a place near Rochester. Cloveshoe was certainly either in Mercia or on the borders of an adjacent kingdom, as the kings of Mercia took the lead in the councils held there.

St. Gregory and St. Augustine, "who first brought to the English nation the knowledge of the faith," should be kept throughout England, and the names of both saints inserted in the Litany. Ethelbald, in atonement for his acts of spoliation, agreed that thenceforth all monasteries and churches should be exempt from taxation.

Papal Legates.—Whether the results of the Council of Cloveshoe answered the expectations of the Holy Father, it is impossible to decide. About forty years later, two papal legates were sent to England by Pope Adrian I., with the intent, as the old Saxon Chronicle says, "to renew the faith and peace which St. Gregory sent us by Augustine the bishop." These legates were most respectfully received. They brought with them a code of laws for the improvement of ecclesiastical discipline, with which they proceeded first to the court of Northumbria, afterwards to that of Mercia. In both places the king, the archbishop, and bishops of the province, with all the people present, after the *capitula* had been read aloud in the Latin and Saxon languages, solemnly promised "to obey them in all particulars in humble submission, with all the devotion of their minds and the utmost of their strength." The chief personages affixed their signatures, drawing the sign of the holy cross with the thumb of their right hand in attestation of their promise. That the custom of ratifying deeds and documents by tracing a cross, or by simply laying the finger on the red or gold cross made by the scribe on the parchment, was in ordinary use amongst the Anglo-Saxons, is shown by the charters and other instruments preserved from that time. To bestow her sanction on this pious usage, the Church in the ninth century issued a decree to the effect that all documents bearing an authentic sign of the cross were binding.[1] Under the first Norman kings this manner of attestation was laid aside, and waxen seals took its place. Strangely enough, the old custom which grew out of their Catholic belief still lingers amongst Englishmen, and he who cannot write makes a cross to authenticate the deed on which another inscribes his name.

Offa and the Lichfield Bishopric.—In this same assembly of Calcuith, held 785, Offa, the king of Mercia, in proof of his devotion to the Holy See, promised a yearly benefaction from himself and his successors of 365 mancuses[2] towards the support of pilgrims, and to furnish lights for the church. Two years later this powerful monarch caused considerable trouble to the Archbishop of Canterbury by taking forcible possession of lands in Mercia appertaining to the metropolitan see, and by his endeavour to erect Lichfield into an archbishopric. It was offensive to his pride that the seat of archiepiscopal power over the Mercian clergy should be in another kingdom than his own. (In 735 the see of York had been made an archbishopric.) Failing in his attempt to obtain the transfer of the metropolitan dignity from Canterbury to Lichfield, he applied anew to Pope Adrian, asking him to send the pallium to the latter see, pleading that the see of Canterbury was too extensive to be governed properly by a single prelate. The Pope granted his request; but

---

[1] *Cf. Church of our Fathers*, vol. iii. pt. 2, p. 116.

[2] A mancus was the eighth part of a pound, equal to thirty silver pennies.

on the death of Offa, finding that he had been deceived, rescinded the decree and restored the province of Canterbury to its former extent.

Peter's Pence.—Towards the close of his reign of forty years, partly to atone for the crime of his consort, who, with his connivance, had caused a neighbouring monarch to be murdered, partly to secure special privileges for the abbey which he had built at St. Alban's, Offa went on pilgrimage to Rome. Whilst there he increased the revenues of the school for English students, founded some time previously by Ina, king of the West Saxons.[1] Offa also introduced into his kingdom the payment of the Rome-scot or Peter's Pence, the tax of a penny levied yearly on every household possessed of land to the value of thirty pence.[2] He attributed the success of his arms to the intercession of St. Peter, and it was gratitude that induced him to promise the yearly pension already mentioned of 365 mancuses to the church of the Apostle. That he faithfully fulfilled his engagement we know on good authority; but after the death of his son, the sceptre passed into the hands of a prince who did not deem the grant binding on any but his direct heirs. Ethelwulf, the father of Alfred the Great, made a somewhat similar bequest, charging his heirs with the obligation of sending to Rome yearly three hundred

---

[1] Matthew Paris, in his *Chronicles*, says: "The Anglo-Saxon school was founded in Rome in order that the kings of England and their race, as well as the English bishops and students, might resort there to be instructed in the doctrines of the Catholic faith, lest anything faulty or contrary to the Catholic faith might grow up in the English Church, so that confirmed and strengthened in a lasting faith they might return to their own country."

[2] *Cf. Blessed Peter and the English People*, by Cardinal Vaughan.

silver mancuses: one for the personal use of the Pontiff, one to supply oil for the lamps in St. Peter's—the want of which was often lamented by the Popes[1]—a third for the same purpose in the church of St. Paul. These benefactions were distinct from the Rome-scot, which was a national tax, established by royal authority and regarded as one of the dues of the Church, to be paid during the interval between the feast of St. Peter and the 1st of August.

The Danish Invasion.—Shortly before Offa was gathered to his fathers, a dire calamity befell the Church and the whole nation of the Anglo-Saxons. The Danes, a wild race of pirates who had long infested the northern seas, began to make harassing incursions on the coasts of Britain and Gaul. They swooped down on the shores of Northumbria; the prospect of plunder directed their attack, carnage and devastation marked their steps. St. Hilda's monastery afforded them the largest booty; the monks and priests made a feeble resistance, but the fierce marauders despatched them without ceremony. They utterly destroyed the monastic buildings, filled their ships with spoil, and sailed away. Emboldened by the success of their first expedition, two years later, in 795, they landed on Lindisfarne. That venerable pile, once honoured by the presence of the Apostles of Northumbria, and sanctified by the remains of St. Cuthbert, became the prey of the barbarians. The peaceful occupations of the monks afforded them no protection; it excited the scorn, as their religion excited the hatred, of these worshippers of Woden and Thor.

[1] *Cf.* Letter of Leo III. in Wharton's *Anglia Sacra* (vol. i. p. 461).

Nothing was reverenced; nothing was spared. The altars were polluted and overthrown; the monks, amid cruel insults, were put to the sword, or cast into the sea, or carried off into hopeless slavery. The vengeance of St. Cuthbert, adds the chronicler, fell upon the spoilers. On the neighbouring coast the inhabitants flew to arms and slew the Danish leader. The pirates took to their ships, but even on their own element they were no longer safe. A tempest swallowed up nearly all their army; those of the survivors who were driven back upon the land were destroyed by the people.

The news of this disaster filled the nation with the utmost grief. Lindisfarne had been to them an object of peculiar respect. Alcuin, hearing of its destruction at the court of Charlemagne, shed tears of sorrow. He wrote to the monks of Wearmouth and Jarrow, bidding them be warned by the fate of others, and urging them to seek the mercy of God by prayer and fasting. He predicted that this incursion was but the beginning of sorrow; and the event verified his words. Within a few months from the date of the letter a Danish squadron entered the mouth of the Tyne, and both those monasteries, the monuments of Benedict Biscop's zeal and King Egbert's munificence, were reduced to ashes.

For some fifty years the Northmen continued their ravages; and although when Egbert in 830 assumed the supremacy of the whole island more organized resistance was offered to them, they contrived, even when beaten back to their ships, to secure sufficient plunder to encourage them to fresh incursions. In the reign of Ethelwulf, the successor of Egbert, they swept up the Thames and pillaged London and

Canterbury. The king fought strenuously in the defence of his realm, and the danger to the Christian faith from these heathen assailants roused the clergy to his aid. St. Swithun, Bishop of Winchester, the brightest light of the English Church in the ninth century, became his counsellor; Alstan, Bishop of Sherborne, joined his armies in the field. A complete victory over the Danes in 851 gained a short respite from their ravages.

King Ethelwulf.—The pious king Ethelwulf took advantage of this period of tranquillity to undertake a journey to Rome. He was accompanied by his son Alfred, whom he had on a previous occasion sent to the Holy City, when Leo IV. adopted him as his son, conferred on him the sacrament of confirmation, and also by his father's request the regal unction, in order to secure his succession to the crown. "To the glory of God and the honour of St. Mary His Blessed Mother," Ethelwulf rebuilt the school and hospital of the Anglo-Saxons in Rome, and offered rich gifts to the Holy Father, amongst which were a crown of pure gold, cups and images of the same precious metal, four dishes of silver-gilt, and vestments of silk with clasps of gold. On his return to England he made the payment of tithes, which had been an accepted law of the Church, a law of the State as well, thus supplying the Church with the power, often lacking to her, of enforcing her right. This custom of giving for ecclesiastical purposes a tenth part of the produce of the land had been established by Theodore and confirmed by the Legatine Council of 787.

Fresh Troubles from the Danes. — Before Alfred ascended his father's throne a fresh series of depredations on the part of the Danes brought, as the Anglo-Saxon Chronicle says, "strife and sorrow all over England." Their fury was directed against everything connected with the Christian religion; the wealth of the churches continued to allure their rapacity; one after another the celebrated monasteries were devastated, and those monks who escaped slaughter deplored in terrified astonishment the rapid depopulation of their order. Tynemouth was the first abbey of importance that was pillaged. From its smoking ruins the invaders directed their course to Lindisfarne. The monastery had been rebuilt, and was again the home of a colony of monks. A party of the inmates, together with the bishop, fled before the arrival of the Danes, carrying with them the uncorrupted body of St. Cuthbert and the head of St. Oswald, with which for nine years they wandered from place to place to elude the vigilance of their persecutors. Meanwhile a party of marauders marched southward, spreading devastation on their way. The abbey of Bardney was the first to experience their rapacity. Thence they proceeded to Croyland, where the abbot was slain at the altar, and the pavement of the sanctuary bestrewn with the corpses of the monks. Medeshampsted (afterwards called Peterborough, because by favour of Pope Agatho its church was endowed with privileges for pilgrims like to those of St. Peter's at Rome) with its magnificent fabric and unequalled library, was levelled with the ground, not a single human being found within its walls escaping slaughter. The great and opulent monastery of Ely shared a similar fate—in fact, the same cruel work was wrought in almost every religious house throughout the land.

In the province of East Anglia, Edmund, the young king, was taken captive, and brought before the Danish leaders. He was offered his life and the safety of his subjects if he would renounce Christianity. On his refusal he was bound to a tree and shot with arrows, and afterwards beheaded. The tree to which he was fastened stood till about forty years ago, when it was struck by lightning. An arrow-head, found embedded in its heart, is still preserved in the British Museum. His martyrdom after this mode made Edmund the St. Sebastian of English hagiology. In later days his figure was seen in the painted windows of every church along the east coast, and the stately abbey of Edmundsbury rose over his relics.

King Alfred.—When, on the death of his brother Ethelred, Alfred succeeded to the throne, he subjugated the Danes by slow degrees, after almost unexampled sufferings and struggles. Having overthrown them in battle, he made terms with the survivors, as is well known, allowing them to settle in England on condition that they should conform to the Christian faith and respect the property of the Church. This means of obtaining a cessation of the horrors of war was not altogether a benefit to the Anglo-Saxons. Although the rite of baptism had entitled the settlers to the name of Christian, their manners and beliefs were still those of pagans, and their intermixture with the natives augmented the demoralization inevitably resulting from the protracted contest with a foreign foe. During the past years little attention had been paid to the administration of justice; habits of predatory warfare had introduced a spirit of independence; the laws of the

Gospel, the regulations of ecclesiastical discipline were disregarded—in fact, the morals of many of the people were scarcely superior to those of the naturalized Danes. Learning and religion were alike paralyzed, and a firm hand and vigorous energy were required to reform the corrupt manners and revive the piety of England.

Alfred put aside every personal aim and ambition in order to devote himself to the welfare of his subjects. Taking the bishops for his principal counsellors, he drew up a new code of laws on the basis of the Decalogue, making the infringement of ecclesiastical canons punishable by the civil power. The bishoprics that were vacant were filled up, and new sees founded out of the larger dioceses. With the exception of one Welshman, the celebrated Asser, Alfred found no scholars in the country capable of aiding him in the education of his people and imparting instruction in the schools he established for the sons of nobles. He therefore introduced foreign teachers, and to promote learning invited men of letters to his court. His own life was a model of devotion and regularity. Amid the manifold duties of the State he set aside fixed hours for his daily religious duties and reading the Psalms. It was his custom to carry about with him wherever he went the holy relics of some saints, and to spend hours prostrate in the church seeking the divine guidance in prayer. "As long as I have lived," he said, when his death drew nigh, "I have striven to live worthily." The marked diminution of crime, and the return of his people to orderly and pacific habits, proved the success of his efforts.

Odo's Reforms.—The degeneracy consequent on

the calamitous period of the Danish invasion was not confined to the laity. Through the destruction of so many monasteries, the religious life had fallen into disrepute, and few were found willing to embrace it. The monks who survived had acquired a taste for roving; the seclusion of the cloister, the restraint of the rule, had become intolerable to them; some had engaged in secular professions. Nor was the effect of the troubles which had befallen the country less deplorable in regard to the secular clergy. Although their ranks had not been thinned by wholesale massacre, as was the case with the regulars, yet numbers had perished by the sword of the barbarians, and most of the ecclesiastical seminaries, from which the bishops selected subjects for ordination, had been destroyed or dispersed. The consequence was that the dearth of pastors was sorely felt. To supply the want, clerks of an inferior grade, even though married, were raised to the diaconate and priesthood. Although marriage after ordination was still strictly prohibited, according to the doctrine and practice of the Anglo-Saxon Church from its origin—no mention of a married priest being found in any document for three hundred years after the arrival of Augustine [1]—yet these newly-made presbyters, if previously married, were permitted to retain their wives. The canons, indeed, required that they should separate from them, but through the relaxation of ecclesiastical discipline this rule was much neglected. Example and impunity propagated the evil; married priests became sufficiently numerous to become a serious scandal. The reform of these and other abuses was first attempted by Archbishop Odo.

[1] *Cf.* Lingard, *Anglo-Saxon Church.*

This prelate, the son of Danish parents, and repudiated by them on account of becoming a Christian, had been educated by one of Alfred's nobles for the priesthood. In his youth he was regarded with great veneration by King Alfred, and in the reign of his successor he was raised to the episcopate and made Archbishop of Canterbury.

St. Dunstan.—But the work inaugurated by the wise regulations and resolute action of Odo was to be taken up, vigorously pushed forward, and carried to completion by one of the greatest of English Churchmen and reformers. Dunstan, a youth of noble birth, had at an early age been dedicated to the service of our Blessed Lady in the abbey of Glastonbury. He received his education from some Irish scholars who had taken up their abode there, and under their tuition made extraordinary progress.

In addition to his high literary attainments, he excelled in painting and engraving, was an admirable musician, and a skilful worker in brass and iron. These accomplishments, united to most engaging manners, brought him into notice at the court of King Athelstan, his kinsman, whither he was taken whilst quite young by his uncle Athelm, then Archbishop of Canterbury. The favour with which he was regarded excited the jealousy of the courtiers, and Dunstan was accused of magical arts. He retired to the house of another uncle, who was Bishop of Winchester, but even there the malice of his persecutors pursued him; he was dragged from his horse and trampled in the mire. A long illness was the result of this treatment, during which Dunstan vowed to renounce the brilliant future open to him and to become a monk. On his recovery he received from his uncle the religious habit, and not long after the sacrament of orders. For some time he lived as a recluse in a cell he constructed for himself at Glastonbury. It was during this period that the legend would have us believe there occurred those wrestlings with the evil one, when the tempter assumed a visible shape and was combated with material weapons, none other, in fact, than the iron tongs which Dunstan employed when heating the metals he wrought so skilfully. However this may be, he learned to subdue his passions and to contemn riches; for, on a lady of royal lineage, who had been charmed with his conversation and edified by his virtue, making him her heir, he distributed the wealth that thus accrued to him to the poor, besides settling on the Church the patrimony which devolved upon him at his father's death. From this seclusion he was called by King Edmund, who conferred on him the office of Chancellor, and made him Abbot of Glastonbury. Dunstan at once expelled from the abbey the secular clergy who were in possession of it, and collected a company of monks, to whom he gave the Benedictine rule. After Edmund's death he enjoyed the friendship of his successor, Edred, who desired him to accept the vacant bishopric of Winchester, in acknowledgement of his labours for the repression of vice, the encouragement of learning, and the restoration of order in the kingdom. This Dunstan declined, as his time was fully occupied with attendance on the king and the government of his monasteries.

On the accession of Edwy, a youth of sixteen, a change took place in the abbot's fortunes. The young king had contracted an illicit union with

Elgiva, a princess more beautiful than virtuous. For the sake of her company he absented himself on his coronation day from the banqueting-hall, where his nobles were assembled to do him honour. Indignant at this discourtesy, they deputed Dunstan to bring him back to fulfil the duties of royal hospitality to the chief men of the realm. The boy-king resented this interference with his liberty, nor did the fair object of his affections allow him to forget the affront. At her instigation Edwy accused the minister of malversation in his office; and to escape his persecutions Dunstan was obliged to fly to Flanders, where he took up his abode in a well-ordered Benedictine monastery. He profited by his residence there to acquaint himself thoroughly with the rule, which he desired to see strictly observed in the English cloisters. During his exile his two monasteries of Glastonbury and Abingdon were dissolved by Edwy's command, and the monks he had collected, with the view of resuscitating the order, were dispersed.

When Edgar was placed at the head of affairs, Dunstan was recalled, and appointed to the bishoprics first of Worcester and then of London. These he held until the see of Canterbury became vacant through the death of Odo in 960. Elfsin, bishop of Winchester, was chosen to fill it, but he perished in the snow whilst journeying across the Alps at a dangerous season to obtain his pallium from Rome, and Dunstan was elevated to the primacy. The customary visit to Rome to receive the pallium from the hands of the Pope was promptly accomplished; he then applied himself to effect the reformation of the clergy in England. In carrying out his plans he was ably seconded by Oswald, nephew to Archbishop Odo, in whose favour he resigned the see of Worcester, and Ethelwold, whom he consecrated in 963 to the bishopric of Winchester. Supported by the authority of the king, whose closest friend and adviser he became, Dunstan acted with the utmost energy and decision. The secular clergy who had usurped the place of the regulars and possessed themselves of the abbacies belonging to them were expelled; those who were married, and who refused to separate from their wives, were deprived of the power of exercising their ministry. All those whose manner of life was discreditable to the cause of religion were first reprimanded, then severely punished. During the Danish invasions and the sanguinary struggles of the preceding years, many of the Church lands and revenues had been confiscated or seized by the nobles and other laymen. The king voluntarily gave up the estates that had fallen to the Crown, and enjoined upon his subjects to restore the property thus unjustly acquired. In cases where a stubborn thane refused to comply and despised the ecclesiastical anathemas, he purchased the lands himself and restored them to the Church. In a few years the great abbeys of Ely, Peterborough, Thorney, Malmesbury, and others, rose from their ruins, and were peopled with men of talent and sanctity, many from the highest classes, and all eager to labour for Christ in the religious state.

Bishop Ethelwold. Monastic Reforms.—Bishop Ethelwold was a leading man in the monastic revival which took place in Edgar's reign. His unflinching determination equalled that of the archbishop himself. The clergy of Winchester were more than ordinarily relaxed in discipline and oblivious of the obligations of their high calling. The canons who had replaced the original monks were men of dissolute habits; it is recorded of them that " they left to substitutes the duty of attendance in choir and the ministry of the altar; often absenting themselves for seven years from the sight of the Church, they spent when and as they thought proper whatever they received from their prebends. The church was stripped bare within and without" (*Annal. Winton.*, p. 289). After frequently admonishing them to amend their lives, the bishop resorted to more stringent measures. One day in Lent, when they were assembled for service, he entered the choir, attended by a royal deputy, carrying a number of Benedictine cowls, which he bade them assume at once, with the obligations they entailed, or quit the church. Three only yielded; the rest in sullen discontent left their stalls. Their places were supplied by a body of monks from the monastery of Abingdon.

Encouraged by this success, Bishop Ethelwold proceeded steadily in the work of reformation and expulsion. The communities of religious women had not suffered less than those of men from the ravages of the Danes. Compelled by the destruction of their houses to mix again with the world, the nuns lost their religious fervour, engaged in the pleasures of a secular life, and in some cases contracted nominal marriage. But these evils were remedied to a great extent under the patronage of Alfred and his queen Alswitha. By them the nunneries of Shaftesbury and of St. Mary at Winchester were founded, and it was easy to people them with Anglo-Saxon ladies of distinction. Of the former of these Alfred's daughter assumed the government; to the latter his consort retired after his death. Her declining years were solaced by the company and the virtues of her granddaughter Eadburga.

The story of Eadburga is curious. It was the wish of her father, King Edward, to devote her to the cloister from her tenderest years; but he hesitated to subject his child to such moral compulsion as this might involve.[1] After some deliberation, he committed the decision of his scruples to a singular experiment. Eadburga, when three years old, was conducted into a chamber, in one corner of which had previously been placed a collection of trinkets attractive to the feminine fancy, in another a chalice with the book of the Gospels. It so chanced that the child ran first to the latter, whereupon the father, clasping her in his arms, exclaimed, "Thou shalt receive the object of thy choice, nor wilt thy parents regret, if they yield to thee in virtue." She was entrusted to the care of the nuns at Winchester, and became eminent among the sisters for her tender piety and extraordinary self-abasement. It is noteworthy that the monasteries of the early centuries in England numbered more royal and noble personages among their inmates than was the case in any other country. Misfortune did not compel them to enter the cloister; the thirty kings and queens who, within two hundred

---

[1] The custom of offering young children to be devoted for life to the monastic profession was early adopted in the Christian Church, in imitation of the oblation of the prophet Samuel. The determination of the parents was considered in some sense binding upon the child until Celestine III. (1191-8) clearly defined the right of all who had been dedicated to the cloister in this way to decide the matter for themselves on attaining years of discretion.

years, laid aside the crown and sceptre to serve God in poverty and obedience, did so when no shadow rested upon their throne, no great sorrow had turned for them all earthly joys into bitterness.

Bishop Ethelwold founded two new abbeys at Winchester—one for monks, another for nuns. The deportment of the latter was regular and edifying; but the pomp assumed by the abbesses, who were all of high rank, shocked the austere notions of the prelate, who was labouring to revive the original discipline of the Benedictine rule. We are told that at the court of Edgar he met the Abbess Edith, the daughter of the king, whose splendid dress accorded ill with the profession of poverty. "Daughter," he observed to her, "the Spouse whom you have chosen delights not in external adornment. It is the heart He demands." "True, father," the abbess replied, "and my heart is given to Him; while He possesses that, He will not be offended with external pomp." Edith, although she made this reply, profited by the reproof addressed to her by the bishop; within the walls of her convent she was distinguished by the austerity of her life, while her liberality in relieving the needs of the indigent proved the solidity of her virtue. The Anglo-Saxon Church enrolled her name in the catalogue of the saints, and she is commemorated with peculiar praise in the Roman martyrology.

Meanwhile the dispossessed canons carried their grievances to the king, and pleaded for restitution, although those who had been ejected had been provided with pensions by the kindness of the bishop. A council was called at Winchester to investigate the matter, and settle the differences between the seculars and the regulars. The council seemed inclined to decide in favour of the former, when a voice from the crucifix (which also served as a pyx) is reported to have been heard saying: "All is well, make no change" (*Absit ut fiat. Judicastis bene; mutaretis non bene*). This turned the scale in behalf of the regulars, and the council was dissolved. Some four years later (978), the complaints of the clergy and the clamour of their friends were revived, and another council met at Calne. In the midst of the debate the floor of the room gave way, and almost all present, with the exception of the archbishop who clung to a beam, were precipitated to the ground below. This accident, regarded as an interposition of Providence, put an end to the contest.

Dunstan's Disciplinary Zeal.—Whilst Dunstan laboured to restore monastic discipline and raise the character of the secular clergy, he did not neglect the morals of the laity. He had the courage to reprove and correct the passions of his sovereign, and imposed on him a severe penance of seven years' duration, to atone for the scandal he had given by forcibly carrying off from a convent a young lady of rank entrusted to the care of the nuns. On another occasion he excommunicated an earl who had contracted marriage within the prohibited degrees of consanguinity, and who turned a deaf ear to the archbishop's expostulations. The earl appealed first to the king, then to the Pope: the former requested, the latter commanded Dunstan to restore the culprit to communion. Conscious that the Holy Father had been deceived by misrepresentations, the prelate was inflexible. "When I see the sinner penitent for his fault, I will obey," he replied; "till this happens, God forbid that I should allow him to continue to transgress the law of God, for fear of any mortal man." In so acting he was in no sense guilty of disloyalty to the Pope; he was but carrying out what he felt convinced would be the Pope's desire, did he know correctly the circumstances. The nobleman repented, abandoned the unlawful union, and publicly asked pardon of the primate.

In 988, Dunstan had grown very feeble, and as the festival of the Ascension approached, he received a supernatural intimation that he should then for the last time appear in the cathedral. He preached that day with unwonted vigour and eloquence on the bliss of heaven, and after giving the episcopal benediction, informed his clergy and people that they would see him no more. Feeling his strength to be failing, he retired to his apartment, where he spent the remainder of the day and the one following in exercises of devotion. On Saturday morning, after receiving Communion, he uttered aloud a hymn of praise to God, and expired in the sixty-fifth year of his age.

St. Dunstan was the principal figure in the history of the tenth century, and, notwithstanding his vigilance and severity, was for many years a most popular saint in this country. Under his rule no less than forty-eight monasteries were rebuilt or erected. In his opinion the monastic system was a necessary factor in the recovery of England from the desolation and darkness brought on it by the Danes.

CHAPTER VII.

RESTORATION OF TRANQUILLITY.

St. Elphege and the Danes.—Towards the close of the tenth century the Danes resumed their habits of depredatory invasion, and England again became the constant scene of war and rapine. In the year 994, Olaf, king of Norway, and Sweyn, king of Denmark, sailing up the Thames with more than ninety vessels, attacked the city of London, and set it on fire in several places. It was the feast of our Lady's Nativity, a day kept as a high festival; the pious Londoners were in the churches at their devotions, when the news came that the assault was being made. Surprised, but not panic-stricken, they hurried to the walls; and with such marvellous ease did they succeed in extinguishing the flames and repelling the foes, that they hesitated not to ascribe their victory to the assistance of the Virgin Mother of God. Elsewhere it was otherwise. From London, the Chronicle says, the Danes marched southward, and wrought the utmost evil that any army could do, by burning, plunder, and slaughter. Ever and anon a feeble effort was made to withstand them, but such attempts produced no effect save that of adding to the distress of the people, and emboldening their persecutors. The natives in despair sought to purchase peace with money; but the payment of enormous sums only procured a temporary cessation of hostilities. At length, in accordance with King Ethelred's orders, the men of West Sussex rose on St. Brice's Day, November 13, 1002, and pitilessly murdered the defenceless and unsuspecting Danes settled amongst them. This act of treachery brought about its own punishment. The invaders returned in greater numbers than before, actuated this time as much by desire for revenge as by greed of plunder.

For four years Sweyn marched through the length and breadth of Wessex, lighting his war-beacons as he went in blazing homesteads and towns. Then for a heavy bribe he withdrew, to prepare for a later, more terrible, and more systematic onset. Again the enemy met with no resistance; they overran East Anglia, Mercia, and besieged the city of Canterbury, regardless of truce and tribute. The archbishop, Elphege, venerable alike for age and virtue, exposed his life for his flock. He went to the camp of the Danes to treat with the leaders, and preached to their followers with such success, that the pagans feared the loss of so many comrades would interfere with their career of pillage and bloodshed. The city was delivered into the hands of the invaders by a traitor; the archbishop was taken prisoner, and compelled to witness the conflagration of his cathedral and the sack of the city. Suffering from a severe wound, he was taken up the river to Greenwich by his captors, who offered to set him at liberty for the sum of three thousand pounds of silver. But he answered that the life of a decrepit old man was of little value, and firmly refused to use the revenues of his afflicted church for his ransom, or to allow the church plate to be sold for the purpose. Treasures consecrated to the service of God, he said, must not be given to pagans. After seven months had elapsed, he was carried into the banqueting-hall where the Danish chiefs had held a carouse, and told he must pay the ransom or forfeit his life. "Gold, bishop, gold!" was the cry that he heard on all sides. "I have no gold to give you," he replied, "but the gold of divine wisdom. I offer to teach you the knowledge of the true God; if you are deaf to my voice, you will experience the effects of His justice." He could say no more; the chieftains rushed in fury from their seats, and taking up the bones with which the ground was strewn after their feast, they pelted him with these and other missiles. He sank bleeding to the ground, and one, more merciful than the rest, put an end to his suffering by a blow from his battle-axe. In more sober moments, the Danes felt some compunction; they allowed the body of the prelate to be honourably interred in London. It was afterwards brought in state by Cnut to Canterbury, and there laid in its last resting-place.

Some years later the successor of the murdered prelate ordered a special fast with processions, confession of sins, and satisfaction, before the feast of St. Michael, for the purpose of imploring the aid of the chief of the heavenly hosts. Every religious congregation was charged to sing a mass daily for the king, to use the collect against pagans, and to recite, while stretched prostrate on the ground, the psalm, *Domine quid multiplicati sunt*—" Why, Lord, are they multiplied that afflict me" (Psa. iii.). These religious preparations for the struggle were accompanied with more military valour than had been till then exhibited. Edmund Ironside made so determined a stand, that, although not strong enough to repel the invaders, he was able to make an agreement with Cnut, the son of Sweyn, for a peaceable division of the land, with the right of succession for the survivor. Shortly after this pacification Edmund died, and Cnut became the ruler of England, 1016.

King Cnut, 1016.—During this most calamitous period the administration of justice had been to a great extent suspended, and universal license prevailed. In consequence of the depredations of the Northmen, and the exactions made in order to raise the sums they demanded, the most opulent proprietors had been reduced to penury, the scarcity being so great that the Danes were compelled to quit the island in search of provisions. Meanwhile, the bishops did not relax their vigilance to prevent the decline of the ecclesiastical discipline which had been revived under Dunstan: the regulations enacted in the national synods would have done credit to an era of order and fervour.

The Church and country began to recover at once upon the accession of Cnut. A heathen when he first came to England, a nominal Christian when he ascended the throne, he became the model of a wise and good monarch. The society which was impotent to withstand his arms had the power to humanize and elevate him. He proved himself a true friend to the Church, a liberal benefactor, a prudent guardian of her best interests. He restored the monasteries which had been overthrown in his own or his father's wars, and erected churches at Assandun and other places where his principal battles had been fought, appointing to them ministers who should, throughout all succeeding ages, make supplication to God for the souls of those who had fallen there. In memory of St. Edmund, whom an earlier generation of Danes had slain, he raised a magnificent edifice, which he largely endowed, at Bury St. Edmund's, the scene of his martyrdom, placing there an abbot and monks. Cnut's care for the Church was not confined to her outward organization or temporal possessions. A number of ecclesiastical laws were passed in the Witenagemote convened by him. The code of which we speak earnestly exhorts to religious obedience and holy living; to careful preparation for receiving the sacraments; to strict observance of the fasts, and the payment of Church dues.

Busy as Cnut was with the affairs of the kingdoms of England and Denmark, he yet found time to make a pilgrimage to Rome. The letter he wrote thence to the English bishops and people speaks well for the nobility of his character and his piety. He tells them he thanks God for having allowed him to visit the shrine of the Apostles to pray for the forgiveness of his sins and the welfare of his people; he expresses his firm belief in the power of the successor of St. Peter to bind and loose, and adds that on this account he thought it highly useful to solicit his patronage with God. He restores the payment of Peter's Pence, which had been neglected of late, and declares he will put an end to all unjust taxation in his realm. "I have vowed to God to lead a right life in all things," he writes, "and administer just judgement to all." Cnut's reverence for the see of Peter was equalled by his devotion to the Mother of God. He celebrated her festivals with special honour, generally going to some monastery for this purpose. Ely was a favourite resort of his. The annals of the abbey record that one day, when he was being rowed down the river, the sound of the monks' chanting was borne across the water. The king immediately ordered his barge to be turned to the bank, that he might join in the service he loved so well to hear. As he listened to the distant melody he composed the following verse:—

> "Merrily sung the monks of Ely
> When Cnut the king rowed thereby:
> 'Row, ye knights, near the land,
> 'And hear we these monks sing.'"

The following well-known anecdote is also related of him. One day when on the beach near Southampton, desirous to rebuke the flattery of his courtiers, he caused a chair to be placed close to the water's edge, and addressing the waves, bade them forbear from wetting the feet of one who was their lord and master. The rising tide soon forced him to withdraw; then, turning to the half-civilized warriors around him, he said: "Ye see how weak is the power of a king, since the waves will not hearken to my voice. Honour God only, and serve Him; Him all things obey." From that day forth Cnut refused to wear his crown; he placed it with his own hands on the head of the crucifix in the roodloft of the old minster at Winchester.

During the brief reigns of the two sons of this good king, only signs of retrogression as regards Church matters can be perceived. Archbishop Ethelnoth, to whose counsels Cnut always listened with respect, died shortly after his patron; his successor in the see of Canterbury bore a less high character. We hear of the bishoprics being held in plurality and sold for money. Stigand, the priest of Assandun, was appointed to a bishopric, but before his consecration it was given to a competitor who offered a larger sum for it.[1] Harthacnut sold the see of Durham to a secular priest named Edred; but the divine judgements fell upon the latter for this act of simony, and he died suddenly a few months after his installation.[2] As soon as Harthacnut was dead, 1042, the nation unanimously chose Edward, the son of Ethelred, to be king. To enforce the ancient laws, to promote the general peace and welfare of his subjects, to aid the restoration of ecclesiastical discipline, were the object of this monarch's incessant prayers and exertions. By the abolition of the oppressive tax known as the Danegeld, and by great acts of charity, he so endeared himself to his people, that peace and liberty seemed inherent in his name. In later years, when smarting under the oppression of the Norman kings, the English used to cry: "Give us the good laws of Edward the Confessor!"

Edward the Confessor, 1042.—The personal character of Edward was one of great sanctity. He possessed the gift of prophecy and miracles. He was the first of our kings who was considered to have the gift of curing by touch the king's evil. One day, whilst leaving mass, he saw in spirit the unhappy fate of Sweyn, the King of Denmark, who, while preparing for a descent upon England, fell into the sea and was drowned. Edward announced this event to his courtiers on the day that it happened. At

[1] Freeman's *Norman Conquest*, vol. i. p. 505.   [2] *Ibid.*, p. 527.

another time he saw our Lord upon the altar, gazing at him with a smiling countenance, and bestowing on him His benediction. This vision was seen at the same moment by Leofric, the good Earl of Mercia, who was worshipping by the king's side.

Normans appointed to Dignities.—Although Edward gained the affection of his subjects by his virtues, he gave umbrage to the clergy and the nobles by the introduction of Normans to ecclesiastical dignities. Ever since his youth he had lived in exile, a period of twenty-seven years, at the court of Normandy, with the relatives of his mother, Queen Emma, who was a Norman princess; and his sympathies were naturally with the people amongst whom he had been brought up, and by whom he had been befriended. His tastes were Norman, he spoke the Norman language, and he gradually raised to some of the highest posts in Church and State his Norman favourites. When the see of Dorchester became vacant, a Norman was appointed to fill it, and the see of London was bestowed on Robert, a monk of Jumièges (a monastery on the Seine), who had become an intimate friend of the king during his exile. Doubtless in so doing Edward was actuated less by motives of personal favouritism, than by the hope of infusing fresh life and vigour into the Church in England, and of correcting abuses and reviving ancient discipline. Besides, increased intercourse with the continent would serve to eliminate an insular spirit, and prevent the little divergences of ritual into which, from their isolated position, the Anglo-Saxons were inclined to drift. But the English clergy were indignant at the appointment of Normans to their benefices; thus on the death of Archbishop Eadsy, in 1050, the cathedral chapter, in order to exclude Robert, the Norman bishop of London, from the archiepiscopal throne, hastened to elect one of their own monks, Elfric by name, to fill it. However, the king took no heed of their choice, and in mid-Lent of the following year, the Chronicle tells us, he held a council in London, and appointed [1] Robert Archbishop of Canterbury. Now Elfric was a kinsman of the powerful Earl Godwin, father-in-law to the king, and the head of the national party; consequently the earl did not feel very amiably disposed towards the prelate for whose sake Elfric had been set aside. Shortly after Robert's return from Rome with the pallium, a dispute arose between him and Earl Godwin about some lands adjacent to the estates of the see of Canterbury, and party feeling ran high. But the earl had at that time some differences with the king; he and his family were banished from the kingdom, and for a time the Normans seemed to triumph. In the following year the tide of popular feeling turned; the earl was restored to his possessions, and the aspect of things was changed. Archbishop Robert and other foreign prelates, accused of stirring up strife between the king and his subjects, were forced to fly; they escaped with difficulty over the sea. Thereupon Stigand, the bishop of Winchester, was intruded into the primacy.

[1] When it is stated that some prelate was appointed to a see by the sovereign, it must be understood that this is only a compendious mode of statement. The king's appointment would not by itself have been held to confer the necessary jurisdiction. That came always from the confirmation by the metropolitan, supervening on election by the chapter, or else from appointment by the Pope as the higher authority, who could always, if he deemed it advisable, supersede the lower.

Stigand.—Stigand, when bishop of Elmham [1] (East Anglia) was the chaplain and chief adviser of Queen Emma, the consort of Ethelred, and afterwards of Cnut. He was involved in her disgrace when, on the accession of Edward, she was deprived of her estates —partly illegal grants made to her by Harthacnut— and, enough being left for her maintenance, she was ordered to live in retirement at Winchester for the remainder of her days. She is supposed to have mixed in politics, and, having transferred her affections entirely to her second husband and her offspring by him, to have neglected the interests of Edward. At any rate she is said to have treated him hardly, and refused either to help him before his accession, or contribute of her wealth to the needs of the State. Stigand was deposed from his bishopric, and his goods were seized, because, as the Anglo-Saxon Chronicle records, " she went just as he advised her, as people thought." His disgrace was however of short duration. The next year he made his peace with the king and Earl Godwin, regained his bishopric, and began to climb the ladder of preferment, for in 1047 he was translated to Winchester, one of the four most important sees of the realm, and attached to the court. On the flight of Robert, Stigand, as has been said, thrust himself into his place, and took possession of the pallium Robert had left behind him. Meanwhile Robert carried his griefs to Rome; but while on his way back, bringing with him a papal letter, he died at Jumièges. The election of Stigand had been uncanonical; Pope Alexander II. suspended him from the exercise of his episcopal functions; and although he continued to retain the name

[1] This see was in 1101 transferred to Norwich.

and enjoy the revenues of the primate, his position was felt to be at the least equivocal, and bishops would not receive consecration at his hands.

Aldred, Archbishop of York.—One of the foremost statesmen and prelates under Edward the Confessor was Aldred, who in 1060 was raised to the see of York. His character offers strange contradictions, and it is difficult to judge aright his busy and erratic career. Previously to his preferment he had been holding two bishoprics, that of Hereford and that of Worcester. The former he resigned, the latter he determined to retain, and procured a letter of sanction from the king to that effect. But when he journeyed to Rome, according to custom, to receive the pallium, in the company of two bishops-elect—Gisa of Wells and Walker of Hereford—who sought consecration, and of Earl Tostig, who was bound for the Papal Court on the king's business, Pope Nicholas II. refused to sanction so irregular a proceeding as the holding of two bishoprics. The two bishops-elect were consecrated, but Aldred was deposed, as he was besides convicted of having exercised unworthy means to obtain promotion. Scarcely had the travellers quitted Rome than they fell into the hands of a party of bandits, who despoiled them of everything but the clothes they were wearing. They returned to the city, having no money to pursue their homeward journey. The powerful earl of Northumbria remonstrated against the misgovernment which allowed such lawlessness at the very gates of the city, and threatened that the payment of the Peter's Pence should be stopped, if restitution were not made. The Pope, moved by the plight of the travellers, or by Earl Tostig's representations, appeased the anger of the latter with presents, and reconsidered Aldred's case.

At length he consented to confirm his election, on the sole condition that Aldred should surrender the see of Worcester. Aldred submitted, and returned rejoicing to York. He was followed immediately by two cardinals, of whose proceedings we know nothing more than that they approved highly of the choice of Wulstan as the successor to Aldred at Worcester, and assisted at his consecration.

Wulstan was a man of holy and mortified life, and most careful as to the fitness of those whom he ordained to the priesthood. It is recorded of him that he had a remarkable reverence for cemeteries; he said doubtless many who slept there were saints, and he forbade any man to ride through them. As a preacher he had a high reputation; it was through his reiterated and eloquent protestations that the shameful traffic in English slaves in the Bristol Channel was stopped, although it had proved too strong for repeated legislation on the part of Ethelred, Cnut, and Edward. Immediately after his appointment to the see, which he occupied with great reluctance, Wulstan found himself engaged in a struggle with the archbishop, who, although he had relinquished the bishopric in obedience to the Pope and to the canons, endeavoured to retain a considerable portion of the revenues. It cost Wulstan a long contest to recover his rights, nor did he regain all the estates that belonged to him until the question had been pleaded before a synod in William's reign, and sentence given in his favour.

If Aldred seems to have been a despoiler of the see of Worcester, he was also its guardian. A soldier before he was a priest, he knew not fear, and did not hesitate to brave the terrible sheriff, Urse by name, who encroached on the church lands, building his castle close to the walls of the cathedral, so that the fosse of his fortress ran across the monks' burying-ground. To a Latin or French speaker the name of *Urse* (bear) might have prompted an easy play on words; to the English prelate it suggested a happy rhyme; he rebuked the sacrilegious intruder in the words :—

"Hightest thou Urse?
Have thou God's curse!"

He dared do more than this: on one occasion he reproved the imperious Conqueror himself, about three years after he ascended the throne of England. Aldred was present in his metropolitan city when one of the great festivals of the Church was approaching; a large supply of wheat and provisions for the feast was being brought in from the episcopal lands in the neighbourhood. The sheriff, William of Malet, going out of York, met the waggons, and although told who was their proprietor, he seized the whole of the stores, bidding his servants carry them to the king's storehouse. The archbishop demanded restitution, but as none was made, he went at once to London, where the king then was. The historian records that he first went to perform his devotions at St. Peter's at Westminster, and then proceeded to the palace, where, robed in full pontificals, he entered the royal presence. William rose to greet him and give him the kiss of peace, but the high-spirited prelate refused his salute. He reminded the king how when as a stranger, by God's permission he won the kingdom, he had given him his blessing and placed the crown on his head. "Now," he said, "I give thee a curse instead of a blessing, as a persecutor of the Church and faithless to the oaths thou swearedst before the altar." William fell at his feet, and asked how he had deserved such a sentence. The nobles who stood by desired to interfere. "Let him lie there, good men," said Aldred; "he lies not at my feet, but at those of St. Peter, whom he has outraged in the person of his successor." Then raising up the king, he told his story. The next day he went back to York in safety and honour; one of the highest nobles being sent with a royal letter ordering that everything that had been taken away should be restored, even to the cords wherewith the sacks were tied. From that day forth no man durst touch the property of the Church.

But we are anticipating, and must resume our account of the events that preceded the Norman Conquest, for which Edward the Confessor was in a measure preparing the way by encouraging the immigration of Normans and so accustoming the English to the rule of foreigners. The marriage of Emma of Normandy to Ethelred in 1002, had been the first step in this same direction, as on this connection by marriage Duke William founded his claim to succeed Edward, whose cousin he was.

Westminster Abbey.—During his exile King Edward had made a vow that, should he regain his throne, he would in thanksgiving make a pilgrimage to the Eternal City. But when, after his accession, he was about to carry out this resolution, the Witan were so strongly opposed to his leaving the kingdom, on account of the danger to which his absence might expose the crown, that the Pope, Leo IX., absolved him from his vow, on condition that he should give to the poor the money which he would have expended, and either build or restore a church in honour of St. Peter. Edward chose to do the latter; he rebuilt the abbey of Thorney, better known as Westminster, at his own expense. This structure was finished and ready for consecration on Holy Innocents' Day, 1065: Edward was, however, too sick to be present at the ceremony, and Edith, the queen, took his place. He died on the Epiphany of the following year, and was buried before the high altar. The surname of Confessor was given to this pious monarch in the bull of his canonization, issued by Pope Alexander III. about a century after his decease.

William of Normandy, 1066.—Until this new minster was built, Winchester had been the place where the kings were anointed, and it had been the right of the Archbishop of Canterbury to place the crown on the monarch's head. The coronation of Harold, Edward's successor, took place at Westminster, and Aldred, Archbishop of York, officiated, because Stigand was suspended. Harold was not destined long to enjoy his regal dignity. It was wrested from him by Duke William of Normandy, who in the preceding reign had visited England, and obtained, as he asserted, from the late monarch, who was childless, the promise to recommend him to the Witan as his successor. Moreover, Harold himself, when cast by a storm on the coast of Normandy, had been forced to purchase his liberty by swearing— some relics having been surreptitiously placed under his hand to give weight to the oath—that he would support the duke's claim. When William, within a year of Harold's accession, landed in England to enforce his claim by arms, bearing a banner blessed by the Pope, Harold hastily summoned such forces as he could collect to oppose the invader. Before leading his army into the field, he went to pray for success to a church he had erected when an earl, at Waltham. He had enriched this edifice with goodly gifts, and appointed thirteen priests for the service of the altar. In it there was a famous rood, said to be miraculous. As Harold lay prostrate upon the ground, with his arms extended in the form of a cross, he vowed to God that if victory might be on his side, he would give greater gifts than he had already given, and serve God faithfully all the days of his life. None was near save Thurkill the sacristan, who watched beside him. Looking at the crucifix, Thurkill perceived that the countenance of the Christ, usually turned upwards, was now bent down, regarding the royal suppliant with an expression of mournful compassion. From that moment he felt assured that it was decreed by Divine Providence that the king should sustain defeat, and should lose his life in the ensuing battle. This prediction was verified.

William of Normandy wished to receive the crown of England, not as a conqueror, but as a lawful king. It was placed on his head by the Archbishop of York in Westminster Abbey, while all who were present signified by loud shouts of "Yea, yea," their willingness to take him for their ruler. He was, as far as outward ceremonies could make him, the king, the choice of the English people consecrated by the chief ecclesiastic of the land.

CHAPTER VIII.

THE FAITH AND PRACTICE OF THE ANGLO-SAXON CHURCH.

BEFORE entering upon the subject of the manifold changes which the Norman Conquest brought to the Church in England, we will pause awhile in order to inquire what the faith and practice of our Anglo-Saxon forefathers really was.

Unlike the cultured nations of the East, the barbarous peoples of the North, when converted to Christianity, were not given to doubt and disputation. They accepted with childlike, unquestioning docility the doctrines taught to them by the missionaries. The innovations and heresies which disturbed and rent the Church in Africa and the East, were, as the reader will have remarked, hardly heard of in these islands. Even the disputes between the Latin and Celtic missionaries only proved, as has been said, that, while they differed on points of discipline, they agreed on all articles of faith. When Ethelhard, Archbishop of Canterbury, demanded from the prelates assembled in the council of Cloveshoe (747), a declaration of their belief, they unanimously answered, "Know that the faith which we profess

is the same as was taught by the Holy Roman
Apostolic See, when Gregory the Great sent missionaries to our fathers." The profession of faith
which St. Swithin, Bishop of Winchester, made, two
centuries later, to Archbishop Ceolnoth, is drawn up
in much the same terms. The reforms effected by
St. Dunstan affected no article of faith, but were
merely a revival of ancient discipline. It is therefore
needless to enter upon an investigation in regard to
the doctrines which formed the creed of the Anglo-
Saxons. It may, however, be interesting briefly to
note some of the religious observances and pious
customs wherein their simple faith was exemplified,
since many of the usages prevalent in early ages,
have, in later times and under altered circumstances,
undergone change or become obsolete.

Pilgrimages.—The devotion of pilgrimages in
England may be said to be coeval with the introduction of Christianity. To the energetic, adven-
turous spirit of the northern nations it offered a
great attraction, and from the earliest times we
read of converts of distinction journeying to Palestine to visit those hallowed spots to which faith
and piety lent so irresistible a charm — the cave
where the Saviour was born, the mount whereon
He suffered, the sepulchre wherein His body was
laid—although the perils attending such enterprises
were sufficient to daunt the most resolute courage.
Jerusalem was distant from Britain more than 3,000
miles ; it was in the hands of the infidels ; the
traveller had to cross an unknown sea, to make
his slow and tedious way amongst peoples whose
language, customs, and manner of life were un-
familiar to him. Yet, as every one knows, St. Helen,

when seventy years of age, journeyed to Jerusalem, in order to become acquainted with a land so worthy of veneration, and carried thence relics of inestimable value for the Christian. The Welsh bishop St. David, in the sixth century, received consecration from the Patriarch of Jerusalem, while on a visit to the Holy Land. An account, written at the time, is preserved of the peregrinations of St. Willibald in the eighth century, who was so fearless as to start from Rome, with only two companions, on a long and very difficult pilgrimage to the places once sanctified by the bodily presence of the Redeemer.

The Tomb of the Apostles in Rome.—Next after the Holy Sepulchre, the tomb of the Apostles in Rome possessed the greatest hold on the Christian imagination, and the most potent attraction for our forefathers. When the division of the Empire lessened the intercourse between East and West, and the advance of Mohammedanism made travelling more dangerous, Rome gradually supplanted Jerusalem to a great degree as the goal of the pilgrim; if not the theatre of our Lord's sufferings, it was that upon which His Passion had been acted over again in the tortures endured by martyrs and confessors for His sake. The mortal remains of St. Peter and St. Paul reposed within its churches; it was besides the residence of the Sovereign Pontiff. The enthusiasm of the visitors to the Eternal City did much to increase devotion to the successor of St. Peter throughout Christendom, and this it is that makes the devotion to the tombs of saints so powerful a factor in ecclesiastical history. Nowhere were pilgrimages to Rome more popular than in England.

The increase of communication with the continent had rendered Italy more accessible, yet the journey was one of no small difficulty and danger. The pilgrim had to cross mountains, to follow highways infested with banditti, to encounter fatigue, exposure, hunger, and often sickness. A large proportion of those who braved these perils did not live to return to their homes. Yet we hear of kings and bishops, besides knights and burghers, priests and laymen innumerable, who undertook the long journey from their remote island to the ancient capital of the world, drawn by their pious desire to visit the tombs of the Apostles, to pay homage to the successor of St. Peter. No less than eight Saxon kings laid aside their crowns and assumed the pilgrim's habit; of this number, four did not resume their regal state, but spent the remainder of their lives in the Holy City. Bede tells us that as early as 670, Oswy, the king of Northumbria, intended, had he recovered from his last sickness, to go and end his days at Rome. We have spoken of Cadwalla, the warlike king of Wessex; of Offa, whose pilgrimage was of a penitential rather than a devotional character; of Ina, the founder of the Anglo-Saxon school at Rome; of Alfred, the adopted son of Leo IV.; of Cnut, the strong Dane, whose letter, written from Rome, shows us a great king and a great man, moved to the depths of his heart by the power and influence of St. Peter. Still more numerous were the ecclesiastics who wended their way to Rome, to receive consecration, to seek counsel and support, to solicit the Papal arbitration in differences with the secular power. The laity also in great numbers took up the pilgrim's staff and gave evidence of their devotion to the

Apostolic See. Unfortunately there were some among these very pilgrims who by their misbehaviour brought some unmerited disgrace on the rest. St. Boniface confesses with shame and sorrow that in certain cities of Lombardy and Gaul were some of his itinerant countrywomen leading depraved lives.

English Sanctuaries.—But it was not only to Rome, moved by affection to the Holy Roman and Apostolic See, that large numbers of Anglo-Saxons went in pilgrimage. England was a soil fertile in saints, and with the invocation of saints came the impulse to venerate their remains. No sooner had St. Alban shed his blood for the faith than Verulam (now St. Albans), became a British pilgrimage. Edmundsbury attracted many pilgrims to honour the martyr-king who had been slain there. Besides these, many sanctuaries dedicated to the saints sprang up in England, and those who were unable to reach the sepulchre of the Saviour at Jerusalem, or the tomb of the Apostles in Rome, as well as many who had visited those more famous spots, satisfied their devotion by repairing to Our Lady of Glastonbury, the shrine of St. Cuthbert at Durham, of St. John at Beverley, the privileged church of Peterborough, or the famous Peter-minster at York, where the annual tribute of the Peter-penny was laid by each pilgrim on the altar. These sanctuaries, besides many later ones, rivalled, as will be seen in mediæval times, the tomb of St. James of Compostella, in the number of pilgrims they attracted, and the munificence of the gifts that were offered by the faithful.

Devotion to the Blessed Virgin.—Beyond all

the saints who were regarded with peculiar veneration, a high pre-eminence was allotted to the "most Blessed Mother of God, the perpetual Virgin Mary," as Ven. Bede terms her. Her praises were the theme of the Saxon poets; Aldhelm of Sherborne, Egbert of York, Cædmon and Alucin spoke and wrote of her with the enthusiasm of sons. Elfric the homilist gives her the title of Queen of the World. The men of action, and builders of churches, like St. Benedict Biscop and St. Wilfrid, dedicated to her the temples they erected, and placed her image in their sanctuaries. Since the landing of St. Augustine, many a great name which adorned the annals of the Church left a monument to Mary, whether in solid stone or in immortal speech. In every Anglo-Saxon church, if the structure itself did not bear her name, the Lady-chapel at the east end was consecrated to her, or at least an altar was erected in her honour, her effigy adorned the walls. The name of Mary was held so sacred that it was never given to infants. It was invoked in public and private devotions; fasting on Saturdays in her honour was a custom widely prevalent.[1] The laws of King Ethelred enjoin: "Let all St. Mary's feast-tides be strictly honoured, first by fasting, and afterwards by feasting." The principal events of her mortal life were commemorated by four yearly solemnities, in honour of her Nativity, the Annunciation, her Purification, and her Assumption. The Conception of Our Lady was not kept as a festival until the time of the Normans, but we may be permitted to anticipate somewhat, and relate

[1] Witness the proverbial saying: "Qui non indiget Divæ Virginis ope, ejus sabbato non jejunat." The abstinence on Saturdays, a pious custom descending from ancient times, remained in force until Pius VIII. dispensed the English Catholics from its observance in 1830.

in this place a very ancient story which, even if only legendary, at least illustrates the belief of the time.

Shortly after the conquest by the Normans, it was rumoured that the Danes were preparing to make a descent upon the island to withstand the power of William the Conqueror. Accordingly William sent the Abbot of Ramsey to Denmark, to ascertain the truth of the report. Having executed his commission, the abbot was returning home, when he was overtaken at sea by a terrific storm, and a great tempest threatened to overwhelm the vessel. The master and all the crew fell on their knees and cried to the glorious Virgin Mary, the hope of the despairing. Then the abbot saw coming across the water a person in the habit of a bishop, who told him that he should be delivered from the peril of shipwreck if he would promise to hallow the feast of the Conception of Our Lady with all solemnity, and cause it to be preached to the people. The abbot asked when the festival was to be kept, and with what office? "On the 8th of December," was the reply; "and the office shall be the same as that of the Nativity, save that where thou sayest Nativity thou shalt say Conception." Thereupon the figure vanished, and the tempest ceased. The abbot and the ship's company came safely to land, and the abbot notified to the authorities what he had seen and heard.

Amongst the instances of wealthy nobles and landowners who sought to obtain favour with God by the erection of churches or images in honour of His holy Mother, we may select the noble Earl of Mercia, Leofric, and his Countess, Godiva, who, when the abbey erected by Bishop Egwin at Evesham fell into ruins, came forward with their wonted munificence, and about 1010, rebuilt the church. "In it," the Chronicler says, "they caused to be placed a large crucifix, with an image of the Holy Mother of God, beautifully wrought in gold and silver; they gave also a green chasuble, a cope, and many other precious ornaments." Nor was this all that Leofric did for love of God and of Our Lady. On the site of a ruined convent (which gave its name to the town of Coventry), standing on his own lands, he erected a magnificent abbey. The Countess Godiva, who is described as the model of an Anglo-Saxon lady, bestowed all her treasures upon it, giving all the gold and silver she possessed to make covers for the sacred books, crosses, images of the saints, and other "marvellous ornaments" for the decoration of the church. Never before had so splendid an edifice been raised in England. The historian, William of Malmesbury, says that it was so enriched with gold and silver that the eyes of the beholders were dazzled, as though what they beheld was not a reality, but something supernatural. The very beams supporting the shrine were covered with a sheathing of the precious metals. There is no doubt that the pious Lady Godiva took care that the celebrated image of Our Lady of Coventry should hold no inconspicuous place in the church. We know that it was adorned with jewels, its richest ornament being the string of costly stones which Godiva, who used it to count her prayers, desired on her deathbed should be hung around the neck of the statue.

The Use of Beads.—The practice of repeating a certain number of Paters and Aves on a string of beads was of very old date among the Anglo-Saxons.

The Benedictine writers who claim for St. Benedict the honour of being the first to introduce the use of Our Lady's Psalter, as the rosary was originally called, represent it as chiefly propagated in the eighth century by Venerable Bede. It is recorded that the spread of this devotion in England was attended with extraordinary results, and that many victories were gained over the Danes by its means; that the English, moreover, who fled from their own land to escape the violence of the invaders, carried their favourite devotion with them to other countries.[1] The fact cannot be denied that most of the ancient images of the Blessed Virgin in England were represented holding the beads in their hands, and in aftertimes many had them round their necks. We may conclude that Godiva's example was followed by other pious ladies of olden time.

The Anglo-Saxon ladies loved to show their devotion to the Blessed Sacrament by employing their time in the decoration of the altar. They were famed for their excellence in embroidering vestments; in fact, no other country could show anything to compare in costliness of material and skill in workmanship with the vestments they made, which are described as stiff with gold thread, sparkling with pearls and gems, and adorned with figures of the saints wrought in the finest needlework.

Devotion to the Holy Eucharist.—The belief of the Anglo-Saxons concerning the Holy Eucharist was identical with our own. The British converts,

---

[1] The institution of the rosary as a popular devotion throughout Europe in the thirteenth century was owing to St. Dominic, to whom it is recorded to have been indicated by Our Lady as a means of arresting and overthrowing the formidable heresy of the Albigenses in the south of France.

before the arrival of the Saxons, had their altars—
"the seats of the heavenly sacrifice"; the Scottish
priests in the remote island of Icolmkill "celebrated
the sacred mysteries, and consecrated, according to
custom, the Body of Christ," as the contemporary
native writers, Gildas, Cumine, Adamnan, abundantly
testify. The disciples of Augustine, Paulinus, and
Aidan, such as Archbishop Egbert, Eddius, Alcuin,
Venerable Bede, used formulas familiar to ourselves
in speaking of "the holy Body and precious Blood of
the Lamb by whom we have been redeemed, immolated again to God for the benefit of our salvation."
In certain ceremonies of the mass, in the arrangement
of the prayers preceding the canon, slight variations
existed—local uses, which for the sake of uniformity
have been gradually suppressed—but the form of the
mass was substantially the same, and it was never
offered up in any but the Latin tongue. For the
service of the altar the Anglo-Saxon bestowed all
the riches that earth yields. What was done in
wealthy and cultured Rome, our rough forefathers
did in their half-civilized country. If Sixtus III.
(432–440) gave an altar of silver to the basilica of St.
Mary Major, the Saxon king Ina gave 264 lb. of
gold for an altar in the silver chapel at Glastonbury,
besides 2,640 lb. of silver for the church, a chalice
and paten of gold, with images of the twelve apostles
in solid silver. In the church of York stood two
altars entirely covered with plates of gold or silver,
decorated with jewels and precious stones of almost
priceless value. The vessels employed in the sacred
ministry were of the most costly description; this
too, be it remembered, when the precious metals were
rare, and a penny was worth more than a pound is

now. Even liturgical books were decorated with similar magnificence. This was done to testify the profound respect wherewith everything connected with the Holy Sacrifice was regarded. The canons and rubrics relating to the celebration of mass enjoined that "no priest should ever presume to celebrate unless he have all things fitting for the housel [1] ; that is, a clean offlete,[2] clean wine, and water. Woe to him that beginneth to say mass unless he have every one of these. . . . Let them put the sanctuary into the best order ; let there be lights burning in the church when mass is singing." (Canons enacted under King Edgar, Thorpe, vol. ii. p. 253.)

Penance.—The Anglo-Saxon had, like us, both high and low mass, and at the former on Sundays the parishioners, "all men of every order," were by the law of the land commanded to be present. The laws of Cnut enjoin upon Christian men to go to communion three times a year at least—at Christmas, Easter, and Pentecost ; Archbishop Egbert declared that those who did not do so could not be considered as Catholics. (*Excerpt. Egberti*, Thorpe, vol. ii. p. 103.) To this solemnity they were to come fasting. "We enjoin," says one of the canons enacted under Edgar, "that no one unfasting taste of the housel, unless it be for extreme sickness " (*ibid.*, p. 253). They were to prepare themselves for it carefully, with confession of their sins and atonement for

---

[1] For many centuries this was the English name for the Blessed Sacrament.

[2] The bread, unleavened and without salt, cut into circular shape, was called in Latin *oblata*, whence came the Saxon word *offlete*, afterwards corrupted into *obley* in the fifteenth and sixteenth centuries. (Lingard, *Anglo-Saxon Church*.)

them.[1] "Confession," says an Anglo-Saxon writer, "with true penance, is the angelic remedy for our sins." Before the rigour of the penances inflicted in those days, the courage of the modern penitent would quail; but our forefathers submitted to them without a murmur. The doom-book lying open before the priest was supposed to apportion the punishment to the degree of guilt, with due regard to the age, circumstances, and dispositions of the penitent. Sins of frailty were to be expiated by a fast of ten, twenty, or thirty days; while for transgressions of a darker dye a long course of penance was enjoined, extending over five or seven years, or even over a whole lifetime. The austerity of the penance was mitigated as time went on; to the severe regimen of bread and water some more nutritious food was added; the three or six days a week were reduced to one or three; almsgiving, prayers, and other good works—in the case of the wealthy, the foundation of a church or monastery—at first accessories, soon became substitutes for fasting. Speaking of a sinner, the ancient laws of England say, "When a man fasts, let the dishes that would have been eaten be distributed to God's poor, and the days that a man fasts let him abandon every worldly occupation, and by day and by night, the oftenest that he can, let him remain in

[1] "Every sin a man shall confess to his confessor, which he ever committed, either in word, or in work, or in thought.... The confessor shall ask him everything, who imparts his need to him, and enjoin him to hide nothing from him, neither in word nor in work, of what he supposes he may have ever wrought against God's will; and the confessor shall, for everything, declare the 'bot' [penance]" (Thorpe, ii. 429.)

"In the week before Lent, every one shall go to his confessor, and confess his deeds; and his confessor shall so shrive him as he may then hear by his deeds what he is to do" (*ibid.*, p. 433).

the church, and earnestly watch there, imploring forgiveness of God with groaning of spirit, and kneel frequently in the form of the cross." For public sins public penances were imposed even upon the highest in the land; we have seen King Edgar, at the command of Dunstan, lay aside his crown for seven years, and fast two days every week, for having by his example encouraged licentiousness (p. 106). For the guidance of the confessor in such matters, Archbishops Theodore and Egbert severally drew up a handbook, or penitentiary. The forty days of Lent were devoted to the performance of the penitential works laid upon the open offender. Barefoot and bareheaded, clothed in sackcloth, he came to the church door on Ash Wednesday, and being led by the bishop into the church, cast himself on the ground, and with outstretched arms recited the seven penitential psalms. After being sprinkled with holy water, he was led out again, not to be re-admitted until Holy Thursday. By the end of the twelfth century public penance had disappeared, unless on certain very grave occasions.

Communion.—Although they believed as firmly as we do that the Body and Blood of the Lord is received under one kind, yet during the Anglo-Saxon period, in fact, until the eleventh century, the faithful usually communicated under both species—provided, that is, that they made their communion during the time of mass. The priest administered the offlete, the deacon the consecrated chalice. This chalice had two handles, by which it was carried to the people kneeling at the foot of the altar, and each one drank of its sacred contents, not by putting his lips to the brim, but through a long narrow tube or reed, made of gold, silver, or ivory. Not until the Council of Constance (1414) was a formal decree issued prescribing communion in one kind only, although the danger of desecration on the one hand, and on the other the fear lest, if every one communicated under both kinds, the belief in Our Lord's whole presence in either species should die out, had led to its disuse in many places. From the very first, communion was given to the sick under one kind only, the hosts reserved for this purpose being kept in a pyx made of gold, generally in the shape of a dove, which was suspended over the altar. In another point of discipline the custom of early times differed from our own. The Sacred Host used to be given to the faithful into their hand, the women not receiving it upon their uncovered palm, but using a small linen napkin, called *dominicale*, for the purpose. Bede (*Ecclesiastical History*, bk. iv. c. 20), describes Caedmon on his death-bed as receiving the Eucharist in his hand, as if it were the practice of the time. A council in Rome, about 880, prohibited the priest from placing the Eucharist in the hand of any lay person, and commanded him to place it in the mouth.

The Clergy.—As a body the clergy stood high in the social scale. Their dignity as ministers and stewards of the holy mysteries, the valuable services they rendered to the laity, their learning, their celibacy, the ascetical course of life they usually followed, gained for them universal respect. An archbishop ranked as an atheling, or prince of the blood royal; a bishop was the equal of an earl, or ealdorman; a presbyter of a thane or noble. The name of *preost*, or priest, was employed to denote any, even the lowest, cleric; those who had received priest's orders were termed presbyters, or mass priests, and the rules regulating the duties and conduct of the latter were very stringent.

The sources whence the parish priest derived his means of subsistence were—(1) The produce of a small piece of land attached to the church; (2) the voluntary oblations of his parishioners; (3) the tithes, payment of which, at first voluntary, was afterwards rendered compulsory. These tithes were to be divided into three parts—for the maintenance of public worship, the relief of the poor, the support of the clergy. Besides this tax, every householder had to pay *kirk-scot*, or first-fruits, at Martinmas; *light-scot*, a silver penny at Candlemas, Easter-eve and All Hallows, to furnish tapers for the altar; *soul-scot*, the fee at burials; and *Rome-scot*, or Peter's-penny, payable in the week ending August 1st. We may here mention two privileges connected with the Church, of great value in semi-barbarous days—that of sanctuary, which offered to the fugitive an asylum for three days from the vengeance of his enemy within the precincts of the church; and the peace of the Church—the suspension, that is, of every feud and dispute—on Sundays, holy days, and during Advent and Lent.

Gilds.—Gilds, which in mediæval times became so prominent a feature in the social life of this country, were very numerous in Anglo-Saxon times. As early as the reign of Ina, the word gild (from *gilden*, to pay) was used in the sense of a society of contributing members, associated for mutual help and assurance. The first charter extant of a gild dates from the reign of Cnut, when Orcy gives the gildhall at Abbotsbury in Dorsetshire, "for God's love and

St. Peter's," to the *gyldscipe* of the place. At all times the religious element entered largely into these associations, but this was more especially the case in early days. On the feast-day of the fraternity, all the gildsmen and women went in procession to the church, to hear the mass of the gild-priest. Many were especially established to promote the honour of the Blessed Virgin; the rules of all enjoined devotions and orisons, care of the sick and aged, and principally, above all other works of Christian charity, care for the dead. On the decease of a gildsman, his fellow-members were summoned to assemble together for the purpose of accompanying his corpse to the place of burial and giving it honourable interment; it was binding on them also to recite certain prescribed prayers for his soul. The rules of the Gild of Abbotsbury provided that on the death of one belonging to it, each member should pay one penny for the good of his soul before the body was laid in the grave. For neglecting to do this a fine of three times the amount was imposed. When a member of the Gild of London died, each of the survivors was obliged to give to the poor a loaf of bread for the benefit of his soul. At one time it was a general custom that persons attending the funeral of a relative or friend should contribute a donation of money or bread on his behalf, to be distributed among the poor who were present. This was the origin of *doles* in England, which consisted of loaves of bread, before the distribution of which certain fixed prayers were recited.

Prayers for the Dead.—The monuments and annals of the Celtic and Anglo-Saxon Churches testify indisputably that prayer for the souls of the departed was from the very first a recognized duty and constant practice of Christians in these islands, as it was of every other land whither the faith had been carried. Traces of it are found in the earliest inscriptions of sepulchre and memorial stones. On an ancient cross in Cardiganshire may yet be seen, in Hiberno-Saxon characters, the request that whoever reads those words would ask a blessing on the soul of the man interred on that spot. In a monastery in Pembrokeshire a stone, assigned to a date shortly after the final departure of the Romans from Britain, still stands, bearing an inscription entreating all who pass by to pray for the soul of one Catuconus. Similar examples may be seen at Iona, Lismore, and other places in Scotland and Ireland. Ven. Bede begs of the monks of Lindisfarne that, in consideration of his having written the life of St. Cuthbert, they will, at his death, offer prayers and masses for him as for one of their own body; Alcuin calls upon his former scholars at York to remember him in their prayers, when it shall please God to withdraw him from this world. The King of Kent and Bishop of Rochester, writing together to Lullus, an Anglo-Saxon, the successor of St. Boniface in the see of Mayence, agree that when either of them departs to another life the survivors shall assist him with their prayers and oblations. The monks of Iona were exhorted to display as much fervour in chanting the office for the dead as if each one were reciting it on behalf of his own particular friend.

This belief in the great benefit the dead derived from the prayers of the living exercised a powerful influence on the manners of the people. So anxious were our pious forefathers to secure for themselves during their lifetime the certainty of a remembrance after death in the prayers of the Church, that no effort was too severe, no sacrifice of worldly goods too great, to compass the desired end. In this view how many churches were built, monasteries endowed, munificent offerings made to shrines! Those who had little of this world's wealth wherewith to purchase eternal treasures, made pilgrimages, offered the produce of their land, or the labour of their hands, with the same object. Persons of rank and distinction earnestly desired to obtain a place of sepulture in churches much frequented, not from pride, but in the hope that the sight of the monuments erected over their ashes might silently solicit for them the suffrages of the faithful. The records of past centuries tell of bequests innumerable to churches and monasteries with the express obligation that the clergy should pray for the soul of the donor, and large sums of money were left to the poor on the same condition.

The deep conviction felt by our forefathers of the importance of prayers for the departed made them no less solicitous to procure them for the souls of others than for themselves. Hence, on the death of a relative or a member of a community, the survivors sought to make his demise known as speedily and widely as possible. In the eighth century it was already customary to announce a death to all who lived in the vicinity by the ringing of bells; sometimes the burning of a bright light was employed for the same purpose. The death of a priest, regular or secular, or any person of high position or eminent virtue, was immediately notified by letter to all the bishops; and each bishop, on receiving the message, was bound to make it known to all the parish churches and religious houses in his diocese. Somewhat later, religious communities adopted the method of sending a circular letter to all houses of their order, and any others with whom they had formed a spiritual association for mutual assistance. These circular letters consisted of a long strip of parchment rolled round a small cylinder of wood, which had a knob at each end to prevent the roll from slipping off. The messenger fastened this *rotulus*, as it was called, by a cord round his neck, and journeyed from convent to convent, from church to church, throughout the land, allowing as short pauses for rest as he could. The roll taken from his hands was read aloud by the head of the house to the assembled monks, who forthwith recited the office for the dead for the repose of the soul of the person departed. The prior or abbot then inscribed his name and the date of reception upon the parchment, with a promise of prayers. Very generally the name of some inmate of the monastery or benefactor recently deceased was added, for whom in his turn prayers were implored. Thus the list of names for whom suffrages were asked lengthened as the roll was carried on its way. The number of these circular letters known to be still extant is about one hundred. Many are of great length, having as many as five or six hundred signatures attached to them. One preserved among the Durham MSS. is thirty-nine feet long and nine inches wide.

Allusions are constantly found in Anglo-Saxon liturgical books to a register of the departed, preserved in the principal churches, designated the Book of Life. These books, or diptychs, stood on the high altar, and it was customary, immediately after the words *in somno pacis* in the mass, for the deacon to read from them the names of deceased dignitaries or benefactors of the Church. To obtain a place in these obituaries was a privilege greatly coveted. Kings and nobles frequently put a clause in their wills to this effect.[1]

The following narrative, related by Bede, illustrates the belief in the power of the Holy Sacrifice to relieve and release the souls in purgatory :—

Amongst those who were left for dead at the close of the battle fought between the kings of Northumbria and Mercia on the banks of the Trent, in the latter half of the seventh century, was a young Northumbrian thane called Imma. The whole night he lay senseless amongst the heaps of dead. Coming to himself, he bound up his wounds as well as he could ; then, after resting a while, he got up on his feet and continued to move a short distance in search of his friends. Being observed by the men of one of the Mercian nobles, he was seized and carried before their master. Fearing to acknowledge his rank, he said he was only a poor countryman, who, to earn a living for himself and his wife, had come to sell provisions to the soldiers. The earl ordered him to be taken care of. When his wounds began to heal, he was always bound at night to prevent his escape ; but always, soon after his keepers had left him, his chains fell off. The earl at last asked him how it was, and

---

[1] The catalogue of the dead, given out to be prayed for on Sundays, began during the Anglo-Saxon and continued throughout the Norman period of our Church history, to be called the bede-roll. " Bidding the beads" consisted (1) of prayers for different personages of position in church and state in general who were living ; (2) for certain individuals who were dead.

whether he carried about him some charm for loosening fetters, such as fables spoke of. He replied that he knew nothing of such arts, but that he had a brother in his part of the country who was a priest, who, he well knew, thought he was slain, and frequently said mass for him; "and," he added, "were I now in another life, then my soul would be freed by his intercessions."

From his speech and general appearance it had long before this been suspected that he was not what he called himself. One day the earl took him apart, and promised to do him no harm if he would say who he was. Imma replied that he was one of Egfrid's thanes. "You deserve indeed to die," answered the earl, "because all my brothers and kinsmen died in that battle. However, not to break my plighted word, I will not slay you." He therefore sent him to London and sold him as a slave to a Friesian merchant. Still his chains fell off as before. His new master tried many different kinds, but all alike relinquished their hold. He therefore exacted an oath from his captive that he would send him his ransom, and then set him free. Imma obtained the money from the King of Kent. Returning home, he related to his brother, who was Abbot of Tunnacester, all that had happened. The abbot had heard that Imma was slain, had gone to the field of battle to search for his body, and having carried to his monastery and buried a corpse which he took for that of his brother, had frequently said mass for his soul's deliverance. The very time at which the fetters mostly fell off was the third hour—that at which the mass was usually celebrated. "Many," adds Ven. Bede, "hearing these things, were inflamed in faith and pious devotion to pray, or give alms, or offer to the Lord the victim of the sacred oblation, for the deliverance of their friends who have passed from the world; for they perceived that the health-giving sacrifice was available to the everlasting deliverance both of soul and body."

That the "month's mind," or thirty days' prayer on behalf of the dead, was devoutly observed in Anglo-Saxon times, we learn from the writings of Archbishop Theodore and St. Dunstan. The latter mentions mass being said daily for thirty days on behalf of one who was departed. One of St. Boniface's canons [1] enacts that for thirty days the friends of any one deceased should offer prayers and fast for the good of his soul. Archbishop Theodore's *Liber Pœnitentialis* is still more explicit. "For seven days after a man's death we bewail all the sins that he committed and that he ought not to have committed; then until the thirtieth day we pray also for those things that he ought to have done and did not do. On the thirtieth day we offer the holy sacrifice for him. For a monk who dies let mass be said on the day of burial, and on the third, the seventh, and the thirtieth days, and afterwards as often as the abbot directs" (Thorpe, vol. ii. pp. 52, 53).

[1] De trigesimis mortuorum (S. Bonif. Op., ed. Giles, t. ii. p. 33).

CHAPTER IX.

CHANGES CONSEQUENT ON THE NORMAN CONQUEST.

William the Conqueror, 1066. His Policy.
—Although William of Normandy was, as we have seen, crowned at Westminster with the full consent of the representatives of the nation, he did not reign as undisputed monarch of England without a struggle. But the insurgents once quelled, his assumption of the regal power and the settlement of his followers in the kingdom was facilitated by the fact that, at any rate to those who were descended from the Danes, the Normans were not an alien race. They, too, were Northmen, a band of Scandinavian pirates originally, who had made their home on a tract of territory granted to them in France. When first the Saxons and then the Danes conquered the island, the Britons, with their purer faith and higher civilization, were the acknowledged superiors, the intellectual masters of the rude barbarians who overcame them in mere warfare. In regard to the Normans it was otherwise. They were equal, if not superior, to the English in language, laws, and customs; and, what is of still greater importance, they were one with them in faith.

The Church had not in her turn, as on former occasions, to conquer the conquerors, to subjugate and bring into her fold those who by force of arms had made themselves masters of the country. In their social and political feelings, however, and their habits of life, the Normans differed vastly from the English, and the blending of the conquerors and the conquered was not the work of a single lifetime. It was accelerated by the consummate policy of William. His desire was to discharge the duties of an English sovereign, and he even tried to learn the language, that he might be able himself to understand the complaints and appeals of his subjects. He may be said neither to have changed nor tyrannized more than his position and circumstances demanded. Yet under him England became more and more Norman, less and less English. By the end of his reign, by merely disregarding the English, rather than by any act of general or violent expulsion, the Normans had contrived to supplant them at least in all the higher appointments of Church and of State.[1]

Not until William was firmly seated upon the throne did he interfere in ecclesiastical affairs, beyond filling up the vacancies that occurred with his Norman friends. It might look like sacrilege when he caused all the monasteries to be searched, but no harm was done to the monks or their possessions.

[1] "One may sum up the change in England by saying that some twenty thousand foreigners replaced some twenty thousand Englishmen, and that these newcomers got the throne, the earldoms, the bishoprics, the abbacies, and by far the greater portion of the big estates, mediate and immediate, and many of the burgess holdings in the chief towns. The English owners had either fallen in battle or fled into exile, or, if they remained, they had forfeited their estates by armed and avowed resistance to the new and crowned king" (*Social England*, vol. i. p. 241).

The religious houses were only visited for the sake of the hoards which wealthy persons, at the time of the invasion, had laid up for safety in the monastic treasuries. These the king looked upon as forfeited goods of rebels, and carried them off accordingly.

Synod of Winchester, 1070.—When William had subdued the disaffected thanes, he applied himself to the reorganization of the episcopate. For this purpose he requested the Pope to send legates to England, and on their arrival a great synod was held at Winchester, 1070. At the opening of the council the legates performed the ceremony of placing the crown on William's head, as a confirmation by papal authority of the consecration he had received from the Archbishop of York at Westminster. They then thus addressed the assembled bishops and clergy: "The Church of Rome has the right of supervision over all Churches, and it behoves her to make inquiry into your deportment and manner of life, you whom she has instructed in the faith of Christ, and to remedy the decline among you of the faith you hold from her. It is to exercise over you this salutary inspection that we, the ministers of the Blessed Apostle Peter, and authorized representatives of our Lord Pope Alexander II., have resolved to hold counsel with you to seek out and uproot the evil things that have sprung up in the vineyard of the Lord."[1] Before this council, several bishops and abbots were arraigned, charged with breach of discipline and unworthiness of life. First and foremost amongst these delinquents was Archbishop Stigand. The accusations brought against him were threefold.

[1] Hook, *Archbishops of Canterbury*, vol. i. p. 524.

1. He had thrust himself into the primacy while Robert was still alive and undeposed. 2. He held the bishopric of Winchester together with the primacy. 3. He had dared to use Robert's pallium, and subsequently obtained one for himself from the usurping Pope, Benedict X., whom "the Holy Roman Church had excommunicated for having attempted to gain access by money to the Chair of Peter." Stigand was likewise accused of simony and grievous covetousness, and being unable to allege anything in his defence, he was canonically degraded, and deprived of all ecclesiastical status. To this punishment the king added that of confinement for the remainder of his life. By universal consent the vacant see of Canterbury was offered to Lanfranc, a monk of the abbey of Bec.

Lanfranc. — Lanfranc was a scion of a noble family in Pavia, well skilled in the traditions of Roman law, who had wandered across the Alps to found a school at Avranches. Attracted by the fame of the sanctity of Herlouin, the Abbot of Bec, he had abandoned honours and dignities to embrace the religious life. His learning rendered the monastery of Bec the most famous school of Christendom. It was with no slight difficulty that, when Abbot of St. Stephen's, Caen, he was induced to accept the archbishopric of Canterbury, to aid in the reform of the English clergy. On his assuming the archiepiscopal mitre he had to contend with difficulties of various kinds. His cathedral church was in ruins, having been burnt to the ground a few years before. The monastic institute was in almost as deplorable a condition as the cathedral, for the body of monks introduced by Archbishop Elfric in 1003 had been reduced in number at the time of Elphege's martyrdom, so that they had admitted into their ranks men who wore the habit but had not received the training of monks, and great laxity in the observance of the rule was the result. Lanfranc rebuilt the metropolitan minster, restored the monks to their full number, and re-established monastic discipline amongst them.

These were not the only troubles the archbishop encountered. William's half-brother Odo, Bishop of Bayeux and Earl of Kent, had seized on many lands belonging to the primatial see as fiefs of his earldom, and had besides appropriated the revenues of the see from the time of Stigand's deposition. It was no easy task to compel him to restore the misappropriations. But the king interfered, and Odo had to surrender to the Church no less than twenty-five estates. Furthermore, a question arose with regard to the respective jurisdiction of the sees of Canterbury and York. Thomas, the archbishop-elect of York, went to Lanfranc to be consecrated, but on his refusal to pay him canonical obedience, the primate would not perform the ceremony. It was not until Lanfranc had argued the point before the council, in the presence of the king (although the decision was not by royal authority) that the question was decided in his favour, and a temporary arrangement effected.

Canterbury and York.—The next year both the newly-consecrated archbishops went to Rome to receive their pallia. With them went Remigius, Bishop of Dorchester, who was accused of having, when almoner at Fécamp, furnished Duke William of Normandy with a well-manned vessel for his expedition against England, on the understanding that, in return, the bishopric of Dorchester was to be given to him. Lanfranc was received with great honour by the Pope, who had formerly been his pupil. The Pontiff rose up to greet him, and anticipated his prostration with an affectionate embrace, saying: "We honour you as our old master, from whom we have learnt all we know." Moreover, as a mark of personal esteem, in addition to the ordinary pallium, he bestowed on Lanfranc another, which he was himself in the habit of using when celebrating mass. The two accused prelates (Archbishop Thomas had also infringed the canons) threw themselves on the Holy Father's mercy, but he referred the decision of their cause to Lanfranc's judgement. Lanfranc pronounced them both to be men of worth, useful to the kingdom; the ring and crozier which they had resigned were therefore restored to them. Archbishop Thomas then begged that the Pope would decide by his supreme authority the relative rights of the archiepiscopal sees of Canterbury and York. For the latter (his own see) he claimed independent primacy on various grounds. The Holy Father wisely ordered the question to be investigated and decided in England, where the facts could be better examined and the rival claims discussed. This was accordingly done at Easter in the following year, when the Witenagemot met at Winchester; the result being that the inherent primacy of Canterbury was acknowledged and confirmed. Thenceforward the ecclesiastical jurisdiction of Lanfranc over the whole kingdom was undisputed.

Separation of Church and Civil Courts.—A memorable feature of this reign was the formation of ecclesiastical courts. In compliance with a custom coeval with the introduction of Christianity among the Saxons, the bishop attended, either personally or by his archdeacon, the chief courts of justice within his diocese. There he presided in company with the earldorman, that they might expound God's law and the world's law. In these courts ecclesiastical pleas were taken first, in which the proceedings were in great measure directed by the bishop; next came pleas of the crown; lastly, the complaints of individuals against one another. It was not easy to show that this judicial interference of the bishops in secular matters was consistent with the prohibition of canons. The papal legates Gregory and Theophylact had in 787 noticed and condemned this practice of Anglo-Saxon prelates, but it was justified in the eyes of the latter in consideration of the benefits resulting from it. It continued in full force until after the Conquest, when the foreign prelates placed by William I. in English bishoprics, protested against a custom which they considered as a desecration of the episcopal office. As a faithful son of the Church, he agreed that its discipline should henceforth be observed.[1] No longer were bishops or archdeacons to hear ecclesiastical causes in the hundred-courts, but in their own courts, and according to the episcopal laws and the prescriptions of the holy canons. No spiritual questions were to come before lay-judges, nor was any sheriff or officer of the king to interfere in matters which ought to be determined by the laws of the Church.

The Ordeal.—While the Church courts were thus placed in a separate and independent position, the clergy were allowed to retain an important part in the ordinary criminal jurisdiction. In cases where nothing but circumstantial evidence could be brought

---

[1] Lingard, *Anglo-Saxon Church*, chap. xi.

against an accused person, the *ultima ratio* was the ordeal. This semi-religious practice prevailed amongst all northern nations that embraced Christianity after the fifth century. Lingard (*ibid.*, chapter x.) terms it "an extraordinary practice which united the most solemn rites of religion with the public administration of justice." For three days previously the accused prepared himself by fasting and prayer: at mass on the third day, at the time of communion, the priest adjured him not to receive the Holy Eucharist if his conscience reproached him with the crime laid to his charge; if he persisted in his denial, the communion was given to him, and he was led to trial. The ordeal was of four kinds, the instruments employed in each being solemnly consecrated by a form of ritual. These were: (1) the *corsned*, or barley-cake, which the accused, if guilty, was unable to swallow; (2) cold water, into which being lowered when bound, if he sank, he was considered innocent, if he swam, guilty; (3) boiling water, out of which a stone was to be taken with the bared right hand; and (4) fire, the test being to lift a red-hot iron and carry it three paces. In each of the two last tests, the hand of the prisoner was sealed up in a cloth for three days, at the end of which if it was found healed, he was declared innocent.

Religious Houses.—The changes introduced by Lanfranc all tended to increase intercourse with the continent, or to break down some national peculiarity. The decree which provided that bishoprics should be removed to the chief cities of the diocese helped to make England like Gaul and Italy. So did the rebuilding of churches and abbeys on a larger scale in stone, and according to the latest continental fashion. On the other hand, monastic chapters in episcopal churches, a thing almost unknown out of England, were encouraged by Lanfranc. The corporate spirit of the regulars was stronger, and their dependence on Rome greater, than that of the seculars. The great danger of the Church in England at that period arose from the degradation of clerical persons and offices. It had to be met by enforcing clerical celibacy and prohibiting simony. The monastic rule was a safeguard against infringement of the laws in both these matters. The government of the religious houses was under Lanfranc entrusted to foreigners. The monasteries were the home of English national feeling. In them some of the noblest-born had found refuge, in them the chronicles of the past were written and preserved. To bring them to greater strictness of life, Lanfranc appointed abbots who ruled with severity. The choice was not always a wise one. In 1082, Thurstan, Abbot of Glastonbury, a monk of Lanfranc's own house at Caen, insisted on the monks giving up the Gregorian chants to which from time immemorial they were accustomed, and adopting a newly-devised Norman mode of singing. They unanimously refused to make the change. The abbot called up his Norman archers (like some other abbots, he supplied a contingent of soldiers to the king) and the monks ran into the church, where they locked themselves in. The archers went up into the choir, and thence they let fly their arrows at the defenceless churchmen, killing three and wounding others. For this cruel and despotic act Thurstan was disgraced, and sent back to his cell at Caen for the remainder of his days: the monks received a reprimand for their disobedience. This was an exceptional case; scenes of blood and sacrilege formed no part of the ecclesiastical reformation of this reign.[1]

The Sarum Use.—The most important liturgical event was the compilation by Bishop Osmund, of Salisbury, of the famous service-books, called, after his see, the Use of Salisbury. They were gradually adopted in the majority of the secular churches throughout the kingdom, the monastic churches naturally retaining their own special service-books. The ringing of the curfew bell, a custom combining a religious practice with civil regulations, was brought over by the Normans.

St. Elphege Vindicated.—Archbishop Lanfranc used to confer on matters concerning the ecclesiastical state of England with his friend and former scholar, Anselm, who, when the saintly Herluin, founder and first abbot of Bec, went to his eternal rest, was elected abbot in his place. The English possessions of the abbey made it necessary for Anselm several times to visit the island of which, fourteen years later, he was to become the chief shepherd. Amongst other matters, Lanfranc consulted him about the reverence paid to Elphege, the archbishop whom the Danes had cruelly slain, and whom he could not regard as a martyr. The prelate, he said, had not died for the faith of Christ, but because of his refusal to pay a sum of money which could only be raised by wrongdoing. Anselm replied that it was as great a thing to die for justice as for truth, and quoted the example of St. John Baptist, who was put to death, not because

---

[1] As soon as the great king William was dead, Thurstan obtained William II.'s consent to his re-assumption of the office whereof he had proved himself so unworthy, it is said by help of his kinsfolk and the more prevailing eloquence of a bribe of five hundred pounds of silver.

he would not deny Christ, but because he would speak the truth boldly; not to defend a dogma, but for the eternal laws of right and wrong. By these reasonings Lanfranc was convinced, and by his orders special honours were paid to Elphege at Canterbury, and his feast was solemnly kept every year.

William the Conqueror held Anselm in high esteem, and greatly valued his advice. It was to him, of all the prelates in Normandy, to whom his thoughts turned, as the chosen physician of his soul, when he lay dying at Rouen. Anselm went to Rouen at his summons, but was himself struck down by sickness, so that he never saw his royal penitent again.

The Conqueror's Death and Character.— William made his peace with God, and the best provision he could for his children and his subjects. On September 8, 1087, in the early morning, the great bell of the minster of St. Mary sounded on the ear of the dying king. He asked why it was rung. He was told that it was the hour for prime. Raising himself on his couch, and stretching out his arms, he exclaimed: "I commend myself to my Lady, the Mother of God, that by her holy prayers she may reconcile me to her dear Son, my Lord Jesus Christ." He fell back, and immediately expired.

"William's education left on his mind," Lingard tells us, "religious impressions that were never effaced. When indeed his power or interest was concerned, he listened to no suggestions but those of ambition or avarice, but on other occasions he displayed a strong sense of religion, and profound respect for its institutions." "He was mild," the Chronicle says, "to good men who loved God, but beyond measure severe to those who withstood his will." His haughty character and imperious temper led him sometimes to invade ecclesiastical rights; but on his deathbed he expressed remorse for his acts of violence, and said he had always honoured Holy Church, and never made traffic of ecclesiastical preferments. In this he spoke truly, and there is no doubt that he was sincere in his desire to fill the bishoprics with such men as would promote the religious improvement of his realm. Those of whom, by the advice of the bishops and abbots, he made choice, were men for the most part well fitted for their office, men of high character and learning. They were, however, almost exclusively foreigners. Gradually, as English bishops died or were deposed, strangers took their places. At the time of the Conqueror's death there was only one Englishman, Wulstan of Worcester, who held a bishopric. The changes effected in this reign naturally entailed some amount of injustice and hardship in particular cases; but the Church on the whole was a gainer. They tended to bring her into more active relations with Rome, and in this lay the secret of her strength. No longer standing, as formerly, apart to a certain extent from the rest of Christendom, she acquired more vigorous life, fuller organization, greater perfection in ritual and discipline.

William Rufus, 1087.—Lanfranc survived his royal patron, and placed the crown on the head of William Rufus, the Conqueror's second son, whom in a letter of instructions to the archbishop, dictated upon his deathbed, he had nominated as his successor. The new king was indeed unlike his father. He was a rough, rude man, of dissolute life, fearing God little and man still less. Conscious of the character of Rufus, whose tutor he had been, Lanfranc obliged him, in addition to the coronation oath, to give a solemn promise that he would govern his people well, and be guided by his advice. Promises had little sanctity in Rufus's eyes, unless they concerned matters of military honour. "Who can do all he promises?" was his wrathful answer when reminded of his own words. However, as long as Archbishop Lanfranc lived, his authority and the reverence due to his age and position were a check upon the king.

The death of that prelate in 1089 removed all restraint upon William's reckless conduct and excessive prodigality. The king's chaplain, a Norman priest of obscure birth, named Ralph Flambard, or the Firebrand, found a means of flattering his vices, and supplying funds for his extravagant expenditure. Hitherto on the death of an abbot or prelate, the care of the temporalities of abbacy or diocese was entrusted to a clergyman appointed by the king, who was compelled to give an exact account of his administration to the next incumbent. Flambard contended that the temporalities of these prelacies were a fief, held of the king, the revenues of which ought, on the death of the tenant, to revert to the Crown until they were bestowed on some one else. On this plea, when an abbot or bishop died, he seized the temporalities and held them for the king. William II. rejoiced in this easy means of acquiring wealth. He kept the vacant bishoprics and abbeys for years in his possession, and when at last a successor was appointed, the new prelate was required to pay a large sum into the royal exchequer. William openly sold benefices to the highest bidder; at his death he had one archbishopric, four bishoprics, and eleven abbeys in his hands, the lands belonging to them being let out to farm. When Lanfranc died, the see of Canterbury was left vacant for nearly five years, in order that the king might enjoy the revenues appertaining to it. This was felt to be a grievous wrong to the whole nation; the Archbishop of Canterbury was the spiritual father of all the faithful in the kingdom, and the chief constitutional adviser of the monarch. The clergy and barons often solicited William to nominate a successor to Lanfranc; at last they begged him to allow prayers to be offered in the churches, that God would vouchsafe, by the appointment of a worthy pastor to the primatial see, to raise the Church from her fallen estate. The king was somewhat angry, but he gave the permission, adding, with a scornful laugh, that let the Church pray as she would, no man's prayers would change his will.

Anselm Archbishop of Canterbury. — The choice of the electors and the desire of the nation had already fixed upon Anselm, the Abbot of Bec, as their future archbishop. Born of noble parents at Aosta, in the north of Italy, he had been dedicated by his mother at his birth to the religious state. His father wished him to follow the profession of arms, and take his place as Count of Aosta at the head of his estates. Anselm, however, showed a marked predilection for a monastic life, and prayed God to send him an illness that would prevent his following the military and courtly career for which his father destined him. This prayer was granted, but it was some time before the object of his wishes was attained. He became one of Lanfranc's pupils at Bec, where he took the religious habit, and, distinguished by his subtle intellect and great learning, stood high amongst the scholars of his day. Gentle and tender, he was at the same time fearless, firm of purpose, a hater of injustice. No fitter champion could have been found to withstand Rufus in his degradation of the Church. One of the barons ventured to mention his name to the king: "We do not know a holier man than Anselm, the Abbot of Bec; he loves nothing but God, it is clear that his heart is set on nothing here below." "No, indeed?" asked the king with a sneer, "not even upon the archbishopric of Canterbury? I tell you he would clap his hands with joy and throw himself into my arms, if he had the slightest chance of mounting so high; but I swear by the Holy Face of Lucca [1] that just now neither he nor any other man shall be archbishop but myself."

Scarcely had these words been spoken when the king was taken dangerously ill, while hunting in the neighbourhood of Gloucester. He was carried to the castle; the clergy and nobles who assembled at his bedside, thinking him to be dying, urged him to provide for his salvation by liberating his captives, forgiving his debtors, restoring liberty to the Church he had enslaved, and, above all, by nominating an archbishop to fill the see of Canterbury. Anselm, who happened then to be in England, was sent for. Alarmed at the approach of death, William made his confession, and promised amendment. A docu-

[1] This was the Red King's usual oath. The object by which he swore was the face of our Saviour on a very ancient crucifix of cedar, said to have been carved by Nicodemus, and brought in 782 to the city of Lucca, where it is still preserved with the utmost care and veneration. *Il Volto Santo di Lucca* has always been highly prized by the inhabitants; it is stamped upon their coins.

ment was drawn up, forgiving all offences against his person, restoring to various churches estates of which they had been deprived, giving proper pastors to the charges let out on hire. A clause was added promising strict observance of justice towards all the king's subjects, and, the Great Seal having been affixed to the parchment, it was laid upon the altar of the chapel. Then the bishops seized the opportune moment to renew their entreaties respecting the archiepiscopal see. In the fervour of a temporary repentance the king acquiesced in the suggestion, and pointed out Anselm as the individual he chose for the office. All present were filled with joy; all except the abbot, who persistently refused to accept the appointment. The bishops and nobles remonstrated, implored, insisted; at length they dragged Anselm to the bedside of the monarch to be invested with the insignia of the episcopate; they forced open his unwilling hand, they thrust the pastoral staff into it, and hurried him off to the church. In vain Anselm expostulated. "What are you doing?" he exclaimed. "I tell you the king's sickness is not to death: you are yoking to the plough a poor weak sheep with an untamed bull. The plough is the Church; in England it was drawn by two stout oxen, the king and the archbishop of Canterbury; the king with secular justice and rule, the archbishop with divine instruction and spiritual government. One of these survives; he has shown the ferocity of a wild bull, and you want to yoke me, a feeble sheep, with him. He will crush me, and the Church will fall into widowhood again, with her pastor still alive."

Six weeks later, the king was well again, and with

the return of health his good resolutions vanished. As if angry with himself for having yielded for a moment, he strove to make matters worse than they had been before. When exhorted by the Bishop of Rochester to take warning by his illness and not defy God again, he impiously retorted: "Know this, O bishop, that God shall never have good out of me for the evil He has inflicted on me!"

Anselm, after going to his abbey to bid his monks farewell, accepted the archbishopric on certain conditions, one of which was the restoration of the lands belonging to the see. William promised to give them up, but sought to evade the fulfilment of his promise. Rather than submit to the spoliation of the Church, Anselm refused consecration. The chief men of state became alarmed lest the archbishopric should continue vacant; the king, under pressure, conveyed the temporalities to the archbishop-elect, who was consecrated as primate of England, and became the king's "man" by feudal law. But he was immediately involved in disputes with the king. On the very day on which he went in procession to the cathedral, amid the acclamations of the people, Ralph the Firebrand arrested him, and summoned him to answer in the king's court for some supposed breach of the royal prerogative. This was a sad presage for the future. Every means was adopted to subdue the spirit of the new archbishop. His tenants were compelled for several months to pay their rents into the royal exchequer. So impoverished were the estates that Anselm found himself without money to defray his household expenses. It was then intimated to him that the king expected from him a present, in return for his promotion.

With great difficulty he raised five hundred pounds: it was scornfully rejected as insufficient. William demanded one thousand pounds; this Anselm could not and would not pay. He distributed the money to the poor, glad to escape the appearance of having entered into a simoniacal arrangement. "As I hated him yesterday," said the king, "I hate him to-day; he shall never be acknowledged as archbishop by me." Thenceforward he used his power to thwart every effort Anselm made for the good of the Church.

Anselm and the Pallium.—The next trouble was caused by the archbishop announcing his intention of going to Rome for his pallium. There was at that time a pretender to the papacy, called, for convenience' sake, Clement V., who had been set up by the Emperor Henry II. of Germany; Urban II. was, however, the one legitimately elected, and generally acknowledged. When therefore the king asked Anselm from whom he was going to procure the pallium, and he answered, "Urban," William flew into a passion, saying that he had not yet acknowledged Urban, and it was treason to call any man Pope in his dominions without his licence and favour. Anselm replied that when Abbot of Bec he had recognized Urban, and he could not now withdraw his allegiance. William retorted that the archbishop could not keep faith towards the king, and at the same time acknowledge the Pope against the king's will. To settle this difficulty a council was called at Rockingham, in Northamptonshire, to discuss the obedience due to king and Pope respectively. A great multitude, both of the clergy and laity, were present.

The archbishop in a dignified speech addressed his suffragans, and explained the cause of difference. He reminded them that it was only through their compulsion, and his confidence in their co-operation, that he had consented, much against his will, to be made archbishop. He entreated them to give him such advice as would neither militate against obedience to the Pope, nor infringe upon his fidelity to the king. But the bishops would not stand by the primate. Led by Flambard, who had been made Bishop of Durham, they all, with the honourable exception of Gundulf, Bishop of Rochester, took the opposite side. They counselled him not to run counter to the king, but to renounce Urban. These subservient prelates, who supported the "arbitrary usages" (*voluntariæ consuetudines*) of Rufus and his father, were yet compelled to acknowledge that Anselm's reasoning "rested on the word of God and the authority of Blessed Peter." Then the primate addressed to them an indignant expostulation: "Since you, who are called pastors of the flock of Christ and the princes of the people, will not give counsel to me, your chief, save according to the behest of one man, I will have recourse to the Supreme Pastor, the Chief of all, the Angel of Great Counsel; and in my cause, nay, rather in His cause, and in the cause of His Church, I will receive from Him counsel that I will follow. He says to Peter, the most blessed of the apostles, 'Thou art Peter, and upon this rock,' &c. He says also to all the apostles, 'He that heareth you, heareth Me, and he that despiseth you, despiseth Me, and he that toucheth you, toucheth the apple of mine eye.' But wherein we must be subject to earthly princes and serve them, the same Angel of Great Counsel teaches and instructs us, saying, 'Render to Cæsar the things that are Cæsar's, and to God the things that are God's.' Wherefore let all know that in the things of God I will render obedience to the Vicar of Blessed Peter: in the things which of right belong to the earthly dignity of my lord the king, I will give faithful counsel and assistance according to my power" (Eadmer, *Hist. Novorum*). Nevertheless, intimidated by the king, whose "men" they were, they were cowardly enough at his command to renounce their allegiance to the archbishop, and declare him outlawed. Their motive for this craven conduct is evident from the language they afterwards used to Anselm. "Lord and Father," they said to him later on, "we know you to be a religious and a holy man, and that your conversation is in heaven. But we are held back by our relations, whom we support, and by many worldly cares, which we love. We cannot, therefore, rise to a sublimity of life like yours, or join you in making scorn of the world" (*ibid.*, p. 399). The conduct of the barons was very different. "He is our archbishop," they said, "the ruler of Christianity in this land, and, as Christians, we cannot refuse his sway." Anselm again asked permission to go to Rome, but as it was not granted, he returned to his see.[1]

The king now changed his tactics. He recognized the lawful Pope, who at his request sent a legate to England with the pallium for the archbishop. William endeavoured to bring about the deposition

---

[1] This prohibition was not based on the plea that the king's authority in spiritual matters was supreme, but that he had a right to keep his counsellors in his kingdom for his service. It was the magnates of the realm generally, not the bishops only, who were forbidden to go to Rome without his leave.

of Anselm by papal authority; finding this step was impossible, he next attempted to get the pallium into his own hands, that he might bestow it on him at his discretion. In this, too, he was unsuccessful. It was finally agreed that the legate should place it upon the altar of Canterbury Cathedral, whence Anselm, according to custom, was to take it as if from the hands of St. Peter himself. Arrayed in pontifical garments, barefoot, for out of reverence he had put off his sandals, he approached the altar, and took from it, with deep emotion, the badge of archiepiscopal authority.

Anselm's Visit to Rome.—William Rufus, although his plan for oppressing the primate had failed, did not cease to persecute him and pillage the Church. In spite of Anselm's remonstrances and reprimands, he continued to lead a life of debauchery, to retain possession of vacant benefices, to prevent the convocation of synods, to let on hire the manors belonging to the see of Canterbury which he had seized. After an expedition into Wales, he complained that the quota of men contributed by the archbishop to the army had been insufficiently supplied with arms and provisions, and for this he cited him to appear before his court. At length Anselm, weary of the struggle with his tyrannical master, and saddened by the sight of so many evils which he could not tolerate but was powerless to correct, asked leave to quit England to seek counsel of Rome. Before leaving he sought the king's presence, arrayed in pilgrim's weeds, and bestowed on him a parting blessing, which the monarch was not hardened enough to refuse.

On reaching Rome in March, 1098, the saint was

received with great kindness by the Pope, who greeted him with these words: " By reason of his great learning we take him for our teacher, and deem him in some sort a compeer, and worthy of veneration as Pope and Patriarch of the new world" (Rule, *Life of St. Anselm*, ii. p. 180).[1] He listened to the tale of his wrongs, approved his conduct, and wrote to the king, requiring that he should be reinstated in all his rights and possessions. When the Council of Bari was called, to discuss the question of the Double Procession of the Holy Ghost, he ordered Anselm to be present. The archbishop spoke with so great learning, judgement, and eloquence, that he silenced the Greeks, and caused the Council unanimously to condemn the heretical doctrine. When the behaviour of the king of England came under debate, the council was won by the charity of the prelate, who cast himself at the feet of the Pope, and entreated him to desist from pronouncing sentence of excommunication on the iniquitous monarch.

For the next two years Anselm lived as an exile at Lyons, where he occupied himself in the composition of several theological and metaphysical works. Meanwhile Rufus spent on his wars or his pleasures the revenues of the Church in England, persevering in the same career until suddenly arrested by death. At the close of a day spent in hunting in the New Forest, he was discovered weltering in his

---

[1] The words thus translated, *alterius orbis Papa*, meant, not that the Pope recognized Anselm as independent of himself, but that Britain, being outside the (Christian) Roman Empire, was another world, and Anselm the highest prelate in it. The see of Canterbury was occasionally, and in a derived sense, accounted a *sedes apostolica*, because established by a missionary sent direct from the Apostolic See. Thus this ascription is itself a witness against " continuity " theories.

own blood, pierced to the heart by an arrow. Cut off
without shrift, without repentance, he found a tomb
in the old minster of Winchester. No bell was
tolled, no prayer was said, no alms were given for the
soul of this enemy of God and man, when his un-
hallowed corpse was laid in the grave. It is said
that when the archbishop heard of his death, he was
greatly dismayed and distressed: bitter tears gushed
from his eyes, and when the bystanders expressed
their surprise, he exclaimed, in a voice broken with
sobs, "To die like that! O that I had died instead
of him!"

CHAPTER X.

THE CHURCH UNDER THE NORMANS.

Henry I., 1100. Quarrel about Investiture.—
The reign of Henry I., who possessed himself of the crown on the death of William Rufus, holds an important place in the history of the Church in England. It was a period of struggle and dispute, in which the sovereign was called upon to surrender a usage which had been practised by his predecessors, but which had degenerated into a most pernicious abuse—the right of investiture, that is, of appointing to ecclesiastical offices, and investing the holders of them with the symbols of their spiritual jurisdiction.

On his accession the new king swore that he would abolish the unjust and evil customs that had prevailed during his brother's reign. "I will make the Church of God free," so ran the charter: "I will neither sell nor put out to farm its property, nor, when an archbishop, bishop, or abbot dies, will I take anything from the domain of the Church until a successor enters upon it." He made it his business to repair the sacrilegious confiscations that had been committed by his predecessor. The Bishop of Durham, the evil counsellor of the late monarch, was imprisoned in the Tower, and Anselm was recalled to England. The archbishop's first relations with the king were very friendly; but when he was required to do homage to Henry, and be reinstated by him in his archiepiscopal estates, he at once refused, intimating his firm resolution to observe the discipline decreed by Rome on this point.

Henry, however, aware that in the days of William Rufus, Anselm had not only received the crozier from the hand of the king, but had also without scruple consecrated bishops who had thus received it, expressed his determination to retain what he asserted to be a prerogative of the Crown.

In order to understand the controversy that ensued upon this point, the reader should know that, according to the ancient custom of the Church, the election of bishops depended upon the suffrages of the provincial prelates. As time went on, the king, desirous to secure the election of an individual who would not be his enemy, claimed the right of approving the person elected, and, in virtue of that right, with his own hand invested him with ring and crozier, the acknowledged emblems of episcopal or abbatial rank. Practically the royal action amounted to a claim to nominate the candidates, since the monarch required the elective body to defer to his wishes, and to obtain this, he would use pressure. The custom of investiture, moreover, tended to produce the impression that the king could convey jurisdiction in ecclesiastical matters, a right which he never imagined himself to possess. Before the significance of this usage had been seen, the royal claim had been tacitly assented to; as has been said, Anselm himself had received investiture at the hands of Rufus. Furthermore, he had done homage to him as archbishop-elect; standing before the king he placed his hands between the king's hands, and pronounced the formula of fealty: this was sufficient to make him the *homo* (man) of the king.

But the treatment of Anselm and other causes led to a decree being made at the Council of Clermont in 1095, forbidding the vassalage of ecclesiastics to laymen, as tending "to place the duty and conscience of Christian bishops under the heel of feudal royalty"; and in the Lateran Council, in 1099, at which Anselm was present, the Church "decided that it must now be a question of principle to preserve the spiritual character of the appointments, and to protest against the shame and mischief of allowing great Church offices to be disposed of by kings and princes without an effort to assert their meaning and sacredness."[1] The prohibitions of former times[2] were renewed, and in the sentence of anathema hurled against all laymen who should nominate to Church offices, all clerics were included who became the "men"—the feudal dependents that is, of laymen—for ecclesiastical dignities.

These facts explain, as Anselm's Catholic biographer tells us, why Anselm, who in 1093 put his hands between the Red King's, so obstinately refused seven years later to do the self-same thing to Henry I. —(1) The Holy See had in the interval forbidden

---

[1] *Social England*, vol. i. p. 254.

[2] The General Council of Constantinople, 869, condemned nomination by laymen; and in 1077 the sentence of excommunication was decreed against the prince who should presume to exercise the right of investiture, and the prelate who should dare to receive it from him (*c.f.* Lingard's History, vol. ii. p. 8).

such a ceremonial act from bishops to kings. (2) He knew too well the high value of precedent not to feel convinced that if the Christian interests of England were not to be placed under the heel of the sovereign, the precedent of episcopal homage rendered to the prince must be broken, and that without delay. The royal investiture of bishops meant, or might any day be made to mean, that bishops received their proper spiritual jurisdiction from the Crown. The whole drift and current of the usage of investiture tended to encourage the heresy that princes were the depositories whence bishops were to derive their spiritual jurisdiction, and Anselm saw clearly that the whole drift and current of the concomitant usage known as homage tended to convert bishops from temporal subjects to spiritual subalterns.[1]

But Henry persisted in his demands, as Anselm did in his refusals, and messengers were sent to obtain a settlement of the dispute from the Papal Court. Meanwhile there was no personal breach between the king and the prelate. Anselm sanctioned Henry's marriage with Matilda (afterwards known as good Queen Maud), the daughter of the King of Scotland, and removed the difficulties arising from her having been placed in a nunnery for safety from the lawless soldiery, where she had worn the veil but had taken no vows. He himself blessed the marriage and crowned her Queen. It was also in a great measure owing to his action that Henry kept the crown in the struggle with his brother Robert, and that the nobles remained faithful to their newly-anointed king.

The answer of the Pope was of course favourable to Anselm. Whilst he highly commended the king for

[1] Rule, *Life of St. Anselm*, vol. i. p. 385.

what he had done to remedy the mischief of the past reign, he firmly refused to concede the right of investiture. Thereupon Henry declared he would forfeit half his kingdom rather than give up one of the usages of his predecessors, or yield a point which his fellow-rulers upon the continent were engaged in contesting at that time; nor, he added, would he tolerate in his kingdom any man who was not his own liegeman. Another attempt was then made to gain the Pope's agreement to the English customs—*consuetudines*, as the royal claims were called—although they were royal usurpations of quite recent origin, and merely called customs because indulged in more than once. An embassy was sent to threaten the withholding of the Rome-scot, or Peter's-pence, and the banishment of St. Anselm from England, if the king's demands were not granted. This application only gave rise to fresh disputes, as some of the ambassadors alleged that the Supreme Pontiff had given them verbal instructions to the effect that, as a personal favour to Henry, he would grant the right of investiture; the others indignantly denied that so contradictory a message had been sent. This necessitated a third appeal to Rome to explain matters.

Marriage of the Clergy.—In the interval, Anselm, by the king's licence, held a council at Westminster (1102), in which many decrees were made, as the Chronicle records, touching the Christian religion. Several abbots, some Norman, some English, were deprived of their staves and their abbacies, either because they had obtained them unlawfully, or lived iniquitously. The most important enactments had reference to the celibacy of the clergy. When Lanfranc was promoted to the see of Canterbury, he had endeavoured, in imitation of St. Dunstan, to enforce the canons forbidding the marriage of the clergy, which under the Saxons had been occasionally disregarded. It was decreed in a synod held at Winchester, 1075, that not only should no married man be ordained priest, but that all those who already were raised to the priesthood, and had married, must put away their wives. Gregory VII. wrote to thank William and Lanfranc for what had been done, and in 1077 he published a Bull ordaining that none should hear mass performed by a married priest.[1] But Anselm found that the Church's law was still oftentimes disobeyed; measures of greater stringency were required to enforce the rule. Accordingly at a synod held in presence of the king, it was re-enacted that no priest, deacon, or sub-deacon, should thereafter enter into matrimony, and that those already married should be compelled to leave their wives, and meet them only in the presence of witnesses. Disobedience was punished, according to its degree, by deprivation or excommunication. This seems to have had the desired effect, and the law regarding the celibacy of the clergy was again happily observed duly throughout England.

The Investiture Question continued.—Henry meanwhile had continued to appoint bishops, although Anselm refused to consecrate them. The Archbishop of York was willing to perform the ceremony, but the firm stand made by Anselm encouraged the bishops-elect to decline to accept from the king the symbols of their spiritual jurisdiction. When, in Lent, 1103, the messengers returned from Rome with letters confirmatory of the Pope's previous written

[1] *Cf. Social England*, vol. i. p. 384.

decision, Reinhelm, bishop-elect of Hereford, gave back the staff he had received from the king. Giffard, whose appointment to the see of Winchester had been one of the first acts of Henry's reign, suffered banishment rather than receive wrongful consecration at the hands of Gerard of York.

Anselm goes to Rome.—At length, after a period of nearly four years had elapsed in constant struggle between the king and the primate, whom nothing could induce to consent to place the Church in bondage to the royal power, Anselm, aged and infirm as he then was, undertook, at the king's request, a journey to Rome. He was to lay the whole controversy before the Pope. He cannot have expected, nor did he wish, to succeed in obtaining a decision favourable to the king's demands. The Holy Father (Paschal II.) gave once more an unequivocal refusal. Anselm did not return to England, as he had been ordered to remain abroad unless he had obtained the Pope's compliance with the royal claims. In his absence, Henry, whose coffers were low, seized the archiepiscopal estates. It was further suggested to him that the law respecting the celibacy of the clergy might be converted into a source of revenue. A commission was appointed with orders to inquire into the conduct of the clergy, and impose a heavy fine on any individual who was found to have transgressed the regulations of the synod. The number of offenders was too small to realize a sum worth having. Thereupon the king caused a certain fine to be levied on every parish priest, irrespective of guilt or innocence. This caused widespread trouble. Some were unable, all were unwilling to pay. In great numbers they were imprisoned or tortured. A deputation of two hundred ecclesiastics, in their robes, waited barefoot on the king and prayed him to release them from this extortion, but without effect. The bishops entreated Anselm to return to the see which was, as he had foretold, widowed during the lifetime of its occupant. The archbishop wrote to the king on behalf of his flock, but his remonstrances were of little avail. At length the Pope threatened excommunication.

The Investiture Question settled.—Henry was not desirous of pushing matters to an extremity. When, his early troubles being over, he was able to apply himself to the consideration of the question, he struck the right line of compromise. He declared himself ready to admit the canonical rights of chapters, the power of the synod to elect, the supreme jurisdiction of the see of Rome. He was also willing to surrender the right of independent nomination. On the other hand, although the bishops might be elected by the chapter, the election must take place at his court. The councils might be held when the bishops chose, but the royal consent must be obtained before the assembly could exercise legislative power. As fealty and homage were feudal duties, it was agreed that every clergyman should pay them before he received the temporalities of his office, while the king consented to relinquish his claim to invest with ring and crozier, which, being symbols exclusively of the spiritual jurisdiction, were not to be given by any lay hand. Henry had a friendly interview with Anselm at Bec, and all dispute was thenceforth at an end. On the 22nd of July, 1105, the king by formal document reconveyed to the primate the temporalities of his see, and in so doing tacitly relinquished the pretensions which had occasioned all these troubles. By his firmness and tact Anselm had won a great victory. He returned shortly after to his see, and seven vacant bishoprics were provided with pastors.

Death of Anselm, 1109.—Anselm only survived this settlement two years. The closing days of his life were troubled by a dispute with the archbishop-elect of York. He had had the satisfaction of receiving from the former archbishop, Gerard, a full profession of allegiance, but this attestation the next-comer, Thomas, wished to evade. To accomplish this, he sought to delay his consecration, as Anselm's life was drawing to a close. Anselm saw through the device, and solemnly charged his suffragans that, in case of his death, they should not consecrate the archbishop-elect without a profession of canonical obedience. They remained firm to the charge, and Thomas was compelled to make the formal promise of obedience.

"In the beginning of 1109," Eadmer, the friend and biographer of Anselm, narrates, " it was evident that the health of the holy archbishop was fast declining. One of those who were with him, seeing his weakness, ventured to say: 'Father and lord archbishop, the Easter court that you will attend is an Easter court with our Lord God.' It was then Palm Sunday. He replied: 'Yes, if it be His will I shall obey it willingly. But were He to let me stay with you a little longer till I had resolved a problem about the origin of the soul, I would gladly accept the boon; for I do not know whether any one will work it out when I am gone.' His intellect remained clear and keen as ever in spite of his physical debility.

On the Wednesday in Holy Week, while he was lying on his bed, and unable to speak, the Bishop of Rochester asked him to give to us who were there, to his other children, to the king and queen and their children, and to all the people of the land who were in obedience to him under God, his absolution and benediction. He raised his right hand as though he suffered no pain, and made the sign of the Cross. One of those in attendance took the Book of the Gospels and read the Passion appointed for the Mass that day. The reader had only reached the words: 'You are those that have continued with Me in My temptations, and I dispose to you, as my Father hath disposed to Me, a kingdom, that you may eat and drink at My table, in My kingdom,' when it was perceived that his breath was failing. He was lifted from the bed to the sackcloth and ashes, and with all his monks gathered round him, he breathed his last breath into the hands of his Creator, and slept in peace."

Anselm was one of the greatest prelates the Church in England has seen. Several miracles are recorded of him; amongst others, that of arresting the progress of a conflagration which threatened to destroy the city of Rochester, where he happened to be passing a few days. He made the sign of the Cross in front of the devouring flames, and the fire died out. He was canonized on the petition of Henry VII., and the chief lesson of his life was his unflinching obedience to the divinely appointed Vicar of Christ.

Canterbury invested with Legatine Authority, 1125.—After the death of Anselm, Henry fell into one of the worst practices of his brother. He kept the primatial see vacant for five years. The revenues were paid into the royal exchequer, but the possessions of the monks of Christ Church were not interfered with. He said that his motive in delaying the appointment of an archbishop was his desire to find a man thoroughly fitted for so important an office. At length a Norman, Ralph of Seez, was chosen. During his primacy and that of his successor, William de Corbeuil, the vexed question of the respective jurisdiction of York and Canterbury again came to the fore. To settle the differences, a papal legate was sent to England. This legate, though only a priest, assumed, in virtue of his legatine authority, a higher rank than bishops and nobles; but when, in a council held at Westminster in 1125, he took precedence of the primate, the latter thought it a humiliation to his order. He went himself to Rome to complain to the Pope, and was by him invested with the powers of a legate in his own person, the privilege to pass down to his successors in the see. Thenceforward the *legatus natus* became a permanent institution in England, until the Reformation. The Supreme Pontiff reserved the right of sending an extraordinary envoy, *legatus a latere*, as his representative, whenever he should deem it expedient. The combination of the legatine with the metropolitan authority at times led to some confusion between the power exercised by the archbishop in virtue of his see, and the power with which he was invested as papal legate.

Scotland and the Pope, 1188.—One phase of the controversy between York and Canterbury concerned the Scottish hierarchy. The northern province of England included all the dioceses of Scotland, and the Primate of England was also patriarch over all the British Isles, for Scotland had no metropolitan of her own, although the see of St. Andrews was acknowledged to have a certain superiority over the other sees. During a vacancy in this bishopric, owing to the resignation of Turgot, the first Englishman who had filled it, Alexander, the King of Scotland, in order to emancipate his bishops from obedience to York, caused Eadmer, a monk of Canterbury (the same who was mentioned above as the friend and biographer of Anselm), to be elected. But Eadmer would only hold the see as subject to the Archbishop of Canterbury, and the latter claimed his obedience on the ground that in his grant of authority over all Britain to St. Augustine, Gregory included Scotland. Alexander would not have Eadmer as a suffragan of Canterbury, so he returned unconsecrated. In 1188, the Pope settled the controversy by declaring the Church in Scotland to be dependent solely on the Holy See.

The ecclesiastical aspect of Henry's reign is further distinguished by an increase in the number of bishoprics. The abbey of Ely was erected by the Pope into an episcopal church, and part of the diocese of Lincoln was detached to form the new diocese. Ely, with its unrivalled minster, its great wealth, its temporal power, became one of the greatest among the English bishoprics. It owed its existence chiefly to Anselm; subsequently to his death Henry endowed another bishopric, obtaining from the Pope the erection of the see of Carlisle, in the land which William II. had conquered, and both he and the present king had taken pains to improve and fortify.

The Cistercians.—The rise of the Cistercian Order gave a special character to this period.

Shortly before the commencement of Henry's reign, the famous Order of Citeaux had its beginning in a foreign land, and before his reign had ended, it had made its way to the country whence its founder had sprung. Stephen Harding, a monk of Sherborne, afterwards of Molesme, left his convent to seek a higher degree of perfection in the new house at Citeaux, of which he became the third abbot. Through him the Order was introduced into England. The Normans had brought with them a strong admiration and zeal for the monastic life, and the rule of St. Benedict, as practised among us at that time, seemed not austere enough for some of its votaries. The new Order, with its greater strictness of life, was welcomed, and became very popular in England. The first settlement made was at Waverley, in Surrey, 1128. Other houses soon arose in different parts of the kingdom, but the Order found its true home in the northern counties. The older Benedictine houses had either been planted in towns, or a town had grown up around the monastic precincts. The Cistercians of set purpose lived in the wilderness, and for the most part pitched their dwellings in lonely places, which often through their labours became spots of striking beauty. Only a few of their houses attained historic fame, but the ruined abbey is more often a Cistercian monastery than any other. The year 1132 witnessed the foundation of the famous Fountains Abbey, near Ripon, by a colony of monks who wished to embrace the new and stricter rule. The prosperity of this house was so great, that it became one of the wealthiest religious houses of the land. (Freeman, *Norman Conquest*, vol. v. p. 233.)

King Stephen, 1135.—Henry had in his last

hours bequeathed his kingdom to his daughter Matilda, and caused the bishops and barons to swear fealty to her. She was, however, supplanted by his nephew Stephen, who hastened to England on hearing that Henry was no more. His coming was hailed by the citizens of London. Anxious to put a stop to the disorder that prevailed in consequence of the king's death and interfered with their commercial transactions, they immediately accepted him for their ruler. Robert, Bishop of Salisbury, supported him, and his brother Henry, Bishop of Winchester, rendered him zealous assistance. Strong persuasions were employed to induce the archbishop to perform the ceremony of coronation; he hesitated to do so on account of the oath of allegiance to Matilda, but finally his scruples were overruled, and he yielded. Stephen was crowned, the bishops and barons swearing to stand by him so long as he should maintain the liberties and the discipline of the Church. This he promised by oath to do.

Quarrel with the Bishops.—For four years Stephen was supported by the clergy. But some of the bishops built castles conspicuous for beauty and strength, and this excited the jealousy of the barons. Stephen was induced to regard these fortresses as a menace to his throne. Like many weak men, he was given to sudden acts of violence. While the Bishops of Sarum and Lincoln were at his court at Oxford (1139), they, together with the Chancellor, were seized, imprisoned, treated with great harshness, and compelled to surrender their castles. This illegal act on the part of the king lost to him the goodwill of the clergy. To them he was to a great extent indebted for his throne, they had helped to maintain him on it; now he had shown himself an enemy of their Order, he had usurped the Church lands, he had laid insolent hands on prelates whose persons were deemed sacred. His brother the Bishop of Winchester, whom Pope Innocent II. had lately made papal legate, expostulated with him, imploring him to make restitution, and alleging that jurisdiction over bishops did not belong to the civil but to the ecclesiastical court. All was in vain. The king was then summoned to justify his sacrilegious conduct before a synod of bishops. He sent certain earls as his representatives, but no reconciliation was effected.

Shortly after, the coming of Matilda to claim the crown of her father on behalf of her son brought upon the country the horrors of civil war. Stephen then had to regret having alienated so large and powerful a portion of his subjects. The Empress Matilda found partisans in the bishops, and for a period of some years, warfare and pillage devastated the country. To such a pitch of misery was the kingdom reduced, that it was commonly said amongst the people that "Christ and the saints slept." "In olden days," says the chronicler, William of Newburgh, "there was no king in Israel, and every one did what was right in his own eyes; but in England it was worse; for there was a king, but impotent, and every man did what was wrong in his own eyes" (*Social Life*, vol. i. p. 257). Large tracts of land went out of cultivation; trade was stopped; there was famine and distress throughout the land.

Archbishop Thurstan to the Rescue.—At this juncture King David of Scotland espoused Matilda's cause, and crossed the frontier with a motley host of Scots and Picts. These wild tribes ravaged the northern counties ; their cruel treatment of the people roused the spirit of Thurstan, the Archbishop of York, who grieved bitterly over the calamities which befell his spiritual children. His heroic conduct is "the one gleam of national glory that broke the darkness of the time." The aged prelate called upon the barons to defend their homesteads. He animated them to give battle for their faith and their country. He unfurled the banner of St. Peter, and those of the three great northern saints—Cuthbert, John of Beverley, Wilfrid of Ripon —and caused them to be nailed to a mast fixed in a car to be placed in the centre of the host. After three days spent in prayer and religious exercises, the forces he had assembled went forth to meet the enemy. Too infirm himself to lead them to battle, he sent the Bishop of Durham before them to Northallerton, where they awaited the onslaught of the Scots. The fierce hordes dashed in vain against the close ranks of the English around the standard, and the whole army fled in confusion to Carlisle. Thus the country was again saved from the invasion of the Scots through the valour of a bishop, as it had been centuries before by the courage of Germanus.

England under Interdict.—In the south, too, a pacification was brought about by Stephen's brother, the Bishop of Winchester. After many vicissitudes of fortune, Matilda withdrew to Normandy, and the strife died out. But the efforts of Stephen to reassert his authority and restore the reign of law were unavailing. Henry of Blois, the Bishop of Winchester, had gone over to the party of his brother, but he possessed too little religious influence to wield a really spiritual power, and it was only in Theobald, the

Archbishop of Canterbury, that the nation found a moral leader. Stephen was impolitic enough to make an enemy of this prelate. On the death of Pope Innocent II. the legatine powers wherewith he had invested the Bishop of Winchester lapsed, and the next Pope, instead of renewing them, conferred the office on Theobald. Henry of Winchester imagined that this was done at Theobald's solicitation, and persuaded the king to forbid him to attend a council held at Rheims, 1148. The primate disregarded this prohibition, and the king banished him. Stephen was, however, not strong enough to carry out such a policy. His domains were laid under an interdict, and his friends, alarmed at the cessation of divine service, compelled him to seek a reconciliation with the archbishop.

St. William of York.—In the northern province there were also troubles. The York chapter had chosen William, the nephew of the king, to succeed Archbishop Thurstan. It was alleged that the king had exerted undue influence to secure the see for his nephew in order to serve his own ends. On this account, although William was distinguished by virtue and holiness of life, his appointment was opposed; an appeal was made to Rome, and the election declared void, chiefly through the influence of the Cistercian Order. The archbishop-elect was deprived by Theobald of his see, to which Murdac, the Abbot of Fountains, was nominated. It was not until the death of his successor, five years later, that William recovered possession of his archiepiscopal chair. His troubles were at an end, but he died thirty days after his enthronement, to the sorrow of all his flock. He had the power of working miracles and the gift of prophecy, and was subsequently raised to the altars of the Church.

The Succession to the Crown.—Although the bishops were averse from warring with Stephen, the result of his conduct towards them was to determine them to secure the succession for Henry of Anjou. Consequently when Stephen required them to crown his eldest son Eustace during his own lifetime, they refused to comply, alleging that it could not be done without the Pope's sanction. It is said that this objection was suggested to the mind of Archbishop Theobald by a young clerk of his household, Thomas à Becket, on whom none then looked as his probable successor in the patriarchal see. The case was laid before the Papal Court, and it was decided that, since Stephen had acquired the crown not by way of inheritance, but by perjury and force, he had no right to transmit it to his posterity. The king's wrath was great. He ordered the bishops who refused his demand to be imprisoned, and their temporalities were for the moment seized. The refusal of the bishops to anoint or crown Eustace made the way plain for the young Duke Henry. Shortly after Eustace was removed by death. Theobald of Canterbury and Henry of Winchester improved the opportunity to reconcile conflicting interests. Stephen was to retain the crown for life, and to adopt Henry as his son and successor. A treaty was made and received with universal rejoicing, for it afforded the hope that an end would at length be put to the anarchy and misery which for nineteen years had held sway in England under the government of this unfortunate monarch. Stephen's death took place not long after, and for a few weeks Archbishop

Theobald acted as Regent. Then Duke Henry crossed the sea; he was welcomed by the people, and solemnly anointed king at Westminster on the 20th of December, 1154.

University Studies.—As a consequence of the Norman Conquest the English Church lost something of her insular character. She was brought by it into more complete fellowship with the rest of Western Christendom, a result to be carefully distinguished from further dependence on the Holy See. Indeed the essential dependence of every local Church on that of Rome was more loyally observed before than after the Norman Conquest. The reign of Stephen was not without its bearing on the ecclesiastical history of the country. As was natural when the civil power was so weak, the ecclesiastical power made rapid strides; the interposition of the Holy See became more often necessary, and the submission to its decrees more absolute. In the reign of Henry I., and still more in that of Stephen, we see the beginning of the system of universities; the first gatherings of masters and scholars, not attached to any great ecclesiastical foundation, not as yet formed into endowed societies. The borough of Oxford, a place sufficiently central for all the land south of the Humber, free from the jurisdiction of any great spiritual lord, was well suited to become the seat of one of these voluntary settlements of students, which, afterwards favoured by kings and nobles and bishops, in the first instance grew up of themselves. In the days of Henry, we hear of the first public lectures in divinity; in the reign of Stephen, amid the clash of arms, we find the first beginning of studies of a more general kind; amid the reign of force, arose the first systematic teaching of law. In Henry's time, the lectures of a Breton named Robert Pulan, who rose to a high place in the Roman Court, made the first beginning of a faculty of theology. In Stephen's time, Archbishop Theobald brought over from Italy a certain Vacarius to begin the first teaching of civil law, which then supplied the method of procedure in ecclesiastical cases. In the following reign the study of canon law, first systematized by Gratian of Bologna, was introduced into England; the clergy then had a code as well as method of procedure of their own.[1]

[1] Freeman, *op. cit.*, vol. v. p. 318.

CHAPTER XI.

SAINT THOMAS OF CANTERBURY.

Henry II., 1154. An English Pope. — The year 1154 was memorable for England, not only because of the death of King Stephen, but as having witnessed the elevation to the throne of St. Peter, under the title of Adrian IV., of the only Englishman who ever sat in the Papal Chair—Nicholas Breakspear, a man whose merits raised him from a humble station in life to the highest dignity in Christendom. In the close of the same year, Henry II., then twenty-one years of age, was crowned at Westminster by Archbishop Theobald. The enmity of the adherents of the late king had been silenced, and public tranquillity maintained, by the vigilance and authority of the archbishop; a fair prospect lay open before the young king. He chose for his Chancellor Thomas à Becket, the young cleric to whose good offices he was indebted in some measure, as we have said, for his succession to the throne.

Thomas à Becket.—The son of a London merchant, Thomas à Becket received his education in the London schools and the University of Paris.

The Archbishop of Canterbury, whose service he entered, pleased with his fine qualities and commanding abilities, made him his secretary, entrusted several important missions to him, and appointed him Archdeacon of Canterbury. When promoted to the post of Chancellor, preferment of all kinds was heaped on him. To the ecclesiastical benefices he already held, others of a secular character were added; thus he acquired feudal rights over considerable territories and bodies of men. The king admitted him to his intimate friendship, and, later on, confided to him the education of his eldest son. Becket dressed as a layman, and took part in all secular amusements and social pleasures, exercising an unbounded hospitality, and living in a style of magnificence which few kings at that time could rival. When he went on an embassy to France, he took with him so vast a retinue, and made so brave a display that people said, "What must the king of England be, if his Chancellor travels in such state?" At Toulouse he appeared clad in breastplate and helmet at the head of his body of troops, and we read of his unhorsing a French knight in a hand-to-hand encounter. Not even the warlike manners of the age can excuse such an infringement of the Church's canons in one who besides being in deacon's orders, was the highest unmitred dignitary in England. Yet despite his love of external magnificence, Becket was diligent in the performance of his official duties, liberal and compassionate to the poor, virtuous, chaste, and even mortified in his private life. He also exerted himself to restrain Henry from the crying sin of the Norman monarchs — that of allowing bishoprics to be long vacant, while the ecclesiastical revenue went to the royal exchequer—besides using his influence with him on behalf of churchmen who had incurred his displeasure. Becket's position was a delicate and difficult one; the king's temper was fiery in the extreme, and although he jested with the Chancellor, and even tore his cloak from his shoulders in the public street to bestow it on a beggar, he would brook no interference, and opposition drove him to great lengths.

In 1161 Archbishop Theobald, who had been primate for twenty-two years, died in the odour of sanctity. The revenues of the see were handed over to the Chancellor's care, and in the following year Henry intimated his wish that Thomas should be the next archbishop. Upon this the Chancellor, looking down at his dress, which was that of a gay courtier, said with a smile, "What a religious man, what a saint you wish to place over that holy see and famous monastery! I am certain that were it so to happen, by God's disposal, the affection and goodwill you now bear me would speedily turn into bitter hatred. I know you would require me to do things which I could never do, for even now you assume an authority over the Church that I could not tolerate." But the king carried his way, for he hoped to find in his friend an ally in effecting some changes he contemplated; and Thomas was in due course elected.

He passed at once from courtly splendour to monastic austerity. If he had till then lived in too great luxury and magnificence for "a servant of the lowly Lord," from that time forth he set himself to give an example to all men of the life a churchman should lead, to conduct himself according to the highest ideal of what an archbishop ought to be. There is no doubt that he had always the liberty of the Church at heart, although in some matters he yielded to the king; but when once he became primate, he applied all the force of his vigorous will to vindicate her right against most powerful and most violent opponents. He knew that a struggle was before him, and prepared to meet it. He was consecrated by his friend Henry of Blois, the Bishop of Winchester. When the ceremony was over the aged prelate said to him, "Dearest brother, you have now the choice: you must lose the favour either of your earthly or of your heavenly king." Upon his knees and with uplifted hands the newly-made primate made answer, "By God's grace and strength I make my choice: never for the love or favour of an earthly king will I forfeit the grace of the kingdom of heaven." Before the close of the year he laid aside his costly attire and valuable furs, to assume the black cappa and linen surplice of the canons regular.

Opposition to the King.—His next step was to resign the chancellorship, both to avoid the obligation of attendance at court, and also because he thought his tenure of this office would be an obstacle to freedom of action in case dissensions should arise between the Church and the Crown. This act and the transformation in Becket's manner of life were very unwelcome to the king, yet for a time the friendship between the two remained unbroken. The friction first made itself felt when Becket, to the great displeasure of the nobles, claimed the restoration of lands which, in the preceding reigns, had been alienated from the Church. Shortly after his position as head of the nation brought him into collision with the interests of the Crown. Henry desired that a certain tax (probably a survival of the Danegeld), which was paid by landowners to the sheriffs on condition that they should protect the contributors from the exactions of their subordinates, should be paid into the royal treasury. To this the archbishop, for the sake of the people, objected, on the ground that the payment was voluntary and conditional, and could not be enforced by law. Thereupon the king, in one of his sudden fits of anger, exclaimed: "By God's eyes the tax shall be enrolled as revenue, and entered in the king's books!" Becket answered: "By the reverence of those eyes by which thou hast sworn, my lord king, it shall not be levied from my lands, and from the lands of the Church not a penny!" "This is the first case," says Dr. Stubbs, "of any opposition to the king's will in the matter of taxation recorded in our national history; and it would seem to have been formally, at least, successful." [1] Thus on the constancy of the archbishop it depended whether the country were illegally burdened or not. Nor was he slack in asserting the spiritual rights of his office; for he excommunicated one of the king's tenants-in-chief, and when Henry bade him absolve him, he answered that it was not the king's business to say who should be bound and who unbound.

Attack on the Liberties of the Church.—The first serious rupture between the king and the archbishop, towards whom the king was beginning to entertain a personal hostility, was occasioned by an

[1] *Constitutional History*, vol. i. p. 463.

attack upon the liberties of the Church. The trial of ecclesiastics belonged of right to the ecclesiastical courts; the king now complained that the immunity from secular jurisdiction enjoyed by clerics often sheltered offenders. He therefore desired that all causes, whether of the clergy or the laity, should equally be judged in the civil court. At a council held at Westminster in 1163, he asked the bishops if they would obey the "customs of his grandfather, and agree that every cleric convicted of crime should straightway be degraded [deprived, that is, of all ecclesiastical privileges and immunities], and given over to the secular officials to be punished as a layman, without any defence from the Church." He also demanded that an officer of the Crown should be present in the ecclesiastical court, to see that no culprit was allowed to escape the just penalty of his misdeeds.

The primate took counsel with his brethren in the episcopacy, but none of them would stand by him. He contended that it was unjust to condemn a man twice for the same fault, first in the spiritual, then in the secular court, and that the sentence of the ecclesiastical authority was adequate. Moreover, he said, the clerks were not subject to the jurisdiction of an earthly king, and the liberty of the Church was at stake. On Henry renewing his inquiry whether they would "obey the customs," Thomas answered that they would do so, saving their order. This was virtually a refusal. The king demanded the withdrawal of this qualifying clause, and Becket wrote to Rome for advice. At a later interview the king taunted the archbishop with his lowly origin, and with showing ingratitude to himself by offering opposition to his will. "Are you not," he said, "the son of one of my serfs?" "In truth I am not sprung," he replied, "from royal race; no more was Blessed Peter, to whom God gave the headship of His Church. I am not ungrateful to you for the favours I have received from you, my lord king, wherefore far be it from me to resist your will, as long as it agrees with the will of God. But it would be good for neither of us were I to leave His will for yours; for in the awful judgement we shall both be judged as the servants of our Lord, and one will not be able to answer for the other."

The Constitutions of Clarendon, 1164.—At length, as the Pope counselled conciliation, and if possible concession for the sake of peace, the archbishop agreed, against his better judgement, to obey the customs as hitherto observed in the realm. Henry then summoned a council at Clarendon, and there, under strong pressure, the primate and his suffragans took the required pledge. The council then proceeded to draw up a body of rules, called the Constitutions of Clarendon. By these Constitutions it was decreed that all cases touching advowsons and presentations were to be tried in the King's Court. The clerk convicted of crime was no longer to be protected by the Church. Appeals from the archbishop were to be final, except when the king on being referred to gave leave to carry them further. No bishop was to quit the realm without obtaining the king's permission. Elections to bishoprics or abbacies were to take place by the chief clergy, but in the king's chapel and with his assent; and the prelate-elect was to do homage and fealty to the king as his liege-lord for his lands before consecration. A royal officer was to be present at all ecclesiastical proceedings, to confine the bishop's court within its due limits. No son of a villein was to be ordained without his lord's permission. All vacant bishoprics were to be left in the king's hands that he might receive the revenues. The privilege of sanctuary was repealed, as far as property and not persons was concerned.

Becket's Resistance.—When the archbishop heard the Constitutions he refused to set his seal to them, and declared he would not assent to them while he had breath in his body. Some of these regulations had never before been heard of. The rest had never been attempted to be put in practice except by such despots as Rufus and Henry I.; they had moreover been firmly resisted by Archbishops Lanfranc, St. Anselm, and Theobald. Henry I. and Stephen had formally abandoned them. Yet they were now to be formally confirmed, as if they had always been the acknowledged rights of the Crown. Bitterly the archbishop deplored his weakness in promising to consent to the "customs," for his conscience forbade him to ratify his promise. For forty days he abstained from offering the Holy Sacrifice until he had obtained the Pope's absolution for his fault. He omitted no means of making peace with the king, and even submitted to the Pope a copy of the Constitutions for his approval—an approval, it need hardly be said, that he was little inclined to give. Henry, in his resentment, subjected Becket to a series of vexations. He summoned him to appear before a council at Northampton, and there endeavoured to crush him by sundry accusations. The primate was charged with perjury, contempt of court, misappropriation of funds during his chancellorship, and, finally, condemned to forfeit his estates to the king. At Clarendon the bishops had sided, although timidly, with their archbishop, for the nature of the dispute forced them to do so. Now that a personal attack was made upon him, they supported the king, whose favour they were anxious to retain. The king aimed at inducing Becket to resign his see, but this he steadfastly refused to do. At a subsequent session of the council, he was impeached for high treason, and declared guilty by the peers of the realm. The Earl of Leicester, as Chief Justice, called on him to hear his sentence. Then the courage of the man rose to its full height. Grasping his archiepiscopal cross, he went in full pontificals to the royal court, disclaimed the right of the king or any layman to judge him, and appealed from their tribunal to the Papal See. Cries of "traitor!" followed him as he retired. At that word he turned, saying that, did not his priestly orders forbid it, his sword should answer that foul taunt. Under cover of the night he rode to Lincoln, and thence to Canterbury, and with a few faithful followers escaped to France in disguise.

Becket in France.—The King of France willingly received the fugitive under his protection. It was an ancient glory of his country, he said, to shelter persecuted churchmen. The sympathy felt for the exiled archbishop was so widespread, that the messengers sent by Henry asking that the "traitor" should not be allowed refuge in the kingdom could not counteract it. Nor did the ambassadors despatched to Pope Alexander III. (who was then at Sens), requesting that he would bid Becket return to England,

and would appoint a cardinal with legatine powers to investigate the charges on the spot, obtain their end. The embassy consisted of several barons and nobles, besides the Archbishop of York, Gilbert Foliot, Bishop of London, who cherished a long-standing personal enmity for Becket, and Hilary, Bishop of Chichester, who had been reproved by him for consenting to observe the royal "customs." The Pope showed great kindness to Becket, and refused to send him back to his persecutors. Having read the Constitutions of Clarendon, His Holiness declared them to be utterly inadmissible. Yet he was desirous to pursue as conciliatory a course as possible towards the king, the more so because at that time an antipope, upheld by the Emperor of Germany, had led many of the children of the Church from their allegiance to himself. Recent events in England had shown that the power of Henry was sufficient to plunge all his dominions into schism, if he should become personally alienated from the Vicar of Christ; and the Holy See has ever borne with everything that was not in itself wrong, in order to avert sin. However, the ambassadors met with no success. After their departure, Thomas himself visited the Holy Father at Sens. He then took up his abode in the Cistercian abbey at Pontigny, and devoted his time to study.

Becket made Apostolic Legate. Fresh Troubles.—The disputes between Henry I. and Anselm had been carried on without the king losing his dignity or stooping to any display of personal spite. It was not so with Henry II. He disgraced his cause by acts of petty vengeance and mean persecution. The details of the quarrel are intricate and somewhat wearisome. Henry endeavoured to ruin the archbishop in the estimation of the Pope and of the French king. In neither case was he successful. After two years had passed, Alexander III. confirmed Becket in his primacy, and made him Apostolic Legate. In this latter capacity Becket thought it behoved him no longer to keep silence about his wrongs. He wrote to the king, asking that he might be reinstated in his see, and allowed to discharge his duties; but, as the archbishop would concede nothing Henry would not consent to a reconciliation. Becket then thought fit to utter sentence of excommunication against the Bishop of Salisbury, who had been disobedient to the Pope's injunctions, and also against several nobles who had, during his absence, usurped possession of lands belonging to the see of Canterbury. The king retaliated by driving into banishment all who were connected with the primate by blood or friendship, without distinction of age, sex, or rank. The list of proscription contained four hundred names; and the sufferers were obliged by oath to visit the archbishop, and importune him with the history of their wrongs. Day after day crowds of these victims, amongst whom was the archbishop's sister with her infant family, besieged the door of his cell at Pontigny. This did not content Henry's resentment. He informed the monks that if they continued to grant a shelter to the "traitor," he would confiscate all the lands of their order in his dominions. The archbishop was consequently compelled to quit his retreat; Louis immediately offered him a residence in the town of Sens. There he spent the last four years of his life. Continual injustice at home, continual intrigues abroad; the Pope deceived by the king's messengers, or unfaithfully served by his own legates; Henry appealing to the Holy See, assenting to its decrees when they appeared to be in his favour, and evading them when they were against him; Becket harried by his enemies, and abandoned by his friends: such were the events of those four years. Nothing moved the resolution of the archbishop; his cause was identified with that of God and the Church.

Henry illegally crowned.—At length a fresh insult was offered to the archiepiscopal see. Henry had determined upon the coronation of his eldest son, the ill-fated Henry. It was not a sudden resolution; nine years before, on the death of Archbishop Theobald, he had procured a brief from the Pope, empowering him to select any prelate whom he thought proper, to perform the ceremony. This was only in force while the see of Canterbury was vacant; therefore, as soon as the king's design transpired, Alexander III., at Becket's solicitation, sent a letter forbidding the Archbishop of York, or any other bishop, to usurp an office which belonged of right and exclusively to the Archbishop of Canterbury. Henry prevented this prohibition from reaching England; having assembled the bishops, he laid before them the permission granted on the death of Theobald, and desired Roger, the Archbishop of York, who had long been an opponent of the primate, to crown his son. Nor was this all; the usual coronation oath to maintain the liberties of the Church was omitted, and another substituted in its place, to observe the royal customs.

Becket returns to England.—This brought matters to a crisis. Louis, affronted because his daughter, the consort of the prince, was not crowned at the same time, threatened war; and Alexander III., thinking the time for forbearance was at an end, determined to extend the censure of the Church to Henry himself. He therefore informed him that unless the primate and his fellow exiles, who had been already six years in banishment, should return to England, and be put in possession again of their rights and land and churches, within forty days, he would lay the kingdom under an interdict, and the bishops under sentence of excommunication. Henry was alarmed; he yielded, and showed a desire for peace. A meeting was arranged between the kings of France and England in a meadow on the borders of Touraine. This meeting Becket, though uninvited, attended, to show his willingness to meet the Pope's wishes, and contribute to bring about a reconciliation. The king greeted Becket with the greatest friendliness and courtesy; he shook hands with him, and conversed with the same easy familiarity as though nothing had occurred to disturb their former intimacy. The archbishop alighted from his horse and threw himself at the king's feet; but the latter insisted that he should remount, saying, "My lord archbishop, let us renew our ancient affection for one another; only show me honour in presence of these bystanders." He acceded to all the archbishop's requests, promising to make restitution to the Church of Canterbury for all the injuries it had sustained, and to allow the papal sentence against the unfaithful bishops to be carried into execution. All seemed satisfactorily settled; but Thomas à Becket knew the king's character too well to cross the Channel until every acre of land belonging to his see had been restored.

The Pope and cardinals shared this distrust; in fact, months elapsed before the royal engagements were fulfilled; and when at last, with the terrors of an interdict hanging over his head, the king gave up the lands, the rents had been previously levied, the corn and cattle carried off, and the buildings were left in a dilapidated state. At last the Sovereign Pontiff urged Becket, in spite of the king's evident duplicity, to return to Canterbury. When he took leave of the king, Henry refused to give him the kiss of peace, as he had before refused in presence of his courtiers. "Go in peace," he said to him, "I will see you at Rouen or in England." "My lord," Becket answered, "my heart tells me you will never see me again alive." "Do you think I am a traitor?" rejoined the king. "Far be it from you, my lord," was the prelate's reply. So they parted. But Becket knew well what was before him. "I am going to England to die," were the last words he said, when bidding the Bishop of Paris farewell.

The archbishop had received from Alexander III. letters of suspension against the Archbishop of York, and of excommunication against the bishops of London and Salisbury. These he sent before him, that they might be declared before his arrival. It was towards the close of 1170 when he landed at Sandwich. Seven years of dreary exile had passed since he sailed from England; his return was hailed with joy by the inhabitants, and when he approached his cathedral city, the Kentish men flocked to meet him with uproarious welcome. The bishops sent on the following day to ask to be freed from their censures; Becket, whilst willing to make every possible concession, preferred to leave the matter in the

Pope's hands. Roger of York, overruling the others, burst into loud complaints of the primate's love of power and thirst for revenge; he accused him to the young prince of violating the royal privileges. All three, instead of pleading for themselves at the one legitimate tribunal, the Chair of Peter, crossed over to Normandy to demand redress from the king. The latter, irritated by their representations, exclaimed in his wrath: "Of all the cowards who eat my bread, will no one free me from the insolence of this low-born priest?"

The Murder of the Archbishop.—Four knights heard this passionate outbreak of their master's anger, and emboldened by it to outrage, crossed the sea, and forced their way into the archbishop's palace. Their names were Richard le Breton, Reginald Fitzurse, William Tracy, and Hugh de Moreville. A stormy conversation ensued, in which Fitzurse said, "From whom do you hold your archbishopric?" The archbishop replied, "Its spiritualities from God and my lord the Pope, its temporalities and possessions from the king." Fitzurse thereupon said, "Do you not acknowledge that you have all from the king?" to which the archbishop rejoined, "By no means; but we must give what is the king's to the king, and what is God's to God." The knights then withdrew to arm, and Becket was persuaded by his clerks to take sanctuary in the cathedral. As he reached the steps leading from the transept to the choir, his pursuers burst in, shouting, from the cloisters. "Where," cried Fitzurse, in the dusk of the dimly-lighted minster, "where is the traitor, Thomas Becket?" The primate turned resolutely back. "Here am I! no traitor, but a priest of God," he replied: and again descending the steps, he placed himself with his back against a pillar and fronted his foes. "You are our prisoner," shouted Fitzurse. The four knights tried to drag him from the cathedral, but he shook them off. They insisted that he should immediately absolve all whom he had placed under ecclesiastical censure; this he refused to do, until they promised satisfaction. "Then die!" a voice exclaimed. "In defence of the Church I am willing to die," the prelate rejoined. "Strike, strike!" retorted Fitzurse, and blow after blow struck Becket to the ground. "Into Thy hands, O Lord, I commend my spirit," he ejaculated. Then Le Breton dealt him a blow so violent that his head was cleft in two, and the assailant's sword fell broken upon the marble pavement. A retainer of the murderers with the point of the sword scattered the primate's brains on the ground. "Let us be off," he said, "the man will never rise again."

Thus, at the age of fifty-three, perished this great prelate and saint, a martyr to his duty, the preservation of the immunities of the Church. The brutal murder sent a thrill of horror through Christendom; the moment of his death was the triumph of his cause. His personal virtues and his exalted station, the dignity and composure wherewith he met his fate, the sacredness of the place where the crime was committed, contributed to inspire men with aversion for his enemies and veneration for his character.

We are told that in infancy Thomas à Becket imbibed a very deep devotion to the Blessed Virgin through the teaching of his mother, and that in his youth he received some signal marks of her favour. He is believed to be the author of hymns in honour of his great patroness; and it is recorded that the favourite devotion wherewith he was wont to invoke her, was the salutation of her seven temporal joys. Once when he was repeating these joys, she appeared to him, and asked why he only celebrated her earthly joys, and not those also which formed her crown in heaven? On his replying that he knew them not, she told them to him, and he composed a Latin hymn to celebrate them, which has been preserved in one of the great libraries at Rome.

The King's Penance. The Papal Settlement.—When Henry heard what had occurred at Canterbury he was filled with remorse. He knew that his rash words had suggested, if they had not authorized, the deed, and that the archbishop's murder would be a stain upon his character, though he disavowed any evil intention. For forty days he did penance, fasting on bread and water. Fearing the papal indignation, he sent envoys to Rome to assert his innocence. At first these envoys could not obtain an audience. The Pope, on receiving the news, was plunged in grief, for he attributed the sad event in a great measure to his leniency in dealing with the adversaries of Becket. He secluded himself entirely during eight days, and gave orders that no Englishman was to be admitted to his presence. At length he consented to receive the embassy that came to plead for the English king. By their negotiations they averted the excommunication which was to avenge the deed of blood. Alexander III. excommunicated the murderers of Becket, and laid Henry's French dominions under an interdict. For a whole year the desecrated cathedral was placed under a ban. By virtue of powers conferred on them by the Pope, the archbishops of Sens and of Rouen absolved the Archbishop of York, on his swearing that he had not received the papal prohibition before crowning the young prince, that he had not bound himself to observe the Constitutions of Clarendon, nor in any way caused the archbishop's death. The bishops of Salisbury and of London were also absolved on taking the same oath. The archiepiscopal see was vacant for two years and three months. When the Prior of Canterbury begged for free election, the king tried to persuade the monks to appoint the Bishop of Bayeux, a man who was the very opposite of Becket. The elections for the vacant suffragan sees then took place, and the names of those chosen to fill them prove that it was still easier to obtain promotion by having taken the king's part than by having suffered with the martyr in the late struggle. Most of the new bishops were the worst enemies of Thomas. Richard, the Prior of Dover, was nominated to the see of Canterbury; on the young king protesting against the election, he went to Rome, where he was consecrated by the Pope.[1]

The Shrine of St. Thomas à Becket.—Before the new archbishop was installed in the see of Canterbury, Becket was canonized. Numberless and striking miracles took place at his tomb; for centuries his shrine was the most venerated in England. The offerings made at it were of immense value; the shrine itself is described as being of unrivalled magnificence, surpassing all others in the world for

---

[1] The four murderers of à Becket were shunned by every man. Tradition says that after a year had elapsed they went to Rome, and by order of the Holy Father made a pilgrimage to Jerusalem as their penance, and died shortly after.

costliness and beauty. It was covered with plates of pure gold, set with large and beautifully sculptured gems. This shrine was not spared when sacrilegious hands were laid on the property of the Church, and so completely was St. Thomas regarded as the champion of the Church's rights, the protector of all who resist attempts of the secular power to exercise spiritual jurisdiction, that the despoiler waged war against his very name. Henry VIII., thinking that men would be stimulated by his example to brave the ecclesiastical authority of the sovereign, summoned St. Thomas into court, as if he were a living man, and after a mock trial, caused sentence to be pronounced "that Thomas, some time Archbishop of Canterbury, had been guilty of contumacy, treason, and rebellion; that his bones should be publicly burnt, to admonish the living to their duty by the punishment of the dead." [1]

The King's Absolution.—In 1174, Henry II. was recalled from Normandy to England, to repel an invasion of the King of Scotland. Directly he landed he made a pilgrimage to the tomb of St. Thomas. He entered Canterbury barefoot, in the guise of a pilgrim, visited the scene of the martyrdom, which he watered with his tears, and prayed long in the church. Meanwhile the Bishop of London proclaimed to all present the contrition felt by the king for the hasty expressions which led to the crime, the full satisfaction he was prepared to make, and the offerings he would give in atonement. His shoulders were then bared, and kneeling down,

---

[1] St. Thomas of Canterbury is considered as the patron of the English secular clergy. His feast is celebrated as a double of the first class.

he received from each prelate five, and from every monk three, strokes of the scourge.

The death of Becket, moreover, led to the surrender on the king's part of much for which he had been striving. The Constitutions were partially annulled, and liberty of canonical election was restored. About three years after his public penance, when the Pope's legate had come to England to arrange the Church's affairs, Henry pledged himself that no clergyman should be arraigned before a lay tribunal, except for transgression of the laws of the forest, or for lay service due for a lay fief; that no bishopric or abbey should be in the hands of the king for more than a year, unless from manifest necessity; that the murderer of a clerk, in addition to the usual punishment, should forfeit his inheritance for ever; and that the clergy should never be compelled to take part in battle.

Henry's unhappy End.—Some time previously, the young prince had taken up arms against his father, and his example was followed by his brother, afterwards the famous Richard Cœur de Lion. These rebellions led King Henry to write a letter to the Pope, which shows how submissive he could be to the Holy See, when it furthered his interests, and did not interfere with his passions. "The realm of England is in your jurisdiction," he writes to Pope Alexander; "and I am bound to you alone by feudal obligations. Let England now experience what the Pope can do, and since he does not use the arm of flesh, let him defend the patrimony of Blessed Peter with the sword of the spirit" (Fr. Morris, *Life of St. Thomas*, p. 442).

In vain did Henry invoke the papal authority to

shield the country from the unnatural attempts of his deluded children. The rebellion of his sons, who joined with his foreign foes and with those disaffected barons who were willing to transfer the crown from the brow of a vigilant monarch to that of a thoughtless youth, harassed and embittered the later years of his reign. In this we may see the just retribution of an offended God. We quote the words of a non-Catholic writer:[1] "Thomas à Becket was murdered in Canterbury Cathedral; the judgement of the Most High begun to fall upon the guilty king and his accursed progeny. Since then everything seemed to have gone wrong. The last six years of Henry the Second's reign were years of piteous misery, shame, and bitterness. His two eldest sons died in arms against their father. The two younger ones were Richard and John. History has no story more sad than that of the wretched king, hard at death's door, compelled to submit to the ferocious vindictiveness of the one son, and turning his face to the wall with a broken heart when he discovered the hateful treachery of the other."

[1] Jessopp, *Coming of the Friars*, p. 29.

CHAPTER XII.

STRUGGLES BETWEEN CHURCH AND STATE.

Longchamp, Bishop of Ely, 1189.—The history of the expedition to the Holy Land, upon which Richard I. embarked immediately after his accession to the throne, is well known to the reader. The fruitless nature of this crusade, by which his name has been rendered memorable, and the circumstances of his captivity in Germany which followed upon it, need not be entered upon here, except in so far as the absence of the king and the expenditure necessary to maintain his armies affected the ecclesiastical history of the country. Whilst the monarch was away, a period of four years, the government passed almost entirely into the hands of churchmen. Richard, on his departure, confided the administration to William Longchamp, Bishop of Ely. A man of humble birth, he had risen by rapid steps, being made first chancellor, then justiciary, and finally, at the king's request, papal legate in England and Scotland. Thus he found himself at the head of both Church and State. He is said to have exercised his twofold power in a harsh and despotic manner; this gave occasion to John, the king's brother, to assume the character of a defender of the rights of the people, and to head a revolt against his authority. At length all parties united against the chancellor; he was deposed from his office, and compelled to leave the kingdom. Meanwhile Archbishop Baldwin had been elected to the see of Canterbury on the death of Richard, the successor of St. Thomas. He joined his royal master in Palestine, and fell whilst fighting at the siege of Acre, in 1190. His primacy was marked by no event of importance.

Hubert, Bishop of Salisbury. Papal Condemnation of his civil Position.—For three years the archbishopric was vacant, the revenues being confiscated to defray the expenses incurred by the crusade. At length the suffragan bishops and the monks of Christ Church, in obedience to the royal behest, elected Hubert, Bishop of Salisbury, to be primate. This prelate was appointed chief justiciary, or judge and governor of England, and his character as archbishop seems almost entirely merged in that of king's minister. He excommunicated John, and on Richard's return, placed the crown on his head at his second coronation at Winchester. When Richard almost immediately again quitted England, to chastise the perfidy of the French king, Hubert virtually became viceroy of the kingdom. His position was not altogether a pleasant one. He had constantly to find large sums of money for the king, who ever and anon pressed him for fresh supplies. England had already been drained of money to furnish the king's ransom, and men did not submit to fresh exactions without murmuring. The taxes pressed heavily on the poorer classes, and in 1196 a revolt was raised in London, where the richer citizens were accused of throwing the burden of taxation on the poor. The leader of the discontented citizens was a demagogue named William Fitz-Osbert, who by his inflammatory addresses threw the whole city into a ferment. Archbishop Hubert thought it his duty to interfere, and after holding an assembly of the principal townsmen, he gave orders to arrest the demagogue. But Fitz-Osbert cleft with an axe the head of the officer sent to take him, and fled for refuge to the church of St. Mary-le-Bow. On the fourth day, the church was, either by accident or design, set on fire; Fitz-Osbert was seized as he attempted to escape, tried for murder, and hanged. During the contest the right of sanctuary had been violated, and that by order of the archbishop, whose duty it was to maintain the immunities of the Church. This, with other grievances, real or alleged, was urged by his enemies on the attention of Pope Innocent III., who in letters to the king and the archbishop, insisted that Hubert should relinquish the secular offices which he held, and confine himself to his archiepiscopal duties. In consequence of this he resigned the post of justiciary, and the Pope recommended that for the future bishops and priests should not take part in civil administration.

Secular Position of the Clergy. Giraldus Cambrensis.—The absorption of the clergy in secular matters at this time occasioned much disedification in England, and was the cause of many evils that oppressed the Church. As far as the State was concerned, the employment of ecclesiastics was no small gain. Besides supplying the country with a succession of highly-trained officers, the Church provided constitutional development. Just as she taught the State at first how to attain unity, so now she afforded it an example of organization and progress. But many a voice had been lifted up to exhort the archbishop and other prelates to attend less to affairs of state, and more to those of the Church. The worldliness and greed of office amongst the higher, and the demoralization of the lower class of clergy, to which this policy gave rise, are denounced in the satires attributed to a witty Welshman, Walter de Map, Archdeacon of Oxford, who freely used his pungent pen to rebuke the ecclesiastical abuses of his day. His friend and countryman, Gerald de Barri, better known as Giraldus Cambrensis, was scarcely less outspoken in his criticisms on prelates and monks. The most amusing writer of his day, an acute observer, refined and learned, he directed his invectives against the system of civil government as well as against ecclesiastical authority. Both these writers generalize too much about the state of the clergy, and exaggerate somewhat for the sake of effect.

St. Hugh of Lincoln.—By far the most important and influential prelate at this time was Hugh, Bishop of Lincoln. A monk of some years' standing in the monastery of the Grande Chartreuse, the fame of his prudence and sanctity had already spread all over France, when Henry II. requested that he might be sent to England to undertake the government of the first house of Carthusians founded in this kingdom, at Witham, in Somersetshire. This foundation at the outset had encountered great difficulties. Hugh set to work to complete the buildings, and by the humility of his deportment and the holiness of his life, he gained the hearts even of the enemies of the foundation. In 1186 he was elected to the bishopric of Lincoln, which then included a large portion of the country from the Humber to the Thames. For seventeen years the see had been vacant; during that period there had been no supervision of the clergy, no ordinations or confirmations, no new churches built, while those that existed were falling into ruins. Hugh restored ecclesiastical discipline amongst the clergy, thoroughly reorganized the diocese, and finished the erection of a magnificent cathedral. He spent much of his substance in relieving the poor, and of his time in visiting the hospitals, and became a splendid example to the other prelates, many of whom had been promoted more on account of the secular services they had rendered to the king than for the spiritual qualities they possessed. Henry II., the most impatient of monarchs and the most uncontrollable in his actions, stood in awe of this holy prelate, and received his admonitions with deference.

The king's foresters were accustomed to exercise an inhuman tyranny in the country, maiming or putting to death without a trial any one who had killed or maimed one of the beasts of the forest. One of the rangers had on slight suspicion laid hands on a cleric and sentenced him to pay a heavy fine. St. Hugh, in consequence, excommunicated the man, nor could the king's solicitations prevail with him to remove the excommunication until the forester acknowledged the crime with signs of repentance. On another occasion, when Henry requested him to bestow a vacant prebend on one of his favourites, the bishop refused, saying the benefices of the Church were for clerks, not for courtiers. And when, on the death of Henry, Richard succeeded to the throne, no man stood before him more fearlessly than St. Hugh, exhorting him to restrain his passions and seek the welfare of his subjects. He did not hesitate to oppose an unconstitutional tax at an assembly held in Oxford, 1198, when it was proposed, on behalf of the Crown, that the barons and bishops should maintain three hundred knights to serve beyond the sea. Hugh of Lincoln answered that though he had come to England as a stranger, he would maintain the rights of his Church, and that though it was bound to do military service within the kingdom, the king could not claim such service in other countries, and that he would not contribute to a foreign war. Another bishop spoke to the same effect, and, their answers coinciding with the interests of the lay-barons, the demand was refused, to the great displeasure of the king. St. Hugh spoke with equal liberty to King John on his accession.

In the first year of John's reign he died. He had been sent on an embassy to Philip Augustus, the King of France, to conclude peace between the two realms, and expired shortly after his return, with the words of the *Nunc Dimittis* on his lips. Some idea of the esteem in which he was held may be formed from the fact that the kings of England and Scotland, three archbishops, a large company of bishops and abbots, with a long train of nobles, attended his obsequies. Meeting the funeral train at the church door, the kings and nobles put their shoulders under the bier as it was carried into the church.

King John, 1199.—Richard I. died as he had

lived, pardoning with kingly generosity the archer who had shot and fatally wounded him, outraging with bitter mockery the priests who exhorted him to repentance and restitution.[1] His brother John, who succeeded him, is described as "the worst outcome of the Angevin race. He united into one mass of wickedness their insolence, their selfishness, their unbridled passions, their cruelty and tyranny, their shamelessness, their superstition, their cynical indifference to honour or truth."[2] At the same time he possessed the vivacity, the cleverness, the love of learning, the profound ability that distinguished his house. His accession to the crown, to the exclusion of his nephew Arthur, brought the elective character of the monarchy into prominence, and Archbishop Hubert, at his coronation with the accustomed solemnity at Westminster, while declaring his election to be strictly in accordance with constitutional usage, made a special appeal to John to observe the oath he had taken. It appeared as though he foresaw the contests that were to come, and strove, as the representative of the English Church and people, to impress on the new king the duty he owed to both. Hubert used his power to restrain John from evil, and the hatred the latter bore to his memory proves that his death, which took place in 1205, was a national calamity.

Election of Bishops.—To explain the unfortunate contest with the Roman Pontiff that ensued on the death of the archbishop, the reader must be reminded that our monarchs at their coronation promised upon oath to respect the prerogatives of the Church,

---

[1] Green, *Short History of the English People*, p. 111.
[2] *Ibid.*, p. 118.

amongst which was numbered the right of cathedral chapters to choose their own prelates. This was a right which the sovereign viewed with jealousy, and on which he encroached without scruple. The bishoprics offered an easy means of remunerating the clerics in his service; and as the baronies attached to them gave their holders considerable influence in the State, the king professed a fear lest they should be given to his enemies. Hence it was required that the meeting of the chapter should be preceded by the royal license, which afforded the king an opportunity of recommending an individual for election ; and that it should be followed by the submission of the bishop-elect to him for approval, thus allowing him the exercise of a veto. So far the practice in England was conformable to that of most Christian countries, but in one point it differed from that of the others. Several of the cathedral churches had originally belonged to monasteries, and were still served by monks, who claimed to exercise alone all the rights of election, and choose one of their own number. With respect to other sees, this claim of the monks was, perhaps, of minor importance, but the Archbishop of Canterbury enjoyed so elevated a station in Church and State, that his election interested both the king and the prelates. The latter strongly objected to having a monk for their primate ; and from time to time an attempt was made by the secular clergy to obtain the removal of the monks from the cathedrals, or, at any rate, to prevent them from electing or being elected bishops. This was based on the plea that their seclusion from the world rendered them unable to judge of the qualifications requisite for the office. But the Pope would not consent to their expulsion, for he knew that however useful worldly experience may be, it is not the chief requisite in the government of spiritual matters; and for every act of spoliation done to the monks, he commanded full restitution to be made. The suffragan bishops, however, claimed the right if not of exclusive, at least of concurrent, election; and that right being fiercely denied by the monks of Christ Church, Canterbury, the contest was renewed at the death of each successive archbishop. Each party asserted that the rights for which they battled had been granted by the Holy See; each denied that the claim of the other had received that supreme sanction. The king confederated with the prelates; to subdue the resistance of the monks, the place of election was fixed at a distance, where only a few could exercise their right in the name of the whole community; and the object of their choice, unless he were the person recommended by the king and chosen by the bishops, was uniformly refused. Still, when ultimately compelled to yield, the monks yielded in such a manner as not to relinquish, by their acquiescence, the right to which they clung.

Election of Reginald to Canterbury.—As soon as the death of Archbishop Hubert was known, the younger of the monks of Christ Church, desirous to have the election as it had been before the Norman Conquest, entirely free from royal interference, assembled at midnight, and, without waiting for the *congé d'élire*, chose as his successor Reginald, their sub-prior. Aware that they would encounter opposition, their only hope of success depended on obtaining the approbation of the Holy See. Reginald was forthwith sent to Rome for confirmation, under a promise that he would tell no one of the honour conferred on him. No sooner, however, had he landed in Flanders, than his vanity overcame his prudence, and he gave out that he was the archbishop-elect. The king, who had hitherto been restrained in his violation of the liberties of the Church and the laws of the land by the authority of Archbishop Hubert, now determined to raise a favourite minister of his own, John de Grey, Bishop of Norwich, to the archiepiscopal throne. He consequently repaired to Canterbury, assembled the cathedral chapter, ordered them to proceed to a canonical election, and recommended the Bishop of Norwich to their suffrages. They obeyed; and John de Grey was enthroned as primate. The suffragan bishops were displeased at not having had a voice in the election, and finally all parties appealed to Rome.

Papal Decision. Langton elected. John's Opposition.—Innocent III. at that time occupied the papal chair. After a long and careful inquiry, he declared that the right of election belonged to the monks, and the bishops had no claim to share in it. He annulled the election of Reginald as altogether irregular, and that of John de Grey, because it had been made before the other was declared void. In order that the see of Canterbury might no longer be left unfilled—two years had elapsed since it became vacant—the Pope ordered the monks sent from England to elect their prelate there and then, recommending to them Stephen Langton, who he thought would be a person acceptable to the king. Personally no better choice could have been made, for Langton was a cardinal of high position and character, who had risen to this dignity through his learning and

the sanctity of his life. But the king was much
enraged at the promotion of this man in the place
of his favourite. In vain did the Supreme Pontiff
try to soothe him; the messengers from Rome were
seized when they landed in England, and thrown
into prison. Innocent III., who had already shown
himself resolved to maintain his authority as Vicar
of Christ, himself consecrated Langton at Viterbo.
The king wrecked his vengeance on the monks of
Christ Church. A body of armed men was sent to
drive them out of their convent; they were compelled to cross the sea, and their lands were taken
possession of for the Crown. When every attempt
to persuade John to yield had failed, the Pope
threatened to lay the kingdom under an interdict,
should he persist in excluding Langton from his see.
John met this threat with defiance, replying with a
counterthreat that, if the interdict were published,
he would expel prelates and clergy, and send every
Italian he could seize in the realm back to Rome
with the loss of eyes and nose.

England under Interdict, 1208.—Innocent was
not a man to draw back from his purpose; at last
the interdict fell on the land. The bishops of London,
Ely, and Worcester, to whom its proclamation was
entrusted, waited on the monarch, and on their knees
conjured him to admit the new archbishop; but
he drove them from his presence with oaths and
insults. On the appointed day the churches were
closed; no bell was tolled; no service was solemnly
performed; the administration of the sacraments,
except to infants and to the dying, was suspended;
the bodies of the dead were interred without prayer
or priest, in unconsecrated ground. This sudden

extinction of the forms and aids of religion struck the people with horror. John alone was unmoved; he retaliated by confiscating the lands of the clergy who observed the interdict, by subjecting them, in spite of their privileges, to the royal courts, and often by leaving outrages on them unpunished. " Let him go," he said, when a Welshman was brought before him for the murder of a priest, " he has killed my enemy!" Two years passed before the Pope proceeded to the further sentence of excommunication. John was formally cut off from the pale of the Church, but the new sentence was met with the same defiance as the old. Five of the bishops fled over the sea; secret disaffection was spreading widely, but there was no public avoidance of the excommunicated king. One ecclesiastic, an archdeacon of Norwich, who withdrew from his service, he ordered to be arrested; and with a refinement of cruelty, sent him a cope of lead " to keep him warm in his prison." Crushed beneath this ponderous garment, his head alone at liberty, the brave man remained without food or assistance—a noble example to prelates and nobles—till death put an end to his sufferings.

Deposition of John.—This state of things lasted four years. At length Innocent III. reluctantly had recourse to the last effort of his authority. At the time when the occupant of the Chair of Peter was regarded as the head of Christendom, he claimed, as the earthly representative of the heavenly monarch by whom kings reign and princes rule (*Prov.* viii. 16, 17), to exercise over Christian princes the power of deprivation and deposition. The Pontiffs were most chary of using this power, and most forbearing towards offenders. They were invariably the supporters of authority and law, yet they firmly opposed tyranny and oppression, and, if necessary, absolved from their allegiance the subjects of a king or emperor who so abused his regal authority as to make his rule an impediment not only to the temporal, but also to the moral and religious welfare of his people.[1] This right Innocent asserted by the deposition of John. Philip II. of France was charged to carry out the sentence; he prepared to invade the kingdom.

John becomes a Vassal of the Holy See, 1213.—John now found himself in evil case. Wherever he turned there was danger: the Welsh were in rebellion, and word was brought him that his barons, many of whom he had deeply injured, were almost to a man conspiring against him. Throughout his reign John was quick to discern the difficulties of his position, and inexhaustible and unscrupulous in the resources wherewith he met them. "When the king

---

[1] "This sense—that the care of the whole world was entrusted to the Pope, that all who refused to acknowledge the primacy of St. Peter's Chair and submit to its authority were in direct opposition to the word of God and to the polity which Christ left on earth—is the keynote to the conduct of the Popes, at this, the highest point of their power and influence. And we do not find that those who held aloof were in any way the gainers.

"The historian of the Byzantine Empire says: 'The Papal Church was at this time often actively employed in defending freedom, in establishing a machinery for the purpose of restraining the abuses of the temporal power of princes. In short, the Papal Church was then the great teacher of social and political reform' (Finlay's *Byzantine and Greek Empires*, vol. ii. p. 345).

"The same writer (*Med. Greece and Trebizond*, p. 76), in speaking of the authority of the Popes in Western Europe during the eleventh and twelfth centuries, says: 'It was supported by public opinion, for both the laity and the clergy regarded them as the only impartial dispensers of justice on earth, as the antagonists of feudal oppression, and the champions of the people against feudal tyranny'" (Luard, *On the Relations between England and Rome*, p. 5).

heard these things," Matthew Paris writes (vol. ii. p. 135), "he was humbled, though against his will, and perturbed in mind, seeing that the peril of confusion hung over him on every side." Not only did he agree to receive the archbishop, and to recompense and restore to their lands the exiled prelates and the monks of Canterbury, but he grovelled at their feet on their return, and promised to submit to all the conditions imposed on him. Furthermore, he solemnly resigned, on May 15, 1213, both crown and realms to the Pope in the person of his envoy, Pandulph, and received them again from his hands to be held by fealty and homage as a vassal of the Pope, promising a yearly tribute of a thousand marks for the kingdom of England and lordship of Ireland. At Michaelmas of the same year, John renewed his submission, to Nicholas, Cardinal Bishop of Tusculum, an envoy of higher rank and more extensive powers. Standing at the west door of St. Paul's Cathedral, he swore that he would be faithful to God, to the Blessed Peter, to the Holy Roman Church, to Pope Innocent III. and his successors, and that he would restore the ecclesiastical laws of St. Edward. The cathedral doors were then thrown open to the faithful for the first time after five years of interdict, and High Mass was celebrated in thanksgiving. The act of John in thus becoming the Pope's vassal has merited for him severe reprobation : Lingard calls it "a disgraceful act" (vol. ii. 331). It certainly was disgraceful in John, for in doing it he was insincere. It was a political manœuvre by which he thought to defeat also the hopes of the king of France ; it was an act of cunning, arising simply out of interest and fear. But was vassalage or feudal dependence upon the

Head of Christendom a disgrace to kings? If so, John was not alone in his shame: it was the condition of most of the princes of Christendom. Nay, they were vassals to one another. The king of Scotland was vassal to the king of England; and the king of England was vassal to the king of France; the one for the lands, whatever they were, which he held of the English crown, the other for his transmarine territories. Both were often seen in public on their knees, swearing fealty and doing homage to their feudal lord. John's own father, Henry, was feudatory of Pope Alexander III.; Richard, John's brother, resigned his crown to the Emperor of Germany, and held it on payment of a yearly rent. John simply did what these had done before him.[1]

It should be remembered, too, as far as Innocent is concerned, that the object he had in view in obtaining a greater hold over the English kings, was to compel them more effectively to do justice to their subjects. It was not papal ambition that actuated the Pope, but the good of the English people.

The oath of fealty to the Pope taken by John was the very same oath which vassals swore to their lord. "By surrendering his crown he bound himself to exercise his royal power in conformity to law. . . . His dependence on the Pope was for the conservation of the liberties of the people. It is acknowledged by all historians that down to the surrender of the crown, the Pope had supported the archbishops, the barons, and the people against the king. He had, *multipliciter et multoties*, as Matthew Paris says,

[1] Manning, *Miscellanies*, ii. 265.

admonished, counselled, expostulated, threatened John, to bring him to law and reason. At last he submitted himself, and the barons were mere counsellors and partakers in his act of submission." [1] Lingard tells us that "the instrument placed by John in the hands of Pandulph was subscribed by himself, one archbishop, nine earls, and three barons." It contained the following words: "By our free good-will and by the common counsel of our barons, we offer and freely grant to God, and the holy Apostles Peter and Paul, and to the Holy Roman Church ... the kingdom of England and Ireland," &c.[2] The cession was therefore made by the counsel and consent of the barons, and from that moment they began to demand the grant of their liberties from the king, and, on his refusal, appealed to the Pontiff as suzerain from the despotic government of his vassal.

Rome would have forfeited its character as the protector of nations if it had failed to receive the penitent on his submission. Thenceforth it was a point both of honour and interest to the Pope to support him. "That it was no nominal submission merely on the part of John, but was made a reality by the Pope during the twenty or thirty years that followed, is clearly seen from the evidence of the papal letters and bulls themselves. England was considered and treated as a fief of the see of Rome, and the greatest anxiety is evinced on the part of the Popes that nothing should disturb the arrangement thus made. The acts of the Roman See in this country show how the Pope exercised his influence in England in minute detail, and exercised exact

[1] Manning, *Miscellanies*, ii. pp. 265, 266
[2] Rymer, *Fœdera*, t. i. p. 176.

superintendence over matters great and small that concerned the Church in this country. . . . Although the delay caused by appeals produced a vast amount of evils, and the Popes were liable to be misled by party statements, we must give them credit for a genuine and earnest desire to promote the peace of the country."[1] The peace was scarcely concluded before John broke it again, and the conflict with the Church, in the person of its primate, for the liberties of clergy and people, began afresh.

Magna Charta, 1215.—From the moment of his landing in England, Stephen Langton assumed the constitutional position of the primate as champion of the old English customs and law against the personal despotism of the kings. As Anselm had withstood William Rufus, as Theobald had rescued England from the lawlessness of Stephen, so Langton prepared to withstand the tyranny of John, and secure on a formal basis the ancient freedom of the realm. He called an assembly of clergy and barons at St. Paul's, and read to them the charter of Henry I. He then bound them by oath to claim the privileges conceded in that charter, and organized a formidable coalition against the king, thus forming what was called "the army of God and Holy Church." John was compelled to yield to their demands; he set his seal to the Great Charter which had been drawn up, and which was solemnly ratified at Runnymede, 1215. Of this charter it suffices to name the first and last clauses, which provided "that the Church of England shall in all things spiritual be free [*i.e.*, from royal usurpation], and hold her rights entire and her liberties inviolate."

[1] *Cf.* Luard, on the relations between England and Rome during the earlier part of the reign of Henry III., pp. 11, 68, 69.

The king, mortified at what had happened, at once sent to Rome misrepresenting the facts, and urging that the Charter should be annulled as an invasion of the rights of the Apostolic See, to which England now belonged. Innocent immediately annulled the concessions extorted from John, and wrote to the barons exhorting them to submit.[1] Archbishop Langton was ordered to excommunicate the disobedient; on his refusal to do so, he was suspended from the exercise of his functions as primate. Nor could he recover the exercise of his authority, though he made personal application at Rome; during the rest of John's reign he remained out of the kingdom.

Stephen's absence was a great loss to the national party, and the last years of the king's rule were sad and troublous. The clergy are said to have been the principal sufferers, as they were known to be as a body in accord with the barons and the nation at large, in its struggle against the royal tyranny, though the absence of their leader hindered them from taking an open part. "The priests," says an historian,[2]

[1] *Cf.* Cardinal Manning on the Pope and Magna Charta, *Miscellanies*, ii. p. 251. The reasons why the Pope condemned and annulled the Charter of Liberties are stated to be the following:—
1. Because the barons had levied war against their sovereign.
2. He was a vassal of the Holy See, and his grant was invalid without the assent of his over-lord.
3. He had taken the Crusaders' cross.
4. Their cause was already in appeal before the Holy See.
5. They had taken the law into their own hands.

Innocent's objection was not to the provisions of the Charter, but to the mode by which they had been extorted without reference to him as over-lord; not to the laws and liberties set down in the Charter, but the rebellious way by which the barons had wrung them from their sovereign. As for the laws and liberties themselves, he invited them to submit their claims to the Holy See, and promised them an impartial judgement.

[2] Roger de Wendover, iii. 351.

"standing at the very altar, shining in their sacred vestments, were continually seized, tortured, robbed, wounded." The death of John in 1216 caused a feeling of relief throughout the land.

Henry III., 1216. Restoration of Religious Fervour.—As soon as Henry III., a child of ten years old, was seated on the throne, principally through the prompt and firm action of the Papal Legate,[1] Langton received permission to return and resume the government of his diocese. He immediately applied himself to the reform of many scandals and abuses that had crept into the Church. To restore religious fervour in the country, he caused the memory of several famous English saints to be revived, by translating their remains to more imposing shrines. Thus St. Wulstan of Worcester, St. Hugh of Lincoln, whose canonization had just been proclaimed (1218), and finally St. Thomas of Canterbury, were translated to more honourable tombs, with magnificent ceremonies, to witness which nobles and prelates came from foreign countries.

[1] There is a remarkable letter of Bishop Grosseteste, written in 1245, thirty years after the accession of Henry III., in which he quotes, in the king's own words, an account of his devotion to the Pope as his spiritual Father, and to the Church as his spiritual Mother, and his grateful recognition of the services rendered to him on his accession to the throne. "To them we will formally adhere both in prosperity and in adversity: on the day when we do not thus, we will consent to lose an eye or even our head; God forbid that anything separate us from devotion to our spiritual Father and Mother. For besides all the reasons which affect us in common with other Christian princes, we are above all others bound by one especial reason; for just after our father's death, while still of tender age, our kingdom being not only alienated from us, but even in arms against us, our Mother the Roman Church, through the agency of Cardinal Gualo, the legate in England, recovered this kingdom to be at peace and subject to us, and crowned us king, and raised us to the throne of the kingdom" (Ep. R. Grosseteste, cxvii. p. 338, *ap.* Luard, *loc. cit.*, p. 7).

In a council held at Oxford in the year 1222, Archbishop Langton caused several important canons or constitutions to be passed, regulating in a very minute manner the duties of the clergy, and providing for the restoration of decent and reverent worship. He died in 1228. It is said that the division of the Bible into chapters was his work.

Oxford and Cambridge.—In the midst of the religious famine which marked the reign of the late king, while the Church was ruthlessly pillaged and her ministers put to rebuke, there was more intellectual activity in the country than there had been for centuries. During the earlier ages of our history, the monasteries had been the chief seats of learning; writing-rooms or *scriptoria*, where the principal works of Latin literature were copied, lives of the saints compiled, the events of history chronicled, formed a part of every religious house. All our men of letters, with two exceptions, from Bede until the Norman Conquest, were clergymen, and principally monks. The Crusades gave a new impulse to the thirst for knowledge in Europe; a fresh fervour of study sprang up in the West from its contact with the more civilized East. English students formed a large element in the foreign schools which bore the name of Universities, and the scholars who lectured in every cloister in our own land drew crowds to their feet. Gradually a number of other schools had arisen, under the superintendence of the secular clergy; when collegiate institutions, like that founded by Harold at Waltham, were alienated from their original purposes to monastic uses, the deprived secular canons set up halls for teaching at convenient centres. It was probably through the fame of such men as Vacarius and Friar Bacon that Oxford, which already in Stephen's reign stood in the first rank of English towns, gained its reputation as a seat of learning. Throughout the peaceful reign of Henry II. it was quietly increasing in numbers and repute, the most famous and learned of English clergy were found within its walls. At the opening of the thirteenth century it was without a rival in our own country, and could compete with the greatest schools of the western world. When, in consequence of the disgraceful murder of three clerics in 1209, the whole body of students who had gathered round the chairs of its teachers dispersed, it is said their numbers amounted to three thousand. The incident which led to their dispersion was this. A student accidentally shot a woman while practising archery. He fled; but the townsmen took three of his fellow-students who occupied the same lodging, and by way of retaliation, with the sanction of King John, who was in the neighbourhood, hanged them, although they were ignorant of what had taken place. The indignant students, together with their masters, forsook the city. Some went to Reading, some to Cambridge, where they opened new colleges; according to Matthew Paris, not a single student remained in Oxford. For five years the city was under a cloud; at length the townsmen were released from excommunication by the Papal Legate Nicholas, on condition of observing certain rules favourable to the students. Oxford was once more re-peopled with scholars, but the colleges at Cambridge remained, and were added to by pious founders. Thus that city also grew into note as a seat of learning.

Dominicans and Franciscans, 1220.—It was about the year 1220 when the Dominican friars first arrived in England. Archbishop Langton received them with cordiality, and took them into his favour. In Oxford they were welcomed with enthusiasm, and were soon surrounded with eager disciples. The popularity they gained by their preaching led to their appointment as theological lecturers, and through their influence the study of theology, which had been almost superseded by that of the canon law, resumed its old supremacy in the schools. About two years after the settlement of the Dominicans at Oxford, a band of Franciscan brethren landed on these shores. These zealous labourers—working for the physical as well as the spiritual necessities of their suffering fellow-men, devoted to poverty, not allowed to erect any but the meanest dwellings, forbidden at the outset to possess books or materials for study—quickly secured a footing in Canterbury and London, and subsequently in the Universities. With the Dominicans, they became a great power in the Church, not merely by moving the laity of every class, particularly the denizens of towns, to confession and repentance, but by stirring up the clergy to efforts after better things.

St. Edmund of Canterbury.—One of those who were mainly instrumental in organizing the nascent University of Oxford was Edmund Rich, afterwards Archbishop of Canterbury and canonized saint. As a boy of twelve years old, he came from Abingdon, his native town, to be educated in a school belonging to the abbey of Eynsham, where his father had retired from the world. His mother was a pious woman, too poor to give her son anything but the hair-shirt he promised to wear every Wednesday, but Edmund was no poorer than his neighbours. He plunged at once into the nobler life of the place, its ardour for knowledge, its mystic piety. It is recorded that when a youth he bound himself to the service of the Blessed Virgin by an eternal compact. He caused two rings of gold to be made, bearing the inscription *Hail Mary*, and secretly, perhaps when at eventide the shadows were gathering in the church of St. Mary, and the crowd of teachers and students had left its aisles, the boy stood before the image of our Lady on the north side of the altar, and, placing a ring on its finger, chose Mary for his bride. That ring could never be withdrawn from the finger of the statue, and all his life long Edmund wore the fellow to it; he expressed a wish to be buried with it, so as to carry to the tomb the pledge of his fidelity to his sacred espousals. On his deathbed he acknowledged that as often as he had in sincerity of heart invoked the aid of the gracious Virgin, she had obtained for him a happy issue out of his temptations, consolation under his persecutions, and a joyful remedy in tribulations.

After completing his education in Paris, where he achieved a great reputation, Edmund Rich became one of the most popular of Oxford lecturers, and contributed to obtain for the body of teachers and scholars that existed there, the corporate character afterwards conceded to them. To him the introduction of the logic of Aristotle is due, and he was the first to possess the title of M.A. in an English university. Ascetic in his life, contemptuous of worldly things, he weaned himself from the love of secular learning and entered the priesthood, but refused to accept the dignities and rich benefices offered him by Archbishop Langton. In 1227 his fame as a theologian caused him to be chosen by Pope Gregory IX. as one of the papal missionaries to preach the Crusade which had been proclaimed by Innocent III. at the Lateran Council. He acquitted himself of his task so well that as many as forty thousand combatants joined the ranks from England. When the see of Canterbury became vacant, Peter des Roches, the chancellor of the kingdom, an unscrupulous and crafty prelate, proposed a creature of his own; but the monks, fearing lest the whole spiritual authority should pass into his hands, refused to elect him, and chose their prior. The Pope, however, rejected this candidate, on account of his age and rusticity. A third nominee he also dismissed; then, well aware how necessary an enlightened and zealous primate was at that time, he ordered the monks to elect Edmund Rich, who was at that time canon of Salisbury.

Edmund reluctantly accepted this dignity. He felt that his conscience would not suffer him to acquiesce in the disorders of the age, and that the gentleness of his character did not fit him for the stern duties of a reformer. In succeeding to the see of St. Anselm and St. Thomas, he inherited their labours and crosses, their unremitting struggle with the spirit of usurpation in high places. Not only was the power of the Crown opposed to him, with its haughty pretensions and impatience of ecclesiastical control, not only were the rude and overbearing barons bent on defying his authority, but, harder still to be borne, the spirit of the world had invaded the Church herself. Relaxation of discipline had crept into the cloister, and was fast undermining the monastic life. Mercenary foreigners, intruded into English benefices, sought only their own gain, instead of feeding the flock of Christ. The people were burdened with heavy taxation, the prelates and clergy being further crippled by the heavy subsidies levied on them to relieve the Pope's necessities.

When a man of Edmund's simple rectitude and elevation of character saw himself face to face with such abuses, he must needs attack and grapple with them. At the time of his elevation to the primacy (1233) Henry III. had just escaped from the trammels of a long minority. He loved to surround himself with foreigners, with whom he constantly endeavoured to fill every office in Church and State. Although he was far from possessing the ungovernable temper of his grandfather, or the irreligious and sad disposition of his father, he was weak and wilful, and, like them, determined to stretch the royal prerogative, and usurp rights which brought him into conflict with the Church. The archbishop addressed to him a strong remonstrance on his neglect of his subjects, the preference he showed for aliens, his practice of keeping episcopal sees and benefices vacant, and otherwise despoiling the Church. By a threat of excommunication, he compelled him to dismiss Peter des Roches, his unworthy counsellor, together with his adherents.

When the king found that the primate was not to be moved from the attitude he had at the outset assumed of defending the rights of clergy and laity against royal oppression, he took the resolution of asking the Pope to send a legate to England. He rightly calculated that the straits to which the Holy

Father was driven by the Emperor Frederick would naturally lead him to conciliate the King of England as much as possible, in order that he might consent to the demand of a tenth of the ecclesiastical revenues which was made on behalf of the see of Rome. In mediaeval times the constitution of the Church took, in a great measure, the feudal form of the secular kingdom, with the Pope for sovereign, the bishops for barons, the clergy for the under-vassals. As the civil ruler demanded subsidies in case of need from his barons, so did the Supreme Pontiff from the priesthood. Year after year the English Church was called upon to contribute to the support of the Holy See—at first because of the Crusades, on the ground that the recovery of Palestine was an object of interest to every Christian, and that as the barons shed their blood in the cause, the clerks should contribute from their revenues. During the long and calamitous contest occasioned by the abominable behaviour of the Emperor Frederick, large subsidies became a necessity. It was right that the needs of the Head of the Church should be supplied by contributions of the whole of Christendom, since his independence was essential to their interests. Yet the increase of appeals for aid roused strong opposition in England, for the nation was already heavily taxed, the king having neglected no means that could be devised to replenish his exchequer. It was on the pretext of raising the money so greatly needed that the Legate was now sent to England, although Henry, who wished to reserve to himself the privilege of levying tribute from the clergy, had with reluctance consented to this tax. His chief motive in desiring the Legate to be sent was the idea that his superior ecclesiastical authority would act as a counterpoise to the archbishop's influence, and serve to nullify his opposition to the royal measures. St. Edmund entered an energetic protest against the presence of the Legate. It proved, as he anticipated, no small embarrassment to him. Although the Legate acted with discretion, yet his authority in virtue of his office enabled him to supersede the archbishop's authority, to annul his decisions and revoke his sentences. At one time when the difficulties of his position pressed hard upon St. Edmund, it was said that St. Thomas of Canterbury appeared to him, bidding him be steadfast and act manfully. Taking his hand, he passed it over his head, that he might feel the scar of his fatal wound, bidding Edmund suffer death as he did, rather than relinquish any of the liberties and franchizes of Holy Church.

St. Edmund's persistent protests were unavailing. "Seeing," says the chronicler, Matthew Paris, "the Church in England to be day by day more trodden underfoot, robbed of her possessions, despoiled of her liberties—life became unsupportable to him, and he could not endure to see the evils which were upon the land." Mortified and baffled on every side; persecuted by the bad; misrepresented by the good; supported by hardly any, even of those who were bound by their sacred office to support him; opposed by the monks, who sought to emancipate themselves from episcopal jurisdiction, and by the bishops, who resisted his attempt to make a visitation of the diocese of London—he presently withdrew from the unequal contest. Like St. Thomas and Stephen Langton, he took refuge within the abbey of Pontigny, which thus for the third time opened its hospitable portals to shelter a persecuted archbishop of Canterbury, forced to exile himself from his native land. Death followed quickly on his flight; he expired at Soissy within twelve months after quitting these shores.

CHAPTER XIII.

GRIEVANCES OF THE CHURCH IN ENGLAND.

Grosseteste, Bishop of Lincoln.—Amongst the suffragans whom St. Edmund had consecrated, there was one as firm as the saint himself, and as staunch an upholder of the rights and privileges of the Church. Robert Grosseteste, who had been made Bishop of Lincoln on account of his scholarly attainments and sanctity of life, was of a sterner character and bolder nature than his primate, and consequently better qualified than he was to initiate and carry out the greatly needed reforms. On being raised to the episcopate in 1235, he made the repression of the abuses that prevailed in his diocese—the largest and most populous in England—his first and immediate aim; his second, that of opposing and preventing the introduction of unfit persons into ecclesiastical offices. To accomplish each of these no little vigour and resolution was demanded. Grosseteste possessed both. He was, as we have said, a man of learning and virtue, and what is more, a man of energy and action. The relaxation of discipline that prevailed may be gathered from his constitutions; they forbid the clergy to haunt taverns, to gamble, to share in drinking bouts; they order them to check the debauchery and riot of the barons, and put a stop to the practice of holding sports and plays in the churches and churchyards. But in the execution of his episcopal duties he was confronted by his own chapter. The canons refused his visitation, on the plea that from the foundation of the cathedral they were exempt from episcopal scrutiny. He had a long suit with them, and the cause was decided in his favour by a definite sentence of the Holy See, establishing the right of bishops to visit their chapters.

The impoverishment consequent on the demands of king and Pope, the negligence and worldliness of the ecclesiastical authorities, the decline of monastic orders into rich landowners, the disuse of preaching and the non-residence of many parish priests, had robbed the clergy of their zeal and lessened their influence. To remedy this evil and introduce a new element into the spiritual life of the diocese, Grosseteste summoned the friars to his aid. The number of these itinerant preachers, who went about amongst the people and appealed to the poor and outcasts, had lately been augmented by the arrival in this country of the Augustinians and Carmelites.[1]

[1] The order of Mount Carmel has peculiar claims on the interest of English Catholics. England was the first European country that gave shelter to its monks when they were driven out of the Holy Land by the Saracens. In England the devotion to the scapular took its origin and received its first extension through an Englishman, St. Simon Stock. It is believed that on July 16, 1250, in the Carmelite Chapel near Cambridge, the ever-blessed Virgin gave him the scapular with her own hands, as a special sign of her favour. The saint invested many laymen with it, amongst others several royal personages—Edward I., for instance, and his unfortunate son, Edward II.

Their preaching was most successful, so that the name of " the Pope's militia " was given them. This was partly because Pope Alexander IV. declared them to be subject to the Holy See, an arrangement by no means acceptable to the parochial clergy, still less to the bishops, of whose authority it rendered them independent.

Bishop Grosseteste soon came into collision with the king. It was the custom of the Crown to withdraw clerics from their ecclesiastical duties to act as ministers, judges, or ambassadors, or, on the other hand, to nominate to benefices royal favourites holding secular offices. This Grosseteste could not tolerate ; and when Henry bade him appoint a forest justiciary to the cure of a church, he firmly declined to comply with the command, unless the clerk should resign his office. In his transactions with the Court of Rome, the prelate exhibited a like inflexibility of character. No man ever possessed a more profound veneration for the See of Peter, or a more exalted idea of its prerogatives. He yielded implicit obedience to its decretals, and maintained as the cause of God the immunity of the clergy from secular jurisdiction. Yet, acting under a strong sense of spiritual responsibility, he did not hesitate to resist unworthy appointments, even when emanating from the authority he venerated so much. Neither Pope nor legate could prevail on him to institute foreign ecclesiastics presented to benefices in his diocese, if he judged them unfit for their duties. When the Nuncio sent a brief whereby a nephew of Innocent IV., a mere boy, was promoted to a prebendal stall in Lincoln Cathedral, the bishop steadfastly refused to admit him, on the ground that, as the order was contrary to the good of the Church and the welfare of souls, he did not consider it as emanating from the Pontiff. The Pope listened to his objections, and withdrew the obnoxious nominee.

Grosseteste did not shrink from carrying out the Pope's demands for subsidies, for he knew that, when in need of aid, the Pope had a right to the goods of the clergy. And when the king wrote to the bishop, blaming him for having undertaken to collect a tax laid on the clergy, consisting of one-third from the resident, one-half from the non-resident, of their revenues for three years, a tax which the king had prohibited, Grosseteste replied that they were bound to assist their spiritual Father, then in exile and suffering persecution (the Papal Court was then still in exile at Lyons). The same view was taken by many noble-minded churchmen, who, although they were friends of constitutional freedom, upheld the duty of supporting the Papacy during its struggle with the emperor. Yet Grosseteste, zealous advocate as he was of the papal claims, did not raise any objection to the reading of a letter of complaint against the exactions of the Legate, by the representatives of the English clergy, at a council held at Lyons, in which it was stated that, in consequence of the suspension of advowsons, Italian ecclesiastics drew over 50,000 marks a year from this country. In fact, some years later, he addressed an indignant protest to the Roman Court, inveighing strongly against the want of zeal in remedying existing evils, and the providing for the Church in England pastors who devoured instead of feeding the flock. "Provided the facts were such as he alleged, there was nothing in this which did not consist with a fervent acknowledgement of the supremacy. The conduct of Grosseteste is illustrative of the boldness, the honesty, and the holiness which gained for him the veneration of his age and almost obtained his canonization. In his utterances we may feel assured that we have reflected the creed which the best of his contemporaries professed. Now in the very letter which contains his refusal to induct into his diocese the papal nominee, he says that to 'the most Holy Apostolic See all power has been entrusted for edification, not destruction, by the Holy of Holies our Lord Jesus Christ'; and that he is ready to obey all apostolic mandates which do not lose their character of apostolicity by being manifestly wrong.' In another letter he says that 'to the Holy Roman Church is due from every son of the Church the most devoted obedience, the most reverential veneration, the most fervent love, the most submissive fear;' because it is to the Universal Church what the sun is to the heavens. Such language is continually occurring in his letters."[1] Grosseteste lived in a time of great abuses, which he valiantly combated, and Protestants on account of this quote him as an opponent of the Holy See. But Mr. Luard, the learned editor of his *Letters*, remarks (p. 20), "No one can exceed Grosseteste in his reverence for the papal power and for Innocent IV. in particular." Grosseteste died in 1253. In the same year England was bereaved of another holy bishop and champion of the Church's liberties, Richard de la Wych, Bishop of Chichester. The friend of St. Edmund, he had been the com-

[1] Fr. Smith's *Alleged Antiquity of Anglicanism*, ch. i. See also *Robert Grosseteste, Bishop of Lincoln*, by Mgr. Croke Robinson (C.T.S.).

panion of his exile, the sharer of his sufferings, and had, like him, incurred the enmity of the king by his strenuous resistance to royal oppression.

The authority of the papacy during the pontificate of Innocent III. and his immediate successors, was recognized as undoubtingly as ever, but an unfortunate quarrel arose which in some respects embittered Englishmen against certain aspects of papal administration. With the Popes, by common acknowledgement, lay the right to supersede the right of presentation to English benefices, the patrons of which held their right of patronage only by consent of the supreme authority, and in the cases in which the supreme authority did not see fit to interpose and exercise the right itself. So much was acknowledged, but the displeasure felt was over the papal exercise of this right of supersession. When foreigner after foreigner was appointed to English benefices by the Holy See, many English ecclesiastics began to think that the necessities of their own land were being subordinated, not so much to the supreme interests of the Universal Church, but rather to the worldly interests of a foreign nation. How far this feeling was well grounded is not so easy to determine: Englishmen are proverbial grumblers as to all that touches their pockets. But it is well to remember that there is another side to the case; and that the Popes were, as a rule, actuated by other motives than ambition and avarice. The correspondence between Innocent IV. and Grosseteste is a witness to this.

Simon de Montfort and the Barons.—The insurrection of the barons against the king under Simon de Montfort, the Earl of Leicester, who had

been an intimate friend of Grosseteste, met with no
opposition from the bishops. On the contrary, when,
after the annulling of the Provisions of Oxford
(measures of reform which the barons had drawn up
in 1258, and forced the king to accept) civil war
broke out, Walter de Cantelupe, the Bishop of
Worcester, after doing all he could to make peace,
openly joined the cause, and threw in his lot with
the Earl of Leicester. The victory of Lewes placed
the earl for a time at the head of the State. He
was anxious for the welfare of the Church; under his
brief ascendency the sphere of ecclesiastical jurisdiction was enlarged, and three bishops were appointed
to inquire into grievances. Cardinal Guido, whom the
Pope sent to restore peace and obtain the release of
the captive king, was refused admission into the
realm; he cited the bishops who were the partisans
of Leicester to appear before him in France, and
sent them back to publish a sentence of excommunication against the barons. The papal rescript was
seized and destroyed, whether against the bearer's
will or not it is impossible to say, by the people
of the Cinque Ports. Seeing any further effort to
set matters right would be useless, the legate returned
to Rome, where he was almost immediately elected
Pope. The earl's government was of short duration:
the next year he was defeated and slain in the battle
of Evesham, and order was again restored. The
legate sent over from Rome suspended the bishops
who had favoured the insurrectionary movement;
the Bishop of Worcester died shortly after, and the
others journeyed to Rome, and there effected their
reconciliation. The legate also did his utmost to
bring the rebellion to an end by ecclesiastical cen-

sures, to re-establish discipline, and to put a stop to the practice of holding more than one benefice.

A period of comparative quiet ensued, despite occasional murmurs; the English nation was devoted as ever to the Holy See, and took pride in being denominated its special daughter. By the Pope's injunction, a tenth part of ecclesiastical revenues was paid to the king by the clergy, who were not unwilling to contribute to the expenditure of their sovereign when the money was not required for foolish schemes of foreign aggression. This subsidy seems to have been partly intended for the crusade in which Prince Edward was about to embark; it may also have been destined to aid in the rebuilding of Westminster Abbey, which was completed in 1269. This edifice was said to surpass all other churches of that day in Christendom.

Edward I., 1272. Spiritual and Temporal Jurisdiction.—The reign of Edward I., who succeeded his father in 1272, is chiefly memorable in ecclesiastical history on account of the border-line between spiritual and temporal jurisdiction being defined in formal documents. The Parliament of 1295—said to be the first complete representative parliament, inasmuch as burgesses and knights of the shire were admitted into the Great Council—was also marked by the presence of the clergy. The king had twice before summoned the higher clergy to take their part in the national government, but not till then was the order issued that two representatives of the parochial clergy were to be chosen from each diocese, to meet with the prelates and representatives of cathedral chapters to "vote for the honour of the Church, the peace of the kingdom, and the comfort of the king." Although forced in Edward's reign to comply with this summons, the clergy sat apart, and their refusal to vote supplies in any but their own provincial synods, or convocations, of Canterbury and York, left the Crown without a motive for insisting on their continued attendance. Their presence therefore became a mere formality; by the end of the fifteenth century it had fallen into desuetude.

Archbishop Peckham and St. Thomas of Hereford. An early act of Edward's reign had checked the acquisition of property by the Church, by passing the Statute of Mortmain. The object of this was to prohibit the alienation by purchase, by gift, or by bequest, under pain of forfeiture, of lands to religious bodies, who were incapable of performing the feudal service due from it to the Crown. In this it is difficult to see more than a jealousy of the rapid growth of ecclesiastical estates, which, displeasing as it was to the barons, who were themselves characterized by a growing passion for the possession of land, was probably beneficial to the country at large. Military service was rendered by Church fees as rigidly as by lay, while the churchmen were the better landlords.[1] This Statute was unsuccessfully opposed by Archbishop Peckham, a Franciscan friar, who had been raised to the see of Canterbury in 1279. Through his action, however, a writ was obtained which defined the limits of ecclesiastical jurisdiction, and ascertained the areas proper to the secular and the spiritual courts. This writ, which had the force of a statute, gave the ecclesiastical judge the right to commit any excommunicated person to prison until satisfaction

[1] Cf. Green, *Short History*, p. 166.

was made to the Church. The zeal of Archbishop Peckham is said to have led him to pass the bounds of his authority over his suffragans, and to lay upon them injunctions which they took as encroaching on their rights. What their grievances were is not recorded, but they were considered of such importance that St. Thomas, Bishop of Hereford, was deputed by the other bishops to lay them before Pope Nicholas IV. This prelate was the eldest son of Baron Cantelupe, Earl of Pembroke. In the reign of Henry III. he had been made chancellor of the kingdom; Edward I. allowed him to retire from this office, whereupon he resumed his studies at Oxford, and in 1275 was chosen to fill the see of Hereford. He proved a resolute defender of the Church property and privileges against some of the neighbouring earls, and was successful in his appeal against his primate. On the return journey he died in Tuscany. The fame of his sanctity had spread far and wide, and there was an immediate desire for his canonization. Amongst the most earnest petitioners to the Holy See for this was King Edward I. himself, who pleaded his personal knowledge of the saint, and the innumerable miracles wrought by him.

Winchelsey resists arbitrary Taxation. — During the early part of this reign the clergy had no cause to complain of excessive taxation. The financial difficulties, however, in which the conquest of Wales and Scotland involved the king, induced him to employ every means to replenish his exchequer. In the view of undertaking a crusade he claimed, with the authorization of the Pope, a tenth part of all ecclesiastical revenues for six years. Somewhat later, when forced into war with France,

Edward seized the treasures stored in the abbeys and cathedrals, and demanded from the clergy half of their annual income. So terrible was his wrath when they resisted this exaction, that the Dean of St. Paul's, who stood forth to remonstrate, dropped dead of sheer terror at his feet. For protection the clergy appealed to the same authority which the king had employed to enforce payment of the tenth. In consequence of this, Boniface VIII., who then filled the Chair of Peter, published the bull *Clericis laicos*, forbidding the clergy of any Christian country to grant, or the secular power to take, taxes from the revenues of benefices without the papal sanction. The archbishop at once promulgated this bull through the Bishop of London. However much he feared to provoke the king, he knew that it was his duty to obey the Pope. "Wishing," his letter to the bishops began, "as is our duty, to execute what is commanded, we enjoin," &c. But the king was urgent: he seized the temporalities, and outlawed the whole body of monks and clergy of the Southern Province. This decree of outlawry was no dead letter; the monks found themselves reduced to beggary. The bishops assembled in council; some, "courting royal and temporal favour," desired to yield, in spite of the apostolic prohibition. But Winchelsey, "a man whom the ancient Church reverenced for his virtues, and sought to canonize,"[1] was not to be moved. He wrote, however, to Boniface VIII. with the most profound profession of obedience and loyalty, begging leave for the clergy to grant a subsidy to the king, on the ground that there was real reason for it. The Pope did not censure a

[1] Smith, *Alleged Antiquity of Anglicanism*, chap. i.

voluntary concession, and the king's demand was compounded with by the grant of a fifth. Here is an extract from Winchelsey's letter to Pope Boniface:

"The Supreme Governor of the world has ordained the Apostolic See to preside on high over the hierarchy of the same world. We, albeit unworthy, assumed into a share of the pastoral solicitude—derived from the citadel of the summit of the Apostolic See, and our Mother the Roman Church, like streams from their source—present lawful petitions, not presumptuously, nor unseasonably, nor arrogantly, but with lowly devotion (*subjectissima devotione*), to which, in spirit prostrate on our knees, we beseech you to give a favourable hearing" (Wilkins, *Concilia*, iii. 233).

Later on, wider measures of arbitrary taxation which were resorted to by the king, provoked general discontent, and led to the assignment of limits to the royal prerogative. The clergy and barons combined together decreed in council that the Crown should relinquish the right to levy taxes without the consent of the nation. Thus the privileges now enjoyed by the country were won from the monarch principally by the patriotic action of churchmen. It will be remembered that Archbishop Langton framed the Great Charter against the abuse of royal authority; Archbishop Winchelsey was the means of fixing the liberty of the subject on a firm and constitutional basis. The Church was in these turbulent times the only counterpoise to the power of the Crown and of the baronage. Her salutary and beneficent influence seemed to keep in check the unruly instincts of the great and powerful, while it alleviated the lot and brightened the days of the toiling serfs.

Winchelsey delated at Rome.—A short time before the death of Edward I., a remonstrance addressed to him by Archbishop Winchelsey, in consequence of the prolongation of the war in Scotland, seems to have recalled to his mind the resistance that prelate had formerly made to his unjust exactions. Edward persuaded himself that he had been hardly dealt with; by representing that he had been deprived of his rights, and that the oath he took on that occasion had been forced from him, he induced the Pope, as over-lord, to absolve him from his obligations. Not content with this, he proceeded to take vengeance on Winchelsey, who was delated at Rome for treasonable intentions, and was accordingly summoned by the Pope to answer to the indictment. Upon investigation he was acquitted, but did not return to England until Edward I. was laid in the grave.

Edward II., 1307.—The weak character of the next monarch caused his reign to be a period of trouble and disorganization. The usual resistance was made to the papal claims for pecuniary aid; while, on the other hand, Archbishop Winchelsey, by the Pope's command, laid a list of ecclesiastical grievances before the king. The complaint was that the collectors of the Pope's tax were impeded in their business; that laymen exercised jurisdiction over spiritual persons; that the property of sees, when in the royal custody, had been grievously wasted; and that the tribute granted by King John to the Holy See had not been paid for fifteen years. The king temporized, promising to remedy these evils. The next year the archbishop and six of his suffragans were chosen to form part of a commission, called "ordainers," to carry out a system of reform. First among the objects which the ordainers swore to promote was the increase of the honour and welfare of the Church; the interference with the spiritual courts, which were to decide in all spiritual cases—such as cases of neglect of churches, perjury, non-payment of tithes, and the like—was strictly forbidden.

Winchelsey died in 1313. Like his great predecessors, St. Thomas and St. Edmund, he was always remarkable for his devotion to the Blessed Virgin. He renewed the injunction that the Conception of Our Lady should be observed as a festival; at every interval of leisure he was found engaged in reciting the rosary.

Suppression of the Knight Templars.—One of the first acts of his successor, Archbishop Reynolds, was to effect the transfer of the property belonging to the Order of Templars. This celebrated order was established in 1118 for the purpose of protecting pilgrims when journeying on the roads which led to Jerusalem. From a band of nine knights their number increased speedily to many hundreds. Their military services and brilliant exploits excited the gratitude and admiration of Christendom; gifts and bequests of money and lands flowed in upon them. Whether they were corrupted by the acquirement of wealth and power, or were the victims of calumny, at any rate the Holy See judged fit to suppress them. In England, as in other countries, they were arrested, and their estates were confiscated; the mildness of the proceedings against them in this country contrasting favourably with the cruelties practised in France. The Council of Vienne had directed that the property of the abolished order, for the sake of preserving it to the purpose for which it was originally destined, should be given over to another military order, that of the Knights Hospitallers. Edward postponed the execution of this decree, for he and his nobles, and even some of the prelates, had appropriated to themselves the tempting spoil. Orders came from Rome that it must be relinquished; yet the archbishop could not induce the king to comply until the Parliament expressly declared that the Pope must be obeyed, and disobedience was punished with ecclesiastical penalties.

Edward III., 1327. Exchequer exhausted by Wars.—The closing years of this unhappy reign offer nothing of importance in regard to ecclesiastical affairs. But when Edward III. had ascended the throne, and shaken off the tutelage of the Queen Regent and her unworthy favourite, the Crown again became involved in disputes with the spiritual powers. The king's ministers were mostly churchmen, whose authority was required to restore tranquillity in the kingdom. Stratford, Bishop of Winchester (who in 1333 was raised to the see of Canterbury), and his brother, the Bishop of Chichester, held for eleven years the post of chancellor, and were obliged to exert themselves to raise money to maintain the war in France, into which the young king had recklessly plunged. At the commencement of this war, to defray the expenses of the expedition, we are told (Spelman's *History of Sacrilege*, p. 192) that the king took the treasure laid up in churches for the defence of the Holy Land, and seized the wealth of monasteries, chiefly those peopled by foreign monks, to pay his soldiers, selling their lands to his subjects.

When the wars were ended, touched with remorse, he granted them all back, an act which the historian calls one of singular piety, though no restitution was made of the proceeds, which had been enjoyed for twenty-three years. For a time the English arms were not successful, and the funds on which the king counted were not forthcoming. Compelled to conclude a truce in 1340, Edward returned to England in high displeasure. The chancellor was displaced, and several other officers of state were imprisoned or fined. The archbishop, who disapproved of the lavish expenditure of money and counselled peace, was, with his brother, marked for arrest; but the king was reminded that a papal constitution forbade him to arrest a bishop. He then published a letter, called the *famosus libellus*, copies of which were sent all over the country, setting forth his accusations against the archbishop; and when Parliament met in the following year, attempts were made to prevent him from taking his seat in the Chamber of Peers. Edward also complained to the Pope, but his charges were too vague to merit formal notice, and, urged by nobles and prelates, he consented to a reconciliation.

The Black Death.—In 1349 a terrible pestilence, known as the Black Death, appeared in England. The eastern counties suffered most from this awful visitation. Not a town or village was spared; more than half the population of the land was swept away. Throughout the country tillage ceased; the industries were paralyzed, the courts of justice were closed; the living scarce sufficed to bury the dead. When, after five months, the scourge was removed, the mortality amongst the priests had been so enormous that the country parish churches were mostly destitute of service. It was reckoned that upwards of eight hundred parishes lost their pastor, and about eighty-three of them were deprived a second time. Some two thousand secular and regular clergy perished thus in the space of a few months. This constituted a severe strain on the reserve force, and the bishops knew not how to supply the deficiency. The difficulty was increased by the mortality amongst the prelates themselves, six suffragans of Canterbury having died of the plague. Their places were filled up by the Pope with "good clerics and doctors"; and a vast number of laymen, it is said, whose wives had perished in the pestilence, presented themselves as candidates for holy orders. Under such circumstances it appears inevitable that there would be a deterioration in the character and fitness of the newly appointed incumbents. It must be owned that a large proportion of the men who presented themselves at that time for admission into the priesthood were of an inferior class, and less well prepared for the ministry than their predecessors, yet nothing is recorded damaging to their reputation. The disastrous effects of the plague were, however, felt in the relaxation of discipline in monasteries; the good fathers, ever zealous in tending the sick and shriving the dying, fell so fast that the cloisters were all but depeopled; nine-tenths of the inmates found a place in the necrology. The religious life of the people suffered severely from the lack of priests; "a religious paralysis," as Dom Gasquet calls it, ensued, and the demoralization of the lower orders of the people was the consequence of the removal of clerical control.

Quarrel about Papal Dues.—The dreadful havoc wrought by this visitation had also a marked effect on the social life of the period. A third part of the land lay uncultivated ; rents were reduced and wages raised, and the whole population, especially the small landowners, were greatly impoverished. Heavily taxed as they still were for the expenses of foreign war, the additional monies levied for the support of the Papacy seemed an intolerable burden. The payment of Peter's-pence, originally fixed, on its introduction by the Anglo-Saxon kings, at the tax of a penny on every householder whose chattels were valued above thirty pence, had by custom been fixed at an annual sum. Thus it remained the same after the lapse of centuries, notwithstanding the augmentation of the national wealth and the number of the inhabitants. The Pontiffs, deeming the annual amount, about £200, inadequate, urged that it should be collected in the manner of the original grant; this demand was, however, strenuously and successfully resisted, as was also the claim made by the Holy Father for the payment of the arrears of the annual tribute promised by King John. During the latter part of Edward I.'s reign this payment had been neglected; but in the reign of his successor the amount that was owing was duly sent to Rome. The tribute was also at first collected under Edward III., until on account of the expenses of the French wars it was again allowed to lapse, and for thirty-three years no payment was made. The claim was renewed by Pope Urban V., who was desirous of removing the papal residence from Avignon to Rome. The exhausted state of his exchequer forced him to apply for pecuniary assistance to the nations of Christendom, and, remembering that the tribute agreed upon had not been paid by England, he naturally called upon the king for the arrears due. The matter was referred to Parliament; but unfortunately the Holy Father was a Frenchman, and in consequence of the war with France, his nationality made him unpopular in England. Besides this, the prolonged residence of the Papal Court at Avignon had tended to make men regard the Pope in the light of a subject of the French king. On the pretext, therefore, that it was contrary to the oath taken by King John and every English sovereign at his coronation, to place himself and his people under feudal subjection to the Holy See, without the consent of Parliament, the demands of the Pope were rejected by Parliament. This decision was quite unjust, seeing that Parliament did not exist in John's days, and, as we have shown, his cession of the crown was made by the advice and with the consent of the Great Council of the Barons. It was, however, considered as conclusive, and the claim seems thenceforth to have become obsolete.

Papal Provisions.—In addition to the demands for money made from time to time in the name of the Holy See, which, just though they were and necessary for the support of the Papal Curia, caused considerable irritation in England, there was another cause which excited discontent. This was the system of provisions, or direct nominations by the Pope to vacant sees and benefices. In order to explain this, the reader must be reminded that in early and mediæval times the bishop had a national as well as a diocesan side, national as well as diocesan responsibilities. He was a feudal lord, seised of extensive lands, upon the vassals of which the king was often dependent for his troops and service (Stubbs, *Constitutional History*, vol. ii. p. 292). The Crown bestowed on the Church

Grievances of the Church in England. 257

endowment of lands, and even cities, for the maintenance of the bishoprics in Saxon times—witness the case of Birinus of Dorchester (Bede, bk. iii, ch. 7), and of St. Edward of Winchester. Prelates, too, often held posts of national trust and influence at the court, consequently their selection was a matter of national not merely of ecclesiastical importance. It would have been unjust and unwise had the choice been left entirely to a small group of monks or canons who might form the diocesan chapter, and could hardly be expected to see beyond local interests. The king, therefore, very properly required that such a functionary should not be elected without his knowledge and approval, so that he might see that at least no person hostile to his interests was raised to a post which would give him lordship over his subjects and a seat in his council. Hence the right of granting a *congé d'élire*, and of royal assent as the lawful part of the sovereign in filling up episcopal vacancies.

It was customary for the chapter, on receiving the *congé d'élire*, to elect the future bishop, and present him first to the king, then to the metropolitan, for approval. In the case of an archbishop, the name of the person elected was sent to the Pope for confirmation. It was this confirmation by Pope or primate which gave to the canonically elect his spiritual jurisdiction. When it had been granted, the new prelate was consecrated, and paid homage to the king, who then delivered over to him the temporalities pertaining to the bishopric which, during the vacancy, passed under wardenship of the king. This, the vicarious or *pallium* method of instituting bishops to English sees, whereby the Holy See granted to the primates of Canterbury and York the power to act as his vicars, was the rule until the middle of the thirteenth century. The practice then began for the king to send with the *congé d'élire* a letter signifying the individual he would accept, thus virtually superseding the right of the chapter to elect as they saw fit. A letter was also written to Rome, in which the king endeavoured to secure the acceptance of his nominee.

Perceiving that this mode of procedure tended to enslave the English Church to the Crown, as it gave the sovereign the chief voice in the appointment of a bishop, and that the kings were in the habit of availing themselves of any pretext for postponing the election for the sake of appropriating the revenues of the see during as long a period as possible, the Popes gradually took the appointments to vacant prelacies into their own hands, and directly, out of the fulness of the apostolic power (*ex plenitudine apostolicae potestatis*)—as the royal writs allow—provided bishops to fill the English sees by what are known as Bulls of Provision. "When a see became vacant, a most exhaustive and searching inquiry was made into its state and condition, and into the merits and qualifications of the person proposed as a successor, by a special commissioner appointed *ad hoc* by the Consistory. A copy of his report, called a Proposition, was placed in the hands of each Cardinal summoned to the Consistory, and in their assembled presence the Pope formally pronounced the sentence of appointment. The Bull, or Brief of Provision, was then drawn up and despatched to the newly-appointed bishop, so that in virtue of it he might receive episcopal consecration, and claim possession of his diocese. Thus five things were involved in the full appointment of a prelate by Provision: (1) presentation; (2) preconization in Consistory; (3) despatch of the bull; (4) consecration and enthronization; (5) restoration of temporalities." The right of nominating to sees rendered vacant by translation had always been reserved to himself by the Supreme Pontiff, on the ground that he alone had the power to sanction a divorce between the bishop and his diocese.

The English monarchs, far from denying the providing power of the Pope, occasionally besought him to exercise it in their favour, sometimes out of a genuine belief in the fitness of the person, sometimes to avoid the necessity of remunerating out of their own exchequer, or with the lands of the Crown, those who had served them; and they frequently in this manner obtained preferment for their own chaplains and friends. Time after time, in the history of every English diocese, we read that the Holy See quashed the elections made by chapters, or over-ruled the sovereign's nomination, and appointed more suitable candidates to the bishoprics, even when the king refused his royal assent, and withheld the temporalities. The case of Richard of Canterbury, in 1174; of Langton, in 1205; of St. Edmund, in 1232; of Peckham, 1270, are a few instances in which the Pope set aside the royal nominee.

It was not so much the provisions to bishoprics that caused general irritation in England as the provisions to inferior benefices. Already in the episcopate of St. Edmund loud complaints were heard on account of the nomination by the Pope of Italian ecclesiastics to English prebends, and in some parts of the kingdom the dwellings of these foreigners were attacked by the populace. "In 1240," Matthew Paris says, "the

Pope sent to the archbishop and bishops of Lincoln and Salisbury requiring them to provide for three hundred Romans in the first vacant benefices, and suspending them from giving away any benefices till that number was provided for." Many of the Italians [1] thus beneficed were ignorant of the language and of the customs of the people, and cared not to acquaint themselves with them, being concerned only with their own temporal interests: or else they were non-resident, and paid a substitute, spending out of the kingdom the remainder of the emolument derived from the post they nominally filled. Once and again a formal but humble remonstrance was laid before the Pope. It was alleged that "the best English livings and prebends were given to foreign, non-resident ecclesiastics, whereby the patrons were deprived of their accustomed rights, and the substance and treasure of the realm, which should be employed in the maintenance of churches, in works of charity to the honour of God and the benefit of the people, were carried out of the country to the prejudice of the king and of his subjects."

To this remonstrance the Popes replied that their predecessors had acted in a similar manner; that they had exercised their right with moderation; that in general they appointed none to benefices who were not the king's subjects,[2] and that when

---

[1] Grosseteste's Letters, p. 443.

[2] It must be remembered that a large majority of the foreigners thus appointed were not foreign to the dominions of the British sovereign on the continent, and that benefices abroad were often held by English ecclesiastics. Some of the most eminent churchmen of our history were "aliens" by birth or education; as St. Anselm and St. Hugh of Lincoln.

they broke that rule, it was in favour of those clergymen who were labouring in Rome and elsewhere at considerable expense and toil in the service of the English Church. "They asserted their duty of watching over the constitution of the sacred ministry and the consequent imprescriptible right to control appointments. They allowed readily, and even as a matter of their *jus commune*, the right of advowson to the founders of benefices, but as a grateful concession for the service rendered, and with the reserve of a concurrent right to be exercised by themselves when expedient in the interests of the Church. The presentation to the bishoprics, according to the *jus commune*, lay with the Chapters. In some countries, but, according to the Roman tradition, never in England, it had been granted by special privilege to the sovereigns; still always subject to the Pontiff's right to supersede."[1]

Thus on the question of *right* the papal action was unimpeachable. If we are to pass judgement on the mode in which the right was exercised in flooding the English benefices with so many foreigners, we shall probably be correct—after making deductions for the exaggerations of partizanship to which writers like Matthew of Paris were very subject—in thinking that the English had fair grounds of complaint. At the same time, much allowance must be made for the difficulties in which the Popes found themselves placed by what Innocent IV. called "the Five Wounds of the Church"—the Tartar invasion, the Greek schism, the progress of heresies, the state of the Holy Land, and the persecutions of the half-infidel emperor, Frederick II.

[1] Smith, *Alleged Antiquity of Anglicanism*, chap. i.

The Statutes of Provisors, 1351, and Præmunire, 1353.—The practice of the Holy Father in disposing of English benefices without regard to the patrons who considered themselves entitled to bestow them at their own discretion, was made matter of discussion in Parliament in the reign of Edward I.; yet little active opposition was offered to his power of appointing until 1343, when Edward III., on the plea that it was not right to suffer foreigners to be supported by the property of the Church at a time when all the wealth of the country was needed to carry on the war with France, determined himself to exercise what he chose to assert to be a prerogative of the Crown rather than of the See of Rome. He was supported by Parliament. In 1351 the Statute of Provisors was passed, enacting that all persons receiving papal provisions should be liable to imprisonment, and that all benefices to which the Pope appointed should be forfeit to the Crown. The immediate, and doubtless the intended effect of this ordinance, was to strengthen the royal power over the Church, not to increase the liberty of the Church; such is the invariable result when the rights of the Supreme Pontiff are resisted or set aside. This effect was still more apparent when, two years later, the Statute of *Præmunire* forbade the introduction into England without the king's consent of any papal bulls or grants which the State might choose to regard as concerned with temporalities appertaining to the Crown, under pain of outlawry, imprisonment, and banishment. It was moreover decreed, but without direct mention of the Papal Court, that any one of the king's subjects who should sue for redress in a foreign court, or induce another to do so, should be put out of the protection of the laws and should incur forfeiture of his goods.

It must not be supposed, says Canon Moyes (*Tablet*, Dec. 2, 1893), that these Statutes of Provisors and of *Præmunire* were passed in a mere spirit of hostility to the authority of the Pope, or that non-residence and plurality were confined to foreigners. Of the primacy of the Pontiff, or his spiritual jurisdiction, there was no question; both of these were repeatedly acknowledged by the Commons and by the king when expostulating as to the manner of its exercise. But it was contended that the Holy Father was surrounded by subtle and rapacious counsellors, who abused his liberality for their own emolument. The enactments we speak of were intended as a remedy for manifold abuses, chiefly caused by so-called Rome-runners—priests thronging to Rome and importuning the Holy See for benefices, to the prejudice of the diocesan and local patrons, and too often obtaining by misrepresentations what would have been denied them had the truth been known. On occasion of the confirmation of the Act in 1365, the preamble states that it is passed "in aid and comfort of our Holy Father the Pope, who would most willingly furnish a remedy, were he thereof rightly informed." The new statutes were accordingly put into execution; "and the same legislators," writes Lingard (vol. iii. p. 132), "who received with deference the doctrinal decisions and disciplinary regulations of their chief pastor, visited with the severest penalties of the law the clergymen who procured from him a benefice in opposition to the rights of the patron."

The Statutes of Provisors and *Præmunire* are often cited as a proof that the English people did not recognize the providing power of the Pope. Enough has been said to show that this was not the case. As a matter of fact, so much were the statutes disregarded, that the Papal Provisions were more numerous after the passing of them than before. The monarchs, as we have seen, though they were frequently offended by the rejection of their nominee, were not in reality hostile to the exercise of the papal power, and after the enactments were made, still asked the Popes to provide for the sees. The bishops formally protested against the statutes, Dr. Stubbs tells us,[1] also against any restriction of the papal prerogative; and both bishops and clergy in convocation petitioned repeatedly for their repeal.

Wealth of Ecclesiastics restricted.—Discontent with the condition of the Church in this country was also increased by the great wealth concentrated in the hands of some of the higher clergy. These often held a considerable number of preferments; William of Wykeham, the king's architect, afterwards Bishop of Winchester, held at one time, while Keeper of the Privy Seal, the Archdeaconry of Lincoln and no less than eleven prebends in various churches. All the great offices of state were, as a rule, filled by prelates and other clergymen, by a custom inherited from the days when laymen seldom possessed the desirable qualifications. Such a spectacle filled the minds of the laity with envy, and they broke forth into complaints. They saw with displeasure that while the nation groaned under heavy taxation, the temporalities of the state went to swell the revenues of ecclesiastical dignitaries. Hence in 1371 the Commons petitioned the

---

[1] *Constitutional History*, vol. iii. pp. 340, 342.

king that the government of the realm should no longer be carried on by churchmen. Laymen, it was alleged, were liable to be punished for maladministration by forfeiture of their goods and chattels; but the clergy were so secured by their privilege, that it was difficult to bring them to justice, whatever had been their conduct while they were in power. "From this great mischiefs and damages had arisen in times past, and more might happen in time to come." Therefore they requested the king that if laymen suitable and able could be found, they, and none other, might thenceforward be employed in the great offices of state. To this the king responded that he would consider the matter, and discuss it with his Council. The result was that a large concession was made to the desires of the petitioners. In consequence of their petition, the Chancellor of State, William of Wykeham, and the Treasurer, the Bishop of Exeter, resigned, their places being taken by laymen. In furtherance of this policy the entire Privy Council of the realm passed into the hands of the laity. In the following chapter it will be seen to what important issues the growing dissatisfaction which prompted this attack upon clerical ministers was destined to lead.

CHAPTER XIV.

WYCLIF AND THE LOLLARDS.

Gathering Clouds of Discontent.—From the earlier annals of the Church it will have been seen that in Anglo-Saxon times both kings and people, after their conversion to Christianity, yielded loyal submission to the See of Rome, prompt and unquestioning obedience to its every decree. In after years, the proud, domineering, restive character of the Normans brought them into frequent collision with the Head of Christendom, and rendered them apt to resist his authority, resent his claims, and encroach upon his rights. From the time of the Conquest there was always in England a party ready to charge the Holy See with a disposition to trench upon the privileges of the sovereign. Many of the nobility, and even some of the bishops, would fain have withdrawn from the rule of the Pope all matters which could under any pretext be considered as belonging to the temporal order. It is enough to refer to the aggressions of William Rufus and his successors, which were respectively withstood by St. Anselm, St. Thomas of Canterbury, Archbishop Langton, and St. Edmund. Yet, in spite of the persistent efforts that were made to curtail the limits of his temporal jurisdiction, the spiritual supremacy of the Roman Pontiff was never contested, nor was his right to legislate in matters of faith and morals called in question. Whatever the political and disciplinary dissensions that had troubled the peace of the Church, for seven hundred years the whole of England had been one in faith and communion with the See of Rome. No disputes had arisen concerning any point of doctrine, no breath of heresy, wafted from other lands, had tainted the ecclesiastical atmosphere of this country. But this happy state of things as regards religious belief was not destined to continue for ever.

In the twelfth and thirteenth centuries, many circumstances combined, as we have seen, to disturb the loyalty which bound the children of the Church to their visible Head, to encourage the spirit of insubordination to his authority, and create a willingness to listen to those who ventured to attack the foundations of the Papacy or the ancient faith of Christendom. The temporary transfer of the Papal Court from the Eternal City to a town in France had robbed it of much of its prestige; the pecuniary exactions levied on all ecclesiastical preferments; the excessive exercise of the right to dispose of all benefices in ecclesiastical patronage; the intrusion of so many foreign ecclesiastics into English livings and sees, gave rise in many hearts to a feeling of animosity towards the occupants of the Holy See, and still more towards his *entourage*, or *Curia*. The grievances were, in truth, not trifling. It is said that the taxes levied by the Pope far exceeded those levied by the king, heavy as these were, and that at one time, no less than twenty thousand marks annually were paid from England into the papal treasury. Another predisposition to heresy sprang out of the unsatisfactory condition of the native clergy. The higher prelates were busied with the cares of political office, and were severed from the lower clergy by the vast inequality between the revenues of the wealthy ecclesiastic and the poor parson of the country. For the sake of money, it was said, "unlearned and unworthy caitiffs" were promoted to benefices of the value of a thousand marks, while the poor and learned could hardly obtain one of twenty. After the pestilence much land fell out of cultivation, and so ceased to yield the tithes; and the impoverished priests left their parishes whenever opportunity offered of obtaining profitable work, or even secular employment, elsewhere. In their absence the churches got out of repair, and the souls of the parishioners were neglected. The spread of learning amongst the laity had raised them to an intellectual level with the clergy, and men like Chaucer were not wanting to castigate with their pungent wit the worldliness, the love of ease, the greed of gain evinced by some churchmen, both regular and secular. All that was required at this juncture to call into activity the latent principle of revolt was the voice of a leader, bold enough to attack the tenets which his countrymen had hitherto revered as sacred. That leader presented himself in the person of John Wyclif, the heresiarch of mediaeval England, one of the most active and mischievous of the many who have risen in rebellion against the Mother who bore them, and one who well deserves to be called the forerunner of the Reformation.

"Every great movement like the sad schism of the sixteenth century invites us to examine its pedigree and make ourselves acquainted with its forefathers. It cannot be regarded apart from the remote events with which it necessarily is connected. To the superficial observer the Reformation seems to stand alone in its solitary independence; but a closer examination will show us that it was but the logical outcome of remoter causes, the gathering in of the harvest of which the seed had been sown by an earlier generation. Our national history points to an individual who may be styled the originator of the Reformation long before Luther saw the light; and to a band of men who, in their turn, accepted and perpetuated the inheritance of evil. Before we may venture to speak of Cranmer and the Protestants, it is necessary that we should know something of Wyclif and the Lollards." [1]

Wyclif.—Wyclif was a man of good family, who had risen to distinction in the University of Oxford. Born in the earlier part of the fourteenth century, he had already passed middle age when he was elected to the mastership of Balliol College, and recognized as one of the ablest of schoolmen and the best disputant of his day. The decay of the University of Paris during the English wars had been the means of transferring her intellectual supremacy to Oxford, and as a scholastic teacher and speculative philosopher Wyclif was no unworthy successor to Roger Bacon, Duns Scotus, and the bold innovator Occam. That the theological opinions of the future reformer, who was destined to attack the creed of Christendom and to break through the most venerable traditions of the past, had as yet excited no suspicion, appears from the fact that he was presented to a benefice of con-

[1] *The Truth about John Wyclif*, by Rev. J. Stevenson.

siderable value. Besides this, Archbishop Islip appointed him Warden of Canterbury Hall, a college he had founded for the advancement of clerical education. On the death of that prelate, a few years later, a dispute arose between Wyclif and his successor, Archbishop Langham. The latter wished to remove Wyclif from his post, on the plea that as the foundation was originally made for the regular clergy, though afterwards transferred to the seculars and endowed out of the revenues of the see, it was reasonable that the monks of his cathedral should resume possession of it. Furthermore he urged that according to the constitutions, the tenure of the wardenship was not for life, as Wyclif asserted, but at the good pleasure of the archbishop. Wyclif refused to give place to the new warden, and the case was brought before the Papal Court. Judgement was given against him, and he was forced to yield to the decision of the Pontiff. There is little doubt that the feelings of resentment and bitter disappointment which his defeat aroused, dictated the envenomed invectives wherewith he afterwards assailed the Court of Rome and the monastic orders.

Wyclif's first Quarrel.—In consequence of the humiliation he had received, Wyclif left Oxford and plunged into the politics of his day. He secured for himself the position of one of the royal chaplains, or "king's clerics," and obtained influence at court as a strenuous opponent of contributions to the papal exchequer, especially the payment of arrears. At that time, as we have seen, through the scarcity of money, such payments were most unpopular. To elevate the temporal power at the expense of the spiritual was the aim of the secularists of the day, and

Wyclif did his best to forward the movement. As yet his quarrel was not with the doctrines but with the practice of the Church. His name appears upon the list of commissioners appointed in 1374 to meet the papal envoys of Bruges, for the purpose of adjusting in an amicable manner the claims of the Pontiff and the rights of the Crown. The result of this commission was not altogether satisfactory, although Gregory XI., who then filled the Chair of Peter, made concessions, and thus it contributed in some degree to bring about an arrangement. The commissioners received a substantial recognition of their services, Wyclif's reward being the rectory of Lutterworth in Leicestershire.

From an attack upon mendicant friars, whom he denounced as "sturdy beggars," Wyclif went on to inveigh against the whole body of clergy. The Pope, bishops, rectors, and curates smarted successively under his lash. His attack upon the endowments of the Church and every ecclesiastical authority within it had its beginning in his disappointed expectation of obtaining the bishopric of Worcester, which had recently been vacant, and to which he had indiscreetly aspired. Every priest, he contended, was bound to imitate the poverty of Christ, consequently the clergy ought to abandon their temporal possessions; and since by not doing so they fell into sin, their parishioners were at liberty to withhold from them their tithes, and set at nought their spiritual censures.

The "Poor Priests."—To disseminate these and similar principles he collected a body of fanatics, whom he distinguished by the name of "poor priests." They were clad in gowns of the coarsest russet, and went barefoot, imitating (as did Wyclif himself to a certain extent) in their manner of life, the austerity of the friars whom he so hotly opposed. These men professed their determination to accept no benefice, and undertook to exercise the calling of itinerant preachers without the licence, and even in opposition to the authority of the bishops. Their sermons, and the tractates that issued from the pen of their master, were calculated to awaken in the people a spirit of insubordination and discontent, of contempt for the authorities, both of Church and State.

Wyclif summoned for Heresy.—No wonder, then, that the incumbent of Lutterworth was summoned in 1377 to appear in convocation before the Archbishop of Canterbury, and Courtenay, the Bishop of London, to answer certain charges brought against him as a teacher of heretical opinions. Wyclif made his appearance under the escort of the two most powerful subjects in England: Lord Percy, the Earl Marshal, and the Duke of Lancaster, the head of the revolutionary party. Fierce words passed between the nobles and the prelates; the Duke of Lancaster resorted to menaces and insults; he is even said to have threatened to drag Bishop Courtenay out of the church by the hair of his head. At last some of the citizens of London, overhearing this language, burst in to their bishop's rescue, and John of Gaunt, who was hateful to them, narrowly escaped with his life. The meeting broke up before a word of argument, of accusation, or defence had been uttered. Wyclif received a reprimand, and an injunction to be silent for the future on those subjects which had given cause for complaint. Meanwhile the death of the king put an end for a time to the inquiry; Wyclif was encouraged to believe himself safe, not only for the present but the future, under the protection of the great Duke of Lancaster.

In this supposition he was mistaken. The heresies which he had taught for long, and with increasing audacity, could no longer escape without attracting public notice. His opinions, either propounded by himself in the university or extracted from his writings, were transmitted to Rome in the form of nineteen propositions; and the Holy Father, dealing with the charge according to the usual forms of ecclesiastical law, ruled that further examination should be made into the truth or falsity of the accusation. Accordingly, towards the end of the year, Wyclif was cited to explain his tenets in presence of the primate and the Bishop of London. This he did in a written document, which is still extant. But the proceedings of the commissioners were abruptly stopped by a message from the court; and the Londoners broke in and dissolved the session. Wyclif counted this second failure in the administration of justice as a fresh triumph.

Wyclif preaches Socialism. — The restless energy of action which marked the latter years of this bold reformer surprises us, not only by its ceaseless activity, but also by the facility with which it originated and carried on to their completion his projects of evil. The principles of insubordination and lawlessness busily disseminated by his emissaries found ready acceptance with the uneducated masses of the people, and they were not slow in reducing them to practice. The inflammatory discourses of the "Poor Priests" fostered the ill-feeling already engendered between landowners and tillers of the soil by the fall in the value of land, the high rate of wages, and the general alteration in the economy of country life consequent on the Great Pestilence. The respect for authority once broken down, and the labourer persuaded that the time had come to assert his independence and throw off the yoke of servitude, social order was at an end. Even in his lifetime the results of Wyclif's teaching were made manifest in the formidable insurrection of the peasantry, the course of which was marked with fire, pillage, and bloodshed. The leader of the insurgents, a priest named John Ball, was one of his foremost adherents; and his most prominent scholar, Nicholas Hereford, is said to have approved the brutal murder of Archbishop Sudbury, who was dragged from his chapel and beheaded on Tower Hill. It was with difficulty that tranquillity was restored to the country.

Wyclif teaches Heresy on the Eucharist.— The revolt of the people created a strong feeling amongst the upper classes against the doctrines of the reformer, and served to deprive him of the support of the party with whom he had hitherto co-operated. But even had it not been for this, their alliance must have been dissolved on account of the new position Wyclif took up. He had already, with what fatal effect we have just seen, attacked the political traditions that had prevailed since the earliest days of the English monarchy; he now attacked the doctrinal principles of belief which had been established amongst us by the Divine Founder of the Church. Some months before the outbreak of the insurrection, he had by one memorable step passed from the position of a reformer of the discipline and political relations of the Church to that of a protestant against its fundamental dogmas. His subtle intellect was not needed to discern the mainspring of the sacerdotal system, the central doctrine upon which the supremacy of the Catholic Church rested. It was by his exclusive right to the performance of the mystery daily wrought in the Mass that the lowliest priest was invested with a dignity far above that of princes. With the formal and direct attack upon the doctrine of the Holy Eucharist, issued by Wyclif in 1381, began that great movement of religious revolt which, though suppressed for a time, ended, more than a century later, in the severance of the Teutonic peoples from the body of the Catholic Church.

Disturbance at Oxford. Wyclif retracts.— This act was the bolder because he stood utterly alone, and he knew well that it could not be permitted to pass unnoticed. The University, in which his influence had hitherto been all-powerful, condemned his propositions as erroneous, opposed to the decrees of the Church, and contrary to Catholic verity. The Duke of Lancaster went down to Oxford in person, to enjoin him to be silent on a subject whereon he had already given so much offence. Wyclif was presiding as Doctor of Divinity over some disputations in the schools of the Augustinian Canons, when his academical condemnation was publicly read. Though startled for a moment, he protested against the validity of the sentence, and at once challenged chancellor or doctor to disprove his conclusions. He met the prohibition of the Duke of Lancaster by an open avowal of his heresies. The bishops, whose duty it is to watch over the divine deposit of the truth, became alarmed; Courtenay, who had been translated from the see of London to that of Canterbury on the death of Sudbury, interposed his authority. He charged a Carmelite friar, Dr. Peter Stokes, to forbid the teaching within the University of certain erroneous propositions which he specified in detail. Two of Wyclif's most mischievous and active disciples, Hereford and Repingdon, refused to be silenced; the former, in an English sermon delivered in the Church of St. Frideswide, in Oxford, asserted the truth of his master's doctrine, and unsparingly assailed the beneficed clergy, calling them thieves and robbers. In his denunciation of the religious orders, of whom there were large communities in Oxford, he was yet more outspoken. When Dr. Stokes attempted to read the archbishop's letters, he was prevented by a body of armed scholars, who threatened him with death. The archbishop summoned the Chancellor of the University to answer before him for the riotous proceedings, and, the royal council supporting his authority, a mandate was sent suspending Wyclif from the office of teacher, ordering the seizure of all his books and the banishment of all his followers, on pain of forfeiture of the privileges appertaining to the university. Hereford and Repingdon appealed to John of Gaunt for protection, but he denounced them as heretics against the Sacrament of the Altar, whom he held in abomination. Wyclif was obliged reluctantly to submit; he read a confession of faith in the presence of the primate and several bishops, and was ordered to retire to his rectory at Lutterworth. There he was allowed to reside unmolested, and to enjoy the income of his living.

Wyclif spreads Heresy.—But although Wyclifism was thus suppressed in Oxford, its author was not silenced. From his quiet home in Leicestershire he continued to promulgate his tenets by means of the Order of Poor Preachers, whom he organized, and by the tracts which he issued one after another with amazing industry. He no longer looked for support to the learned or wealthier classes on whom he had formerly relied; his daring denials of Catholic truth were not confined to the small circle of scholars who still clung to him; he appealed to the people at large. The classic language in which he had addressed his academic hearers was flung aside, the schoolman was transformed into the pamphleteer. His tracts were written in the tongue of the people, the rough, clear, homely speech of the ploughman and trader of his day, coloured with the picturesque phraseology of the Bible. Having once cast off the safeguard and restraints of unquestioning belief, Wyclif's mind worked fast in its career of scepticism. Pardons, indulgences, absolutions, pilgrimages to the shrines of the saints, veneration of their images, worship of the saints themselves, were successively assailed. An appeal to the Bible as the one ground of faith, coupled with an assertion of the right of every instructed man to examine the Scriptures for himself, threatened the very groundwork of dogmatism, and found a ready response in the pride of the human heart.

Wyclif dies at Mass.—Two years after Wyclif's expulsion from the University, the judgements of God fell upon him, and silenced for ever the impious tongue that had dared to attack the sacred mysteries so dear to every Christian heart. On Holy Innocents' Day, 1384, whilst he was assisting at his curate's mass in the little church of Lutterworth, at the moment of the elevation, when every sound was hushed and every head bent in reverent adoration, a stroke of paralysis deprived him of speech and in part of the use of his limbs. He expired on the last day of the year, at the age of about sixty years. Only a short time before he had declared that "the chief object of his teaching was to call back the Church from that idolatry upon the doctrine of the Eucharist which she had taught and practised for many centuries."

Wyclif not the Originator of Scripture-reading.—If there be one recommendation which has endeared the name of Wyclif to the Protestant world, it is that of being the earliest translator of the whole of the Old and New Testament. The idea that he was so is as general as it is erroneous. Portions of Holy Scripture were early translated into the vernacular. The poems attributed to Cædmon give an outline of Bible history, and close translations of many passages. Bishop Aldhelm published a Saxon version of the Psalms. The Venerable Bede completed a Saxon translation of St. John's Gospel just before his death. Elfric, Archbishop of York, rendered other portions into the tongue of the common people; and the pious King Alfred the Great employed himself in a similar manner. There is a Norman-French translation of the whole of the Sacred Scriptures dating about 1260. Thus it cannot be denied that all at least of the principal portions of the Old and New Testament were familiar to Englishmen long before the days of Wyclif. Nor is his share in the translation attributed to him by any means as large as is supposed. The version of the New Testament may possibly be his; that of the Old Testament certainly is not. As for the particular translation which popularly bears his name, there are strong grounds for thinking it is not really his, but the authentic Catholic translation of his time. Before that period the need of an English translation had hardly arisen, as those who were sufficiently educated to read understood Norman-French.[1]

Equally unfounded is the assertion that before the era of the Reformation the use of the written Word of God by the faithful was systematically discouraged, even prohibited, by the clergy. On the contrary, the study of the Holy Scriptures was not only sanctioned but recommended, provided that the guidance of the Church was not disregarded, and that private readers did not claim the ridiculous right to prefer their own interpretations to the authorized interpretations of the Catholic Church.[2] Wyclif's design was precisely to oppose this sound principle, to assert that the Bible is the sole source of religious truth, and to protest against the authority of the Church in putting her own interpretation on difficult passages and denouncing all other interpretations as erroneous. He claimed for every man the power to judge for himself, and to interpret Holy Scripture according to his private opinion.

Wyclifites, or Lollards.—The truth of the words, "the evil that men do lives after them" is

---

[1] Cf. Dom Gasquet's article in the *Dublin Review*, July, 1894.

[2] Cf. the Encyclical (1893) of Pope Leo XIII. on the study of Holy Scripture, wherein he expresses his desire that this precious revelation of Catholic truth may be more fully opened to the faithful, yet carefully guarded against those who dare to deny its authenticity, or pervert its meaning to the encouragement of new and erroneous doctrines. "Quamobrem diffitendum non est religiosa quadam obscuritate Sacros Libros involvi, ut ad eos, nisi aliquo viæ duce, nemo ingredi possit: Deo quidem sic providente ut homines . . intelligerent præcipue Scripturas Deum tradidisse Ecclesiæ, quâ scilicet duce et magistra in legendis tractandisque eloquiis suis certissima uterentur."

never better exemplified than in regard to the teachers
of error, and Wyclif proved no exception to the rule.
All the religious and social discontent of the times
floated instinctively to this new centre. At first the
movement met with encouragement from the nobles,
for the Lollard [1] preachers levelled their fiercest
invectives against the opulence and luxury of ecclesiastics,
declaring that all the taxation and other
evils oppressing the nation arose from the wealth of
the Church. In this doctrine the worldly-minded
among the nobles saw a pretext for the confiscation
of Church property and the withdrawal of secular
power from the clergy. But the "gospel of equality"
proclaimed by the new teachers had a wider application
than at the outset appeared. The wealth of
landlords was also to be confiscated, on the plea that
they did not ameliorate the condition of their dependents.
Thus the doctrines of the Lollards were found
to be subversive of civil government and social order,
as well as of religion and morality, and both clergy
and laity were roused to take active proceedings
against them. In 1387 the Lords and Commons
united in a petition to the king for legal redress. It
was stated that many unlicensed persons were in the
habit of itinerating from place to place and preaching
heresy, not only in churches and churchyards, but at
fairs and markets, and in public places generally.
The tendency of the discourses of these men was to
engender discord between the different estates of the
realm and to cause disturbances among the people.

---

[1] *Lollard*, a word which probably means "idle babbler," was the
name given to the followers of Wyclif. Pope Gregory XI., playing on
the word, speaks of them as "*Lolium inter purum triticum*"—tares
or cockle among the pure wheat.

Measures were accordingly taken which, it was hoped, would curb the growing evil. The bishops were enjoined to punish the delinquents with the utmost rigour of the canon law. The Archbishop of Canterbury thought it his duty to make a personal visitation of his diocese. In several towns which he passed through he caused convicted Wyclifites to do public penance, and for a time this put a stop to unlicensed preaching, and to the outbreak of disturbances.

In its religious development Lollardism proved a far more formidable power than in its social aspect. Wyclif had been treated with extreme moderation, and the seeds which he had sown broadcast had taken deep root in England. Left comparatively undisturbed in their first growth, they could not after his death be eradicated. From an early stage of its existence the mischief of his teaching had shown itself by a diminished attendance at mass and a growing disregard of the sacraments. Until the time of which we speak, the parish church had been the house of God, to which His children had resorted as a privilege and a blessing. The sacraments had always been regarded as the divinely appointed channels for the communication of divine grace through the ministry of the priest, who was looked upon as the teacher and best friend of the people: and although statutes against alleged papal aggressions were multiplied, they were disregarded for the most part, and probably had not the sympathy of the body of the people. This state of things the tenets of Wyclif's disciples were calculated to destroy. They hesitated not to proclaim consequences their master would have glossed over. They denounced the clergy as mercenary shepherds, usurpers of the patrimony of the poor; they disparaged holy orders, proclaiming that the virtuous laymen was more competent to administer the sacraments than the worldly-minded priest—a doctrine which strikes at the very root of the Church. Unfortunately at this time the great schism of the West, which tore asunder the Christian world into two great divisions, tended to diminish the respect felt not only for the Holy See, but for ecclesiastical authority in general. The Lollards could count among their friends some influential knights, and some courtiers in whose eyes the political power of the bishops was their greatest sin.

Action against Lollardism.—In 1382 an act against the heresy had been passed, by which it was ordered that, on a certificate from the bishop, the chancellor should commission the sheriffs to compel the persons accused to satisfy the requirements of the Church. It was repealed in the same year at the petition of the Commons, as not having been passed with their assent. This abortive attempt at legislation had emboldened the Lollards, and the bishops showed no desire to promote extreme measures against them, for they generally recanted when ecclesiastical pressure was brought to bear upon them. Hence they increased in numbers and in political courage and weight. Their views became more advanced, and were enunciated with extreme boldness. In 1394, during the king's absence in Ireland, they brought a bill into the House, petitioning Parliament to aid them in reforming the Church. This bill contained a declaration of their opinions, under twelve heads. Of these the principal ones were—a denunciation of the endowments of the Church, and of the priesthood conferred by the ritual of that Church; an objection to celibacy amongst the clergy and monks; denial of transubstantiation; repudiation of exorcisms, blessings of water, oil, &c., as practices of necromancy; condemnation of the holding of temporal offices by prelates and clergy; of auricular confession, pilgrimages, the veneration of images; and finally of war and criminal executions, as being contrary to the law of the gospel. Effectually to secure the publication of these "conclusions" they were not only presented in Parliament, but affixed to the doors of St. Paul's and Westminster Abbey. The Lollards seemed to court strife, and as their audacious manifesto was made public, it could not be left unnoticed by the civil power. The king therefore, on his return, called together some of their chief supporters, reprimanded them severely, and ordered that their teachers should be expelled from the University. This had the effect of temporarily checking the spread of these heretical and revolutionary opinions. Soon afterwards the Pope despatched letters to the king, requesting him to aid the episcopate in their attempts to repress the "pestilent and contagious sect."

Henry IV. Archbishop Arundel's activity against Lollardism.— But the political convulsions of the latter years of Richard II.'s reign crippled the action of the bishops, and impeded the carrying out of ecclesiastical discipline. Arundel, the Archbishop of Canterbury, was accused of conspiring against the king; the latter procured his impeachment and banishment for life, with forfeiture of his temporalities. Arundel betook himself to the Pope. The Pontiff, desiring neither to offend the king nor desert the archbishop, translated the latter to the see of St. Andrews in Scotland, and appointed Walden, the king's treasurer, to the see of Canterbury. The effect of this was to create a union between Arundel and Bolingbroke, who was also in exile—a union which quickly culminated in the return of Bolingbroke, and the abdication of Richard in his favour. Bolingbroke, who now assumed the crown under the title of Henry IV., had obtained the support of the clergy on condition that he should act vigorously against the Lollards; hence immediately upon his accession, he announced himself as the protector of the Church. The practical immunity enjoyed by the disciples of Wyclif during the first years of their existence, and the futility of the efforts of the prelates for their suppression at a subsequent period, is to be accounted for by the fact that there did not exist in England at that time any machinery for bringing severity to bear upon heretics. Up to this period it is doubtful whether any one had been capitally punished for heresy. There was no statutory power to arrest and try, far less to punish with death, the propagators of soul-destroying errors. It was only when rebellion and outrages of all kinds were becoming every day more and more common, that the severer penalties of coercion were introduced to repress the disorders which an unrestrained licence of thought and speech had brought into existence. It was held that nothing short of capital punishment would suffice to stop the progress of the sect, and a new law was therefore required to enable the secular arm to support the bishop's censures.

Burning of Heretics.—The Parliament of 1401 is chiefly known in history for the action taken against the Lollards. This was prompted by Archbishop Arundel, who was restored to power, and was throughout his career their unflinching enemy. With the consent of the king, the lords and the commons, a statute was passed (*de hæretico comburendo*), which provided that the impenitent heretic, convicted before the spiritual court, was to be delivered over to the secular authorities, who should "cause him to be burnt in some conspicuous place, that such punishment might strike terror into the minds of others." All heretical books also were to be destroyed. Thus, for the first time in English history, the statute law of the land took upon itself to inflict capital punishment on those who had been condemned by the ecclesiastical tribunal.

Sir John Oldcastle.—The first to suffer under this new statute was one William Sautrey, who two years previously had been convicted of heresy, and deprived of his living by the Bishop of Norwich. On his recantation he had been set at liberty, and migrated to London, where he obtained a chaplaincy, and again taught the doctrines he had renounced. Examined, degraded, and condemned, he was burnt as a relapsed heretic at Smithfield. A layman of note, Sir John Oldcastle, was the next to incur the terrible penalties of the act, although his offence was chiefly political. He had made himself the patron of the itinerant preachers, and his residence became their headquarters, whence they issued on their mission in the neighbourhood, setting at defiance the prohibitions of bishops and ecclesiastical officers. When arrested and brought before the primate, he conducted himself with insolence, and was committed to the Tower. But while the execution of his sentence was suspended, in the hope that by gentleness he might be recalled to his duty, he contrived to escape, and rallied round him some bands of Lollards, who seem to have conceived the design of dethroning the king. Like that of the anarchists of modern times, the object of these misguided men was "to destroy the Christian faith, the king, the spiritual and temporal estates, all manner of policy and law." Having taken up arms against the government, the insurrectionists mustered in St. Giles's fields, where they were attacked and dispersed. Sir John Oldcastle and other ringleaders were taken prisoners, tried, and executed, being first hung as traitors, then burnt as heretics (1417). This rebellious movement on the part of the Lollards had the effect of adding to the vigour of the penal laws already in existence. A more stringent statute ordained that the king's officers of whatever grade were to apprehend Lollards and deliver them over to the bishops within ten days, and that conviction of heresy was to entail forfeiture of life and of estate.

Wyclif the Precursor of Luther.—With the death of Sir John Oldcastle the political activity of Lollardism came to an end, while the action of the bishops, though it failed to extinguish it as a religious sect, succeeded in destroying the vigour and energy which had marked the outset of its career. Numerous cases of trials and punishment are to be found recorded during the next hundred years, for the doctrines of Wyclif were still cherished and propagated by his followers. Formulated with a certain degree of consistency, and not a little exaggerated, they were handed on until they became the common property of the Reformation, and triumphed under Henry VIII

"We have but to go to Lutterworth, and there we shall see the spot whence sprang those principles of evil, religious evil, political evil, social evil, which, ever since the days of John Wyclif, have waged such an unceasing warfare against the sceptre of the prince, the tiara of the Holy Father, and the teaching of the Catholic Church."[1] His doctrines, carried to Germany, also influenced Huss and Luther, and returned thence at a subsequent date to England. It is noteworthy that at the press established by Tyndal at Antwerp, reprints were made of Wyclif's tracts.[2]

[1] *The Truth about Wyclif*, p. 190.
[2] Green, *Short History of the English People*, p. 342.

CHAPTER XV.

CONDITION OF THE CHURCH BEFORE THE REFORMATION.

Evils of the Statutes of Provisors and Præmunire. We have now reached the period immediately preceding the (so-called) Reformation, and will inquire into the state of the Church in England at that time. During the latter half of the fourteenth century, the statute against Papal Provisions, enacted by the Parliament in the reign of Edward III., met with little opposition from the Popes. Now and again they raised their voice against this restriction of their rights, but during the continuance of the dispute over the Papacy, it was necessary to pass over many abuses, and to avoid all measures which might induce the English sovereigns to espouse the cause of the rival line. Moreover, as has been remarked (p. 264), the statute was from the outset little more than a *brutum fulmen*, so impossible was it to resist the Pope, without whose consent the valid title to ecclesiastical jurisdiction could not be obtained. At length the reiterated complaints of patrons concerning the manner in which it was set aside or evaded, led to fresh legislation on the subject. When the Parliament met in 1390, it was decreed that every person accepting a benefice contrary to the statute, was to suffer forfeiture of goods and banishment for life. Nine years later the Statute of *Præmunire* was confirmed, and rendered more stringent. By virtue of this Act, every one who should appeal to Rome concerning matters claimed by the kings as belonging to the temporal order, could be severely punished and outlawed; and any person bringing into England a papal sentence or excommunication to defeat the execution of the statute, would incur forfeiture and death. Against this last clause the clergy protested, on the ground that it "tended to restrain the apostolical authority, and subvert ecclesiastical liberty."

Experience began, too, by this time to show that these statutes operated, in a way that had not been anticipated, to the depression of learning. The deterioration observable in the Universities since they had been enforced, was such as to induce the authorities to present a petition to Convocation, setting forth that when the Popes were permitted to confer benefices by provision, they had for the most part given the preference to men of talent and industry, and of high standing in the University. This had had the salutary result of affording a stimulus to learning, and multiplying the number of the students, whereas since the passing of the Act their members had been neglected by the patrons: consequently the students had disappeared, and the schools were nearly abandoned. No measures were taken at the time, but the evil continuing to increase, the House of Commons, sixteen years later, struck by the condition of the Universities, petitioned the king for the repeal of the statute against provisors. The king replied that he had referred the matter to the bishops. Unfortunately the prelates did not urge the repeal, and thus the opportunity of freeing the Church passed away. A law was however passed in Convocation, obliging every patron for the next ten years to bestow the first vacant benefice in his gift, and after that time the second, on some member of the University who had taken his degree.

The lower ranks of clergy, and the laity too, found themselves annoyed in many unforeseen ways by the operation of these statutes. Where mention is made of them, it is generally in terms of disapprobation, or even undisguised execration. In a list of accusations drawn up by some insurgents against Henry V., one clause asserts that he "ratifies and supports a most wicked statute, directly against the Roman Curia, and the power conferred by Christ on Blessed Peter and his successors, to whom, from the plenitude of their power, the full and free disposition of all ecclesiastical benefices ought to belong." This document proceeds to point out that many patrons conferred the livings on illiterate and unworthy persons, on their own illegitimate sons and relations, or on men involved with them in heinous sins. Few, it was averred, bestowed them without a compact to receive half or a third of the benefice thus bestowed; so that knights, squires, and merchants, preferred to bring up their sons to some worldly calling, rather than send them to the University to be enrolled among the clergy. Still the statute remained unaltered, the remonstrances of the Holy See being little heeded during the continuance of the Western Schism.

Martin V. and the Statute of Provisors.

When this schism was ended by the election and universal recognition of Martin V. as lawful Pope, the new Pontiff, conscious how greatly the statutes crippled his action as Chief Pastor, wrote to the king, urging their repeal in forcible language. Subsequently, during the minority of Henry VI., he addressed a letter to the same effect to the Regency, and to Parliament. In 1426 he enjoined on Archbishop Chicheley to do his utmost to obtain the abolition of the Statutes of Provisors and *Præmunire*. "By these execrable statutes," he wrote, "the king of England disposes of the Church with his provisions and administrations, just as if Christ had constituted him His Vicar. He makes a law concerning churches clerics, and the ecclesiastical state, draws spiritual and ecclesiastical causes to himself and his lay courts, in short makes provisions about churches, clerics, and the ecclesiastical state, just as if the keys of the kingdom of heaven were put into his hands, and the superintendency of these affairs entrusted to His Highness, not to St. Peter." Moreover he reproached Chicheley for not having, ten years earlier, improved the opportunity which presented itself for the abrogation of the Act, and, for his inaction and indifference on that occasion, deprived him of the dignity of legate.

The Disputes about Provisions no Repudiation of Papal Supremacy.

There is no doubt that there was a strong spirit of disobedience pervading the long course of resistance to the Popes recorded in our history. Nor were our monarchs always actuated by the single-minded purpose of defending their own temporal authority; they sometimes resisted the Pontiff on his own ground of spiritual jurisdiction. But disobedience is not denial of authority. As a general rule, the dispute was, as we have seen, not contrary to, or incompatible with, recognition of the papal supremacy; it concerned (as has been well said) the frontier line between secular and spiritual jurisdiction. Richard II. and his parliament insisted that provisions were an invasion of the temporal jurisdiction, and on that account to be stopped by legislation. The practice of appeals was complained of, but the complaint is of one who admits, not denies, the Pope's right to receive appeals on spiritual matters. It was to prevent an action being brought to the Papal Court, about matters "whereof the cognizance belonged to the king's court," that the statute was passed. Bulls on spiritual matters were constantly entering the country without incurring any opposition. With the Reformation, the operation of *Præmunire* was applied to things confessedly spiritual. Under Henry VIII. it was interpreted to forbid all appeals of any sort. Under Elizabeth it was extended to the refusal to take the oath of supremacy.

Abundant evidence proves that, throughout the Middle Ages, England was constantly loyal to the Holy See. Even when, in 1245, the Parliament was addressing remonstrances to Pope Innocent IV. against the Curia's excessive exactions of money, it did so without in any way deviating from the attitude of respect and obedience to the Apostolic See. "Our Mother, the Roman Church, we love and cherish with all our hearts, as our duty is; and with all the affection of which we are capable we seek to further and increase her honour." In

1337. King Edward III., although the author of the Statute *Præmunire*, recognizes that "the Holy See is divinely constituted in the fulness of power," and he describes the Church of Canterbury as "the devoted daughter of the most holy Roman See" (Wilkins, vol. ii. p. 584). King Henry VI. writes (1422): "From the very cradle of the Christian religion his [the Pope's] authority has been regarded as most manifest, and the plenitude of his power reverenced with all possible veneration."[1] The bishops of the province of Canterbury, under Archbishop Winchelsey, pleading for a mitigation of extortionate taxation, say, "We cast ourselves prostrate at the feet of your Holiness, and implore that you will take into consideration the fervour of our English faith, and that the said kingdom has stood out as specially devoted to the most holy Roman Church." Archbishop Peckham, in referring the appeal of one of his clerics to the Holy See, writes: "We shall be at all times ready to lay our neck under the definitions of the Holy Apostolic See, however much the littleness of our own opinions or the zeal of our feelings might seem to oppose them."

A little later, in 1412, Archbishop Arundel and his suffragans signed a letter to the reigning Pope, asking for a confirmation of their condemnation of the Lollards, and attesting the Catholic faith of the province in a remarkable passage, which concludes thus: "For this is that most blessed see, which by God's almighty grace is known never to have erred from the path of apostolic tradition; which has never been stained or overcome by heretical novelty, but to which, as the mother

[1] *Corr. of Bekynton*, Rolls Series, ii. 30.

(*domina*) and mistress of all other Churches, the excellent authority of the holy Fathers ordained that the greater causes, and chiefly those relating to faith, should be referred for decision and termination" (Wilkins, *Concilia*, vol. iii. p. 350). Chicheley, Archbishop of Canterbury in 1428, writes to Pope Martin V., in words expressive of the traditional obedience of the English Church to the See of Peter; he protests "that there lives not any man who is more anxiously desirous to the utmost of his power than we are to defend the liberties of the Church, or more willing to carry out the commands of the Holy See" (*Ibid.*, vol. iii. p. 472 *seq.*).

The above quotations suffice to show how closely connected England was with the See of Rome. Our country was always regarded as in a peculiar manner under the protection of the Apostolic See; the Popes, one after another, gave to the English people the title of "the singular and special sons of Blessed Peter." Baronius tells us that the English kings were crowned as "the eldest sons of the Church;" and St. Peter used to be invoked as one of the primary patrons of the realm in the old coronation service.

Devotion to Our Lady.—While England professed the true faith, she had three patrons—the Blessed Virgin, St. Peter, and St. George. The two former were her chief patrons from the earliest period; St. George only from the time of the Crusades, when he was invoked as her military patron. Nothing could exceed the devotion of mediaeval England to the Blessed Virgin, or the love wherewith she was invoked (see Bridgett's *Our Lady's Dowry*, passim). At the early dawn the bell sounded its summons to the "Marye-mass," and the people hastened to the magnificent Lady-chapels of the cathedrals, or of their own parish church. This mass did not take the place of the Mass and Office of the day. It was the willing tribute of a devout people to the Mother of Jesus. Day by day the services went on in the choir, at the altar, in the vast naves of the glorious churches of the land. But the Lady-chapel was the scene of Mary's special honour. Her altar was there, her image was there, of precious marble, more often of pure gold or silver, or perhaps of common wood plated with precious metal, or dark and venerable with the lapse of years. Decked in robes of the costliest texture, adorned with sparkling jewels, rare gems, pearls and rings, the image stood beneath a beauteous canopy, or was placed in a richly-wrought tabernacle. The ministers who officiated were set apart for this special duty ; sometimes a single priest, who was our Lady's priest ; sometimes a company of four, six, or eight clerks, for whom the piety of benefactors had provided, that they might stand at Mary's shrine. The Lady-chapel had its own valuable vestments and golden chalice ; wax-candles, from the number of five, to represent her five joys, to that of thirty, burnt during the Mass, and before her effigy ; the lamp that shone there by day, and the "cresset," or torch, that was lighted at night, were in the custody of one whose office it was to guard and keep the chapel. And as day-light began, so eventide ended with Mary's praises : as the shades of night fell, the darkening aisles re-echoed to an antiphon chanted before her altar by priest or clerks appointed for the purpose. The founder's statutes generally required the inmates of every college to meet together on Saturdays and the eve of every feast, to sing in honour of Mary the anthem of the season. Oftentimes it was the voices of children that raised this grateful lay; we read that in the Lady-chapel at Winchester, erected by the piety of William of Wykeham, the charity boys of the priory used to assemble every night to sing the *Salve Regina*, until this practice was forbidden by the commissioners of Edward VI. Had not our liturgical books been almost entirely destroyed by the Reformation, we should know how popular were once the sequences of our Lady, the hymns composed by St. Thomas of Canterbury— *Imperatrix gloriosa, Hodiernæ lux diei*—in our land. The praises of Mary were in every missal and service-book; they were chanted not only by clergy and cantors, but by the people at meetings of gilds and companies, by the labourer in the fields, by the children on their way to school.

Order of the Garter.—And what was true of the daily liturgical life of the country, was true also of its political and social life in the widest sense. We are told that the Order of the Garter was founded by Edward III. to the honour of the Blessed Virgin, and that "out of his singular affection for her he had wished her to be honoured by his knights"; and on our Lady's festivals the knights, during the divine offices, bore on their right shoulders golden figures of the Mother of God. The seals of great cities were stamped with her effigy; the church bells bore an inscription consecrating them to her holy name. When King Henry VI. founded his great college of Eton, he dedicated it to the name of the " Blessed Mary." At Winchester, as in Oxford, her statue was placed in a niche over the principal entrance to the colleges founded by William of Wykeham, where they may still be seen; and until recently, at Winchester, the students used to raise their caps as they passed under the doorway, though ignorant of the ancient devotion to which they were witnessing. Henry V., the hero of Agincourt, led his troops to battle to the war-cry: "Our Lady for her dowry!" We learn from the Constitutions of Archbishop Arundel that England gloried in the title of "Our Lady's Dowry" at a date prior to that of this battle, at any rate in the time of Richard II., who resigned his sceptre in 1399. Shortly after, at the desire of his successor, Henry IV., the Archbishop of Canterbury appointed that, as hitherto the Gabriel bell had been rung, and the angelic salutation had been said throughout Europe only in the evening, thenceforth in England the bell be rung in the early morning also, and the same prayers recited. The reason he assigns for this is that "we in England, being the servants of her special inheritance, and her own dowry, ought to surpass all other nations in the honour paid to our heavenly sovereign." The common conjecture is that Richard II. consecrated the country to our Lady in 1381, on the occasion of his almost miraculous deliverance, after imploring her help, from the hands of the rebellious peasantry. Froissart tells us that on the eventful morning when the young king set out to encounter the infuriated insurgents, he and the nobles who were with him, heard mass in Westminster Abbey, and after that, went to kneel before an image of our Lady, called

Our Lady of the Pewe. This image (a *pietà*), the historian says, "is famous for miracles and graces, and the kings of England place great confidence in it. The king then made his prayers before the statue, and made an offering of himself to our Lady. Then he mounted his horse and rode towards London." He could not but attribute to these prayers and to this offering the marvellous turn of fortune that immediately followed.

Our Lady of Walsingham.—This shrine was but one of the many famous sanctuaries which abounded in this country, to which royal and noble personages, and crowds of pilgrims, continually flocked. Of these the most popular was Our Lady of Walsingham. So strong was the affection of the common people for this Norfolk shrine, that in the wild but poetic imaginings of the time, the Milky Way was piously thought to be placed in the heavens to point out the way to the sacred spot, and on this account it was in ancient times called "Walsingham Way." The sanctuary consisted of a little chapel, similar to the Holy House of Loreto, enclosed within a spacious church, and richly decorated with brilliant gems, with gold and silver. Scarcely less popular were the sanctuary at Glastonbury, venerable for its great antiquity; the church of All Hallows in London, celebrated on account of a miraculous image, placed there by King Edward, in gratitude for his victories over the Welsh; Our Lady of Grace, at the north door of St. Paul's Cathedral; Our Lady of Ipswich, of Lincoln, of Coventry, of Doncaster, and many others. Amongst these, far away to the west, among the hills of Glamorgan, was Our Lady of Penrice, marked still by a holy well. The latter we find mentioned in one of the scurrilous ballads composed at the time of the Reformation.

> To Walsingham a-gadding, to Canterbury a-madding,
>   As men distraught of mind ;
> With few clothes on our backs, but an image of wax
>   For the lame and for the blind,
> To Thetford, to Ipswich, to Oxford, to Shoreditch,
>   With many mo places of price ;
> As to Our Lady of Worcester, and the sweet Rood of Chester
>   With the Blessed Lady of Penrice.

The mention of a wax image is an allusion to the custom in the Middle Ages of placing waxen effigies in churches; these images either represented benefactors, or were thank-offerings on the part of persons who had received favours at the shrine. They were dressed like living persons, and were allowed to remain in this place until they perished from age. In connection with all these shrines mention is made of special offerings for lights. The pious custom of burning tapers before her image was a most common method of testifying veneration for our Blessed Lady. At Lincoln, to take one instance out of many, we find it recorded that St. Hugh, for the glory of the Virgin Mother of the True Light, endowed the treasury of the cathedral with revenues for this purpose, so that, as the historian adds, "the lustre of the tapers with which the cathedral was illuminated during the offices of night might vie with that of the rays of sun, with which it was lit by day." In many chapels the Lady-light was supported by one of the gilds, some of these being founded for that express object. Henry VIII., in the days of his piety, used to keep candles, called the king's candles, before Our Lady of Walsingham and of Doncaster; and the Earl of Northumberland maintained lights at the same sanctuaries all the year round. Lands too were given or bequeathed for this purpose, by nobles or wealthy traders, and these gifts and legacies, as we learn from the chronicles of the time, were on no niggardly scale.

The offerings made by the pilgrims of every class and condition who annually resorted to these favourite sanctuaries were so great that, in one instance, in 1411, it is recorded that the Archbishop of Canterbury had to arbitrate as to the disposal of them. By no nation in Christendom was more done than by Catholic England for the adornment of the house of God, as we learn from the inventories of the rich vestments and sacred vessels which once belonged to the cathedrals. The mere weight of gold and silver taken from monasteries and churches by order of Henry VIII. was something enormous. The shrines of Our Lady, beloved by the English people, and enriched by their piety, were not spared by that impious monarch. The chronicles of the city of Lincoln record that in 1531 he visited that city. Whilst he was kissing the crucifix presented to him by the bishop, and walking with the Queen Catherine of Arragon to the chapel of the Blessed Virgin, to pay his devotions before the famous image, his sacrilegious eyes were noting avariciously the riches of the cathedral. Shortly after, these treasures were all seized for his Majesty's use. By virtue of the decree authorizing the spoliation of the cathedrals, the shrine was taken down, and the silver image. At the same time there was taken out of the cathedral about 220 lb. of gold and 350 lb. of silver, besides a great number of pearls and precious stones of great value, the offerings and bequests of the faithful. But of these spoliations we shall speak later on.

Gilds.—The gilds which, it will be remembered, were first founded under the Anglo-Saxon kings, became an important factor in the social and religious life of the centuries immediately preceding the Reformation. The range of their provident care was exceedingly wide; the gild stood like a loving mother, assisting her sons in every circumstance of life, and caring for them after death. There were social gilds and religious gilds, craft gilds and merchant gilds, gilds for the relief of poverty, old age, sickness. All of these had a religious colouring, and were for the most part under the patronage of Holy Mary or Blessed Peter, as well as of some saint appropriate to the calling of the members. The combination of religion with the occupations and relaxations of daily life was a marked feature of these gilds. They knew God, and served Him with cheerfulness. They gave to Him the first place; they went in solemn procession to the gild churches, they founded masses, erected altars, and placed stained-glass windows in our cathedrals. A yearly requiem was sung for all deceased brethren, and a distribution of alms was made to the poor to pray for their souls. Nor were their good works confined to their members. We read of one gild that daily fed with bread, fish, and ale, as many poor persons as there were brothers and sisters in the gild. Others provided lodging for poor strangers, almshouses for the destitute, dowries for necessitous maidens. Nor did they restrict themselves to corporal works of mercy. In 1352 the Gild of Corpus Christi, at Cambridge, obtained the king's permission to found a "House of Scholars," now known as Corpus Christi College, and free schools were established and maintained by many such associations. The festivals of the gilds were held on the day of their patron saint; the day began with mass and a procession, then came the feast and often a miracle play, intended not merely to please the eye, but to inculcate religion and morality. The hours of toil were fixed from daybreak till curfew, and a strict rule was made that no work should be done on Sundays or festivals. The Saturday half-holiday, swept away at the Reformation and only recently re-introduced, was universal in the thirteenth and fourteenth centuries.

The Reformation abolished the whole system of gilds. Henry VIII. needed money, and an Act was passed for the dissolution of hospitals, gilds, and fraternities. They were opportunely found to have misapplied their possessions in various ways, and this was to be rectified by all their possessions being applied "to the maintenance of the Crown." This shameless spoliation of the property of the poor and thrifty was justified on the ground that they "maintained and upheld superstitious practices."

Predisposing Causes of the Reformation. 1. Social Distress.—The acts of Henry VIII. and his successors, which resulted in the overthrow of the Faith in England, would not have been possible had there not been a reverse to the fair picture we have shown; attendant on the bright light, there was, unhappily, a dark shadow. Side by side with obedience to the voice of Christ's Vicar, devotion to the Mother of our Redeemer, love for the house of God—then, as now, the distinctive marks of a good Catholic—which characterized the English nation, there existed an evil temper of discontent and criticism amongst a large proportion of the people. The origin and causes of this are not difficult to trace. First and foremost amongst them was the material change which passed upon the social state of England after the ravages of the Black Death. The partial suspension of religious care and teaching through the sudden removal of at least two-thirds of the clergy, the diffusion of Wyclif's pernicious doctrines at the very juncture when the poverty and distress caused by the stagnation of trade and agriculture, and the altered relations between the labourer and the employer of labour, had prepared men's minds to receive them, occasioned general demoralization. Notwithstanding the efforts of good men, religion declined amongst the people. Then followed all the evils of civil war. The long-existing quarrel between the Houses of York and Lancaster broke out into open warfare; for thirty-five years a fratricidal strife deluged England with blood, laid the land waste, impeded the pursuit of learning, the enforcing of ecclesiastical discipline, the free course of religious observances. And when the long bloodshed ended with the enthronement of Henry VII., the flower of English youth had been destroyed and the power of the nobles finally broken, so that the power of the king became sole and supreme.

2. Deterioration of the Clergy.—Far more detrimental to the life of the Church in England than these national calamities, was the deterioration of the clergy which ensued. The pestilence had carried off so great a multitude of priests and of scholars destined for the priesthood, that the standard of qualification for holy orders was lowered. The ranks of the clergy were recruited, as has been said, with men of inferior birth and attainments, whose conduct and prudence was untried. The evils resulting from this was hardly felt at first, but after a time the character and conduct of many churchmen was such as to warrant, to a certain extent, the charges brought against them by the Wyclifites in their forcible and extravagant language. Already in the reign of Henry IV. we are told that "the clergy of England had passed the meridian of their greatness, and were on their declination. The people left off to admire them as they had done, and began little by little to fall off from them in every place, being distracted, though not wholly led away, by the lectures, sermons, and pamphlets of them who laboured for an alteration in religion."

3. **Wealth and Secular Employments of the Clergy.**—The great wealth of the Church revenues enjoyed by a large number of ecclesiastics also served to render them an object of envy to the people. When Henry IV. pressed for subsidies, the spoliation of the clergy was openly advocated, and a bill was introduced into Parliament by the famous Lollard, Sir John Oldcastle, which proposed that the king should take their temporalities, on the ground that "they had grown to such pride that it was charity to deprive them of their riches." It was alleged that from the superfluous revenues of the Church, if they were applied to purposes of general utility, the king might maintain fifteen earls and seven thousand knights and squires for the defence of the kingdom, besides endowing a hundred hospitals for the relief of the poor. This

confiscation was averted by Archbishop Chicheley, who suggested that the possessions of the alien priories, or priories dependent on foreign abbeys, should be seized. The immunity, or benefit, as it was called, of the clergy, mentioned in a previous chapter, was another cause of offence. It was a standing grievance to the laity, the more so because the privilege was no longer confined to priests, but extended to clerks in minor orders, and by them not unfrequently abused. The mild punishments of the ecclesiastical courts carried little dismay into the ranks of disorderly clerics. Privileged as they were from interference from the world without, the clergy, by their control over wills, contracts, marriages, and by the dues they exacted, penetrated to the very heart of the social life around them. On the other hand, their moral influence was rapidly declining; they had but little power to restrain the vices of the higher classes, the insubordination of the lower. The more opulent churchmen were often seen with curled hair and hanging sleeves, imitating the costume fashionable in the knightly society which they frequented. The bishops were, for the most part, conspicuous for their high character and their scholarship; but their entanglement in secular affairs withdrew them from their spiritual duties, and tended to render them worldly-minded, and subservient to the king's despotic will. The position of bishops as statesmen was particularly galling to the nobles, especially when men of low origin were raised to the prelacy. Notwithstanding the effort made in 1376 to check, if not to prohibit, the tenure of state offices by ecclesiastics, in consequence of which William of Wykeham and other prelates had been removed from the ministry, the evil had continued, so that in the reign of Henry VII. the clergy in England were absorbed in secular employments, more completely, perhaps, than at any other period. The Archbishop of Canterbury was Lord Chancellor until relieved of that post by Wolsey. Wolsey held, either together or in succession, the sees of Tournai, Lincoln, York, Durham, and Winchester; in the meanwhile he was acting as a lay statesman. Fox, Bishop of Winchester, was Lord Treasurer; other bishops filled the offices of Secretary of State and Master of the Rolls. Among the lower clergy a large proportion were employed in diplomatic, civil or legal offices, and were in possession of two or more benefices.

To the existence of this demoralization amongst the clergy, the very possibility of the so-called Reformation in England is traceable. Dom Gasquet, when commenting on the unsatisfactory condition of the clergy at the time when Henry VIII. began his evil course, quotes the following passage from Bellarmine: "I declare that false teaching, heresy, the falling away of so many peoples and kingdoms from the true faith, in fine, all the calamities, wars, tumults, and seditions of those distressing times, take their source from no other cause than because pastors, and the other priests of the Lord, sought Christ, not for Christ's sake, but that they might eat His bread. For some years before the Lutheran and Calvinistic heresy, as those testify who were then living, there was in ecclesiastical judgements hardly any severity, in morals no discipline, in sacred learning no teaching, towards holy things no reverence. The renowned glory of the clergy and sacred orders had perished;

priests were despised, laughed at by the people, and lay under grave and constant infamy" (*Concio de Dom. Laetare*, ap. Gasquet, *Monasteries*, vol. i. p. 20). This is very strong language, and as the words are spoken of other countries beside our own, we will hope that they represent the state of things upon the continent rather than amongst ourselves.

4. Effects of Rival Claimants to the Papacy.
—It must be remembered that the respect for ecclesiastical authority in general had been lessened by the unhappy schism (to use the popular misnomer) in the Papacy. The doubtful election of Popes, and the existence of one or even two claimants to the Chair of Peter in addition to its lawful occupant, had the effect of emboldening men to withhold obedience to the Vicar of Christ, and the source of the supreme pontifical authority became in some places a matter of academical discussion.

"Uncertainty," says Pastor, "as to the title of its ruler is ruinous to a nation; this schism affected the whole of Christendom, and called the very existence of the Church into question. The discord touching its Head necessarily permeated the whole body of the Church; in many dioceses two bishops were in arms for the possession of the episcopal throne, and two abbots in conflict for an abbey. The confusion was indescribable." "It is impossible to deny that by weakening the reverence for papal authority, this (so-called) schism paved the way for the real schism that rose a century later, and is still continuing."[1]

The Church not opposed to Learning.—
It has sometimes been alleged that the Church was antagonistic to the advancement of learning. No

[1] *Cf.* Rev. S. F. Smith, *The Great Schism of the West.*

statement can be more false. We have seen how, up to a recent period, the most illustrious men of letters, the lecturers at the universities, were almost exclusively ecclesiastics, either regular or secular. In the seclusion of the cloister the leisure of the monks was employed in transcribing valuable manuscripts, or in penning erudite treatises on subjects philosophical, theological, or scientific. Even the mendicant orders could not resist the general passion for knowledge, so that friars were reckoned amongst the most eminent of the schoolmen. Bishops were foremost in the ranks of patrons of learning; witness the numerous schools and colleges which owe their foundation to prelates. In 1314 the Bishop of Exeter founded Exeter College, Oxford; in 1361 Archbishop Islip founded Canterbury Hall. And on the suppression of the alien monasteries, although the revenues were informally granted to the king, a considerable portion of the wealth thus obtained was devoted to educational purposes. William of Wykeham founded Winchester School; and, later on, New College, Oxford, was built by him from the funds of his diocese. Eton College and King's College, Cambridge, were endowed from the revenues of suppressed priories; from the same source Archbishop Chicheley founded All Souls', Oxford, in commemoration of those who had been killed in the French wars; Waynflete founded Magdalen College; Fox, Bishop of Winchester, Corpus Christi; and Bishop Alcock, Jesus College, Cambridge. In spite, however, of these and other institutions for promoting the education of the laity, the period during which England cowered beneath the scourge of civil war, or slumbered under the apathetic rule of Henry VII.,

The Church before the Reformation.

was marked by the gradual decline and ultimate stagnation of learning, as well as by the general decadence of morals. Literature had reached a low ebb when, at the close of the fifteenth century, a wave of the great intellectual movement, which took place upon the continent, reached our shores. Of this movement, and its bearing upon the Church in England, we have now to speak.

CHAPTER XVI.

EVENTS IMMEDIATELY PRECEDING THE SCHISM.

The Renaissance, or Revival of Letters. Warham. Colet.—Among the preludes to the momentous religious changes of the sixteenth century, the great intellectual revolution known as the Revival of Letters holds an important place. It commenced with the revival of the study of the ancient classics in Italy. On the capture of Constantinople by the Turks in 1453, the westward flight of its Greek scholars opened anew the science and literature of the old world, and brought a fresh influx of vitality and vigour to Europe, at the hour when the intellectual energy of the Middle Ages was in its decline. Florence, long the home of freedom and art, became the centre of this renascence: thither, ere long, crowds of foreign students flocked to learn, from the teachers who had settled there, Greek, which was considered as the key of the new knowledge. Amongst these came scholars from Oxford, Grocyn, Linacre, and pre-eminently Colet, whose lectures, on their return, marked an epoch in the history of our literature. In England, as everywhere else in Europe, there was a growing thirst for knowledge; Colet's lecture-room was crowded with old and young; "the whole university," Erasmus says, "went to hear him." The teachers of the "New Learning," as it was called, found a patron in Archbishop Warham, who filled the see of Canterbury from 1503 to 1533. During his prelacy the universities flourished afresh. Immersed as he was in the business of the state, Warham was no mere politician; and he took a personal interest and share in the new movement of thought. In the simplicity of his life he offered a contrast to the prelates of his time, caring nothing for the pomp and worldly pleasures in which they too often indulged. His favourite relaxation was in the company of the learned, and many a poor scholar received from him substantial support. Erasmus, on his visit to England, termed him "one of the best of men," and "an honour to the realm; wise, judicious, learned, and modest." [1]

The revival of letters in England assumed a different aspect from that which it had taken in Italy; one more practical in its bearing on the religious life of the nation. The introduction of a new era of religious thought was principally the work of Colet, who, with his friends Erasmus and More, stands foremost amongst the educational reformers of the day. The only son of the Lord Mayor of London, Colet in his youth studied scholastic theology, and went afterwards to complete his studies in France and Italy. He drank in with avidity the lore of the new teachers, but with him the study of pagan classics gave place to reading the early Fathers of the Church. The knowledge of Greek was for him the key to a better understanding of the New Testament, the

[1] Ep. clxvii. ap. Froude, *Life of Erasmus*, p. 91.

opening out of a view of religious beliefs, more practical, and, as he imagined, better suited to the needs of the times than that which had satisfied preceding centuries. His dislike of scholastic theology, with all its subtle distinctions, burst forth in the lectures on St. Paul's Epistles which he delivered at Oxford, when he bade men "keep to the Apostles' Creed, and about the rest let men dispute as they will." It is a pity he formed this superficial view of the value of scholastic distinctions; still his intentions were good, and by his efforts to advance classical and exegetical studies he did a good work. Such was his repute that Henry VIII. created him Dean of St. Paul's. His first step was to restore discipline in the chapter, which had all gone to wreck; his second to carry out his designs of educational reform. To this end, with the large fortune he inherited from his father, he founded and endowed a grammar school within the shadow of his cathedral, for 153 boys. Above the headmaster's chair was an image of the Child Jesus, with a scroll, bearing the words: "Hear ye Him."

Colet's discipline was not popular with the chapter of St. Paul's. They complained to the bishop, and he to the primate; but the latter sided with Colet, who moreover was strong in the king's protection. By the archbishop's permission he addressed the convocation of clergy, exhorting them in unsparing terms to take thought for the reformation of the Church. "No heresy," he declared, "is so fatal to us, and to the people at large, as the depraved lives of the clergy." The accumulation of benefices, the luxury, avarice, and worldliness of prelates, must be abandoned. Care should be taken for the ordination and promotion of worthy ministers; residence should be made obligatory; a higher standard of practice enforced. Thus Colet sounded the note of reform; for he, with many others, felt persuaded that without a radical alteration of existing abuses, a catastrophe was not far off. Unfortunately he did not content himself with promoting the reform of discipline. Erasmus states his friend to have been "a man of genuine piety"; but he admits that his opinions were "peculiar," that he "hated scholastic theology, had a particular dislike of bishops, and did not believe many things generally taught." [1]

Erasmus.—If the support given by the primate to Colet was marked, still more so was the patronage he extended to Erasmus, who, by birth a Dutchman, came while young and comparatively unknown to Oxford to acquire a knowledge of Greek, and speedily rose to be the most distinguished man of letters of his day. Though as regards his own personal life somewhat of a time-server, he ruthlessly assailed the prevalent abuses. In his commentary on the New Testament, published with the tacit approval of Archbishop Warham, and dedicated by consent to Pope Leo X., he complains of "a priesthood who thought more of gold than of books; of the degradation of spiritual life, of the vain observances and scandalous practices of the religious orders": unfortunately he also stigmatized the pious customs and time-honoured devotions of the faithful as "superstitions." When, after writing this inflammatory book, Erasmus left England for the last time, about 1513, he little thought that he had done much to raise the storm in which his friends More and Fisher were to perish.

He believed that a peaceful reformation was at

[1] *Lif of Erasmus*, p. 92.

hand, that Pope and princes, and the wisdom of the laity, were about to make an end of ecclesiastical abuses." [1] And when, later on, he saw the work of demolition beginning, he hoped each step would be the last: that England, which he loved so well, which he termed "the home and citadel of virtue and learning," might be spared the convulsions he saw hanging over Germany. But there is no denying that Erasmus's New Testament, and his writings generally, had given the first impulse to the great upheaval. On this account Erasmus was denounced as "a sower of heresies"; it must however be remembered that he was the friend of Charles V. and other princes and prelates of known orthodoxy, a pensioner of cardinals, a declared opponent of Luther. "I am well liked at Rome," he writes. "The cardinals and the present Pope [Leo. X.] treated me like a brother. The English bishops are proud of my acquaintance. The Archbishop of Canterbury [Warham] could not have been kinder had he been my father." [2]

There is no doubt that Erasmus's desire and hope for a general reformation, and especially for the correction of abuses among the clergy, undertaken with moderation by the Church itself, was shared by the Pope and cardinals, as well as by all who desired the advance of religion. The idea of reform was kept steadily in view, but, as will be seen, it was not carried out till a later period owing to the opposition of the sovereigns of Europe and the Lutheran party.

Thomas More.—The religious tendencies of the revival of learning in England assumed a less destructive aspect in another of its representatives, the pious,

[1] Froude, *Life of Erasmus*.
[2] Ep. viii. Second Series, *ap.* Froude, p. 163.

gentle, sweet-tempered Thomas More. Even before he went to Oxford, while in the household of Cardinal Morton, where he spent his boyhood, More's remarkable talents had raised the highest hopes. "Whoever may live to see it," the grey-haired statesman used to say, "this child now waiting at table will turn out a marvellous man." When a student at Oxford, through the charm of his manners, his intellectual gifts and high attainments, he took a prominent place in the group of scholars assembled there. With Erasmus, then a man of established fame in the world of letters, his senior by thirteen years, he formed a friendship that only ceased at his death. On leaving the University at the age of eighteen, he was known throughout Europe as one of the foremost figures in the new movement; later on in his *Utopia*, a Latin romance, he embodied the dreams of social, religious, and political reform which it aimed at realizing. At one time desirous of becoming a monk, More schooled himself by austerities for the rule of the Carthusians; but he allowed himself to be persuaded that this was not his vocation, and at his father's wish embraced the legal profession and entered on political life. He rapidly rose into repute at the bar, but having incurred the displeasure of Henry VII., he was compelled to withdraw from public life until the death of that monarch introduced a new order of things.

Henry VIII., 1509.—The accession of Henry VIII. was hailed with an universal outburst of joy. The avarice and extortions of his predecessor on the throne had so disgusted the people of England, that the advent of the young king was hailed as the return of the golden age. Thus Thomas More regarded it;

his feeling broke out in Latin verses wherein he sings of glorious days to come, and celebrates the gentleness, the clemency, the cultivation, the piety of Henry VIII. This poem reads strangely in the light of his after history, but at the commencement of his reign the king was of a temper, as Cardinal Pole afterwards confessed, "from which all excellent things might have been hoped." His beauty of person and skill in martial accomplishments seemed matched by the generosity of his character and the nobleness of his political aims. Though fond of pleasure he was most observant of his religious duties, his custom being to hear two or three masses every day, "even," as his chronicler adds, "on those days which were devoted to the pleasures of the chase." Himself no mean scholar, Henry's sympathies were from the first openly on the side of the new learning, and through all the changes of his terrible career, his court was the home of letters. Hence during the early years of his reign, the intellectual movement, which had been held in check during the lifetime of Henry VII., by the suspicion and ill-will of that monarch, flourished apace, and spread far beyond the bounds of Oxford. Aided by the influences of the times, the diffusion of knowledge was rapid and extensive; books, heretofore the property only of the few, were by the invention of printing brought within the reach of the many, and an eager thirst for learning took possession of the minds of men.

The Humanists.—But the dream of a new age, of the regeneration of society, introduced peaceably by the progress of culture, the growth of letters, the reform of abuses, the revival of ecclesiastical discipline, was not to be realized. Upon the continent, unhappily, greater liberty of thought was to become a factor in the encouragement of license, the corruption of morals, the destruction of religious unity. The Humanists, so called from their almost exclusive study of the humanities, began to show a spirit of irreverence towards the institutions and teaching of the Church. The Latin of the Middle Ages, which, judged apart as an instrument of exact thought, was a language of great excellence, and, in the hands of a writer like St. Thomas of Aquin, of beauty, was alleged to have lost its classical purity; and criticism of the phraseology of the schools, of the dry terms of the mediæval theologians, was extended from the language employed to the subject-matter it embodied. Hence the divine science of theology met with neglect and depreciation. When Luther raised the standard of insurrection against the Church, a party was found ready to rally around it. Men whose writings had been arrested or condemned by the censors of books, sought to free themselves from what they denominated the thraldom of the Papacy.

England Loyal to the Faith.—In England, however, their protest as yet awoke no echo; its only effect was to rouse a spirit of opposition. Luther's works were solemnly burnt at Paul's Cross, heretical publications were ordered to be delivered up, fresh decrees were issued for the prosecution of heretics in the bishops' courts. The young king himself, proud of a theological knowledge in which he stood alone among the sovereigns of Europe, entered the lists against Luther by publishing a treatise from his own pen in defence of the Seven Sacraments, wherein the errors of the heresiarch were refuted. For this he was rewarded by Leo X. with the title of Defender of the Faith—a title which is still retained by our English sovereigns. The insolent abuse of the reformer's answer brought More and Fisher into the field of controversy. Later on, these two courageous men were destined not merely to use the pen, but to lay down their lives for the sake of the truth. Little could it then be surmised that Henry, the enemy of religious innovation, the upholder of orthodoxy, would be himself the one to remove the bulwarks of the citadel he was defending. Only the keen eye of Sir Thomas More discerned the unreliability of the king's character, his heartlessness and selfishness, and foresaw that if opposition were offered to him he would not hesitate to act upon the maxim: *Suprema lex regis voluntas.* Roper, the son-in-law and biographer of More, relates that one day, when he spoke to him of the happy state of the realm in having so Catholic and zealous a prince, Sir Thomas expressed his misgivings as to the future of England in these words: "And yet I pray God that we may not live to see the day in which all this will be changed, and in which we shall be glad to be permitted to possess our own churches and our own religion in peace." It will be necessary to narrate as briefly as possible the circumstances that led to the fulfilment of these prophetic words, and brought about the severance of England from the unity of Christendom.

Catherine of Arragon. Anne Boleyn.—Upon his accession to the crown, at the age of eighteen, Henry VIII. had married the Princess Catherine of Arragon, the affianced bride of his elder brother Arthur, who had died young. Catherine had been married to the deceased prince, and was thus incapable of marriage with Henry. The impediment however, being of ecclesiastical not divine law, could be, and was, removed by a dispensation granted by the Pope. Five children, three sons and two daughters, were born to Henry; they all died in infancy, with the exception of the Princess Mary, who subsequently ascended the throne. The king's disappointment at having no male heir was great; he had not been a faithful husband during eighteen years of wedded life, and now the faded charms of the queen, who was considerably his senior, had no attraction for him. He conceived a violent passion for one of the ladies of her household, the famous Anne Boleyn; and she, although a person of no very severe morals, saw her opportunity, and, warned by the fate of her elder sister Mary, refused to have any connection with him excepting that of wedlock. Henry consequently bethought himself of setting aside his marriage with Catherine as invalid. He professed to have scruples as to the lawfulness of his marriage with his brother's widow, and asserted his persuasion that the death of his sons was a judgement of heaven on account of this illicit union. Whether in this he acted on his own initiative, or whether the idea was suggested to him, it is impossible to determine. He consulted his favourite minister Wolsey on the subject, and together they concerted a plan by means of which the king's object might be attained.

Wolsey. A Divorce mooted.—Wolsey, the son of a wealthy burgher of Ipswich, had early mounted to power through his ambitious character and extraordinary abilities. Already in possession of the deanery of Lincoln, one of the wealthiest preferments of the English Church, when Henry came to the throne (1509), he rose to the post of chaplain and almoner to the young king, was made Bishop of Lincoln, and in 1514 raised to the archiepiscopal see of York. His qualities as a statesman gave him the highest place in the royal favour, and during fifteen years he virtually governed the kingdom, for he possessed the rare art of guiding his sovereign while apparently he was guided by him. Henry continued to reward his services. When Archbishop Warham gave up the seals of office, Wolsey was created Chancellor; as such he stood at the head of public justice, while his elevation to the cardinalate, and to the office of Legate *à latere*, rendered him supreme in the Church. Thus all authority, secular and ecclesiastical, was concentrated in his hands. When the notion of a divorce[1] was proposed to this all-powerful minister, political reasons induced him to promise his aid to the king. He saw in it an opportunity of supplying Catherine's place with a sister of the king of France, and thus dissolving the alliance with the Emperor Charles V. But he fatally mistook the king's intentions. The passion for Anne Boleyn, despised by Wolsey as a mere intrigue of gallantry, was a serious matter with Henry, who before it became generally known that a divorce was in agitation, openly announced to the Cardinal his resolve to

[1] Following the usual custom, we shall speak of the desired separation as a divorce. But it is necessary to keep in mind the distinction between a true divorce, which purports to dissolve a previously existing marriage, and a declaration of nullity, which declares that a marriage previously supposed to be sound was in reality null and void from the first. The Catholic Church never dreamed of attempting to give a true divorce, and Henry knew this too well to solicit it. What he asked for was a declaration of nullity. This, however, is often popularly called a divorce, and we shall employ the term in this sense.

marry her. Accordingly it was agreed that Wolsey as Legate should cite the king to appear before him to answer for having espoused his brother's widow. The king alone appeared, as Catherine was kept in ignorance of the plot until June 22, 1527. "In the Royal Council the divorce received no support. The most learned of the English bishops—Fisher of Rochester—declared openly against it. The English theologians who were consulted on the validity of the papal dispensation which had allowed Henry's marriage to take place, referred the king to the Pope for a decision of the question."[1]

Appeal to Rome.—In May, 1527, the Pope was in dire distress, through the capture and sack of Rome by the army of the Emperor with every circumstance of atrocity. Henry pretended to induce the French to come to the rescue of the Holy Father, and while Wolsey went to the French court the king despatched in July envoys to Rome to open negotiations with the Pope, and endeavour to obtain a legal declaration of the invalidity of the bull of dispensation on which his marriage with Catherine rested. Clement VII., who then filled the Chair of Peter, appointed an inquiry to be made in England, and sent Cardinal Campeggio as his legate. After considerable delay, the Legatine Court was opened in June, 1529. Both king and queen appeared before it; the queen only to appeal from it to the Pope in person. Thus nothing was decided, and the Cardinals agreed upon an adjournment for the sake of consulting the Pope as to the judgement to be pronounced. Fisher, Bishop of Rochester, made an able speech in defence of the queen, showing her to

[1] Green, *Short History of the English People*, p. 322.

be a legitimate and true wife, on account of which he incurred the enmity of the king.

Wolsey's End.—Wolsey's failure to obtain the divorce lost him all the favour he had enjoyed. Furious at the frustration of his will, the king dismissed him from office, and at once prosecuted him for transgression of the Statute of *Præmunire* by his exercise of papal jurisdiction within the land in his capacity of legate, although this had been done not only with the king's consent, but at his instigation. Few events in our history are more pathetic than the suddenness with which this great Cardinal and Chancellor fell. Surrounded by enemies, watched by spies, betrayed by those he trusted most, in one day he found himself stripped of his power, banished from court, a prisoner in his own house. He narrowly escaped impeachment, pardon being granted only on condition of the surrender of all his vast possessions to the Crown. Permitted to retire to his archbishopric, the one dignity he was suffered to retain, he spent the last year of his life in visiting his churches, confirming children, serving the poor; thus affording a picture of Christian humility. But his popularity in the north excited the jealousy of his political rivals; he was arrested on a charge of high treason. Already broken by his labours and crushed by the humiliation of his fall, this was for the old man a sentence of death. On his way to London an attack of illness forced him to stop at the abbey of Leicester. "Brethren," he said to the monks who met him at the gate, "I am come to lay my bones amongst you." On his deathbed his thoughts turned to his past career, and he expressed the regret it caused him in the well-known words: "Had I but served God as diligently as I have served the king, He would not have given me over in my grey hairs. But this is the just reward for my pains and study, not regarding my service to God, but only my duty to my prince."

Cardinal Wolsey had been a bountiful patron of learning: he founded several scholarships at the universities, and invited learned foreigners to lecture there. His foundation at Oxford, whose name of Cardinal College has been lost in its later title of Christ Church, is a splendid monument to his memory. But the best eulogium on his character is to be found in the contrast between the conduct of Henry before and after his fall. Whatever faults of ambition and worldliness are imputed to Wolsey, it must be owned that as long as he was at the right hand of the king and governed his counsels, the royal passions were confined within certain limits. No sooner was his influence removed than they broke through every restraint, and by their caprice and violence terrified all but the most intrepid into acquiescence and submission to the tyrant's overwhelming despotism.

On the question of the divorce being laid before the universities, Henry, by means of coercion and bribery, obtained a certain number of favourable opinions. At Cambridge, in February, 1530, when Gardiner and Fox requested the opinion of the University on the question, an answer was twice given against the king's contention. It was only at the third time that the vote was asked, that a conditional affirmation was carried by a bare majority. At Oxford, by excluding a great majority of the Masters of Arts, thirty-three signatures were obtained to the same conditional reply that Cambridge had given.[1] At Bologna Henry got the opinion of five friars, given secretly, and disowned by the university as soon as it was known. At Paris, when he had bribed the French king to put on pressure, he got a small majority. That these majorities were obtained by gross bribery and chicanery is not an allegation, but a fact recognized by all competent historians. Learned men and theologians on the continent were consulted, but the decisions were mostly the reverse of what was desired. Luther, in his reply to the request for a judgement, says : " Rather than sanction such a divorce, I would give the king leave to take another queen as well, and have two queens at the same time." The real motive of the king in desiring the divorce was easily discernible through the thin disguise wherewith he affected to cover it, namely, the scruples of a timorous conscience and the danger of a disputed succession. Above all, the iniquity of the proposal rendered it most unpopular amongst the people.

Henry's Dealings with the Clergy. The Title " Head of the Church." (1531.)—On Wolsey's disgrace, the chancellorship was offered to Sir Thomas More. He accepted the office—at that juncture of affairs a difficult and dangerous post—principally in the hope of carrying out in a spirit of loyalty, not hostility, to the Church, the religious reforms demanded by Colet and Erasmus. The necessity for reform now occupied the attention of Archbishop Warham. A Convocation, or Provincial Council, of Canterbury, drew up a code of decrees and instructions for prelates and pastors, for religious orders,

[1] See Brewer, *Calendar*, iv.

preachers, and schoolmasters, as excellent and as full as could be desired. But the king had other matters in hand than the moral reform of clergy or laity. The decrees were scarcely committed to paper before, by artifices and threats, he first deprived the clergy of their liberty, and then cast them headlong into schism and heresy, as we are now about to relate.

Wolsey had felt the need of taking stringent measures to remove existing scandals, and in view of this had, in 1527, in virtue of his legatine powers, convoked a synod. This council had come to nothing: its sittings were prorogued at first on account of the prevalence of an alarming epidemic, termed the sweating sickness; afterwards the miserable affair of the king's divorce came to thwart the project. The holding of that synod was the pretext for Wolsey's prosecution—most unjustly, for it had been done with the consent and at the desire of the king. It now suggested a plan of humiliating the clergy and enriching the royal coffers at their expense. This was to convict them as a body, under the same Statute of *Præmunire*, for having acknowledged the legatine authority. A writ was accordingly issued against the clergy in 1531, and the penalty of conviction was confiscation of all their goods and imprisonment at the king's pleasure. Had they made an united stand against this absurd and tyrannous charge, it would have been impossible to proceed with it. The Convocation hastily assembled, and weakly and foolishly offered the enormous sum of one hundred thousand pounds by way of compromise, or to purchase a pardon. Henry refused the proposal, unless in the preamble to the grant a clause was introduced acknowledging the king to be "the protector and only supreme head of the Church and clergy of England." Three days were spent in consultation, argument, and conference concerning this new and strange demand. At length it was agreed that the clergy should yield to it, provided the king allowed the insertion of these conditional words: "*quantum per legem Christi licet*"—"as far as the law of Christ will allow." It is plain, Dr. Lingard remarks, that the introduction of these words seemed to invalidate the whole recognition, since those who might reject the king's supremacy could maintain that it was not allowed by the law of Christ. But Henry was as yet timid and wavering; he sought to intimidate the Pope, but had not determined to separate from his communion. The title of Supreme Head, when first claimed by him and conceded by the clergy with the qualifying clause was not meant to be a denial of the higher rights of the Holy See to decide in questions of faith and matters spiritual. It was not, in fact, at the time understood to include headship in spirituals; but the vagueness of the term constituted its danger, as Fisher pointed out, since it might be made to mean anything, and cover the assumption of authority, disciplinary or doctrinal. At any rate, it was intended to prepare the way for resistance to the Holy See, should the desired divorce be decided against in Rome.

Hardly and with great reluctance as the Convocation of Canterbury had agreed to acknowledge the king as Supreme Head, still greater was the difficulty experienced in gaining the consent of the Convocation of York. Bishop Tunstall, who presided, strongly opposed the claim, on the ground of the ambiguity of the title. All resistance was, however, subdued, the clergy being allowed to compound for a fine of £18,840.

The Pope's Attitude.—Meanwhile Queen Catherine had, as we have seen, appealed from the legatine court held in London to the Holy See, for judgement in her behalf. Thereupon Clement VII. published a Bull prohibiting any person or court, except those authorized at Rome, from deciding the question of the divorce. Moreover, when the queen wrote to announce to him her expulsion from Court, and prayed him no longer to refuse her justice, he rebuked Henry for his relations with Anne Boleyn and forbade him to abandon Catherine or contract a new marriage. Henry revenged himself by prohibiting the usual payment of annates, or first-fruits of benefices, which for several centuries had been regularly transmitted to Rome. He also despatched Cranmer, a creature of his own, who had risen into notice through having disputed the authority of Pope Julius II. to grant the dispensation for the king's first marriage, to the continent, to endeavour to obtain learned opinions sanctioning the divorce. The result was, as before, unfavourable; all Christendom condemned his cause.

The annals of ecclesiastical history furnish no record of any matrimonial suit which entailed embassies so innumerable, a correspondence so voluminous, theological and judicial investigations so extensive, diplomatic negotiations so complicated, as did that of Henry VIII. The matter in itself was neither intricate nor obscure. The duplicity of a voluptuous monarch, determined to gratify his wishes at any cost, the intrigues and servility of courtiers and prelates, the use of bribes and undue pressure, magnified the affair into a question difficult of solution, and involving momentous issues. Nothing is more apparent than that Clement VII. was actuated only by conscientious motives in declining to decide in Henry's favour, that he entertained kind feelings towards Henry, and was willing to go to the utmost limits of indulgence and compliance. In the hope that the king's infatuation for Anne Boleyn would prove evanescent, he tolerated every delay that Henry's advocates put in the way of a final decision, for six years postponing the decision, and bearing patiently Henry's reproaches and uncourteous words, lest he should accelerate the threatened schism of England. On one point he was immovable—in upholding the inviolability of the marriage bond; and in this the whole Papal Curia agreed with him. He firmly refused to sanction the severance of the nuptials lawfully contracted, and, in obedience to God's law, he braved the monarch's displeasure.[1]

It has been said that had Clement followed a different policy, and taken decisive measures at the outset, he would have served justice better and saved England to the Church. Over and over again he was threatened by Wolsey and by the king's agents that to refuse the

---

[1] According to the doctrine of the Catholic Church, the impediment against marriage with a deceased brother's wife was, and is, existent; but at the same time it is of ecclesiastical, not divine, institution, and hence can be dispensed by papal authority. If a dispensation has been obtained, and the impediment thereby removed, the marriage between the two parties, when once contracted, is absolutely indissoluble. No power on earth, the papal included, can, without grievous sin, attempt to set it aside. Now such a dispensation had been issued by Julius II., and therefore the Pope was bound not to allow of the dissolution of the consequent marriage.

king's demand was to lose the allegiance of England. The disobedience shown by Henry was such as might well have justified a sentence of excommunication. But Clement was not a Gregory VII., and the judgement passed upon him by many writers is that during the whole progress of this unhappy question he contrived more and more to weaken his own authority until it was finally repudiated. Still it is easy to reason thus when a course of policy has been unsuccessful. The times did not perhaps admit of the stringent measures of former days. Some years later St. Pius V. was blamed for being too firm towards Henry's daughter Elizabeth, and for forgetting that the days of Hildebrand had gone by.

Cranmer, Archbishop of Canterbury. His Oath, 1532.—On the archbishopric of Canterbury becoming vacant in 1532 by the death of Archbishop Warham, Henry immediately bestowed it on Cranmer, who had been carrying on futile negotiations at the Papal Court to obtain a sanction of the divorce. The chief qualifications for the post that this man possessed were complete subservience to Henry's will, and readiness to employ any means towards the desired end. Before he could be invested with the dignities and privileges of the primacy, it was necessary that he should take the oath of canonical obedience to the Pope, and yet the whole of his future policy was to be based on repudiation of the Pope's authority. In order to get over this difficulty, previous to his consecration he made a protestation, in the presence of four witnesses only, that he did not intend to bind himself to do anything contrary to the laws of God, prejudicial to the rights of the king, or prohibitive of such reforms as he might think needful in the Church

—these "reforms" being, as he knew at the time, the separation of England from its obedience to the Holy See. Afterwards he proceeded to the high altar, and on his knees took the following oath: "I will be faithful and obedient to the Blessed Peter, the Holy Apostolic Church of Rome, and our Lord Pope Clement VII. and his successors. I will not consent, either by advice or act, to any injury being done to them in any manner. . . . I will carefully preserve, defend, increase, and promote the rights, honours, privileges, and authority of the Church of Rome, and of our Lord the Pope and his successors." The ceremony then followed, Cranmer, on the faith of the oath just publicly taken, receiving from the hands of the papal delegates, who knew nothing of his secret protestations, the pallium which the Pope had sent him. Dr. Lingard's remark on this extraordinary proceeding of the great English reformer is unquestionably just—"Oaths cease to offer any security, if their meaning may be qualified by previous protestations, made without the knowledge of the party who is principally interested."

Cranmer pronounces in favour of a Divorce.—The day of Cranmer's consecration was an evil one for England. Shortly afterwards he pronounced Henry's marriage with Catherine void, on the ground that Pope Julius II. had exceeded his powers in granting a dispensation for a union forbidden by the laws of God and of nature. Henry had anticipated this declaration by a private marriage with Anne Boleyn in the winter of 1532. He now proceeded to celebrate his nuptials in public. At these he desired Sir Thomas More, with whom he was on terms of affectionate friendship, to be present. More's refusal to comply with this invitation earned for him the implacable hatred of the newly-made queen. So long as the question of the divorce was undetermined, he had assisted Henry in his endeavours to procure a decision; but when it was clear that the final decision of the Holy See would be adverse to the king's wishes, More had to choose between his conscience and the honours of the world. He consequently resigned the chancellorship and retired into private life.

Cranmer crowns Anne Boleyn. The Pope's Action, 1534.—Cranmer's next step was to place the crown she had so long coveted upon Anne's head. This he did in direct defiance of the Supreme Pontiff. Clement annulled his proceedings, issued a brief of censure against him, and excommunicated Henry and Anne, unless they separated within a fixed time. It was not, however, until March, 1534, that, in a consistory of Cardinals, definite and final judgement was pronounced, declaring the marriage between Henry and Catherine to be canonical and valid, and ordering the king to take Catherine back as his lawful wife.

Henry's Resolve.—When Henry found that his last hopes of a decision in his favour in Rome were at an end, and that the formal censures of the Holy See were pronounced against him, the opposition to his wishes roused his haughty spirit, and he resolved to sweep away the papal power in England. The transfer of the highest spiritual authority from the Papacy to the Crown, and the consequent erection of a new and independent Church within the realm in place of the old, will form the subject of our next chapter.

CHAPTER XVII.

THE ROYAL SUPREMACY.

Establishment of the Royal Supremacy.—
It has already been said that when the admission of the king's headship over the Church was required of Convocation, no allusion whatever was made to the Pope, nor was any definition made as to what was involved in the term. Pending the issue of the deliberations in Rome on the divorce suit, Henry had contented himself by asserting his authority in an ambiguous phrase, capable of a twofold interpretation. Had the ultimate decision been other than it was, he would probably not have proceeded further on the road of schism. But now occurred that which the bishops had foreseen as possible, and had endeavoured to guard against. The royal authority was substituted for the pontifical, the Church prostrated at the foot of the throne. In a word, "the English Church was to have for its jurisdictional axis the king instead of the Pope." In 1534, an Act of Parliament ordered that the king "shall be taken, accepted, and reputed as the only Supreme Head on earth of the Church of England." All the functions of government, that is, in the ecclesiastical as well as in

the civil order, thenceforth belonged to the sovereign, to be exercised by himself in person, or by others under his appointment ; the authority over all persons and in all causes, both secular and religious, was vested solely in the Crown. Thus the assumption of the title of Supreme Head at last revealed itself as aimed expressly at the supreme jurisdiction of the Pope. But as it might seem that a parliamentary statute did not commit the Church, especially as less than a third of the prelates joined in its enactment, in the same year formal renunciations of papal authority were obtained, under stringent pressure, from both Convocations and from the two Universities. By a mere exercise of arbitrary power, all the clergy, regular and secular, were required definitely to abjure their allegiance to the Vicar of Christ, and to accept a layman, self-appointed, in his place, under penalty of imprisonment and death.

Fisher stands firm.—It might be imagined that the hierarchy of England would have risen against a demand so unprecedented, so repugnant to the tradition of centuries, so contrary to the law of Christ. But it was not so. Fisher, the holy and learned Bishop of Rochester, alone of all the prelates, refused to commit so grievous a sin against the Faith. When the Oath of Supremacy was tendered to him, he would not take it. Notwithstanding his age and the great esteem in which he was held, he was forthwith committed to the Tower, for it was high treason to withstand the king's command. The lesson intended was not lost. When commissioners were appointed to require submission from the friars and monks, there were some noble exceptions, but by many, alas! the formulas were signed almost without resistance. Few were met with who refused the oath of obedience, although, as one of the commissioners stated, "some have sworn to it with an evil will, and slenderly taken it."

The Pulpit utilized by the King.—The king did not rest satisfied with declarations and oaths which he quite understood to be unwilling and insincere. An order was issued to the bishops, abbots, and parish priests, to preach sermons against the usurpations of the Papacy and in defence of the new dogma, the bishops being held responsible for the obedience of the clergy under their orders, as the sheriffs were held responsible for the compliance of the bishops. The common people, being at this period without those means of information which are now universal, were more dependent for instruction upon the pulpit than we can well imagine. This one source of knowledge was now poisoned for them. Non-resident and non-preaching clergy had of late years left their flocks in dense ignorance. These pastors, who had long been dumb dogs, were now forced by the royal lash to bark at the Vicar of Christ. Almost the solitary example of zeal and activity in those evil days was displayed on this introduction of schism. Printed copies of a declaration of the king's supremacy were read to the people, and preachers inculcated on the minds of the simple folk the errors propounded in the books and pamphlets daily published against the sovereignty of the Apostolic See. It was known that the way to gain the king's favour was to decry the person, to repudiate the authority, and as far as possible to banish the name of the Pope, from the land which owed its Christianity and its civilization to the Holy See.

It may seem strange that these new theories were accepted by the nation. "But the uninstructed, who formed the great majority, may well have failed for a long time to perceive that schism had been contracted. Henry at first made no substantial alterations in the service-book. Although the name of the Pope was ordered to be struck out, mass was offered up the same as ever; there were still the seven sacraments, the invocation of saints, the celebration of the traditional festivals. On the other hand, the significance of bulls of confirmation, of oaths of supremacy, and similar forms, would not be appreciable to people of a humble class of society. They would perceive there was something wrong, some serious quarrel with the Pope on the subject of the divorce. But its practical bearing on their own position would be beyond their comprehension. Even those who did comprehend that a separation from the unity of Christendom was involved, may be excused if they did not at once deduce a consequent obligation to withdraw from communion with schismatics. It was not easy to determine what should be done, and while men are in perplexity, the *status quo* continues." [1]

The Acquiescence of the Bishops.—For the conduct of the bishops, however, it would not be easy to find excuse or palliation. What Fisher knew, they knew; what he did, they were bound to do; even like him to shed their blood to defend the unity of the Church. Had they all been as dauntless as he was, not even the audacity and obstinacy of Henry could have prevailed against a united episcopacy; for the clergy and religious orders would have stood firm at their example, and the

[1] *Alleged Antiquity of Anglicanism*, chap. iii.

people would have rallied to their defence. The only thing that can be said for them is that they did not perhaps at first understand the true nature of the new act, nor realize that the royal supremacy included the power of defining the doctrine of the faith and sacraments, and that the king's will would become law by sheer means of royal proclamations. Moreover, owing either to the false principles which had become current since the disputed succession to the Papacy, to the want of deep theological studies at the universities, or to the contempt of ancient ways which, as we have seen, then prevailed among the disciples of the Renaissance, the importance of the supremacy of the Holy See for the maintenance of unity was less felt than in former times in England. Opposition to papal authority was familiar to men who were themselves firmly attached to the Catholic faith and to the Holy See. The course of this history will have testified to the tendency continually manifested in this country towards what has since been called Erastianism; the undue intrusion, that is, of lay and secular power into the province of the spiritual power. The long struggle against the separate jurisdiction for clerks and laymen; the Statute of Mortmain, enacted to restrain the transfer of lands to the Church; that of Provisors, which took from the Pope and conferred upon the king the right of disposing of English benefices; that of *Præmunire*, whereby appeals from the king's court to that of Rome were rendered penal, all point the same way. The repeated attempts to extend the royal prerogative when the temporal and spiritual jurisdictions came into collision, culminated in the assumption by Henry VIII. of the ecclesiastical headship, a thing in itself without precedent and at variance with all traditions.

The minds of men had also been to some extent prepared to acquiesce in Henry's religious supremacy by the long tenure of supreme ecclesiastical authority in the kingdom by Wolsey. In virtue of additional faculties, which he had asked for, and presumed erroneously that he had obtained, during the imprisonment of Clement VII., he exercised almost all the prerogatives of the Supreme Pontiff within the realm, and all appeals to Rome were consequently suspended. In raising his favourite to the head of the Church and State, the king was simply getting all religious and civil authority — never before united in one person—within the reach of his own grasp. The transfer of these from his subject to himself was no difficult task, for Wolsey's wealth and power were held merely at the royal pleasure, as was proved by the suddenness wherewith he was deprived of them. Thus, to a large majority of those most concerned in it, the change did not at the time appear so fundamental as in reality it was. Not until men had time to reflect did the profound significance of the Act of Supremacy force itself upon them.

Henry's Despotism.— There is no doubt how Henry understood his new office, and the radical changes consequent on it. " Measures were taken to stay the inflow of jurisdiction from Rome by prohibiting the bishops-elect from procuring bulls of confirmation. In the following year those who had previously received bulls were required to surrender them into the hands of the king, who had succeeded to the authority which the Pope had lost." [1] All

---

[1] *Alleged Antiquity of Anglicanism*, chap. iii.

ecclesiastical legislation and spiritual jurisdiction was thenceforth to emanate from the royal power, no exception being made for any collateral and independent authority appertaining to the archbishop. Henry was, moreover, prepared to vindicate his new headship with something more than mere enactments. Arbitrary legislation, arbitrary imprisonment, arbitrary executions, acts of unscrupulous tyranny sanctioned by an obsequious parliament, were to mark the remainder of his reign. The terrible penalties attached to high treason were to be inflicted on all who ventured openly to deny his ecclesiastical supremacy.

But the penal statutes, although they might enforce conformity, were powerless to produce conviction. In spite of the servile compliance of the prelates, and the external submission of the clergy at large, adherence to the old belief in the supremacy of the Sovereign Pontiff was cherished at heart. Though an appearance of conformity was obtained, there remained a large number who refused to identify themselves with the schism. The Carthusians, men distinguished amongst other monks for their sanctity and austerity, had, after a stubborn resistance, acknowledged the royal supremacy. Before many months had elapsed, recognizing their error, they came forward to retract their oath. Committed to prison and brought to trial, they were neither to be persuaded by argument nor subdued by terror. Three priors, with two other monks and a secular priest, all men of good character and learning, were cruelly put to death in May, 1535, being hanged and then disembowelled before life was extinct. Blessed Thomas More, from his prison-cell in the Tower, in which he too had been cast for refusing to take the oath required of him, beheld the noble band on their way to execution, dragged on hurdles along the ground. "Dost thou not see," he remarked to his daughter, who was allowed to visit him, "that these blessed fathers be now as cheerfully going to their deaths as bridegrooms to their marriage."

Fisher's Martyrdom.—The fearless death of these monks, and of a second band who suffered in the following month, some of whom were personally known to him, helped also to raise the thoughts of Bishop Fisher from his dungeon in the Tower to the glory which was preparing for him in the courts of the celestial city. For eighteen months already this saintly prelate had languished in a noisome prison, on insufficient diet, without a fire in winter or clothes to protect him from the cold. Aged as he was, and enfeebled by sickness, it was a wonder that he did not succumb to his suffering during those long and weary months, during which he was furthermore deprived of all external help and of the consolations of religion. In June, 1535, an event occurred that accelerated his doom. The news reached England that he had been created a cardinal by Pope Paul III., who had succeeded Clement VII. in the Pontifical See. The Pope was proposing to hold a council, and since it was desired that cardinals of every nation should be present at the council, he thought it necessary to raise some Englishman to the purple. Hearing that no prelate in the realm was to be compared to Fisher in wisdom, learning, and virtue, his choice fell on him. It was thought that this would give the king pleasure, whereas it exasperated him. "Paul may send him a hat when he will," Henry is reported to have said, "but I will so provide that whensoever it cometh he shall wear it on his shoulders, for head he shall have none to set it on." Accordingly Fisher was tried and condemned, the only crime of which he was accused being the denial to the king of the new title of Supreme Head of the Church. The sentence pronounced against him was that he should be "drawn on a hurdle to the place of execution [Tyburn], hanged, cut down alive, his members cut off and cast into the fire, his bowels burnt before his eyes, his head smitten off, and his body quartered." These atrocious penalties were afterwards commuted to decapitation on Tower Hill, not from any respect for his dignity as a cardinal, or clemency on the king's part, but merely because it was feared that he was too weak to reach Tyburn alive. We must perforce linger a moment over the details of his glorious martyrdom and that of his companion and fellow-sufferer, Blessed Thomas More.

At five o'clock on the morning of the day fixed for his execution, the Lieutenant of the Tower went to the cardinal's cell, to tell him that it was the king's pleasure that he should suffer death that forenoon. "If this be your errand," Fisher replied, "you bring me no great news, for I have long time looked for this message. And I most humbly thank the king's majesty that it pleaseth him to rid me of all this worldly business, and I thank you for your tidings." He then inquired at what hour he was to leave the prison, and on hearing it was not until nine o'clock, he asked to sleep a little longer, as by reason of his infirmities, not for any fear of death, he had had little rest that night. He then lay down and slept soundly for more than two hours. On being waked, he called

for his best apparel, and dressed himself carefully,
remarking that on the day of his nuptials it behoved
him to use greater cleanliness for the solemnity. A
copy of the New Testament was in his hand when
he approached the scaffold. Opening it for the
last time his eye fell upon the words: "This is life
everlasting, that they may know Thee, the only true
God, and Jesus Christ whom Thou hast sent. I
have glorified Thee on earth, I have finished the
work Thou gavest me to do" (St. John xvii. 3-5).
Thereupon he closed the book, saying: "Here is
learning enough for me to my life's end." With an
alertness which astonished those who knew his
debility, he ascended the steps to the scaffold; the
sun shining brightly in his face, he was heard to
murmur: "Accedite ad eum et illuminamini, et
facies vestrae non confundentur" (Ps. xxxiii. 5).[1]
After addressing a few words to the people, he laid
his head on the block, and as his historian adds,
his immortal soul mounted to the joys of heaven.

It is said that Anne Boleyn ordered the head of
the saintly cardinal to be brought to her, and, after
looking at it for a time contemptuously, uttered these
words: "So this is the head that so often exclaimed
against me! I trust that it shall never do me more
harm," and, striking the mouth with the back of her
hand, received from one of the teeth a wound that
left a scar until her death. Nor did Henry's unrelenting rage end with death. He was not satisfied
unless the dead body was exposed to every kind of
contumely. He ordered that it should be stripped
of all its clothes and remain uncovered on the place

---

[1] "Come ye to him and be enlightened, and your faces shall not be confounded."

of execution as a spectacle to the people, and no one dared to approach it for fear of the tyrant, except those whose office was to outrage it. At night the remains of the blessed martyr were tumbled into a grave dug by the halberds of the watchmen, without a shroud or anything usual at a Christian man's burial. The head was placed on a pole on London Bridge, beside those of the Carthusians who had been executed before him. Although the season was the height of summer, it daily grew fresher and more comely, the colour being better than in his lifetime. This was accounted a miracle, and so many persons thronged to see the strange sight, that the passage over the bridge was rendered almost impassable. At the end of a fortnight, therefore, it was removed, and in its place that of Blessed Thomas More was set up.

Martyrdom of Thomas More.—As the foremost layman in England, More had been summoned from his retirement at Chelsea, where he occupied himself with literary pursuits, to take the Oath of Supremacy. As yet it had been tendered only to the clergy, not to the laity; and it was thought that if More did not resist it, no other layman would. On his refusal he too was lodged in the Tower. When arraigned as a criminal at the tribunal where he formerly sat as sole judge and arbitrator, he made so eloquent a defence, showing that he was innocent of having made any attempt, or even of having expressed a desire, to deprive the king of the title of Head of the Church, his only offence being silence, that he was on the point of being acquitted. But the solicitor-general bore false witness against him, and the same hideous sentence was passed on him as on his fellow-martyrs; it was, however, commuted to decapitation. The king, who was fond of More, and had often enjoyed his society, made every endeavour to gain his compliance, at whatever price. At the very foot of the scaffold a courtier came up, promising him, in Henry's name, restoration of liberty, wealth, position, office, even the royal favour, if he would change his mind. Under More's gentle and sunny nature lay a stern inflexibility of resolve. "It is beheadal or hell," he replied, and turned to ascend the scaffold, meeting death with constancy and cheerfulness.

By these executions the king proved that neither virtue, talent nor learning, past favour or services, could atone in his eyes for the crime of denying his supremacy. More and Fisher saw him introduce a principle which might be, as in fact it ultimately proved, the source of every error. They died not merely for maintaining doctrines or defending Catholic traditions; they died for something more fundamental still : for the divine constitution of the Church, the pillar and foundation of all truth for upholding the Pope's supremacy, and resisting the usurpation by the civil power of sovereign authority over the Church. Full well they knew that, once deprived of the solid basis upon which for ages it had rested, and placed upon the slippery sands of human authority, the edifice of the Church in England would speedily crumble beneath blows aimed at it by the soul-destroying hand of heresy and unbelief.

Thomas Cromwell.—The framing of the statutes whereby the royal supremacy was established in England, was chiefly the work of one Thomas Cromwell, a man of low origin, who had formerly been in Wolsey's service. When the estates belonging to the

Cardinal were forfeited, he had, by royal permission, retained the administration of them. Clever, prompt, ruthless, and remorseless, Cromwell exactly suited Henry, and his rise was extraordinarily rapid. He became Chancellor of the Exchequer, Master of the Rolls, Secretary of State. When the king, having neither law nor precedent to guide him in the duties of his new capacity, needed a new officer for the conduct of ecclesiastical affairs, he chose the man whose counsels had first suggested the appropriation of the supremacy, and whose industry had carried the attempt to a successful termination. To Cromwell, under the title of royal vicegerent or vice-general, he delegated his spiritual jurisdiction, giving him autocratic and irresponsible power to treat all causes ecclesiastical, to redress heresies and abuses in the Church, to issue censures and inflict punishments, to confirm elections, and to present to benefices and prelacies. As a proof of the view he took of the nature of the supremacy as the source of all ecclesiastical jurisdiction, Henry gave his vicar precedence of all the lords spiritual and temporal, and subjected to him all orders of clergy, the archbishops not excepted.

It was with difficulty that the clergy suppressed their murmurs when they saw supreme ecclesiastical authority over them exercised by a man who had never taken orders, or graduated in any university; who in his youth had been a soldier of fortune in Italy, a "ruffian," as he himself once owned to Cranmer, in the most unscrupulous school the world contained. But their degradation was to go a step further. Cromwell received special authorization to undertake a visitation of the entire English Church, and in the meanwhile, in order to test the sincerity of the bishops' submission and extort from them a practical acknowledgement that they derived their authority from no source but the Crown, they were required temporarily to surrender to the king all their right of jurisdiction, as if subjected to the penalty of suspension. To this the archbishop and the other prelates submitted humbly; until, on their presenting a petition to be restored to the exercise of their usual powers, they were, in the king's name and as his delegates, reinvested with authority to ordain priests and discharge all the other episcopal duties. In this manner the whole liberties, powers, and privileges of the clergy were swept away at a blow. The one great institution which could offer resistance to the royal will was struck down.

The Dissolution of the lesser Monasteries.— The object of the visitation was thus plainly shown to be not to enforce greater strictness of discipline, but to exact more complete acceptation of the royal supremacy. A further aim was to bring about the dissolution of the monasteries, and thus place the wealth of the religious bodies at the disposal of the Crown. This proposition when made by Cromwell was welcome to Henry. The royal treasury was empty, and no readier source of replenishing it was at hand than by the plunder of the monasteries. By this means a vast spoil might be gathered in with very little difficulty.

The suppression of monasteries was, as we have seen, no new thing in England. The property of several alien priories had been seized by Edward III., on the plea that they were the cause of much money being sent abroad without any return being made, and that it was a shameful thing, during the progress of the French wars, that the revenues of England should be enriching a hostile nation. This precedent was followed by Richard II.; and in 1414 an Act of Parliament ordered the suppression of a considerable number. Henry V. is said to have suppressed 190 foreign foundations. At the time of which we are speaking, Cardinal Wolsey was the first to set an example of dissolving the English monasteries. The number of these houses had of late years multiplied greatly and their wealth had increased; in many discipline was relaxed, and it was felt that the labours of foreign monks as transcribers and teachers was less necessary than formerly. It was with the sanction of the Holy See that Cardinal Wolsey dissolved seven or eight of the less important monasteries, in order that with their revenues his college at Oxford and the school he was erecting at Ipswich might be endowed. But the suppression of monasteries by King Henry VIII. was wholesale and indiscriminate; it was suggested by motives of avarice, and conducted with cruel injustice, in a spirit of hostility to the religious orders. The work was begun by Cromwell in 1535 by issuing injunctions which he knew the monks could not possibly accept; this he did in the hope of driving them to surrender or to open revolt. Even Protestant historians designate his proceedings as "acts of flagrant injustice, done in the outraged name of religion and law." He next appointed as commissioners to inquire into the condition of the religious houses, four men of very equivocal character, who sought not the improvement but the spoliation of the institutions they visited. The report these commissioners drew up was laid before Parliament, with a petition that all the smaller monasteries throughout the kingdom, whose income did not exceed £200 a year, should be suppressed. These smaller houses were, it was alleged, given up, far more than the larger ones, to sloth and immorality. Small credence must be given to the charges brought against their inmates, for little could be substantiated to their discredit, and few persons were found desirous of abandoning the religious life.

Not without extreme difficulty, and after a long debate, did the Bill for the dissolution of these lesser monasteries, and the transfer of their property to the Crown, pass the House of Commons. The king's threats alone availed to carry it through. By this measure about 376 communities were dissolved, and an addition of £32,000 was made to the yearly revenue of the Crown, besides the sum realized by the sale of valuables, amounting to about £100,000.

In eighteen months after Cromwell's work of destruction began, all the smaller monasteries were things of the past: picturesque ruins replaced magnificent structures which had been the homes of learning and piety. Any attempt made by the monks to conceal their treasures was punished with death; twelve abbots were executed without mercy. Friendless men and women were turned adrift on the world, disgraced with false accusations, without means of support, except, perhaps, some miserable pension, or the alms which the charitable bestowed on them.

Resistance. The Pilgrimage of Grace.—Still this was but the beginning of sorrow. A rebellion broke out in the north, where the monks were very popular, which soon assumed formidable proportions. From the borders of Scotland to the banks of the Humber, the inhabitants in general bound themselves by oath to stand by each other " for the love which they bore to Almighty God, and the faith of His holy Church, for the restoration of the Church and the suppression of heresy." The whole nobility of the north took up arms; thirty thousand " tall men and well horsed moved southward, demanding reunion with Rome, and redress for the wrongs done to the Church." This enterprise, of which Lord Darcy was the leader, was styled the " Pilgrimage of Grace." The banners bore the effigy of Christ crucified, the chalice and host, and other sacred emblems. Wherever the insurgents came, the ejected monks were reinstated in their monasteries. Henry gave the Duke of Norfolk, who headed the royal forces, full power to treat with the leaders; a free pardon was offered to the insurgents, and accepted by them on the understanding that their grievances should shortly be patiently discussed in the parliament about to meet at York. But Henry, relieved from apprehension, neglected to fulfil his promises. Some of the nobles again took up arms, and this was made the pretence for the withdrawal of every concession. The leaders were arrested, and sent up to London to be executed, others were hanged by scores at York, Hull, and Carlisle; and the insurrection was followed with ruthless severity in all the northern districts.

Spoliation of the greater Monasteries.— Cromwell saw in this rising a pretext for attacking the more wealthy monasteries, which had till then been spared, because their abbots and priors possessed greater influence and superior means of defence. On the plea of inquiry into what complicity they might have had in the insurrection, a fresh visitation was set on foot. By one expedient or another, all the great abbeys of the north were successively wrested from their proprietors, and transferred to the king's ownership.

The success of the commissioners in the north stimulated the industry of their colleagues in the south of England. They proceeded from convent to convent, soliciting, requiring, compelling the inmates to submit to the royal pleasure; each week was marked by the surrender of one or more religious house. If persuasion, intrigue, intimidation failed, recourse was had to violence. A search was instituted, and the discovery of any treatise in favour of the papal supremacy or the validity of the king's first marriage, any charge, real or fictitious, that could be brought against them, was taken as a proof of the monks' adhesion to the king's enemies, of their disobedience to the statutes of the realm. In vain large bribes were offered to Cromwell in the hope of obtaining better terms; he accepted them without hesitation, thus enriching himself and his friends enormously, but continued on the same course. If the abbot and the leading brethren were refractory, they were punished with imprisonment during the king's pleasure. Some, like the Carthusians confined in Newgate, were left to perish through hunger and neglect; others like the abbots of Glastonbury, Reading, and Colchester, were executed as felons and traitors. The fate of the abbot of Glastonbury will serve as an instance of the way in which individuals who resisted the Commissioners were treated. A man of eighty years of age, Richard Whiting, was known far and wide for his rare learning, extreme piety, and hospitality; he was also the head of a college where some three hundred youths were educated. Cromwell's agents, having despoiled the time-honoured abbey, after a mock trial dragged the aged abbot, whom they accused of concealing some of the sacred vessels of the church, on a hurdle through the streets of Glastonbury to the Tor Hill. There he was literally butchered, his body being divided into four quarters to be exhibited at four of the neighbouring towns, while his venerable head, impaled on a spear, was placed over his own gateway.

During these proceedings, which lasted five years, the religious bodies, instead of combining for their common defence, seem to have awaited their fate with the apathy of despair. A few wealthy houses sought, through the agency of their friends, to purchase exemption with offers of money and lands, but the rapacity of the king refused to accept part when the whole was at his mercy. He caused an artfully-devised bill to be brought into Parliament, vesting in the Crown all the property of the monastic establishments that already had been, or should thereafter be, dissolved. The torrent of wealth poured in upon the Crown by the spoliation of the monasteries has seldom been equalled in any country by the confiscations following a subdued rebellion. The value of the Church plate was of course immense, besides the images of gold and silver and pearls and precious stones of incalculable price, the offerings and bequests of the faithful. The vestments of the priests, the carved stalls, the lead from the roofs, the bells from the belfry, were all carried off and sold to the highest bidder. The work of destruction appears to have been pursued in as wanton a manner as possible; the axe and mattock, says Spelman, ruined almost all the chief ecclesiastical ornaments of the kingdom. The costly libraries were destroyed, books being part of the booty; stores of precious manuscripts and rare printed volumes were sold as waste paper, or sent over the sea in shiploads. More than a thousand chapels and chantries were looted and destroyed, together with the religious houses, through the insatiable avarice of the king by the sacrilegious hands of his commissioners.

Such was the royal extravagance, however, that within a few years all the substance thus brought to the king's treasury was exhausted. The spoil was to a great extent shared among his courtiers, into whose laps, we are told, he flung half the property of the Church. Something like a fifth part of the actual estates in the realm was transferred from the holding of ecclesiastics to that of nobles and gentry. Not only were the old families enriched, but a new aristocracy arose through the enormous grants of Church land made to the dependents of the Court and the upholders of the king's ecclesiastical policy. The property thus bestowed on laymen brought with it a curse, not a blessing. Temporal disasters, a violent or otherwise miserable death, the absence of male issue, were judgements which often fell upon those who robbed religious houses, or who grew rich upon the spoil taken from the Church.

Cromwell's End.—Cromwell himself, the instigator and chief promoter of the iniquitous spoliations, which it is impossible to palliate, much less to excuse, was speedily overtaken by the fate he had prepared for many others. Created Earl of Essex, having the office of Lord Chamberlain added to his other appointments, enjoying the immense wealth he had appropriated out of the spoils of the monasteries, he appeared securely established in his new and dazzling fortunes, when the judgements of God suddenly fell upon him. The king had, by his persuasion, married by proxy, whilst she was still on the continent, Anne of Cleves, a Dutch princess, awkward and ill-favoured, to whom he at first sight conceived a strong dislike. In his anger and annoyance the king turned upon his favourite. Cromwell was charged with betraying his duty as Vicar-General, with receiving bribes, encroaching on the royal prerogative, and encouraging heresy. By a bill of attainder, a most unjust procedure, but one of which he could not complain—since he had employed it against men, and women, too, of birth, education, and virtue infinitely superior to his own— he was doomed to the scaffold. Arrested at the council table, Cromwell was utterly unprepared for his downfall. By a strange nemesis he passed to execution suddenly, almost untried, and certainly unheard in his own defence. The nobles sprang on him with a fierceness that told of long-suppressed hatred. "Is this," he cried, "my guerdon for the services I have rendered? Make quick work with me, and let me not languish in prison." Quick work was made. The king stripped him of every office, of every privilege and title that had been conferred on him, and a burst of popular applause hailed his execution.

Results of the Dissolution of Monasteries. —Not the religious communities alone, but the whole kingdom, suffered from the acts of confiscation and robbery of which Cromwell had been the instrument, and the flagrant injustice and cruelty which even Protestants condemn. From the first permanent introduction of Christianity into Britain, the monasteries had been a most necessary and useful part of the Church system, centres of religious life and teaching, homes of sanctity, of learning, of prayer. Nor were the occupations of their inmates exclusively of a spiritual and intellectual nature; the monks tilled the soil, cultivated waste lands, taught the unskilled natives useful arts, and raised magnificent abbeys, unequalled for architectural beauty by the structures of later times. The abbots and priors were good and kind landlords; their gate was ever open to the needy and suffering. Thousands of poor were employed, fed, and clothed by the monasteries. The Church was the easiest of landlords, the great dispenser of charity. At every religious house throughout the land daily relief was given to the necessitous; all the larger ones had a hospice where travellers were entertained, an infirmary where the sick were tended, or a school where the children of poor gentlemen were educated free of charge.[1] In imitation of the abbeys, the palaces of the bishops, the houses of the clergy, the castles of the nobles, the homes of the faithful, maintained all the year round the Christian law of almsgiving, and the poor were regarded and ministered to as the brethren of Jesus Christ. But when the monasteries had been wrecked, the churches plundered, chantries and chapels suppressed, works of charity innumerable extinguished, the poverty of England began. Faith declined and want increased;

---

[1] *Cf.* Spelman, *History of Sacrilege*, p. 232.

the bishops and clergy were commanded to stir up the charity of the rich towards the poor, yet the intervention of public law for their succour became necessary. In the reign of Elizabeth an act of parliament made the relief of the poor compulsory, and England for the first time had a Poor Law.

No wonder that all the miseries which fell upon the "meaner folk," as they were termed, in consequence of the dissolution of the monasteries, drove them into rebellion. Revolt was everywhere stamped out. The king, either to lull his own conscience or to stifle the murmurs of his subjects, gave back several hospitals and charitable foundations in London to the poor who had been robbed of them. A portion also of the property rudely wrested from the Church was applied to the creation of six new bishoprics—the first created since the reign of Henry I.—and also to the endowment of certain schools and colleges. Trinity College, Cambridge, was founded principally out of monastic revenues.

No Precedent for Henry's Supremacy.—Non-Catholics, who refuse to recognize in the occupant of the Chair of Peter the Vicar of Jesus Christ, the divinely appointed teacher and ruler of the Church, are wont to assert that in establishing the royal supremacy over the Church in England, Henry VIII. was but reviving and restoring to the Crown an ancient prerogative which belonged to it by right, and had been usurped by the Bishop of Rome. In this, as we have seen, they are quite mistaken. The supreme headship of the Pope is an integral and essential part of Catholic belief, the keystone of the arch on which the edifice rests; and it was acknowledged as such expressly as well as practically, over and over again, by pre-reformation kings, prelates, and others. Nor was Henry contented that his royal supremacy should consist in seeing that all Church laws were properly carried out, in regulating the nomination to bishoprics, in defending the (supposed) rights of the monarch against the aggressions (as they were termed) of a foreign potentate. He claimed the right to supersede all ecclesiastical canons, and to govern in matters spiritual autocratically, according to his own absolute and irresponsible will. For this no one will be found to allege warranty of law or sanction of custom. By a policy as daring as it was unscrupulous, all the bulwarks of liberty were overthrown. The reader will not be surprised to learn from the following chapter that Henry, after demolishing the defences, attacked the citadel of the Faith. He proceeded to make his own judgement the standard of orthodoxy, and claimed the right of dictating the form of doctrine to be held and taught throughout the land.

CHAPTER XVIII.

CHANGES IN DOCTRINE.

Cardinal Pole's Mission.—It must not be supposed that the events happening in England passed unnoticed at the Papal Court. The schism of the English Church, the long series of profane and sacrilegious deeds committed with the king's sanction and at his command, deeply grieved the Supreme Pontiff. When the blood of the first martyrs, shed for their adherence to the Holy See, cried aloud for vengeance, he prepared a bull of excommunication against Henry. Motives of prudence, however, induced him to postpone its publication, since he feared lest, under existing circumstances, it might increase the irritation of the king rather than bring him to repentance. After the insurrection had taken place in the northern counties, he considered an opportune moment had come to attempt a reconciliation. For this object he employed the instrumentality of Cardinal Pole, and invested him with the necessary powers. This prelate, whom his opposition to the king's ecclesiastical policy had exiled from his country, was a lineal descendant of the House of York, and consequently a kinsman of the reigning monarch. Born in 1500, he was educated at Oxford, and afterwards sent to Italy, where the brightest and happiest years of his life were spent amid a circle of chosen friends. At the age of twenty-nine he returned to England, and when the see of York became vacant by the death of Wolsey, Henry desired to bestow it upon Pole as the price of his approval of the project of the divorce. His refusal to accept this bribe, and his outspoken denunciation of the servility, the ambition, the intrigues of the prelates about the Court, awoke the animosity of the despotic monarch; and Pole, judging that his resistance to the royal designs could effect no good, obtained permission to return to Italy. A treatise which he wrote at Henry's desire, on the Unity of the Church, did but increase that monarch's enmity to him, since he treated the burning questions of the day, the supremacy and the divorce, in a manner directly hostile to the king's views.

On the proposal of a council *de emendanda ecclesia* made by a committee formed in 1536 by Pope Paul III., Cardinal Pole was summoned to Rome to take part in its deliberations.[1] Shortly before this time he had been raised to the cardinalate, on account of the renown he had acquired for erudition and virtue, and because the Pope thought his elevation

---

[1] The deliberations of this council unfortunately came to nothing, owing to the obstacles placed in the way by the Emperor, the King of France, and the Lutherans. The proposed reforms were, besides, too radical and incisive to meet the approval of the majority of the cardinals, who thought it better to try and amend matters quietly and gradually. Those who took this view were perhaps right; yet, by the postponement of stringent measures, the enemies of the Church were emboldened to sneer at her pastors as men who loved darkness because they feared the light (*Cf*. Fr. Zimmermann, S.J.: *Kardinal Pole, sein Leben und seine Schriften*, p. 126).

might be advantageous to the oppressed Church in England. For whilst absent from his native country, her needs and her troubles were ever near Pole's heart; he watched with keen anxiety the course of events, and bitterly deplored her alienation from the Holy See. Accordingly he was nominated Papal Legate, and was proceeding to England to attempt to effect a pacification; but the hostile attitude of the king, who set a price upon his head, prevented him from entering the kingdom. He returned to Rome with his mission unaccomplished. Henry meanwhile, unable to reach the cardinal, wreaked his vengeance on his mother and brothers, the former of whom—Margaret, Countess of Salisbury—as is well known, was executed at his command, and is enrolled amongst the beatified English martyrs.

Alteration of Doctrine.—From the time of the abolition of papal authority and the substitution of the civil power in its stead in the government of the Church, until the close of Henry's reign, the creed of the Church of England depended on the caprice of its supreme head. From the primate to the lowest deacon, every minister derived from him his right to exercise spiritual functions. The voices of the preachers were the echo of his will. He alone could define orthodoxy or declare heresy, change the forms of worship or decide the articles of belief. Through the exercise of these powers a number of holidays were abolished, which the king considered superfluous as regarded religion, and prejudicial as regarded the trade and industry of the people. The clergy were ordered to discourage the reverencing of images, and to remove what might be abused to the occasion of idolatry. Thus some of the most celebrated shrines were demolished; images of our Blessed Lady, long the objects of veneration to the faithful, were stripped of their costly vestments and committed to the flames. The smouldering embers of Lollardry needed but this breath to kindle them afresh; the followers of Wyclif, who sympathized with the German Reformation, rejoiced to insult the faith that had long held them in subjection. Latimer, the Bishop of Worcester, was one of the most zealous promoters of the new changes. He dragged from its pedestal in his cathedral the time-honoured figure of our Lady, at whose feet so many a devout pilgrim had bent the knee to implore the aid of the Help of Christians. Contemptuously designating it, on account of its size, as "the great sibyl," he counselled Cromwell to turn it to some good purpose, blasphemously adding, "She hath been the devil's instrument to bring many to eternal fire." Then he proposed to send it to London to be publicly burnt, remarking, with disgusting impiety: "She, with her old sister of Walsingham, her younger sister of Ipswich, and their two other sisters of Doncaster and Penrice, would make a jolly muster at Smithfield."[1] The relics of the saints were in some places snatched from their reliquaries and flung upon the ground. It was suggested to the king that as long as St. Thomas of Canterbury was venerated as the champion of the liberties of the Church, men would be stimulated by his example to defy the ecclesiastical authority of a secular ruler. Thereupon the name of the saint was erased from the calendar and the service-books as that of a

[1] Green, *Short History*, p. 345.

traitor; his bones were torn from the stately shrine in which they reposed, and publicly burnt [1]; all images and pictures of him were destroyed, whilst the gold and jewels that adorned his tomb were conveyed in twenty-six carts to the royal treasury. Tyndale's writings, and his version of the Holy Scriptures, disfigured by unfaithful renderings and by annotations calculated to mislead the ignorant, had been placed in the hands of the people; and the indiscriminate reading of the sacred volume in the vernacular, which had formed a powerful weapon in the hands of the German reformers, provoked many an unseemly controversy and violent attack upon the doctrines of the Church.

The Six Articles.—At length a profane assault upon Transubstantiation, that centre of the Christian's faith, aroused the resentment of the king. The work of innovation was proceeding too rapidly to please the Head of the Church; religious toleration was not part of his system. He did not approve of the teaching of the Lutheran divines; besides, they had opposed him in the matter of his second marriage. Remembering his title of Defender of the Faith, Henry prepared to suppress by force the opinions he had formerly combated by argument. Tyndale's Bible was prohibited, a more correct translation being promised in its place. Permission to read the Scriptures in private was denied to all except persons of education and of gentle birth. The doctrines impugned were reasserted in six articles, which established—1. The Real Presence. 2. The non-

---

[1] Doubt has been thrown upon this by a recent writer, but Fr. Morris gives the evidence. It is also stated in the Bull of Pope Paul III. See *Life of St. Thomas Becket*, p. 484.

Changes in Doctrine. 361

necessity of communion under both kinds. 3. The celibacy of the clergy. 4. The binding nature of vows of chastity. 5. The use of private masses. 6. The necessity of auricular confession. The penalty for denying the first was death at the stake, and the others imprisonment and forfeiture of goods. The refusal to hear mass was accounted as felony. Archbishop Cranmer at first strenuously opposed the new code, as he was himself privately married; but at the peremptory command of the king he accepted it, and, with others of the bishops, expressed and supported doctrines in direct variance to those he had formerly publicly maintained. Shaxton, Bishop of Salisbury, and Latimer, Bishop of Worcester, whose language had been too intemperate to be revoked, were compelled to resign their sees. Moreover, when a colony of German Anabaptists landed in England, and began to propagate their erroneous tenets, they were instantly apprehended and admonished; those who refused to recant were condemned to the flames.

The King's Book.—These measures filled with alarm the teachers and advocates of the reformed doctrines; they saw that their only security was in silence and submission to the king's will. Some years later what is known as "The King's Book" appeared, containing a code of doctrine and ceremonies to be believed and observed. This was the one authorized standard of English orthodoxy. In it Catholic doctrines were more or less exactly taught, but the royal supremacy in matters spiritual as well as temporal was strongly enforced. Hitherto England had received for its faith whatever the Catholic Church proposed; now it was compelled to receive whatever Henry decreed. The Convocation of Bishops nominally discussed the decrees, but it was only the monarch's servile instrument; for the king of England had become a despot, and the people had shrunk into a nation of slaves.

Henry VIII.'s policy of combining Catholic teaching with Protestant government of the Church ended only with his life. It is said by some that at the beginning of his last illness he expressed a wish to be reconciled with the See of Rome, but that the bishops, afraid of the penalties, evaded the subject, with the exception of Bishop Gardiner, who advised him to consult his Parliament. The king was constantly attended by his confessor, heard mass daily in his chamber, and received the Holy Eucharist under one kind; but what were his sentiments on his death-bed is not known with any certainty. He expired in January, 1547, and was succeeded by his son, Edward VI., who was then a child.

Edward VI., 1547. Further Changes in Religion.—Ever since the separation from Rome, two religious parties had been struggling in England to gain the ascendency and win the royal favour. The men of the old learning, as it was termed, looked upon Archbishop Cranmer as their most dangerous enemy, since the correspondence he kept up with the German reformers showed what were his real opinions, while he apparently moulded his ideas in conformity to the king's will. Now that Henry was dead Cranmer had no further need for disguise; his own party, a strong and energetic minority in the nation, rose into power. Under the rule of the Duke of Somerset, the protector, the protestantizing of England advanced with rapid strides. Cranmer broke openly with the old religion. "This year," says a contemporary, "the Archbishop of Canterbury did eat meat openly in Lent in the Hall of Lambeth, the like of which was never seen since England was a Christian country" (Green, *Short History*, p. 350). This significant action was followed by a succession of sweeping changes. The first act of the council nominated to represent the young king during his minority, was to require the bishops to take out anew from the Crown letters patent of jurisdiction. This issuing of letters patent was a device previously invented by Cromwell to assert the supremacy of the Crown. Another step was to establish a royal visitation, in order to enforce on the clergy obedience to injunctions which gave directions as to the performance of the clerical functions, and the acceptance of a Book of Homilies to be read in every church on Sundays, giving instruction on Christian doctrine. Meanwhile all preaching was inhibited by the royal decree, except where licenses had been granted by the Lord Protector. Gardiner, Bishop of Winchester, a champion of the old order of things, made a vigorous protest against these and other measures of the council, urging that no important alterations should be made until the king came of age; but his remonstrances were unavailing, and he was flung into prison. Bonner, Bishop of London, offered a less resolute opposition; on being arrested he withdrew his protest.

When Parliament met the work proceeded swiftly; the lands of those chantries, hospitals, and gilds, which, although given to Henry VIII., had escaped his rapacious grasp, were seized to pay the legacies left by the late monarch. This was the first of a series of acts of spoliation of the Church to be continued throughout the reign. The legal prohibitions of Lollardry were, moreover, removed; the Six Articles of the preceding reign were repealed; by a royal injunction all pictures and images were banished from the churches; bishops received orders to abolish in their respective dioceses the custom of bearing candles on Candlemas Day, of receiving ashes on Ash Wednesday, of carrying palms on Palm Sunday. A bill was passed permitting priests to marry, and ordering that communion should be administered in both kinds. The services were to be performed in English, and in 1549 a new liturgy, called "The Book of Common Prayer and Administration of the Sacraments," compiled by a commission consisting of six bishops and six doctors, besides Archbishop Cranmer,[1] was ordered to be used throughout the land. A new catechism embodied the tenets of Cranmer and his friends; and such of the prelates who, struggling feebly for the Catholic faith, ventured to remonstrate, were forced to submit or committed to the Tower. Ridley was made bishop of London in place of Bonner, who for preaching the Catholic doctrine of the Sacrament of the Altar remained a prisoner until the king's death.

Popular Dissatisfaction.—It may well be supposed that the introduction of changes so radical in faith and ritual could not be effected without great difficulty. It required the exercise of all the royal power and authority to abolish the use of Latin, and

---

[1] Strype in his Life of Cranmer (*Eccl. Mem.*, vol. ii. p. 85) states that the commissioners for drawing up the Order of Communion were "most of the bishops and several others of the most learned divines of the nation," together with Archbishop Cranmer. For the authors of the First Prayer book he assigns "the same bishops and divines" (*Cf.* Gasquet, *Edward VI. and Book of Common Prayer*, p. 140).

suppress the old rites and accustomed ceremonial of the Church. If the priests submitted to perform the service in the vernacular, it was often the mass translated. Those who consented to use the new liturgy continued to combine with it the old ceremonies. The laity, if compelled to attend the services, would make no offerings towards the new rite called the Lord's Supper. At length the popular indignation broke out in open rebellion. Religious discontent was aggravated by agrarian discontent. The common people found that the new proprietors of the Church lands did not pay the same attention as the old to the wants of the poor; this neglect rendered them yet more intolerant of the innovations in religion, and led them to complain yet more loudly of measures which increased their temporal misery, at the same time forcing on them practices of worship foreign to their habits and feelings. In most of the midland counties the peasants rose in revolt, partly on political grounds, but chiefly on account of the "laying aside of the old religion, of which, they said, because it was old, and the way their forefathers worshipped God, they were very fond." In Cornwall and Devonshire the outbreak assumed the most dangerous shape. Armies were formed, and it was only with the aid of foreign troops that the insurrection was suppressed. Priests were hanged from their church towers; a bloody assize completed the pacification of Devonshire.

The insurgents demanded that the new service should be laid aside, "since it is like a Christmas play," and the old service again used, with the procession, in Latin. In the fifteen articles of complaint (afterwards reduced to eight) which they drew up they asked "that priests should live chastely," also that at least two abbeys should be re-established in each county. One of the articles regarded the ceremonies of the Church. It ran thus: "We will have holy bread [1] and holy water every Sunday, palms and ashes at the times accustomed; images to be set up again in every church, and all other ancient old ceremonies used heretofore by our mother Holy Church." This demand was answered by Archbishop Cranmer in a strain, as his chronicler [2] informs us, " of happy perspicuity and easiness," his design being "to expose the abuses and corruptions of popery; what need there was that such matters should be abolished as the Pope's decrees, solitary masses, Latin service, hanging the Host over the altar,[3] sacrament in one kind, holy bread and holy water, palms, ashes, images, the old service book, praying for souls in purgatory." In his reply he reproaches the petitioners for "refusing the true heavenly Bread of Life except at Easter, and utterly refusing the Cup of the Most Holy Blood, and instead of these desiring to eat often of the unsavoury poisonous bread of the Bishop of Rome, and drink of his stinking puddles, which he nameth holy bread and holy water." Even if allowance be made on account of the different times in which he lived, one can hardly think this language becoming to one in Cranmer's position, or to the nature of the petition of

---

[1] The distribution of blessed bread (the Eulogia) after mass on Sundays and holy days was from the earliest times an invariable usage in England. It was reckoned with other "popish practices" to be done away with under the First Prayer Book of Edward VI., and, although temporarily restored among other Catholic rites in the reign of Mary, was finally abolished under Elizabeth's rule.

[2] Strype, *loc. cit.*, vol. ii. p. 117.

[3] The Blessed Sacrament used to be reserved in a pyx of the form of a dove, suspended above the high altar.

the rebels. It serves to show the character of the man who filled the highest post in the Church of England, and the lengths to which he went.

Co-operation with Foreign Protestants.—With their triumph over revolt, Cranmer and his Genevan colleagues advanced boldly in the career of innovation. Foreign divines of every sect and every nation were welcomed in the palace of the archbishop. He procured for them livings in the Church and protection at court, his object in surrounding himself with them being that they might help him to assimilate as far as possible the Church of England in doctrine and practice to the Protestant Churches abroad. With them he formed a sort of Protestant Council, to consider the status of the Reformation, as a counter-demonstration to the work of the Catholic theologians assembled at the Council of Trent. The sacerdotalism which was of the very essence of the old Pontifical being intensely displeasing to their Protestant minds, a new one, entirely purged of that offensive doctrine, was devised to take its place. A crowning defiance was given to the doctrine of Transubstantiation by an order to demolish the stone altars, and replace them by wooden tables, "decently covered," which could be placed wherever the minister thought fit. This enactment not only produced the greatest disorder in the ritual of the Church, now, alas! become a city of confusion, but was also the fruitful parent of sacrilege and profanation. Robbery of sacred things prevailed everywhere. "Information was given to the Council," says Fuller, "that private men's halls were hung with altar-cloths, their tables and beds covered with copes instead of carpets and coverlets. Many drank at their daily meals out of chalices."

New Prayer Book, 1552.—At the instigation of the foreign divines, who detected in it several points worthy of censure as upholding the old superstitions, a careful revision was made of the new Common Prayer Book, although at the time of its issue it had audaciously been said to be drawn up "by aid of the Holy Ghost and with one uniform agreement." Every change made in the Second Book, published in 1552, marks a very decided advance in Protestant sentiment as compared with the first (1548). Maskell tells us that in arrangement and contents the English communion service is to be regarded as a composition of the sixteenth century, not to be traced to any early form.[1] About the same time the forty-two articles of religion, since reduced by omissions to thirty-nine, were constructed as a complete confession of the doctrine adopted by the Church of England. To these the clergy were requested, but not compelled, to subscribe.

The Down-grade.—The work of Cranmer and his allies had been greatly facilitated by the fanaticism of the young king, who was bent, under the influence of his instructors, on religious reformation. But the course of the Reformation was hastening too far in the direction of the Genevan model, and the daring speculations of the followers of Calvin and Zwinglius awoke alarm in the minds of the more orthodox, and thereby favoured the Catholic reaction which took place in the succeeding reign. Green tells us :[2] "Men heard with

---

[1] *Ancient Liturgies of the Church in England*, p. xli.
[2] *Short History*, p. 352.

horror that the foundations of faith and morality were questioned, oaths denounced as unlawful, community of goods raised into a sacred obligation, the very Godhead of the Founder of Christianity denied. The repeal of the Statute of Heresy left the powers of the common law intact, and Cranmer availed himself of these to send heretics of the last class without mercy to the stake; but within the Church itself the primate's desire for uniformity was roughly resisted by the more ardent members of his own party. Hooper (originally a Cistercian monk, later on a zealous champion of Calvinistic views), when named Bishop of Gloucester, refused to wear the episcopal investments, denouncing them as 'the livery of Babylon.'" Several sees were left vacant, for want of divines of sufficiently advanced opinions to fill them. Ecclesiastical order was almost at an end. All teaching of theology at the Universities ceased; the number of students had fallen off.

Plunder of the Church.—The intellectual impulse of the New Learning had died away. A portion of the plunder taken from the Church was, it is true, employed in the foundation of eighteen grammar schools. This measure was destined to throw a lustre over the name of Edward VI., but it had no time to bear fruit in his short reign. The endowments of these institutions, moreover, which scarcely exceeded £20 per annum, were taken from the funds of the gilds of the several towns where they were erected. Other charitable institutions were sacrificed to satisfy the greed of a host of nobles, whose fortunes were built up with the last spoils of the Church. Even ultra-Protestant writers are obliged to confess this. "The untimely death of

Edward VI.," writes Bishop Burnet,[1] "was looked upon by all people as a just judgement of God upon those who pretended to love and promote a reformation, but whose impious and flagitious lives were a reproach to it. The open lewdness in which many lived without shame or remorse, gave occasion to their adversaries to say they were in the right to assert justification without works, since they were to every good thing reprobate; while their gross and insatiable scrambling after the goods and wealth that had been dedicated with good designs, though to superstitious usages, made all people conclude it was for robbery, not reform, that their zeal made them so active."

"One great sin of the Reformation," writes a more recent Protestant historian,[2] "was the confiscation of so large a portion of the property of the Church, for the aggrandizement of temporal ambition, and the enriching of the nobles who had taken a part in the struggle. Almost all the social evils under which Great Britain is now labouring may be traced to this fatal and iniquitous spoliation, under the mask of religion, of the patrimony of the poor, on the occasion of the Reformation." The possession of these ill-gotten gains frequently brought, as has been already said, a curse upon their owners, in the shape of temporal disasters. It also proved a formidable obstacle, as we shall presently see, in the way of the national reunion with the Holy See, for avarice hardens the heart, and dread of losing this world's goods blinds the eyes against the recognition of the truth.

[1] *History of the Reformation*, vol. iii. p. 216.
[2] Sir A. Alison, *History of Europe*, vol. xii. p. 384.

Before proceeding to consider the restoration of the Faith in England under Queen Mary, let us listen to the testimony of one more Protestant writer regarding the moral results produced by the Reformation. "To the people of England it had brought misery and want. The once open hand was closed; the once open heart was hardened. The ancient loyalty of man to man was exchanged for the scuffling of selfishness. The change of faith had brought with it no increase of freedom, and less of charity. The prisons were crowded, as before, with sufferers for opinion, and the creed of a thousand years was made a crime by a doctrine of yesterday. Monks and nuns wandered by the hedge and the highway as missionaries of discontent, and pointed with bitter effect to the fruits of the new belief, which had been crimsoned in the blood of thousands of the English peasants."[1]

Accession of Mary, 1553.—The death of Edward VI. in 1553 was a crushing blow to the hopes of the reforming party, and their ill-advised attempt to set aside the succession of the Princess Mary only made matters worse, for by it the cause of the Reformation was in a measure identified with that of rebellion. The public voice was unanimous in support of her rights. Mary had throughout her brother's reign adhered firmly to the Catholic faith, refusing to yield in any point to the religious changes authorized by law. She had mass regularly said for her by her chaplain, which was at first winked at, until the bigotry of the young king took scandal at it, and he determined to make her yield. A promise having been given to the Emperor that she should not be disturbed in her religious

[1] J. A. Froude, *History of England*, vol. vi. p. 28.

duties, the Council endeavoured to persuade Edward to remain quiet, but he would not consent. Mary had to endure a continual persecution because she remained inflexible; her chaplains and servants were sent to prison. Bishop Ridley visited her and offered to preach before her. She would not listen to him, and the harsh treatment she received only served to strengthen her detestation of the new doctrines and practices to which she was expected to conform. And now the cause of her rival, Lady Jane Grey, for whom the Duke of Northumberland endeavoured to secure the crown, was espoused by the Protestant party. Archbishop Cranmer, as one of the Council, signed the settlement, and Bishop Ridley preached in her favour at St. Paul's Cross, exhorting his audience, as they prized the light of the Gospel, to oppose the claim of the Popish princess. But the torrent of his eloquence was poured forth in vain; Mary was everywhere received with enthusiasm, and after the lapse of a few days was firmly seated on the throne. The position of ecclesiastical parties was now to be reversed; the new queen made no disguise of her attachment to the ancient faith, and her desire to see her realm reunited to the See of Rome. The manner in which she set about the accomplishment of this work it will now be our business to show.

CHAPTER XIX.

REUNION WITH ROME.

Mary's Caution. — On her accession to the throne, Queen Mary might perhaps have at once carried out her determination to restore Catholic worship in England had it not been for the counsels of the Emperor Charles V., who advised her to act with prudence and caution, and to abstain from making any important alterations without obtaining the consent of Parliament. It was in compliance with his wish that she allowed Archbishop Cranmer to officiate according to the new rite at the interment of the late king in Westminster Abbey, though at the same time she caused a solemn dirge and high mass to be chanted for him in the chapel of the Tower, at which the nobility and courtiers were present to the number of three hundred persons. She issued no order for the disuse of the English liturgy; she expressly declared that it was not her intention to compel her subjects to any change of religion; but she heard mass in her own chapel, and did not conceal her desire that her example should be imitated. One of the first acts of the queen was to release the five imprisoned bishops, and restore them to their sees. This was done by means of a lay commission, the same agency that had been employed to depose them. All, in fact, of the early proceedings of her reign were in strict accordance with the laws, and were sanctioned by the precedents, of her two immediate predecessors.

Cranmer, Ridley, and Latimer confined for Rebellion.— Yet the well-known attachment of the monarch to the ancient faith became the cause of great uneasiness to the reformed preachers, who, perceiving that their good time was over, endeavoured to arouse the zeal and religious animosity of their hearers against the Catholic faith. A trifling incident furnished Mary with abundant reason for imposing silence on them, by forbidding, after the example of King Henry, preaching in public without a license. A fanatic threw a dagger at one of the royal chaplains, who, preaching at St. Paul's Cross, inveighed against the late innovations in doctrine. A tumult ensued, which gave occasion for the issue of a royal proclamation forbidding all unlicensed preaching and public discussion of subjects likely to cause religious dissensions "until such time as further order might be taken by common consent." This prohibition was disobeyed by the leaders of the Protestant party, with the result that many of them were arrested and placed in confinement. Archbishop Cranmer and Bishop Ridley were also committed to the Tower for complicity in the movement to place Lady Jane Grey on the throne, and for preaching in her favour; and Latimer, who in King Henry's reign had been deprived of his bishopric for refusing to accept the Six Articles, and who now probably had imitated his metropolitan, was imprisoned for his "seditious demeanour." Others of lesser degree met with the same fate, unless they kept quiet, or, like the foreign teachers, preferred to quit the country.

The real obstacle in the way of reconciliation with Rome, on which the queen had set her heart, was not any opposition likely to be encountered in the re-introduction of Catholic worship. The new service was, it is true, everywhere established by law, but it had been embraced through compulsion rather than conviction. The great majority of the people were in favour of the Latin service; all their habits, prepossessions and beliefs, leading them to prefer the form of worship with which they had been familiar since their infancy. But, with the upper classes particularly, another argument had weight. It was thought that the restoration of ecclesiastical property was essentially connected with the recognition of the papal supremacy. The spoils of the Church were now by sales and bequests divided among thousands; in fact, almost every family of opulence in the kingdom had reason to oppose a measure which would involve, according to the general opinion, the surrender of a part, if not the whole, of its possessions. The Council resolved therefore to proceed cautiously in the endeavour to restore the religious status of former times.

Repeal of Acts of Edward VI.—When Parliament met, an act to annul the divorce of Henry and Catherine, and establish the queen's legitimacy passed as a matter of course. A Bill was then laid before the two Houses for the repeal of all the acts made concerning religion in the time of Edward VI. This did not touch the question of the royal supremacy, nor the alienation of Church property; it simply proposed a return to the condition of things at the close of Henry's reign. It was passed, though not without what the French ambassador described as a " marvellously violent debate," lasting eight days. A body of injunctions was published, the most important of which were that the oath of supremacy was not to be demanded of ecclesiastics; married priests were to be removed from their benefices; the festivals, processions, and ceremonies restored; and the people compelled to attend mass. All this was not effected, as Mary said when writing to Cardinal Pole, "without strife, embittered disputation, and on the part of the faithful strenuous efforts"; the reason being that that Parliament was stocked with the class enriched from the spoils of the Church property.

Cardinal Pole.—The Church of England had now returned to the condition in which it was in the latter days of King Henry VIII. This however was far from satisfying the aspirations of the queen, who desired the papal supremacy to be fully recognized, and the Church property which had been confiscated to be restored to its original uses. Had this been attempted at the commencement of her reign, it would very probably have ruined all; and Bishop Gardiner, her chief adviser, was too wise to encourage so rash a proceeding. He had, however, to contend not only against the queen's own wishes, but also against the influence brought to bear upon her from abroad by Cardinal Pole.

Reconciliation with Rome.—The news of the accession of Mary had been received with great joy at Rome, and the Supreme Pontiff, Julius III., had immediately appointed Pole legate to England with fullest powers. Pole wrote to Mary congratulating her, telling her of his appointment, and desiring to know her mind as to the way in which he should act. Anxious as he was to promote the reconciliation of his country with the Holy See, he yet hesitated, since he was still under attainder, to leave his retreat without some information as to the prudence of the step. By means of an emissary he learnt that Mary was determined to bring about the submission to Rome, but that the state of feeling in the country was such as to render it impossible to do anything further at present in that direction. She herself, she said, had been obliged, although reluctantly, to assume the title of Head of the Church, and it would hardly be safe for Cardinal Pole to come to England just then. The cardinal was by no means pleased with this communication. He answered in a tone of reprimand, pointing out to Mary that she could not expect obedience from her subjects while she herself set an example of disobedience to the Head of Christendom. Another reason why the presence of Pole was not desired in England at that time was the disfavour with which he regarded the Spanish alliance. But this marriage, highly unpopular as it was, obtained the sanction of Parliament, and was solemnized in July, 1554.

It was hoped that the meeting of Parliament in November of that year would witness the complete reunion of England with the Holy See. To accomplish this was a somewhat hazardous task, since a large and influential class were, as we have said, opposed to it from motives of interest. They had shared in the plunder of the Church, and would not consent to the restoration of a jurisdiction likely to call in question their right to their present possessions. Hence, though the attainder of Cardinal Pole was repealed, and there was nothing to keep him any longer out of England, Bishop Gardiner, who knew well the temper of the nation, took care that he should not come until he was amply provided with powers to confirm to their holders the abbey and Church estates. In view of this, negotiations were carried on with the Court of Rome. At first the legate had been authorized by the Pope "to treat, compound, and dispense" with the possessors of ecclesiastical property as to their rents; then this power was extended from rents to lands, tenements, and titles. Even with this Gardiner was not satisfied. He knew it to be the opinion of Pole that all the parochial livings ought to be restored, and a dispensation depending on his good pleasure implied a considerable amount of uncertainty. At length Pope Julius signed a bull, empowering the Legate "to give, alienate, and transfer" all Church property to its actual possessors, to be retained without scruple of conscience. Armed with this welcome document, he arrived in England.

Mary's Leniency.—In the presence of the king and queen he addressed the Houses of Parliament, and exhorted them to repeal the laws enacted against the papal authority, and to accept the reconciliation he was commissioned to grant. The next day the motion for reunion was carried almost unanimously. In the House of Lords, not a single voice was raised against it; in the Commons, out of three hundred members, only two demurred, and these afterwards withdrew their opposition. It was resolved to present a petition in the name of both Houses to the queen, stating the regret they felt for the defection of the realm from the communion of the Apostolic See, and their readiness to repeal every statute that had caused that defection, in order to be received back into the fold of the Church. This was done on the following day, November 30, 1554, when the whole assembly, on their bended knees, asked absolution of the cardinal. Rising, with extended arms, he absolved all those present, and the whole nation, from all heresy and schism, and restored them to the communion of Holy Church, in the name of the Father, the Son, and the Holy Ghost.[1] "Amen" resounded from every part of the hall, and the members, rising from their knees, followed the king and queen into the chapel, where a *Te Deum* was chanted in thanksgiving for the event. The next Sunday the legate made his public entry into the metropolis; high mass was celebrated in St. Paul's Cathedral, the whole court being present; and Bishop Gardiner preached a sermon in which he bitterly lamented his conduct under Henry VIII., inviting all who had fallen like him to rise with him, and return to the one fold of the true Shepherd. Thus by the consent of Parliament and the joyful acquiescence of the people, England became once more a Catholic country. Would that the reunion thus happily effected had been permanent! In a few short years, alas! as we shall see, all the good was to be undone, and the nation plunged once more, this time irretrievably, into schism and heresy, at the arbitrary word of an impious woman.

[1] This public absolution of the public sin of the nation did not affect individuals, each of whom had afterwards to apply for personal absolution, showing the requisite dispositions.

Various statutes were then passed, re-establishing in England the whole system of religious polity which had prevailed for so many centuries previous to Henry VIII. The clergy made a full and formal submission to the See of Rome; and the Roman Pontiff was acknowledged as chief Bishop of the Christian Church, with authority to reform and redress heresies, errors, and abuses within it; appeals to him from the spiritual courts were again allowed. Cardinal Pole, desirous for the restoration of ecclesiastical discipline and order in the country, and the remedy of spiritual evils, convoked a synod, wherein many necessary regulations were passed. Non-residence and pluralities were forbidden to the clergy, and their abstention from the pursuit of any secular business was rigorously insisted upon. Decrees were passed against simoniacal and other malpractices; moderation in dress and amusements was enjoined on priests. A new catechism was to be compiled, and a fresh translation of the Bible undertaken. The neglect of preaching had been one of the greatest evils of the past century; from many pulpits the Word of God was never heard; others were silent except on the Sundays of Lent. This important duty was urged upon all who had the care of souls: pastors were to preach every Sunday, warning their flocks against error, or at least read aloud homilies drawn up by the authorities. The catechizing of children was also to take place in the church every Sunday and holyday. Regulations were also made for the education of boys, and the proper training of candidates for holy orders.

Mary's Leniency.—The return of England to the unity of Christendom, the marriage of the queen, the consequent possibility of the crown remaining in her family, which would of course be Catholic, and the reintroduction of the worship they condemned as idolatrous, caused great dissatisfaction amongst that section of her subjects who still professed the reformed doctrines. Disappointment embittered their zeal; they heaped upon the Pope, the queen, the bishops, every opprobrious and irritating epithet language could supply. Ferocious and scandalous words were soon accompanied by ferocious and scandalous deeds. A priest was attacked and wounded whilst giving communion to the people; two of the queen's chaplains were insulted and stoned. The reformed preachers prayed openly for the queen's death; they denounced her as the cruel Jezebel and ungodly Athalia, who by God's laws and man's ought to be punished with the severest judgements. It could not be expected that, in such an age, attempts like these to excite to rebellion and contempt of religion and authority should be tolerated. Accordingly, soon after the queen's marriage, the question of the punishment of these seditious heretics was debated in the Council, and the advisability of bringing them to justice was laid before the queen. Her answer deserves to be recorded. "Touching the punishment of heretics, methinketh it ought to be done without rashness, not leaving in the mean time to do justice to such as by learning would seem to deceive the simple; and the rest so to be used that the people might well perceive them not be condemned without just occasion; by which they shall both understand the truth, and beware not to do the like. And especially within London, I would wish none to be burnt without some of the Council's presence, and both there and everywhere good sermons at the same time." This qualified and reluctant consent on Mary's part is sufficient evidence against the theory that the cruel burnings which ensued had their rise in the malignant and bloodthirsty spirit of the queen.

Prosecution of Heretics.—Although it had been held in the last reign that heresy was a crime punishable by death, it was deemed advisable to revive the three statutes formerly enacted to suppress the dangerous and revolutionary doctrines of the Lollards. For this purpose an act was passed in Parliament. The year 1555 opened for the reformed preachers with a lowering aspect; before the close of the first month the storm broke over them. The three propositions applied as the test of heresy were: (1) Whether the true and natural Body and Blood of Christ were present in the Holy Eucharist; (2) whether the substances of bread and wine cease to exist after consecration; (3) whether the Mass be a propitiatory sacrifice for the sins of the living and the dead. Those who denied these propositions were (if in holy orders) degraded from their office, and handed over to the secular arm. The first prosecutions were conducted before Bishop Gardiner, who was Chancellor. At their conclusion he, who was known to be a most tender-hearted man, too full of compassion for the office he bore, eagerly transferred the ungracious task to Bonner, the Bishop of London, in whose diocese the Council sat. This prelate, in spite of the character for cruelty which his official prominence in the work of death earned for him, as a man was never a zealous persecutor. He evinced the greatest distaste for his task, and soon, as we are told, "seemed sick of it," so that a special reprimand from the Council was necessary to rouse him to the performance of his duty. One day after he took his seat on the bench, a Spanish friar, Alphonso di Castro, confessor to King Philip, in a sermon preached before the court, strongly denounced the proceedings against the Protestants as contrary to the spirit as well as the text of the Gospel, and called on the bishops to instruct the ignorant, and not seek the death of their misguided flocks.

Ridley and Latimer burnt.—This sermon at once produced a great impression. For some weeks all executions for heresy were stayed, and, had the fanaticism of the reformed preachers permitted them to remain quiet, it is probable no more would have taken place. But the extreme language in which they indulged, and the detection of a new conspiracy which had been organized in the eastern counties, led to instructions being given to the magistrates " to watch over the public peace, to apprehend the propagators of seditious reports, the preachers of erroneous doctrines, and others who assembled secret meetings." Such amongst them as were accused of heresy were to be sent to the bishops, " that they might by charitable instruction be removed from their naughty opinions, or be ordered according to the laws provided in that behalf." The bishops manifested such reluctance to deal with those persons who, in obedience to these instructions, were handed over to them, that the Council again interfered, and ordered them to show greater zeal and diligence for the preservation of the peace of the realm. This was the signal for fresh convictions, and until the end of the reign the persecutions were continued with more or less vigour. About two hundred in all fell victims to the laws against heretics. Amongst these the most prominent were Archbishop Cranmer, and Bishops Ridley, Hooper, and Latimer. In the preceding reign they had concurred in sending to the stake those who differed from them; they were now compelled to suffer the same cruel punishment they had so recently inflicted on others. Ridley and Latimer were burnt in Oxford, opposite Balliol College. Every effort was made to save them, and pardon was offered to them at the last moment, provided they would recant. But they refused, and were chained together to the same stake, exhorting one another to be firm. The explosion of a bag of gunpowder, tied round their necks, speedily ended their suffering.

Cranmer's Death.—In the case of Cranmer, some delay had been caused by the necessity of sending to Rome for the Pope's sentence; as an archbishop who had received his pallium from Rome, his judgement rested with no meaner tribunal. When his condemnation was announced to him, his resolution gave way. He flattered himself that a pardon would be granted if he would recant certain passages in his writings and sermons; and, loving life more than his opinions, with craven cowardice he signed no less than six different recantations of the doctrines which he had been industriously propagating—nay, forcing upon others—for upwards of twenty years. Each recantation was more humiliating than the others; he admitted he had been a persecutor of the Church, a blasphemer, everything that was most vile. All this was of no avail. The looked-for pardon came not. First among the many decisions in which the archbishop had prostituted justice to

Henry's will stood that by which he annulled the king's marriage with Catherine and declared Mary illegitimate; the last of his acts had been to join in the shameless plot to exclude her from the throne. These deeds were enough of themselves to render his life forfeit, but his political offences might be overlooked, it was said, had he not been author of the schism in the reign of Henry VIII., and of the change of belief in the reign of Edward. Such offences required that he should suffer " for example's sake."

When the day of execution came, and he found there was no more hope of saving his life, Cranmer, embittered by disappointment, determined that he would not gratify those who were anticipating from him a fuller acknowledgement of his misconduct. At the stake he repudiated his recantations, declaring, though untruly, that they had been wrung from him; and, placing his right hand, the instrument as he said of his error, in the flames, he held it there without wincing until it was consumed.[1] Whether we regard these recantations as sincere or insincere, our opinion of the man must be of the poorest. If sincere, his subsequent retractation must have been insincere; if insincere, how base was his cowardice by the side of the courageous consistency of Fisher and More. Nor can we indeed have much pity for the man who was only undergoing what he had without hesitation inflicted on others; they, however, being made to suffer for fidelity to the faith of their forefathers, he for having been a leader in the terrible policy of

---

[1] This is generally said, and is supported by what purports to be the testimony of eye-witnesses. It is however not easy to understand how it could have happened, as Cranmer would have been bound to the stake before the fire was lighted around him.

forcing by terrorism on a whole nation the unwilling abandonment of its ancient faith. If he had been beheaded as a traitor, it is probable no one would have pitied him.

Cardinal Pole.—Pole took but slight part in these condemnations for heresy. He counselled the queen to exercise moderation and leniency in bringing back her people from schism, and he frequently rescued from the stake those who had been sentenced to death. After the execution of Cranmer, he succeeded him in the see of Canterbury. It was no easy task to repair the havoc made under the rule of Henry VIII. and Edward VI. Pole met with contradiction and difficulties in quarters where they might least have been expected. The energy and unsparing zeal wherewith he exerted himself for the amelioration of the condition of the clergy, the reform of discipline, the advance of learning in the Universities, the spread of Catholic truth by means of sermons and devotional works, the revival of the monastic orders, rendered him one of the truest benefactors of his country. However, notwithstanding his exemplary life and the esteem in which he was held by all good men, he was subjected to persecution and cruel accusations. In spite of all that he had formerly suffered for his attachment to the Catholic creed, his bold defence of the Church in his writings, his labours for the restoration of the Faith in England, the charge of holding heretical opinions was brought against him, he was deprived of his office of Legate *a latere*, and summoned to Rome to clear himself before the Inquisition. The queen expostulated, stating that the control of a legate was necessary in England, and representing the triumph that would be afforded to unbelievers, and the corresponding discouragement to the faithful, should the man who was the chief representative of Catholicism in England, and working effectively for its progress, find himself under the painful necessity of defending his own orthodoxy. Certain that the Pope had been grossly deceived by false statements, she caused the messenger bearing the papal letters recalling Pole and conferring the legatine authority on a Franciscan friar, to be arrested at Calais, and his despatches to be forwarded secretly to her. Thus they never reached the hands of the persons for whom they were intended; and while matters were in suspense, the death of the queen, and of Cardinal Pole, who survived her scarcely twenty-four hours, altered the aspect of affairs.

Restoration of Ecclesiastical Property. Mary's Death.—Shortly before the close of her reign, Mary judged it her duty to restore as far as possible to the Church such ecclesiastical property as had during the late reigns been vested in the Crown. With the consent of Parliament a yearly revenue of about sixty thousand pounds, the proceeds of abbey lands, was placed at the disposal of the cardinal-archbishop for the benefit of impoverished clergy. The exaction of the first-fruits was also discontinued. In her last illness Mary edified all around her by her piety and her resignation to the will of God. Her chief solicitude was for the stability of the Church, and her disappointment at having no heir was aggravated by her suspicions of the insincerity of her sister, who, though she conducted herself outwardly as a Catholic, was thought to be favourable to the reformed opinions. A presentiment, too soon to be justified, that the work she had accomplished for religion would not be permanent, prompted her to require from Elizabeth an avowal of her real sentiments. The princess declared herself to be a true and conscientious believer in the Catholic creed, and asserted her readiness to confirm her words by an oath. On November 17, 1558, Mary received extreme unction, and peacefully expired as the benediction was pronounced at the end of the mass, which was said daily according to custom, in her chamber.

Prosecutions under Mary.—"The death of the queen," writes Dr. Lee,[1] "was indeed a misfortune to England. By it all the regulations of law and morals effected by Cardinal Pole were practically brought to naught, while the irreligious disorders of the preceding reign were restored and renewed. The virtues and noble qualities Mary exhibited, her charity to her dependents, her love and condescension towards the poor, the efficiency wherewith she performed her royal duties, would have made her name venerated by posterity, had it not been for the severe punishments inflicted by the then existing laws upon heretics, and other perverse and misguided people during that disturbed period, which moreover have been greatly exaggerated by John Foxe and his numerous followers." The cruelties practised, it cannot be denied, are most deplorable, and in the light of the present day, reflect dishonour on those who advised and carried out such merciless measures. But the blame of them cannot be ascribed to the queen herself. Considering the intolerance of the age, and the great provocation given by the Reformers,

[1] *Life of Cardinal Pole*, p. 240.

it would have been remarkable if Mary had acted otherwise. She had met with neither pity nor courtesy from those who professed the reformed doctrines when they were in power; she had been insulted and abused by the Protestant prelates; she had seen the Catholic bishops imprisoned for years, the ancient faith proscribed, an armed force resisting, in the name of Protestantism, her lawful rights. In spite of this, she continued opposed to the revengeful effusion of blood, although urged by her counsellors to extreme measures. There were members of her Council who had conformed under the rule of Henry or Edward, and were prepared to turn their coats again under Elizabeth. To this class, so careful of their own skins, mercy for others was unknown. Their policy and advice, rather than the disposition of the queen, or the intolerance of the Catholic episcopate, were the cause of the sufferings for religion during this reign.

It must moreover be remembered that the principles of religious toleration as now recognized were, in the sixteenth century, not only almost unknown, but reprobated as dangerous and wrong. Next to professing and disseminating religious error was the guilt of those who permitted it to exist, and who, having the power of punishing heretics, refrained from its exercise. Toleration was regarded as a proof of indifference; and it was argued that if treason and disrespect to earthly powers incurred severe penalties, much more ought these to be inflicted on persons who by their maintenance of false doctrine imperilled souls, and did despite to the majesty of heaven. Such sentiments were not peculiar to Roman Catholics, but were held equally by the Reformers, who, during their ascendency, displayed the same persecuting spirit which they formerly condemned, burning Anabaptists, and preparing (by the canon law drawn up by Cranmer shortly before King Edward's death) to burn Catholics at the stake, for no other crime than adherence to religious opinions differing from their own. The extirpation of erroneous doctrines by the sword or the stake was inculcated as a duty by the leaders of every religious party. Every sect, when it had the power, adopted similar means of repressing those who opposed it. In 1553, Calvin, the head of the Protestants of Geneva, caused a Spaniard to be burnt for heresy. In a letter he wrote to the Protector in the reign of Edward, this passage occurs: "As I understand, you have two kinds of mutineers against the king and the estates of the realm; the one a fantastical people who, under the colour of the gospel, would set all in confusion; the others are stubborn people in the superstition of Antichrist of Rome. These altogether do deserve to be well punished by the sword. Of all things let there be no moderation. It is the bane of genuine improvement." [1]

Thus it will be seen that persecution, not merely punishment, but privation of life, was inculcated even more strongly by those who rejected than by those who asserted the papal authority; those whose tenets rested on the sand of private opinion went to as great or greater lengths than those whose creed was securely based on the Rock of Peter. It seems strange that the former should have been oblivious of the fact that in disallowing liberty of conscience, and that freedom of thought which permits every variety of

[1] MSS. Ed. VI., vol. v. 1548.

heterodox speculation to lift its head on high, they were denying the principle on which their own existence depended. And as in the past, so in the present, Catholics must and do allow willingly the fair-minded tolerance they receive at the present time from a vast number of Protestants, and the latter in their turn will acknowledge that Catholics of the present day are singularly liberal in their disposition. Meanwhile a class of ultra-Protestants still exists, whose doctrinal standpoint is the same as that of the persecuting Reformers, and who persistently demand from the legislature a relentless persecution of Catholics, such as is cruelly exercised by themselves in private to the best of their opportunities.

The number of the persons who suffered death for religious and seditious opinions are acknowledged by non-catholics to have been largely exaggerated by Foxe and his literary partisans. It is, besides, a significant fact that, except the four heretical bishops, they include not a single individual of rank, opulence, or importance. Members of the higher classes who professed the reformed doctrines under Edward VI., and returned to them under Elizabeth, without exception embraced the ancient creed when re-established under Mary, if not from conviction, from motives of policy and convenience. The victims of persecution came from the lower orders of society. In the following reign, as will be seen, the reverse was the case. Of the reformed clergy a few suffered under Mary; others who refused to recant sought an asylum abroad, and met with a welcome from the Genevan theologians. The demon of discord, however, interrupted their harmony; dissensions and mutual reproaches soon divided the petty sects. Hence when the exiles hastened home, on hearing that heresy and schism again prevailed in unhappy England, they were far from being of one heart and one soul. Nor did they meet with as cordial a reception as they anticipated from the Protestant monarch who had ascended the throne.

CHAPTER XX.

RELAPSE INTO SCHISM.

Elizabeth, 1558.—On the death of Queen Mary the vacant throne was immediately taken possession of by her half-sister, the Princess Elizabeth. Her title rested upon no more secure basis than the will of Henry VIII., but it passed unchallenged by any active rivalry, all parties seeming to unite in admitting her right to the crown.

Recent historians are agreed that, at the accession of Elizabeth, the sympathies of the nation were with the Catholic religion; but what the sentiments of the new queen were was at first a matter of conjecture. She was an adept in the art of dissimulation, and had early begun to practise it. During the reign of Edward VI. she had professed Calvinistic opinions; when Mary sought to withdraw her from the new to the ancient form of worship, she feigned to see her errors, and embraced the faith of her forefathers. As the reader will recollect, with solemn asseveration she assured the queen that she was a devout Catholic and intended always to remain one. Nevertheless, others besides her sister were not deceived into the belief that her professions were genuine; thus when she ascended the throne, both Catholics and Protestants fixed their eyes on her with anxiety, not knowing whether they had more to fear or to hope.

Restoration of Protestantism.—It is probable that at heart Elizabeth was destitute of all religious sentiment, and in her own mind was indifferent to either form of belief and practice. For Protestantism in itself she certainly felt no attraction; from its harsher manifestations she was decidedly averse. She placed herself at its head merely because circumstances seemed to indicate that this position would afford her the best chance of giving stability to and extending her sovereignty. She loved, as did her father, to play the tyrant, and the ecclesiastical policy she determined to pursue was in principle identical with his, although worked out under other conditions. Her subjects were not long left in doubt as to her intentions. Elizabeth did indeed continue to assist at mass, and occasionally to communicate. She buried her sister with all the ceremonial of the Catholic ritual, and she ordered a mass of requiem for the soul of the Emperor Charles V.; but her choice of Sir William Cecil as Secretary of State, and the addition to her Council of eight new members, all of whom were known to hold the reformed doctrines, gave the Catholics grave apprehensions as to the principles on which the government was to be conducted. These fears were confirmed when the new Council drew up a document headed, "A device for the alteration of religion," which was to be submitted to Parliament when it next met. Then it was seen that the religion of the realm was to be altered, and this all-important question was to be discussed by a body of laymen, not by the prelates and clergy. Meanwhile the queen was counselled to intimidate the clergy by prosecutions under the *præmunire* and other penal laws, "that they might abjure the Pope of Rome, and conform to the new alteration." This alteration for the present was to go no farther than that "the communion be received as the queen pleased, and that if more chaplains than one be present at the mass, they do always communicate with the officiating priest in both kinds." Moreover Bishop White, of Winchester, was imprisoned on account of something that displeased the queen in his sermon at the funeral of the late sovereign, and Bishop Bonner was treated with marked disfavour.

Coronation according to Catholic Rites.—

Five weeks after the queen's accession came the festival of Christmas, when it was usual for one of the bishops to say mass in the royal chapel. Before the mass, when Oglethorpe, the Bishop of Carlisle, stood vested at the altar, two messengers from the queen forbade him to elevate the Host at the consecration. He replied that he knew what ceremonies were customary in the Catholic Church for the celebration of the Holy Sacrifice, and her Majesty must pardon him if he continued to say mass as he had been wont to do. As he was firm in the right, so was Elizabeth resolute in the wrong; when the gospel was ended she rose and left the church, "satisfied with a mass of the catechumens."[1]

---

[1] The Spanish ambassador, De Feria, says that when the queen sent him word not to elevate, the bishop replied that she should be the mistress of his goods and life, but not of his conscience; whereupon she left the chapel after the gospel. (Simancas doc. *ap.* Bridgett. *Queen Elizabeth and the Catholic Hierarchy*, p. 64.)

Alarmed at this innovation, which was practised by the queen's chaplains at her command, the bishops conferred together whether they could in conscience place the crown on the head of a princess who might object to some part of the coronation service as ungodly and superstitious, and who, if she did not refuse to take, certainly meant to violate, the oath binding her to maintain the liberties of the Church. The result was that the whole episcopate, with one exception, refused to officiate at her coronation. The Bishop of Carlisle was prevailed on to perform the ceremony, not as a favourer of heresy, but lest, if the queen were made angry, she should have more excuse for overthrowing the religion of those who refused to anoint her. She was however compelled to take the oath, and to conform to the rites of the Catholic pontifical. It is alleged that the grief Bishop Oglethorpe felt at having separated himself from his colleagues accelerated his death.

First Parliament. Acts of Supremacy and of Uniformity, 1559.—Parliament opened on January 25, 1559, the queen assisting in state at the Mass of the Holy Ghost; a sermon was preached in the queen's presence by a married priest lately returned from abroad, exhorting to the reformation of religion and the removal of idolatry. This was sufficient to indicate what the royal pleasure was, and there was no doubt that it would be carried out by a subservient majority. *Qualis rex talis grex*,[1] is a saying that might have been intended expressly for the English people, since they of all other nations are most readily influenced by those who rule them. After the recognition of the queen's legitimacy, the

---

[1] "As is the King, so is the people."

settlement of ecclesiastical matters was taken in hand by Parliament.

The queen's ministers had secured the return to the House of Commons of members on whose votes they could rely. Five new peers had been created, well known to be favourable to the new religion. Two bills were introduced into the House of Lords— one, the Act of Supremacy, and the other, the Act of Uniformity. By the first, the acts of Henry VIII. rejecting the papal authority, and conferring on the sovereign the headship of the Church, were revived, except that instead of the title of "Supreme Head," Elizabeth preferred that of "Supreme Governor." By the other bill, the Second Prayer-Book of Edward VI. was ordered to be used throughout the kingdom instead of the mass. Heath, the Archbishop of York, Scot, Bishop of Chester, and Fekenham, Abbot of Westminster, made eloquent and forcible speeches against both these bills. In February the two Convocations of Canterbury and York drew up a calm but unmistakable declaration of their firm adhesion to the Pope, and to the doctrines of the ancient faith. This was subscribed to by the Universities of Oxford and Cambridge, and presented to the queen and to Parliament. Some of the lay lords also spoke against these bills. It seemed in March very doubtful whether the bills would pass, when the queen's advisers hit upon an ingenious device for diminishing the Catholic majority. During the Easter vacation a conference was ordered to take place between the Catholic bishops and the Protestant divines, on such points as the use of Latin in public prayers, &c. Bacon was moderator, and on the bishops protesting against some ruling of his, two of them were committed to the Tower, and three others were bound to attend the court daily, to await sentence. This was continued until the dissolution of Parliament. In the meantime, the two bills were passed by "the Lords Temporal," all the bishops that were able to be in their places entering their protest against them. Even so, the Act of Uniformity was only carried by a majority of three; but by this contrivance the whole work of Queen Mary was undone, and England was again formally severed from the unity of Christendom.

Elizabeth's Supremacy repudiated by the Bishops.—Elizabeth was resolved to lose no time in availing herself of the supremacy of authority over the Church wherewith the Houses of Parliament had invested her. In March the Act became law, and during the following summer Royal Commissioners were employed throughout the length and breadth of England in extorting from the reluctant clergy, from clerical bodies and the heads of religious houses, the declaration that the Bishop of Rome had no authority within the realm, and the recognition of the sovereign as supreme head, without the qualifying clause ("as far as the law of Christ will permit") which in 1531 had been admitted. The oath was first of all tendered to the bishops. Only sixteen out of the twenty-four were then in possession; at the accession of Elizabeth six sees were vacant, and the subsequent death of two more prelates had raised the number to eight.

"When the violent and uncontrolled passions of Henry VIII. rose up to destroy the unity of God's Church, only one member of the English hierarchy remained faithful to his trust. It will be remembered that Blessed John Fisher stood alone in his refusal to incur the guilt of schism, and suffered death in consequence. His blood was not shed in vain, for when the policy of Elizabeth led her again to break with the Holy See, of the whole episcopate only one member proved faithless. Kitchin, Bishop of Llandaff, consented to take the oath, and was suffered to retain his see. The rest imitated the constancy of Fisher, if not to martyrdom, yet to the endurance of deprivation of their bishoprics, poverty, and imprisonment."[1] "The fundamental changes introduced under Edward VI., always in virtue of the royal supremacy," says the same writer in another place,[2] "had opened their eyes as to its true nature. The logic of facts taught them that the royal supremacy included the power of defining the doctrine of faith and of the sacraments, and having discovered the error into which they had fallen, they were led to reconsider the subject, and look more deeply into the provisions made by Jesus Christ for the unity of His Church. Some of the bishops who refused to admit the supremacy of Elizabeth were taunted with fickleness and inconsistency, since they had easily admitted and even warmly defended that of her father. So far as they were inconsistent, it was with the inconsistency of a sincere repentance." One of these was Tunstall, the aged bishop of Durham. The north was the great stronghold of Catholicism, and the influence he exercised over clergy and laity alike was well known. In order to keep him out of the way, the queen had exempted him, on the pretext of his great age, from attendance in Parliament. But when tidings reached

---

[1] Bridgett, *Queen Elizabeth and the Catholic Hierarchy*, Preface. *Life of Fisher*, p. 324.

him of the intended visitation of his diocese, the old bishop wrote to Sir W. Cecil, telling him that if it were to extend to the pulling down of altars, the defacing of churches, the removal of crucifixes, he could not assent to it, for he would never agree to have any new doctrine taught in his diocese. Notwithstanding this protest, he was one of the bishops whom Elizabeth "in the plenitude of her power" ordered to consecrate Parker to the archbishopric of Canterbury. He declined to act on this commission, and nothing remained but to summon him to London and exact from him the oath of supremacy. On his refusal to take it he was deposed and placed in close custody in Lambeth Palace, where he died some six weeks after, in the eighty-fifth year of his age. Of the other prelates, three contrived to leave the country; the remainder endured years of weary imprisonment before a modified form of restraint was conceded to them. The Bishop of Lincoln was confined in jail for twenty-four years, others for a shorter period; several died of maladies contracted during the time of incarceration. These penalties were not inflicted because of offence against any statute, but because the government considered that the imprisonment of men so conspicuous and so "stout in papistry" might serve as an example to all who were inclined to be obstinate.

Many did indeed prove "obstinate" in their adherence to the ancient Church. In general the deans, archdeacons, prebendaries, canons, the heads of religious houses, with the leading members of the Universities, peremptorily refused the oath and declined to accept the new Articles, thereby sacrificing their offices and emoluments, in some cases their personal liberty. The great bulk of the inferior clergy left the commissioners' summons unheeded, and did not present themselves to take or refuse the oath. Some adopted the Prayer Book, through dread of poverty, others in the hope that the change would be but temporary; at any rate, it is certain that a considerable proportion of those who acquiesced in the innovation remained Catholic at heart. A learned non-Catholic has said, "What is commonly affirmed, that all the clergy conformed to the new order with the exception of two hundred, cannot possibly be true. This estimate represents very nearly the bishops and other dignitaries who are known to have refused the oath. The great number of ordinations held in the early years of Elizabeth's reign, at most of which as many as one hundred and fifty priests and deacons were admitted to holy orders, and the large proportion of churches which still remained unserved for lack of ministers, prove the inaccuracy of the assertion. In the year 1565, in some dioceses a third part, in others half, of the parishes were still without rectors or vicars, though the want was in some supplied by a curate. Moreover we find at a later period the number of Roman priests who were still living in seclusion is spoken of as considerable." [1]

Parker's "Consecration."—The duty of providing a new hierarchy for the reformed Church now devolved upon the queen. To supply pastors for the vacant sees a selection was made out of the exiles who had hastened back from the continent, and the clergymen who had, during the previous reign, distinguished themselves in England by their

---

[1] See article by Mr. Pocock in *The Guardian*, Nov. 23, 1892.

adherence to the new liturgy. At their head Elizabeth resolved to place Dr. Parker, a married man, formerly chaplain to her mother, Anne Boleyn. In obedience to a *congé d'élire*, he was chosen to fill the see of Canterbury by the Chapter, only a small part of whom, however, took part in the election. An order for his consecration was then issued under the Great Seal. But by whom was the ceremony to be performed? The old Catholic episcopate had been swept away by Elizabeth; of the bishops who had held office in Queen Mary's reign, sixteen survived, but they all save one, Kitchin, Bishop of Llandaff, were in prison. By the revival of the ecclesiastical code of Henry VIII., the law required that four bishops should take part in the consecration; the queen, therefore, in virtue of her ecclesiastical authority, commissioned four prelates—of whom Tunstall was one—to perform the ceremony. They all declined to do so. A second commission was accordingly issued to seven others, including the Bishop of Llandaff, commanding four of their number, on their allegiance, to consecrate the archbishop-elect. Barlow, formerly Bishop of Bath and Wells, and Hodgkins, who had been consecrated to the suffragan bishopric of Bedford under Henry VIII., with Scorey and Coverdale who had been appointed under Edward VI. and consecrated by the Edwardine Ordinal, declared themselves willing to act on this occasion. Neither of the four was in possession of a see, nor had they any jurisdiction. In the chapel of Lambeth Palace nevertheless they met, and laid hands on Parker according to the form prescribed in the Ordinal of Edward VI. A few days later Parker, as Archbishop, confirmed the election of Barlow to the see of

Chichester, and of Scorey to that of Hereford; then taking them for his assistants, he proceeded to consecrate to the vacant sees several of the most prominent Protestant divines.

The Catholics of England could not regard men thus intruded by the secular arm into the place of the imprisoned bishops as the lawful successors of the apostles, nor could they for many reasons acknowledge the validity of the form of their consecration.[1] Nay more, even according to the law of the land it was doubtful if they were legal bishops, since the law, in this respect unchanged since the time of Queen Mary, recognized no other form than that of the Catholic Church. In order to quash this objection an Act of Parliament had to be passed, establishing the legality of the previous consecrations, and ordering that the Ordinal of Edward VI. should thenceforward be used.

The last English Bishop.—The last survivor of the English hierarchy died in 1585. It was Goldwell, Bishop of St. Asaph, one of the three prelates who found a refuge abroad. With the exception of the

---

[1] First and foremost, the rite employed was not the ancient rite which, as the only one handed down to the Church by an immemorial tradition, was the only one which could be treated as in any sense trustworthy. Secondly, this new rite was once constructed by Archbishop Cranmer and his friends, on the essentially Protestant principle of excluding whatever phraseology involved a sacerdotalist conception of the priesthood. Thirdly, the episcopal consecration of Barlow was at the best most doubtful, and yet he was the principal officiant at the consecration of Archbishop Parker (from whom all subsequent Anglican Orders are derived). Hodgkins, one of the assistant bishops, was indeed a truly consecrated bishop beyond all doubt, but there is small probability for the notion that an assistant bishop's part in the ceremony has the effect of independently conferring orders. Since these words were written, the Bull *Apostolicæ Curæ* has settled that Anglican Orders are null and void on the first two grounds mentioned here.

brief interval of Mary's reign—during which he returned to his country, was consecrated, and given the see of St. Asaph—the last fifty years of his life were spent in exile. With him ended the long line of bishops who for nearly a thousand years, from St. Augustine downwards, had ruled and fed Christ's flock in England.

As to the belief in an apostolical succession, it is not, as the Anglicans of the present day are compelled to admit, to be found in any of the writings of the Elizabethan bishops. The queen and her ministers regarded the bishops merely as officers of the State. The two ideas concerning her own supremacy, which Elizabeth had most at heart, were that the bishops were her delegates, and that Church property was an excellent quarry for replenishing her finances. In regard to the latter point, she was as bold a plunderer as her father had been, and carved out rewards for her ministers from Church lands, with a total disregard for the rights of property. The new bishops, on their appointment, found not only that the ecclesiastical revenues restored by Queen Mary were re-annexed to the Crown, but that by a new Act the queen was empowered to take the episcopal manors, giving in exchange for them certain tithes. Her well-known reply to the Bishop of Ely on his venturing to remonstrate against this spoliation, illustrates what she meant by her ecclesiastical supremacy: "Proud prelate, I would have you know that I who made you what you are can unmake you, and if you do not forthwith fulfil your engagement, by God I will immediately unfrock you!" But she would allow no plunder save her own; and required order and decency to be observed in the outward arrangements of the Church. If she had no convictions she had taste, and that taste revolted from the violence of the foreign reformers, the bareness of Protestant ritual, and, above all, from the marriage of the clergy.

The Change of Religion. Sacrilege and Immorality. — Immediately on the use of the new Prayer Book becoming obligatory, the work of pulling down images and destroying altars had begun. The gorgeous vestments of the ancient worship were cut up for gowns for the clergymen's wives; bonfires burnt in the streets of London, fed with roods and sacred images; the Blessed Sacrament was removed from St. Paul's; the Grey Friars of Greenwich, the Black Friars of Smithfield, the monks and nuns of Syon and the Charterhouse left the country; the monks of Westminster were driven out; the abbot of Westminster was deposed and imprisoned. These extreme measures did not please Elizabeth. She would not give up the crucifix and lights in her chapel. She said the commissioners had exceeded their injunctions, and declared it to be her will that the roods which had been taken from the churches by their over-zealous action should be restored. The bishops were compelled to minister in Catholic vestments, much to their annoyance. When the Dean of St. Paul's, preaching before her, spoke irreverently of the sign of the cross, she rebuked him from the window of her pew, and bade him "leave that ungodly digression." Lest the changes should be too striking, the fasts were to be observed, the old festivals were to be kept, the bread used in the Lord's Supper was to be circular in shape, and music was to be retained in the churches. The marriage of the clergy was neither allowed nor forbidden ; the country clergy were let alone, but wives and children were not permitted to appear within cathedral closes or academical colleges, since her Majesty held that their presence within these precincts gave no small offence to the intent of the founders, and to the quiet and orderly profession of learning. This order excited great indignation among the bishops.

If we were engaged in recording the history of the religion established in this realm by the will of the sovereign and the authority of Parliament, we should have a sorry tale to tell of internal dissension and strife of sects—of fanaticism on the one hand, of apathy and neglect of religious observances on the other. The widespread refusal of the clergy to conform caused great difficulty to the newly appointed bishops. To provide the vacant parishes with ministers, they were constrained to have recourse to the ranks of the illiterate. Rather than suffer the people to remain without Protestant supervision they ordained not merely candidates who had not had a university education, but craftsmen and mechanics, whose want of cultivation, with their manner of performing their official duties, proved " very offensive to the people and the wise of the realm." All sorts of disorders crept in, and the bishops had to rebuke in forcible language the proceedings during the time of divine worship. The effect of the religious changes introduced by Elizabeth was, on the nation at large, most lamentable. While material prosperity marked her rule, the standard of piety and morality sank very low, according to the testimony of the Reformers themselves. The state papers of this period also bear witness to the deterioration of morals and the licentious manners of the people. In 1561, the Bishop of Hereford, writing to Cecil, says that his cathedral is a very nursery of blasphemy, immorality, pride, superstition, and ignorance. Some years later a writer, addressing the same bishop, contrasts the listlessness of the service and the disregard of the truth of the Gospel in his day with the fervour of the frequent services and the zeal and devotion he could himself remember in the dark days (so he termed them) of Queen Mary.

Thus from the commencement of her reign, as we have seen, Elizabeth introduced innovations in doctrine and discipline, until an external change of religion was effected throughout the kingdom. The Sacrifice of the Mass was interdicted, the use of the ancient liturgies abolished, the prelates and dignitaries of the Church deprived of office and imprisoned; but to root out the Faith from the hearts of the people was a less easy matter. Since a large proportion of the clergy remained Catholic—some indeed conforming outwardly, others abstaining from the performance of any sacred function, in the hope of obtaining from the Holy See a dispensation—it may be assumed that similar dispositions prevailed to a great extent amongst the laity. A small number kept true to the Faith at all costs, and refused to attend the Protestant worship; a large majority concealed their hostility to the new doctrines and ritual, and yielded outward conformity out of deference to the times, while they preserved their Catholicism in secret. Persons whose position enabled them to do so, left the country at the time of Easter to avoid receiving communion according to the new rite. In some churches the altar was left standing, and the Catholic ornaments were kept in concealment, ready for the mass at an hour's notice, should opportunity occur.

Attendance at Protestant Services forbidden to Catholics.—That the great bulk of the laity conformed outwardly it is impossible to deny. Martyrs are seldom other than a small minority, and attendance in the parish churches was enjoined under penalties. To avoid these penalties some Catholics thought it might be lawful to attend, arguing that the mere fact of their presence did not involve an approval of the services. But the attendance in question was prescribed by the authorities as a formal mark of adhesion to the new order, a fine of twelve pence being inflicted for every case of absence on Sundays and holydays. The more conscientious Catholics saw it in this light, and in the fourth year after Elizabeth's accession they addressed a request for guidance in this matter to the Council of Trent. In this they stated that they would continue to absent themselves from the Protestant worship at all risks, if the Council judged right; but that they would be only too glad to escape the penalties of recusancy if this were possible without sacrifice of conscience. The Council could not sanction the practice, and the result of its reply was a marked increase in the number of recusants. Those who had gone to church, believing this to be consistent with the refusal to conform, ceased to attend when they found that it was not so. Still the duty was hard, and the practice was not finally abandoned until later, after much remonstrance and exhortation, and an express prohibition from Pope Pius V.

Coercion by the Queen.—Obedience to this order was regarded by Elizabeth as an act of defiance,

Relapse into Schism.

and heavy fines were levied on all who absented themselves from divine service in the ordinary churches. Shortly after an insurrection took place in the north, set on foot by the great Catholic lords, instigated by the presence in England of Mary, Queen of Scots, whom they desired to liberate from captivity. The principal object, however, for which they took up arms was to obtain liberty of conscience and restore the old customs and usages of religion. The revolt proved abortive, owing to the inaction of Catholics in other parts of the country; and the ruthless measures of repression taken by Elizabeth showed that the clemency that had till then characterized her rule was no longer to be looked for. The adherents of the nobles who had taken part in the rising paid for the attempt in bloodshed and ruin; the subsequent executions, amounting to no less than eight hundred, struck terror into the survivors. The disaffection of the Catholics was met by imposing on all magistrates and public officers the obligation of subscribing to the Articles of Religion, by which the sacraments were repudiated, and the mass declared to be a blasphemous fable. This measure served to place the administration of justice and order in the hands of their Protestant opponents.

Elizabeth's Excommunication.—It was the cruelty of Elizabeth towards her Catholic subjects which induced St. Pius V. at length to issue a bull of excommunication against her. His predecessor, Pius IV., had, on his elevation to the papal throne in 1559, written to her in a conciliatory spirit, striving to recall her to the communion of the Church, and inviting her to send delegates to the Council of Trent. These overtures had been rejected, and the

Papal Nuncio forbidden to enter England. St. Pius V., on his succession, finding her to be so determined an adversary to the Catholic religion, saw no reason for further leniency; he therefore in 1569 published a bull (*Regnans in excelsis*) whereby, after the enumeration of her offences, he deposed her, and absolved her subjects from their allegiance. Elizabeth herself affected to ridicule the sentence pronounced against her, but it alarmed her, and roused her to more definite action, the issuing of more rigorous enactments. The comparative immunity of Catholics from active persecution during the early part of her reign had arisen partly from the connivance of the gentlemen who acted as justices of the peace, partly from her own indifference. She was content at first to play a waiting game. She thought it wiser not to resort to stringent measures that might drive a large portion of the nation to desperation. She trusted to the gradual extinction of the Catholic priesthood, and the growth of a new Protestant clergy to supply their place; the dying out of those in influential positions whom she might replace with creatures of her own. She preferred to leave time to do its work in accustoming the laity to the change of religion, leading them into conformity through force of association, wearying recusants into attendance at the state services by the fines imposed on them. The rising generation would have less vivid memories of Catholic days, and prove more pliant to her hand.

Priests remain Faithful.—But it was not so easy to eradicate the old Faith. The Marian priests who had not acquiesced in the changes imposed on them worked bravely to keep up the Catholic spirit among the people. "For the first sixteen years of the schism," we are told,[1] "from 1558 to 1574, the preservation of the Faith was due to the priests, some regular, but mostly secular, ordained in the previous reign, and to them alone. Some of these, from the prisons to which they were consigned for the remainder of their days, bore witness to the Catholic faith for which they suffered. Others, exiles from their native country on account of their religion, aided from abroad, by their writings, the Catholic cause in England. But a large number, especially of the parochial clergy, remained steadfast at their posts, and through the long night of danger and persecution watched, like true pastors, over their flocks. Of one of these, the Douay Diary records that he had laboured for sixteen years in England at the peril of his life, reconciling to the Catholic faith those who had gone astray and animating others to perseverance; and many more there were whose names have not been recorded, and whose quiet labours were seen only in their fruits." Dr. Dodd says[2]: "There was not a province throughout all England where several of Queen Mary's clergy did not reside, and were commonly called the old priests. They served as chaplains in private families. Again, several Catholic clergymen found such friends as to be permitted to enjoy sinecures without being disturbed by oaths and other injunctions. Great numbers of the most eminent clergymen went abroad; and there was scarce any university in France, Italy, or Flanders, but one or more might be found in them. A great many indeed still remained in England, and

[1] *Douay Diaries, First and Second.* Edited by Thomas F. Knox, D.D., preface, p. lxi.
[2] *Church History*, vol. ii. p. 8.

conformed for a while, in hopes that the queen might relent, and things come about again. But their hopes vanishing, they forsook their benefices and followed their countrymen over-seas." With regard to the state of the Universities, he says: " In the beginning of the reign of Queen Elizabeth, the University of Oxford was so empty after the Catholics had left it after the alteration of religion, that there was very seldom a sermon preached in the University Church of St. Mary. Bishop Jewel and Archbishop Parker complain that the Universities are left in the most lamentable condition. The persons left were so few and so illiterate that an order was sent out for every one to con over the lessons, being unable to read them distinctly otherwise; also for liberty to make use of the Common Prayer in the Latin tongue, there being some danger of losing that language in the University. Only two theologians remained who were able to preach."

Further Persecution.—Many of those parish priests, too, who submitted to exchange the chasuble for the surplice, to use the Prayer Book instead of the Missal, preserved the same tenour in their teaching. They hoped that as Mary had undone the work of Edward, so a Catholic successor would reverse the changes of Elizabeth. On this account they were anxious to obtain from her a declaration that Mary Queen of Scots was the next heir to the throne. At first, also, the queen played with the hopes of her subjects for a Catholic reaction, by talking of her marriage with an Austrian Catholic prince; and again when, later on, she listened to the proposals of the Duke of Anjou. But since the publication of the Bull, every day made it more difficult for

Catholics to reconcile devotion to their religion with loyalty to their queen. New and tyrannical laws were issued. It was made treason to declare in any work that the queen was a heretic or schismatic, no less than to declare her a tyrant and usurper. It was made treason to bring from Rome to England, or to use, any writing or instrument from the Pope, whatever its contents; or to give or receive absolution in virtue of any written jurisdiction from the Holy See. The mere fact of possessing an Agnus Dei, beads, pictures, or crosses, blessed by the Pope or priests deriving their authority from him, subjected the owner to the penalties of *præmunire*. All individuals above a stated age were compelled not only to attend the services, but to receive communion after the new form. Nor were persons who had left the country to escape these enactments beyond their reach; unless they returned within six months after they had received warning to that effect, even had they procured a license to leave, their goods and chattels and the revenues of their lands were forfeited to the Crown for life. Every form of worship but that established by Government was proscribed: thus the Puritans also incurred penalties, but their grievances were nothing in comparison with the sufferings of the Catholics. The wealth of the latter presented an alluring bait to their persecutors, and the heavy fines levied on recusants replenished the royal exchequer and filled the pockets of informers, even before the more brutal and bloodthirsty persecution commenced which struck terror into the hearts of the Catholics and roused the indignation of Europe.

As early as 1563, the Emperor Ferdinand had interfered on behalf of the English Catholics. In different letters he had recommended to the queen the practice of toleration, solicited her indulgence in favour of the imprisoned bishops, and exhorted her to grant one church at least in every populous town for the exercise of Catholic worship. But Elizabeth, far from relenting towards her Catholic subjects, grew more embittered as time went on. In the twenty-third year of her reign she took upon herself to determine that in the case of any man absolving from sins, with faculties from the Pope, or reconciling any person or persons with the Roman Church, it should be high treason to the reconciler and the reconciled, and to all who abetted or lent themselves thereto, and that they should suffer death in consequence. At the same time it was decreed that every recusant above the age of sixteen years, instead of paying twelve pence every Sunday that he absented himself from the Protestant church, as was appointed, should henceforth forfeit and pay £20 every month, and should besides be put in sureties of £200 for his good behaviour. Those who could not pay this sum were to forfeit two-thirds of their lands and goods yearly.

But what caused the "terrible thundering statutes" (as a writer of the time calls them) to be enacted against both priests and laymen, was the education of candidates for holy orders in English seminaries abroad, in view of returning to minister to the faithful in their own country. Of this we shall proceed to speak in the following chapter.

CHAPTER XXI.

PERSECUTIONS.

The Seminary at Douay, 1568.—In spite of the vigorous laws enacted against all who refused to accept the new religion, half, or as some say two-thirds, of the population adhered to the ancient Faith and the spiritual headship of the Bishop of Rome, if not openly, at any rate at heart. A large proportion of the laity, as we have seen, had the courage to refuse the external conformity required by the Government. These latter had recourse, as opportunity offered, to the Marian priests, although with peril to the lives of both parties. Even had they not had amongst them these pastors labouring under the authority of the Holy See—had they been obliged to remain, as the faithful remnant of Japanese Christians were obliged to remain, for centuries without pastors—their Catholicity would not have been impaired. The relation to the Holy See was preserved, and this by itself was all that was needed to endow them with the full rights that attach to membership of the Catholic Church. But death annually thinned the numbers of the nonconforming priests, and the bishops of Queen Mary's reign were unable to exercise their powers, owing to the confinement in which they were kept. The two Universities, like all other Church property, had been seized and given by law to the established religion. Thus the gradual extinction of the old priests would have left the faithful without pastors. But the mighty Mother, ever fruitful in heroes and in saints, was not unmindful of her children in their hour of affliction. Dr. (afterwards Cardinal) Allen, a Fellow of Oriel College, who had been driven from Oxford by the Text prescribed in the Act of Uniformity, foresaw the danger, and with the aid of some English priests living in exile, founded a seminary for the education of English candidates for the priesthood at Douay, in 1568. In Rome also, at a subsequent period, the English hospital, which was the successor in a certain sense of the ancient Anglo-Saxon school (represented by the Church of Santo Spirito in Sassia), was through his means converted into a seminary for priests, and opened to English refugees by Gregory XIII. The seminary at Douay, liberally supported by Catholic peers and foreign ecclesiastical bodies, was soon filled with students, animated with zeal for the propagation of that religion for the sake of which they had sought an asylum in a foreign clime. Their object was to study theology, receive holy orders, and return to England, to keep alive the faith of their fellow-countrymen, and reclaim those who had gone astray. The college at Valladolid was founded somewhat later by Father Persons, S.J., with the same object.

English Martyrs under Elizabeth.—In 1574, the first seminary priests, as they were called, landed in England, to carry the consolations of religion to the afflicted Catholics. Their presence was felt to be an insuperable impediment to the attainment of religious conformity; the system of gradual compulsion on which the queen had relied for the protestantizing of her subjects was foiled, and her resentment was quickened by the thwarting of her will. Unwilling to incur the charge of religious persecution, which she felt to be a stigma on her rule,[1] she chose to regard the seminary priests as political emissaries from Rome, sent over to sow treason, to stir up sedition in the kingdom. With a strange ignoring of the connection between the two things, it was declared that, while every one was perfectly free to hold what religious opinions he chose, freedom of worship was incompatible with order; therefore non-attendance at the services of the established religion was stigmatized as disloyalty. Furthermore Parliament, which, through the working of the Test Act, had become a wholly Protestant body, declared the landing of the priests to be treason, and the harbouring of them felony.

B. Cuthbert Mayne.—The first victim was the Rev. Cuthbert Mayne, the proto-martyr of Douay College. Although this servant of God was the first who suffered the cruel death of a traitor under the new statute, the queen, employing the vast powers conferred on her, had before this, like Herod, stretched forth her hand to afflict some of the Church. Thomas Woodhouse, one of Queen Mary's priests, had been hanged and butchered alive at Tyburn, in 1573, for the denial of the royal supremacy. The fate of Mayne, and of the gentleman who sheltered him, gave an impulse to the work of bloodshed, which

[1] *Cf.* Green, *Short History*, p. 401.

was carried on with pitiless energy. And when, some six years later, two Jesuit missioners—the precursors of many others of the Society of Jesus who shed their blood for the maintenance of the Faith in their native land—arrived in England, fresh alarm was awakened in the Council. More active search was made for recusants; the fines for abstention from church were increased; the gaols became so crowded with poorer prisoners who were arrested for the sake of religion, that the counties complained of the cost of their maintenance.

Jesuits.—The Jesuit missioners were hunted down like vermin. So hot was the pursuit that Father Persons, one of the two who inaugurated the mission, was forced to fly across the Channel; while his companion, Blessed Edmund Campian, whose talents and scholarly accomplishments were of a high order, was within a year arrested and with twelve other priests placed at the bar, accused of having conspired to procure the queen's death, and to stir up rebellion in the realm. No charge could have been more unfounded; all the accused had come with the sole view of exercising their spiritual functions, and had received a strict prohibition from their ecclesiastical superiors against interfering in politics, or under any pretext whatsoever mixing in secular concerns. They were, nevertheless, all found guilty, and suffered accordingly at Tyburn. This was but the prelude to a steady relentless effort to effect the extermination of Catholicism in England. The twenty years that followed saw the execution of more than 150 priests, while as many perished in the filthy and fever-stricken gaols where they were left to languish. By far the larger number of these martyrs died under an Act of Parliament made in the twenty-seventh year of Queen Elizabeth, 1585. This Act made it high treason *ipso facto* to be in England after having been made priest by Roman authority since the queen's accession. The same Act made it felony, punishable with death, to harbour a priest; the difference between the punishment of priest and layman under this Act was that the layman was hanged until he was dead, whereas the priest was cut down alive and butchered under circumstances of revolting barbarity.

Character of the Persecution.—" We find it very difficult," writes Father Morris,[1] " to recognize that a state of things, so very different from our own, existed in our own country, or that such unrelenting severity was the means whereby religious conformity was attained in England. Thousands in those times consented to go to the Protestant Church when they believed it to be a sin to do so—yielding, as they then thought, for a time, till the storm should be overpast. In the vast majority of cases they and their children were lost to the Faith. This being so, all the more honour is due to those who stood steadfast, and have left us an admirable example of courage and constancy, bearing the brunt of an awful persecution for the Faith which we value above our lives." Of this persecution, unparalleled for ferocity in the annals of our country, we will give a few details, although to describe all the sufferings of both priests and laity would fill many volumes. For the ecclesiastics who had been educated abroad to get back into England was no easy matter, as the seaports were watched, and

---

[1] *Troubles of our Catholic Forefathers*, Third Series, Preface, p. viii.

in the very colleges where sacred orders had been received, there were spies to betray the Church students, so that their description might precede them, and they might be arrested on landing. Spies, too, were constantly on the alert, to watch the roads and follow any person whom they suspected. But even if the priest landed safely, and sheltered in some Catholic house, a painful and perilous life was before him. Some remained concealed for months, afraid to move lest they should be seized; others travelled about in one disguise or another, under a false name, a price set on their heads, ministering to the faithful in different places as long as they could elude their pursuers. Hiding-places had to be made for them and for the altar furniture, for at any moment the house might be surrounded and searched. No man suspected of harbouring a priest could enjoy an hour of security; the pursuivants burst open the doors, forced their way into every apartment, tore the tapestry and wainscoting from the walls, broke open closets, chests, coffers, and made every search that ingenuity could suggest to discover either a priest, or books, vestments, chalices appertaining to Catholic worship. The inmates of the house were interrogated and intimidated; their persons were searched under the pretext that superstitious articles were concealed under their clothes. The merest trifle, the testimony of a servant or a child, was enough to make out that they were the entertainers of a priest; the sick and aged were torn from their beds and their homes, men and women of gentle birth were dragged away to prison. The priests, by the means of informers, were sometimes taken in the act of saying mass; not unfrequently the very man who appeared most devout (like the traitor who betrayed Father Campian) would be the one who earned for himself the patronage of the queen's minister, Secretary Walsingham, by calling the local magistrate and the *posse comitatus* to carry off to gaol the celebrant of the mass, with all who assisted at it.

State of the Prisons.—In the prisons the captives were to a great extent at the mercy of their gaolers. If they had not the means to pay the most exorbitant demands, or if they had been committed with strict injunctions that their usage was to be severe, the hardships they suffered were inconceivable, and often caused their death. "It is impossible," says a Protestant writer, speaking of the prisons of York, which differed nothing from those in the rest of England, except that the number of Catholics confined there was greater than elsewhere, "to speak in terms of too strong reprobation of the state of northern prisons in the sixteenth and seventeenth centuries, and of the conduct of their keepers. They were dens of horror, in which men and women were herded together almost without air, light, or ventilation. Some were under water whenever the river rose above its usual level." In the Tower a prisoner could be fairly treated if it was so ordered; but the usage Father Southwell, S.J., the poet and martyr, met with was such, that his Protestant father, who went to see him, could scarcely recognize his son. He found him half-naked, hardly able to speak, swarming with worms. Hastening to the queen, he petitioned her that if his son had committed crime he might suffer death, rather than be confined any longer in that filthy dungeon. All that he could obtain, however, was permission to furnish him with clothes and food. One young gentleman, whose only offence was that of letting Catholics meet at his house for mass, was confined in a cell where the ordinary conveniences and necessaries of life were denied him, and no one was allowed to visit him, so that in eight days' time he was brought to his end, as the chronicler records, by the stench and filth of the place.

All these sufferings were borne with the utmost fortitude and even cheerfulness. Of one martyr, who was so heavily ironed that he was unable to move without assistance, it is told that "a notable person coming up to him in his sickness, and he lying on his bed with his shackles on his legs, shaking them said to his visitor: 'The high priest of the Old Law had little bells about the rim of his vestment, and I stirring my legs, say; *Audi, Domine, haec sunt tintinnabula mea;* 'Hear, Lord, these are my little bells,' signifying that these were as acceptable to God as the sound of those little bells."

Modes of Torture.—Besides fetters, the use of torture was then the practice in England, as in other European countries. It was employed with the most wanton barbarity as a means of extorting information from prisoners, inducing them to incriminate others. The priests, whilst under torture, were asked where they had been entertained, at what houses they had said mass, who had been present, in what places other priests were concealed. A few gave way in the Tower of London under the fearful suffering, and became informers; others, like Campian, though they almost expired in the extremity of torment, refused to speak a word which might bring ruin on the families who had sheltered them, or lead to the apprehension of their colleagues. There were tortures of various sorts. There was "Little Ease," a cell so small that a man could not sit, stand, or lie down in it. There was a thing called "The Scavenger's Daughter," a hoop or circle of iron, into which the whole body was, as it were, folded up, hands, head, and feet bound fast together. Blessed Luke Kirby and Blessed Thomas Cottam suffered it.

The worst torture of all, and that which was by far the most frequently used, was the rack. Of this there were two kinds. One was to be hung up by the hands, and this was so painful a torment that Fr. John Gerard, who underwent it, says that none who have not tried it can imagine how grievous it is. The other was to have cords fastened to the hands and feet and passed over windlasses, by which they could be stretched as tight as the presiding magistrate chose. By this instrument it was that Norton, the rack-master of the Tower, boasted that he had made Blessed Alexander Briant a foot longer than God had made him. Of the other kind of racking we have a sufficient example in the case of Fr. Robert Southwell. He was hung from the wall by his hands, with a sharp circle of iron round his wrist, pressing on the artery, his legs bent backwards and his heels bound to his thighs. This was in the house of the notorious pursuivant Topcliffe, a monster of cruelty, who informed the queen that if it was her highness' pleasure to know anything in his prisoner's heart, this torment would enforce him to tell all. In this Topcliffe was mistaken. The firmness and patience of the gentle Jesuit overcame his tormenter. Topcliffe never allowed him to rest except when he appeared to be dying. Then he would take him down and bring him to himself by burning paper under his nose; this caused him to vomit a quantity of blood, after which he was hung up again. All this time he was so patient, and the expression of his countenance so sweet, that even the servant who watched him began to look upon him as a saint. His only exclamations were, "My God and my all!" "God gave Himself to thee, give thyself to God!" The heroism of the holy man bore this cruelty for four days without betraying one of his benefactors. He was then consigned to his vile dungeon in the Tower, unable to move hand or foot for the terrible agony he endured.

From the prisons a great many of these victims passed to the gallows. They were dragged at a horse's heels, bound upon a hurdle, to Tyburn, the principal place of execution in London. It is interesting to learn how often they succeeded in winning souls on the evening of their martyrdom, often amongst the malefactors who were "in the same condemnation." William Patenson, for instance, the night before his execution was put down into the condemned hole with seven criminals who were also to suffer on the next day; being more concerned for their eternal salvation than for his own temporal life, he so movingly preached to them repentance for their sins and a sincere conversion to God and His Church, that six out of the seven were reconciled by him. The next morning they expressed themselves determined to die in the Catholic faith, as they did, with signs of great sorrow for their crimes, and willing to suffer an ignominious death in satisfaction for them. Father Heath, O.S.F., reconciled in the very cart one of the malefactors executed with him.

The method of hanging in those days was different from our own; there was no drop to cause instant death. Whether the martyr was allowed to hang upon the gallows long enough to kill him, or even to deaden his pain, depended on the sheriff or the hangman. The bystanders were occasionally allowed to interfere. In Father Garnet's case they cried "Hold! hold!" when the executioners made three attempts to cut him down before he was dead. In the majority of cases, however, the sentence of the law—in comparison with which burning seems a merciful penalty —was carried out to the letter; the traitor was first hanged, then cut down alive, disembowelled, dismembered, beheaded, and his head and quarters fixed over the city gates. This ghastly work afforded frightful instances of barbarity. Of one, Roger Cadwaller, it is recorded that when brought to the block to be quartered he revived and began to breathe; before he was stripped naked he came fully to his senses. It was long after they opened him before they could find his heart, which, notwithstanding, yet palpitated in their hands after it was torn out. When Fr. Barkworth, O.S.B., was martyred, he pronounced the words, "O God, be merciful to me!" while the butcher was seeking for his heart. This, together with the disembowelling, was often a long process, during which the martyrs, when their tongues could no longer utter the life-giving name of Jesus, gave signs by their groans of the torments they endured. And those who suffered in this manner were holy men, pure-minded, self-denying, zealous; priests who had come over with their lives in their hands to keep up the faith in England, and the lay men and women who at the hazard of their lives received them and concealed them in their houses.

Every effort was made on the part of the Government to incriminate Catholics, and to prove that their desire for the restitution of the ancient worship led them to plot the subversion of the state and the death of the queen.

The Babington Conspiracy. — Prominent among these efforts were the practices of the Government in connection with the Babington conspiracy. Mary, Queen of Scots, being a Catholic and the next heiress, if not the rightful possessor of the English crown, it was natural that the thoughts and hearts of Catholics, both in England and abroad, should turn towards her; and this the more because of the sympathy which her long captivity, in defiance of all law and justice, was calculated to excite in generous hearts. The result showed itself in many attempts to assist her escape, attempts which, in the eyes of the Government, were deemed conspiracies. Anthony Babington, a young gentleman of property in Derbyshire, was induced by one Giffard to embark all his fortunes in a scheme of this sort. Babington was a youth of high character, and readily assented to the proposals of Giffard, so far as they contemplated the liberations of the captive queen. But Giffard also indicated as a necessary means to the end the assassination of Elizabeth. At this proposal Babington drew back until, by sophistical reasonings, Giffard persuaded him that the deed was to be regarded as a legitimate art of war against a usurper so guilty of injustice and oppression. One cannot, of course, but disapprove of the conduct of Babington in lending his ear to this evil counsel; but his guilt is small by the side of his who wrought on his impressionable young mind. And who was this? Giffard, although by birth and education a Catholic, was, in fact, one of Walsingham's spies; and there can be but little doubt that this base endeavour to entangle Babington, and with him other Catholic young men, and even, if possible, the Queen of Scots, in a scheme of assassination, was a device of the Secretary Walsingham himself. Babington paid for his wicked folly with his life, and it was on the same charge of having sought to assassinate Elizabeth that Mary Stuart was brought to the block. But it is clear from the way in which her trial was conducted that she had done nothing save attempt to escape, which she was perfectly entitled to do. They did indeed cite letters ascribed to her in which the project of assassination was approved, and speak of witnesses who could certify to the part she had taken. But they never ventured to produce the witnesses in her presence, or her original handwriting; whilst, on the other hand, it is certain Walsingham employed persons skilled in imitating handwriting to tamper with the intercepted letters of his victims.

The Spanish Armada, 1588. The work of bloodshed carried on in England, the torture and death of the Jesuits and other martyrs, sent a thrill of horror through the Catholic world. It at last roused into action the hostility of Spain. It broke down the caution and hesitation of Philip II., the chief aim of whose policy was to prevent the triumph of heresy. After the execution of Mary Stuart, the hopes of her adherents, groaning under the severity of the penal laws and despairing of relief from their sovereign, were bound up in him. The history of the expedition, fitted out principally with the object of avenging the blood of the martyrs and restoring papal authority in England, is well known; as are the imprudent haste in the equipment of the Armada, the inefficiency of its commander, the disasters that overtook it before the coast of Spain was out of sight. The only chance of success lay in a Catholic rising throughout England, and at this crisis the hatred of invasion proved stronger than the hope of deliverance from oppression. The loyalty of Catholics was subject to the severest trials under the plea of precaution; crowds of both sexes and all ranks were dragged to the common gaols; the Protestant clergy declaimed with vehemence against the tyranny of the Pope and the treachery of the Papists. But no provocation could urge the Catholic peers to any act of imprudence. They displayed no less loyalty than their more favoured brethren [1]; they, too, armed their dependents in the service of the queen. Harassed by the English vessels, driven by contrary winds on the rocky shores of Scotland and Ireland, the ponderous Spanish galleons were dashed to pieces or foundered in the storm, and thousands of brave hidalgoes, the flower of Spanish nobility, perished miserably in the waters or by the hand of the wreckers.

Fourteen more Years of Persecution. — From the defeat of the Spanish Armada until the death of the queen, a period of fourteen years, the Catholics of England groaned under the pressure of continual persecution. As time went on, penalties were multiplied. The exact number of martyrs is not known, but it is certain that sixty-one priests,

[1] *Cf.* Lingard, vol. vi. p. 505.

forty-seven laymen, and two gentlewomen suffered capital punishment for one or other of the spiritual treasons lately created. Witnesses were for the most part dispensed with; by artful questions the avowal was drawn from the prisoner that he had been ordained beyond the sea, or that he had harboured a priest, or that he admitted the ecclesiastical supremacy of the Pope and denied that of the queen. Any one of these crimes was sufficient to consign him to the scaffold. Life was, it is true, offered on condition of conformity to the established worship, but the offer was generally refused; and the refusal was followed by death, or rather butchery, performed too often, as we have seen, upon the victim while he was still in possession of his senses. Any one contributing to the support of seminaries or religious persons abroad was subject to imprisonment and confiscation of goods. For simple abstention from divine service during the space of three months the recusant was to abjure the realm, or suffer perpetual confinement in gaol until he made declaration of submission and conformity. Many gentlemen were thus reduced to beggary, all their living and goods being taken away, since the sum they were required to pay as fines for their recusancy and that of their families exceeded the amount of their yearly income; and even the members of opulent and ancient houses found themselves ground to the dust.

The frequent domiciliary visits in search of priests were most intolerable grievances. In some cases the pursuivants obtained counterfeit warrants, and under this pretence robbed and rifled houses, carrying away money, plate, all that was of value on which they could lay their hands; and after the gentlemen searchers, as the memorials of the day record, followed hungry rascals who licked up their leavings, sparing neither the silver spoons, linen, garments, nor anything that could be removed. The damage done to the houses in pulling down walls or ceilings, tearing up boards and flooring in search of concealed passages and hiding-places, cost large sums to repair; yet no one might, under pain of high treason, complain of his wrongs or seek restitution and redress. The Act of 1585 against all priests was enforced with renewed vigour in 1592, and they were ordered to quit the country within forty days under pain of death. Some obeyed, thinking it wise to yield to the fury of the times; but the greater number remained to strengthen the courage of the laity, "fearing lest they might be stricken with too great terror, and if deprived of the sacraments and of pious exhortations might lose heart; also lest the sudden flight of all the clergy should seem to arise out of fear and sloth rather than a sound deliberation."

Elizabeth's persecution of Catholics was not the result of religious ignorance or fanaticism. She did not believe in the spiritual supremacy she exercised, and scoffed at the prelates she had created. But her love of power would not allow her to recognize any authority to which hers must yield, or any divinely-appointed law to which her sovereign will must bend. The policy she adopted, however, proved a failure; her project of universal conformity to the form of worship she had established in her dominions was far from being realized. The Protestants were divided into innumerable sects; the Catholics, fined, imprisoned, tortured, deprived of their teachers by the dungeon and the gibbet, were rendered more hostile than ever to the national Church. The unconquerable devotion of the missionary priests, the blood so generously poured out, kept alive the light of faith; in spite of apparent defeat, the Catholic cause held its ground. The number of English seminaries in foreign lands increased [1]; convents were founded in Belgium and France for the reception of English ladies who were called to serve God in the solitude of the cloister; a continual stream of priests from Douay and the other seminaries abroad, as also from the religious orders, supplied the place of those who had fallen in the battle. The miserable end of Elizabeth's life need not be dwelt on here. It was befitting one who for forty years had been a systematic, merciless, persistent persecutor of God's servants and of His Church.

James I., 1603. Hopes of Catholics disappointed.

—The death of Elizabeth and the accession of James I. raised the hopes of Catholics in England. The new monarch, before entering the country, solemnly promised to give them toleration, and for a while after he mounted the throne their persecution was relaxed: but it soon began again with greater severity than before. This was mainly owing to the influence of the Puritans, who were prominent in the king's council and formed a majority in Parliament. The insatiable hatred that animated them towards all Papists caused them to adopt all means that policy could invent or

---

[1] In 1606 a novitiate of the Society of Jesus, specially intended for English subjects (afterwards transferred to Liège), was founded in Louvain by the liberality of a Spanish lady, Doña Luisa de Carvajal, who bequeathed a large sum for the purpose. She herself resided for some time in England, whither she went for the purpose of assisting and pleading for the afflicted Catholics.

power perform to root Catholics and the Catholic religion out of England. James I. found he could not fulfil the promises of toleration he had so lavishly given, without offending the leading members of the Government. In the first year of his reign he confirmed and revived all the laws Queen Elizabeth had made against Catholics, and it was evident that he would not only go forward in the steps of his predecessor in the matter of persecution, but add to the yoke she had laid upon them. Thus the hopes of the afflicted Catholics were soon turned into fears, and their fears into the assurance that far from meeting with any clemency from the king (as they not unjustly expected from the son of such a mother as Mary Queen of Scots), far from receiving any mitigation or alleviation of their burdens and sufferings, worse things were in store for them. Six thousand were presented as recusants in one year; the fine of £20 a month, with an additional £10 a month for the other members of his family, was rigorously demanded from every one, with arrears for the time of suspension; thirteen payments were exacted in the year, the option resting with the king of taking two-thirds of the recusants' land and goods instead of money.

What made things worse was the practice, introduced by James, of farming out Catholics of any means to Scottish adventurers, that they might enrich themselves by exacting these heavy fines from their victims. To send any child for education beyond the seas in a Catholic college or seminary was an offence punishable by a fine of not less than £100; and lest priests should conceal themselves as tutors in gentlemen's houses, it was provided that no one should teach even the rudiments of grammar without a license from the diocesan, under a penalty of forty shillings a day, to be levied both on the tutor and his employer. Worst of all were the visits of the searchers, which became so frequent that no man could have assurance of an hour's quiet or safety within his own home by day or by night, and were conducted with such barbarity and violence, that some of the Scottish gentlemen who accompanied King James to England said that, were they in Scotland so used, they should presently have killed those who entered their houses by force and against their will.

Difficult indeed was it for Catholics to bear such trials, being debarred as they were at the same time from the sacraments and other means of grace, according to the words of St. Bernard: "Woe to them who are called to the works of the strong and are not nourished with the bread of the strong." Acting upon the commands of the Holy See, and the exhortations of the Jesuit and other missioners, they had shown such invincible patience, marvellous long-sufferance, and humble submission to the most cruel and unjust treatment, that it was thought they would never attempt anything in their own defence, how hardly soever they were used. But as Abner said, "It is dangerous to drive people to despair" (2 Kings ii. 26); desperate men will seek a desperate remedy.

Gunpowder Plot.—In these circumstances it is scarcely wonderful that some of the more unruly spirits among the persecuted Catholics should have resolved upon an attempt to better their condition by violence. Their leader was Robert Catesby, who conceived and induced twelve others to adopt the wicked and insane scheme of the Gunpowder Plot. They resolved, by an explosion under the Parliament House, to destroy at one blow both the king and the legislature, to whom they attributed their evils, and then, having seized one of the royal children to be proclaimed as the new sovereign, to take advantage of the confusion which must ensue and obtain their own terms, including a guarantee for toleration. The conspiracy was brought to light on the very day on which the blow should have been struck, though it is highly probable that it had been for some time previously known to the minister, Cecil, who allowed it to go forward for his own purposes. Of the confederates the greater part were captured and thrown into the Tower, a few being slain in the country, whither they had fled. Great efforts were at once made by the Government to implicate leading members of the Catholic clergy, and it was publicly proclaimed that three Jesuit Fathers—Garnet, Gerard, and Greenway—had been the authors and instigators of the whole design. None of the actual conspirators could, however, be induced to accuse them, though torture was freely employed to wring from them the required declaration; and to their last breath on the scaffold, where they expiated their crime, they persisted in declaring that the Fathers were innocent. Of these Gerard and Greenway escaped to the Continent, and, being there beyond the reach of danger, expressed in the strongest terms their horror of the conspiracy, and repudiated all connection with it.

Father Garnet.—Fr. Garnet, after a long search, was at length captured at Hendlip Hall, the seat of a

Catholic gentleman, Mr. Abingdon, in company with Fr. Oldcorne, the chaplain there. Both were brought to London and closely examined in order to obtain evidence against them, Fr. Garnet being interrogated three-and-twenty times. All that could be elicited was that he had a general knowledge that Catesby and others threatened to attempt some violence, on account of the injustice they suffered, but that he had always opposed and denounced any such course, had made them promise to consult the Pope before they would do anything, and had written to Rome urging that so strong a prohibition against all rebellion should be issued as to make it impossible for any calling themselves Catholics to attempt it. He also acknowledged that a short time before the discovery of the plot he had heard of its details in confession from Fr. Greenway, who had been consulted in the same manner by Catesby, but on account of the inviolability of the sacramental seal neither could make any use whatever of this knowledge. Catesby had, however, given permission to mention what he had told his confessor should the matter otherwise become public. This was all that ever appeared to connect the Fathers with the plot, and they both declared that they had done everything which was possible, within the narrow limits allowed them, to prevent its execution. Nevertheless, Fr. Garnet was hanged, drawn, and quartered as a traitor, the Government persisting in the assertion that he had been clearly convicted as the arch conspirator; and the same story has been repeated to our own days, and is still constantly heard. Fr. Oldcorne was also executed as a traitor for having aided Fr. Garnet to escape.

From this account it will be seen that, though the conspirators were Catholics, the Gunpowder Plot cannot justly be charged against the Catholic body or their clergy, and that the Jesuits who suffered for it were the victims of gross injustice. The use made of the plot by the ministers of James I. to excuse their iniquitous policy of persecution was, in truth, even more criminal than the abominable design of the conspirators themselves.[1]

[1] See *What was the Gunpowder Plot?* By the Rev. J. Gerard, S.J., 1896.

CHAPTER XXII.

CONDITION OF CATHOLICS UNDER THE STUARTS.

Revision of the Penal Code.—The late conspiracy, disavowed though it was by the whole body of Catholics, was made a pretext for the enactment of new statutes, which aggravated their sufferings. One would have imagined that it would have proved a warning of the danger of driving men to an extremity by inflicting such severe penalties for certain religious tenets. In this light it was represented to the king by the French ambassador, who urged him not to goad his Catholic subjects into plotting his destruction, but to follow the wiser policy of convincing them that they had a protector in their sovereign. James professed himself an enemy to harsh and cruel measures, but said he could not withstand his Parliament.

The revision of the penal code resulted in greater restraints on the liberty of Catholics. They were forbidden to go beyond five miles from their ordinary dwelling-place without a license signed by four magistrates. They were declared incapable of acting in any civil capacity, of holding a commission in the army, or embracing any profession. Unless they were married by a Protestant minister, neither husband nor wife could assert a title to each other's property; unless children were baptized by a Protestant minister within a month after their birth, the parents were subjected to a fine of £100, of which one-third went to the informer; unless the dead were buried with Protestant rites, in a Protestant churchyard, their executors forfeited the sum of £20. Every household of whatever creed, receiving Catholic visitors or keeping Catholic servants, was liable to pay for each individual £10 per lunar month. Not only was attendance at the public worship required, but the reception twice a year of the heretical communion; the very fact of having a Catholic prayerbook was punished with a fine of forty shillings; if a crucifix were discovered by the searchers, it was to be defaced at the quarter sessions, and thus defaced, the image of his redemption was, by a refinement of brutality and impiety, to be restored to the owner. No details were regarded as too insignificant in the war of the Puritans against the holy sacrifice of the mass. Even altar-breads were carefully looked for amongst "Church stuff;" they are often mentioned in the list of things seized, under the new name of "singing-cakes."

Many Catholics escaped the rigour of these laws by a voluntary exile; with regard to those who remained, Boderie, the French ambassador mentioned above, declares that their fervour and zeal surpassed all that he could have imagined. He was particularly struck with the behaviour of ladies of quality; there were few of that class who were not Catholics.

New Oath of Allegiance.—Another instrument of persecution invented at this time was a new oath of allegiance. Its object was to exact a renunciation of any recognition in the Pope of the right to depose a temporal sovereign, and one of its clauses even went so far as to declare belief in the deposing power to be heretical. Some slight, though only slight, immunity from the severe laws against Catholics was offered to those who would take this oath, the oath being persistently pressed on all. On reference to Rome this oath was condemned as unlawful, but many of the Catholics in England, disregarding the papal prohibition, took it, whilst others courageously refused. Hence a division among the Catholics followed, which is doubtless what the king had in view, but which was one of the saddest episodes of the persecution. The Holy Father, Paul V., in the hope of mitigating the severity of the penal laws, sent an envoy to King James, assuring him of the obedience of his Catholic subjects, expressing the strongest disapproval of the late plot, and soliciting the royal protection for those who were innocent of it. This mission availed nothing: the persecution continued with unrelaxed vigour, and several priests fell victims to their refusal to take the oath.

In one point, however, we must acknowledge that James was less cruel than his predecessor. He disliked the punishment of death, and during the lapse of eleven years, from 1607 to 1618, the number of those who were executed as traitors for the exercise of their functions amounted only to sixteen. Moreover, on the commencement of negotiations for the marriage of his son with a Spanish princess, he granted liberty to the Catholics confined under the

penal laws, four thousand prisoners obtaining release
This, however, was most displeasing to the Puritan
writers, who bitterly lamented that so many idolaters
should be let loose to pollute an atmosphere purified
by the true doctrines of the Gospel. Accordingly,
the failure of the Spanish match was followed by the
presentation of a petition to his majesty that the
laws against Romish priests and recusants should
again be put in force—a petition to which James
assented without much reluctance.

An English Bishop, 1598.—It was about this
date that, for the first time since the extinction of
the ancient hierarchy, the English Catholics had the
benefit of episcopal government. This had been
desired for some time previously, but had not been
deemed expedient by the Holy See, partly out of
fear of an increase of persecution which such a step
would provoke, partly on account of some distressing
disputes among the English clergy over the lawfulness of certain oaths of allegiance and about other
matters. Not deeming the time to have come for
granting a bishop, and yet feeling the necessity of
some fuller discipline, the Pope had in 1598 appointed
George Blackwell as arch-priest. Blackwell unfortunately took a wrong course as to the oath of allegiance, and George Birkhead was substituted in his
place in 1608. Birkhead, dying in 1614, was succeeded by William Harrison, the last of the arch-
priests. In 1623 Dr. William Bishop was consecrated
to the see of Chalcedon *in partibus infidelium*, and
appointed Vicar Apostolic over England and Scotland. Bishop worked zealously during his short
tenure of office, but he died in the following
year, when, after some months' delay, he was suc-

ceeded by Dr. Richard Smith, likewise made Bishop of Chalcedon.

In the following year the prospects of Catholics again brightened, on the proposal of an alliance of Prince Charles to the French princess, Henrietta Maria. An engagement was made on the part of the king that the future queen should have a Catholic household, and that his Catholic subjects should for the future suffer no molestation in their persons, property, or conscience. The marriage took place immediately after the death of James I., and it was hoped that the union of his successor to a Catholic princess would be the means of affording liberty to her co-religionists.

Fresh Martyrdoms, 1628.—On the meeting of Parliament, however, the Puritans, who had formed themselves into a formidable phalanx to show their displeasure at Charles's marriage with a Catholic and the promises he had made to extend toleration to the Catholics in his dominions, insisted on the enforcement of the brutal laws that he would gladly have left in abeyance. A fresh outburst of persecution was the result; a great number became willing confessors, and some received the crown of martyrdom. Amongst the latter was Ven. Edmund Arrowsmith (1628). His hand (doubtless taken off while his quarters were fixed aloft on Lancaster Castle) is preserved in St. Oswald's Church at Ashton-in-Makerfield, in Lancashire, where to this day it works many cures.

With the view of comforting and encouraging his children in England under this renewal of their troubles, the Holy Father, Urban VIII., sent them a pastoral letter. They were before long deprived of their bishop; for the Protestant bishops, learning that a Catholic prelate was in England, induced the king to issue a proclamation for his arrest, and offer a reward of £100 for his capture. He in consequence withdrew to France. A curious story is told showing that the bishop was for a time sheltered by the Marquis de Châteauneuf, the French ambassador, and that Charles I. knew it. One day in Lent the king requested his wife, on account of her state of health, to eat meat, and as the queen scrupled to do so without a dispensation, the king begged the ambassador, who was then at court, to send a servant home at once to get leave from the bishop, adding that he knew very well that he would find him there.

Leniency of Charles I.—When Charles I. signed the death-warrant of priests, it was not from cruelty or fanaticism, but from weakness. The formidable faction of the Puritans, whose great aim it was to exterminate the Church in England, was offended by the moderation and lenity he displayed. He was aware that their intolerant zeal accused him of harbouring a secret design to re-establish the ancient creed and worship, and he thought it expedient to silence this murmur, and to give public proof of his orthodoxy, by ordering the magistrates and bishops to enforce the penal laws. But it was with reluctance that he caused priests who were apprehended and convicted to suffer the penalties of treason merely on account of their religion. Hence during the early part of his reign little blood was shed; some perished in prison, some were sent into banishment, others obtained their discharge. The penury of the royal exchequer forced the king to maintain the old system of fines for recusancy; but he allowed the accused to compound for a fixed sum paid annually, and of this indulgence many hastened to avail themselves. The exaction of these fines was, it is true, irreconcilable with any principles of justice, but while the recusants looked upon this mitigation of their penalties as a benefit, the zealots stigmatized it as a crime in a Protestant monarch.

Laud's Reforms.—What chiefly aroused the animosity of the ultra-Protestants at this time was the action of some of the Anglican prelates, mainly of Bishop (afterwards Archbishop) Laud, whom Charles I. had raised to the see of London, and entrusted with the direction of ecclesiastical affairs. The desire of these men was to draw the national Church farther from Geneva, to bring back much of Catholic ceremonial into her worship, of Catholic doctrine into her teaching. As soon as he was made Bishop of London, Laud asserted his influence to correct irregularities and enforce observance of the prescribed ritual. Certainly the state of things which he set himself to remedy would be simply incredible were it not attested by hundreds of contemporary documents. From these it appears that the ordinary matins and evensong, the services appointed to be said on Sundays, were curtailed in various ways by the minister who officiated; he often wore no surplice, and did not scruple to omit the prayers altogether, to make room for the sermon. The congregation sat, the men wearing their hats or not, as suited their convenience; the communion-table, standing in the body of the church, was made a receptacle for hats and cloaks that were not worn, and frequently used as a seat by persons otherwise unprovided with one. The habit of receiving the communion in a sitting posture had become common, and the sign of the cross was in some places dispensed with at baptism. It was no uncommon thing for cock-fighting to go on in the chancel of the church, the minister and his sons being present and enjoying the sport. These, and other worse sacrileges and scandals, were the results of the "glorious" Reformation, in which many Protestants still exult.

"The aim of Archbishop Laud," Green tells us, "was to raise the Established Church to what he imagined to be its real position as a branch, though a reformed branch, of the Catholic Church."[1] A revival of the ritual of the ancient worship was the first step in the way of reunion, which, he fondly hoped, time would bring about. The great obstacle in his way was Puritanism, and on this, when he became Metropolitan, he made merciless war. Lax or recalcitrant rectors and vicars were suspended or deprived; the ceremonies most offensive to Puritan feelings were strenuously enforced in every parish. Puritans were in power at that time; they saw in the archbishop, who was endeavouring to introduce a higher standard of religious observance in the national Church, a Romanist in disguise, one who was labouring to set up amongst them the "damnable heresies of Popery." The conversion of some distinguished persons about this period increased the general alarm; the Bishop of Gloucester (Goodman); Cressy, a canon of Windsor, and secretary to Lord Falkland; and Woodhead, one of the proctors of the University of Oxford; gave in their allegiance to the See of Rome. Besides these several laymen of note did the same; Sir William Davenant, the poet laureate; Walter Montague, son of the Earl of

---

[1] *Cf. Short History of the English People*, p. 494.

Manchester; and Calvert, afterwards Lord Baltimore, one of the ablest of the Stuart counsellors, known as the colonizer of Maryland, in North America, where he sought for himself and others of his faith liberty for the exercise of their religion. We must also mention Sir Toby Matthews, the friend of Bacon, a skilful diplomatist high in the esteem of James I., who eventually became a priest and (according to Anthony à Wood, though probably incorrectly) a Jesuit.

Supposed Offer of a Cardinal's Hat to Laud.— The alarm was increased when it became known that an accredited papal envoy had received permission to reside in London. Pope Urban VIII. had taken advantage of the presence of a Catholic queen to send a trusty messenger (Panzani) to the Court for the purpose of reporting upon the state of religion in England. Dr. Dodd (*Church Hist.*, iii. 35) says that "Laud was charged with a design of working a reconciliation between the Church of England and Rome. . . . But whatever the archbishop's intentions were, he incurred great odium among the people by his practices and ordinances. What made him most suspected of correspondence with Rome was the offer made him of a cardinal's cap," on the day that the death of Archbishop Abbot opened to him the prospect of the primacy. In his diary Laud writes, "August 4th, 1633. That very morning at Greenwich there came to me one seriously, and that avowed ability to perform it, and offered me to be a cardinal. I went presently to the king and acquainted him with the thing and the person. . . . This offer was renewed," he adds, a few days later (on the 17th), " but somewhat dwelt within me which would not suffer that, till Rome were other than it is." Dean Hook, in his *Lives of the Archbishops of Canterbury* (vol. xi. p. 321), says, "It is difficult to believe that this offer was made with authority." The opinion of Lingard (vol. vii. chap. v. footnote) is that "the proposal of the cardinal's hat came from Queen Henrietta, under the notion that there was truth in the current report of Laud's secret attachment to the Roman Catholic creed." "Very likely," says a more recent writer, "some one, possibly Conn (the legate who succeeded Panzani in London), nay, not improbably the queen herself, may have said something of this sort, 'If you will become a Catholic, I have no doubt I can get the Pope to send you a cardinal's biretta.'" His formal abjuration of the Anglican heresy would obviously have been a *sine quâ non*. As a matter of fact, Laud was no nearer to Catholicism than to Calvinism, though he did his best to bring about a better state of things in the Anglican establishment.

Increase of Priests.—The number of missionary priests in England at the period of which we are speaking, as reported to Rome, was five hundred or more of secular clergy; about two hundred and fifty Jesuits; one hundred Benedictines, more or less; twenty Dominicans and about as many Carmelites, besides a few Capuchins and Franciscans. These men were all spoken of in the highest terms; scarcely any other part of Christendom, it was said, could produce an equal number of priests so ready to suffer and to die in defence of the faith. And this, be it remembered, was at a time (1634) when the storm of persecution had, with the brief interval of Queen Mary's reign, been raging for a whole century.

During the last six years the tempest had, it is true, greatly abated in violence. The Catholics had been left in comparative peace, owing partly to the expostulations of the Pope and of the French king, who reminded Charles of the promises of toleration made at his marriage. He consequently checked the zeal of Archbishop Laud, when, to appease the discontent of the Protestants and shake off the imputations of Popery cast on him by his enemies, he was fain from time to time to enforce the penal laws.

Fresh Persecution of Priests.—When Parliament met in 1640, the persecution of priests broke out again in full force. The cry that religion was in danger from the machinations of Popery was revived: the Commons clamoured for the execution of the statutes of Elizabeth and James. The king, harassed with petitions, gave orders that Catholics should quit the court, and took away the commissions in the army which some few held; he directed that the houses of recusants should be searched for arms, and that priests should be banished from the realm. So unpopular had the queen become on account of her religion, that she began to tremble for her safety; her mother, who had resided in England during the last two years, unable to escape the insults of the mob, was forced to quit the country. In the following year the queen's confessor was sent to the Tower, and her establishment for the service of her chapel was dissolved. Pursuivants were appointed by the authority of the Lower House with power to apprehend priests and Jesuits; amongst others they arrested a priest of the name of Goodman. Captured and brought to trial, he acknowledged that he had received holy orders abroad, and for this reason alone he was condemned to suffer the terrible death reserved for those whose office it was to stand at the altar of God. Charles was desirous of commuting the sentence into either banishment or imprisonment, but this was too merciful for the Puritans who swayed the parliament; they insisted that the law should take its course. Hearing of what had passed, Goodman sent a petition to the king, beseeching him rather to remit him to their mercy than let him live to be a subject of so great discontent between the people and his majesty; adding that God had given him grace to desire with the prophet, that if this storm were raised for his sake, he would rather be cast into the sea, that others might avoid the tempest. This magnanimity put an end to the dispute; Goodman was left in Newgate, whence he contrived to make his escape. During the next twelve months, however, the death-warrants of two priests were signed, and the following year (1642) witnessed the execution of no fewer than eight, in different parts of England.

Catholics side with the King.—In the civil war, which followed upon the disputes between the king and the parliament, the Catholic nobles to a man arrayed themselves under the royal banner. They had long been oppressed and persecuted in virtue of a charge of disloyalty; they now sacrificed their life and property for the king who had sentenced many of their number to death. But their loyalty was a fresh crime in the eyes of the victorious Puritans. They could now be branded as Royalists as well as Romanists, and, thus persecuted on a two-fold ground, exposed to additional obloquy and aggravated punishments.

The priests who suffered death in the course

of the war amounted on an average to three each year; this must be reckoned a small number, when the agitated state of the public mind is remembered, the excited passions, the bitter prejudices, the wild fanaticism that held sway at that period. The entire property of such laity as had borne arms for the king was confiscated; they were exposed (being put out of the protection of Parliament, by public proclamation) to have their houses rifled, their goods plundered, their lives endangered by the soldiers. Under the pretext that the war had been caused by the intrigues of the Catholics, and consequently its expenses ought to be defrayed by the forfeiture of their property, it was ordained that two-thirds of the whole estate, both real and personal, of every papist should be seized for the use of the Parliament; and that under the name of "papist" should be included every person who, within a fixed period, had harboured a priest, been convicted of recusancy, attended at the celebration of mass, caused his children to be educated in the Catholic religion, or refused to take the oath of abjuration. The oath thus designated was one newly devised, by which all the distinctive tenets of the Catholic creed were specifically renounced; and might be tendered at any time to a suspected papist by the municipal authorities.

Persecution under the Commonwealth.—At the close of the civil war, the strife of religious parties in England had resolved itself into what was rather a contest for religious freedom against religious conformity than a struggle of Protestantism against Catholicism. The stubborn, independent spirit of the Puritan rebelled against the episcopal government of the national Church, and prelacy was hated by the zealots almost as thoroughly as Popery. Archbishop Laud, the chief assailant of Puritanism within the Establishment, had, on an accusation of high treason, been consigned to the Tower, where he remained a prisoner for four years. One of the charges brought against him was that he sought to introduce Popery into the Church, in evidence of which the offer made to him of the cardinalate was adduced; but he had no difficulty in proving that he had listened to no overtures that would oblige him to own allegiance to Rome. No charge could be fully substantiated against him, but a bill of attainder was passed, and he died on the scaffold, the victim of fanaticism.

Under the rule of Cromwell, who on Charles's death (1649) assumed the protectorate of the kingdom, freedom of faith and worship was proclaimed for all except Romanists and Prelatists. Episcopacy was abolished, the use of the Prayer-book was proscribed, the bishops were imprisoned; numbers of Protestant rectors and incumbents were deprived of their benefices, and their pulpits filled with Puritan preachers. Catholics were still the victims of persecuting statutes, the same reward being offered for the apprehension of a priest or of his entertainer as that which was granted for the apprehension of a highwayman.

The zeal of the Independents (this name was adopted by the party then in power, in distinction from the Presbyterians and Episcopalians) may not have shed so much blood, but they equalled their predecessors in rapacity. Bare suspicion was sufficient to warrant the sequestrator in seizing his prey; and it is difficult to say which suffered most cruelly—families with small fortunes who were reduced to a state of penury, or members of the working classes, servants, artisans, and even thrifty labourers, who, on their refusal to take the oath of abjuration, were deprived of two-thirds of their hard-won earnings, their household goods, their very wearing apparel. An instance is recorded of a Catholic maid-servant, an orphan, who, in the course of seventeen years of service, had contrived to save the sum of twenty pounds out of her scanty wages. The sequestrators, having discovered with whom she had deposited her money, took two-thirds for the use of the Commonwealth, leaving her the remainder, viz., six pounds thirteen shillings and fourpence. In vain she appealed to the commissioners for redress; she was informed that nothing could be done for her assistance unless she took the oath of abjuration. With such relentless energy did the sequestrators, who received a large percentage of the forfeited property for their pains, pursue their work, that at length a petition for indulgence was presented to Parliament. It was, however, indignantly rejected by the professed champions of religious liberty. Moreover, as a protest against Popery, and Prelacy, which was considered to be akin to it, every kind of sacrilege was permitted. The remains of the painted glass, the carvings and statuary of churches and cathedrals, which had escaped destruction at an earlier date, the old market crosses of country towns, were torn down, broken to pieces or defaced. Well might the faithful in England, witnessing this final triumph of Protestantism, exclaim with the Jews of old: "O God, the heathens are come into Thine inheritance, they have defiled Thy holy temple: they have given the dead bodies of Thy servants to be meat for the fowls of the air; they have poured out their blood as water. We are become a reproach to our neighbours, a scorn and derision to them that are round about us. Remember not our former iniquities; let Thy mercies speedily prevent us, for we are become exceeding poor" (Ps. lxxviii.).

Divine Judgements on the Nation.—The vengeance of God was soon to fall upon the nation which had thus shed the blood of His servants. Not unfrequently His judgements overtook individuals guilty of profanity. We read of a soldier who, climbing upon the rood-loft in a church in order to tear down the crucifix, in mockery struck the side of the figure with his pike. Thereupon blood flowed from the wound, and the soldier, falling backwards on to the pavement, met with instant death. Again, a farmer near Tewkesbury, when the celebrated statue of Our Lady was thrown from its shrine, carried it away, and after a time hollowed it out to make a drinking trough for his pigs. Not many days after, happening to stumble over it, he was precipitated into the well close to which it was placed, and perished miserably by drowning. Many similar isolated instances are recorded. But it is impossible not to see the visitation of God in the three national calamities that befell our fellow-countrymen at this period—the humiliation of the nation in the disastrous naval war with the Dutch; the terrible plague which broke out in the streets of London, and in the course of three or four months carried off a hundred thousand people; and the no less terrible fire which in the following year reduced two-thirds at least of the metropolis to ashes, and brought utter destitution upon thousands of its inhabitants.

CHAPTER XXIII.

CATHOLICS UNDER THE STUARTS (*continued*).

Charles II., 1660. His Leanings to Justice.
—The religious anarchy which prevailed during the Commonwealth ceased on the death of Cromwell (1658). A reaction set in in favour of a tranquil and settled government; Charles II. was recalled, the Episcopal Church re-established. The new monarch had pledged himself to support the national Church, but he was desirous of obtaining toleration for his Catholic subjects. The Stuart princes naturally were disposed to look favourably on Catholicism. During their exile their mother, sister to the French king, had procured their reception at foreign courts; Charles II. was married to a Catholic princess, and he was well aware that the English Catholics had been staunch supporters of his unfortunate father, and had suffered in the royal cause. He deemed himself bound in honour to procure them relief; he knew the execration wherein the penal laws against them were held on the continent, and he had often declared his resolution, should he recover the throne of his father, to mitigate the severity of those barbarous enactments. But the temper of the

nation was not yet prepared for toleration ; jealousy and apprehension of the Catholics was still rife ; and although they were not harassed by quite so severe a persecution, liberty of conscience was denied to them. A measure which the king laid before Parliament, and which would have enabled him to dispense, not only with the provisions of the Act of Uniformity, but with all laws and statutes enforcing conformity in worship or imposing religious tests, was rejected. A proclamation for the banishment of Catholic priests was extorted from Charles ; and by the Conventicle Act (1664), any assemblage of persons for religious services, unless those of the Established Church, was prohibited.

The Test Act, 1673.—The spirit of religious intolerance, which for some years had been abating, awoke to fresh life in 1670. Complaints were made of the growth of Catholicism, and Parliament reiterated the old cry of "No Popery." A suspicion was industriously fostered and became general that a plot was on foot for the re-establishment of Catholicism and despotism ; and some colour was lent to it by the fact that the Duke of York, the king's brother, had embraced the Catholic faith, while the king himself was credited with a secret leaning to it. It was alleged that priests and Jesuits had come over in greater numbers ; that English Catholics more than ever frequented the chapels of the embassies ; that mass was often celebrated in private houses ; that various convents and schools for Papists had been established in the country. Charles, to prove his Protestantism, received publicly the heretical communion, and the Test Act was passed in both Houses (1661) which declared every individual refusing to take the oath of supremacy and allegiance, and to receive the sacrament according to the rite of the Church of England, should be incapable of holding any office, civil, naval, or military. Furthermore, it was required that a declaration, denying transubstantiation and declaring the "adoration" of the Virgin Mary and other saints, and the sacrifice of the mass, to be superstitious and idolatrous, should be subscribed by all persons holding office, under the penalty of a fine of five hundred pounds and various legal disabilities. In consequence of this measure, the Duke of York resigned his office as Lord High Admiral; and Clifford, the Lord High Treasurer, also owned to being a Catholic, and voluntarily laid down his staff of office. Their resignation was followed by that of hundreds of others in the army and the civil service of the Crown.

Titus Oates.—In spite of the Test, it was suspected that men who were Catholics at least at heart still held office in the State. It was even whispered that the king himself was actually a Romanist, and a panic of distrust began. Rumours of plots for the subversion of the Protestant religion filled the air. At this moment of public agitation, a vile impostor came forward to take advantage of the general alarm by the invention of a Popish conspiracy. Titus Oates, a Baptist minister before the Restoration, a curate and navy chaplain after it, left penniless on account of his infamous character, had feigned conversion to the Catholic faith, and had been admitted into the Jesuit College at Valladolid and subsequently into that of Saint Omer. While there he learnt the fact of a meeting of Jesuits in London, which was probably nothing but the usual chapter for the arrangement of matters pertaining to the Society. On being expelled from St. Omer for disgraceful conduct, his fertile imagination magnified this meeting into a plot for assassinating the king, placing his brother James on the throne, and re-establishing the papal rule in England. He alleged, moreover, that the recent calamitous fire of London had been originated by the Jesuits; that they had thrown fireballs to increase the conflagration, with the design of extirpating the Protestant religion.

His story was laid before the king, and afterwards before the council; when made public it heightened the alarm of the credulous multitude, ready to believe anything evil of Catholics. It is probable, however, that this monstrous fabrication would have been denounced as an impudent imposture, and its author dismissed with contempt, had it not been for the seizure of the correspondence of the secretary of the Duchess of York, a busy intriguer, who had endeavoured to procure money from the king of France by offering his services on behalf of the interests of France and of Catholicism. It appeared that a secret treaty had been made between Charles II. and Louis XIV., agreeing that England should not take part in any war against France; that the two sovereigns should mutually aid each other in case of rebellion in their dominions, and that Charles should become a Catholic. These proposals had no connection with Oates's supposed disclosures, yet a passage in one letter was calculated to increase the alarm already aroused. "They had a mighty work on their hands," thus it ran, "no less than the conversion of three kingdoms, and by that, perhaps, the better subduing of a pestilent heresy which had so long domineered over a great part of the northern world. Success would give the greatest blow to the Protestant religion that it had received since its birth." These letters won credit for the perjuries of Oates, who heightened the popular frenzy by adding to his former depositions fresh and more startling revelations, recalling new and more important reminiscences of Jesuit perfidy.

The last English Martyrs.—Warrants were issued for the arrest of innocent persons incriminated by his statements; five Catholic peers, whom he accused of complicity in the pretended plot, were sent to the Tower, two thousand suspected persons were committed to prison. Patrols paraded the streets of London, and orders were given for the disarming of all Catholics, as precautionary measures to guard against the Popish rising declared to be at hand by Oates and other bold impostors, who found profit and popularity in playing the part of informers. The king's ministers fanned the flame. A bill was brought into Parliament for the exclusion of Catholic peers from the House of Lords, and an attempt was made to set aside the succession of James, the king's brother, and heir-presumptive to the throne. Both Houses voted a resolution that "there had been and still was a damnable and hellish plot contrived and carried on by Popish recusants for murdering the king, subverting the government, and rooting out the Protestant religion." The penal laws which had fallen into abeyance were again put in force; a fierce persecution, the last of a long series, broke out against the Catholics. Pursuivants and informers once more clamoured at the gates, rifled every apartment, and spread terror in every Catholic household. First

three, then five Jesuits, convicted on the testimony of
Oates of participation in the conspiracy he invented,
were put to death in London, and besides these the
Catholic lawyer Langhorne, who was condemned
without being heard in his own defence. Eight priests
were executed in many different parts of the country,
the only charge against them being the mere fact that
they were priests. One of the most noted victims
amongst the laity was Lord Stafford, who was
beheaded in 1680. But the sight of so venerable
a victim marked the beginning of the reaction. To
his speech on the scaffold the multitude responded
with shouts of "We believe you, my lord! God bless
you, my lord!" From that time the tide of popular
sympathy began to turn; Oates's statements proved
too much for the credulity of the most prejudiced
juries; horror and remorse on account of so much
bloodshed made itself felt. The last victim suffered
in 1681, when Oliver Plunket, Archbishop of Armagh,
suffered at Tyburn, and gloriously closed the long line
of our English martyrs.

Although Charles II. had not the courage to
confess his faith during his lifetime, yet when he
felt his end approaching he evaded the suggestions
of the bishops that he should receive the Protestant
communion, and eagerly accepted the offer of his
brother to send for a Catholic priest, his one anxiety
being to die in the communion of the Church. The
chamber was therefore cleared of the prelates and
attendants, and a priest named Hudlestone (who
had in 1651 been instrumental in assisting Charles
to escape after the battle of Worcester) was furtively
introduced. He heard the king's confession, reconciled him to the Church, and administered to him

the last sacraments. The utmost precautions were taken to prevent this fact from being known, as the reconciliation of any individual with the Catholic Church was counted as high treason; but concealment was impossible, and in a few days it was announced throughout the palace. It was even asserted that for years previous to his death Charles had been a Catholic, but this statement is quite unfounded.

From the time of Henry VIII., during nearly a century and a half of persecution, English Catholics had been hoping for the recovery of their country to the ancient Faith by the succession to the crown of a Catholic or the conversion of the reigning monarch. At last the former contingency had occurred, and a Catholic sat upon the throne of England.

But a long period of Protestant domination had obliterated from the mind of the nation all memory of the Church that had Christianized the land. In the place of her fair image there was substituted in men's ideas an odious parody of the truth concerning her. Calumny, reiterated through generations of public and private teaching, and emphasized by cruel and unjust legislation, had made Englishmen hate and dread what their forefathers had loved and clung to. Any power for good that a Catholic king might otherwise have had was thus precluded.[1]

James II., 1685. Catholics favoured.—James II. began his reign (1685) by declaring that he would preserve the laws inviolate, and would support and protect the Established Church—a pledge received with general satisfaction, and serving somewhat to dispel suspicions. He even went further in this

---

[1] *Catholic England in Modern Times*, by Rev. J. Morris, S.J.

direction, and, with questionable lawfulness, caused the funeral rites of the late king to be performed according to the use of the Protestant worship, whilst at his coronation, though he caused the communion service to be omitted, he allowed the customary forms to be observed by the archbishop.

The first attempt of the king to legalize the Catholic religion in his dominions was an assault on the Test Act of 1672. By this, as will be remembered, it was ordained that every officer, civil or military, should be required to receive the Protestant communion, and sign a declaration condemnatory of the leading doctrines of the Church of Rome. In defiance of this statute James gave commissions in the army to several Catholics who had faithfully served the Crown on former occasions, without their having previously qualified themselves according to the provisions of the Act. This gave great dissatisfaction to the Parliament, and the bishops protested against the infringement of a law which constituted a bulwark of the Established Church. On the question being laid before the judges, it was decided by them that the king had the right, by virtue of his royal prerogative, to dispense with the laws in particular cases. James, forgetful that "he who goes slowly goes safely and he who goes safely goes far," hastened to take advantage of this judgement of the Bench. Catholics were freely admitted to civil and other posts; four Catholic peers and Father Petre, the queen's confessor, were made members of the Privy Council. The laws which forbade the presence of Catholic priests within the realm and the public exercise of Catholic worship were set at naught; a vicar-apostolic for all England was appointed, with a yearly pension of £1000; a papal nuncio was received at Whitehall as ambassador to the English Court; Benedictines, Carmelites, Franciscans, settled in London, while the Jesuits set up a school in the old Savoy Palace. This school was frequented by both Catholics and Protestants, and such was its success that in a short time the number of the scholars amounted to four hundred. The chapels royal of St. James and Whitehall were opened for Catholic worship, and the king went to mass there in state. Protestant ministers were ordered to desist from controversial preaching, and from denunciations of Roman ritual or doctrine; and penalties were exacted from all who disobeyed this injunction.

Murmurs. Magdalen College, Oxford.—This rash method of procedure excited murmurs, and the leading Catholics represented to the king the danger of acting with such precipitancy. The Vicar Apostolic (Dr. Leyburne, formerly President of Douay College), and the Nuncio who accompanied him to England, were both of them charged by the Holy See to oppose the king's policy, and check his endeavours to force Catholicism on a reluctant nation. And when the king, anxious to wrest the University of Oxford from the hands of Protestants, compelled the fellows and students of Magdalen College to install Dr. Giffard, one of the newly consecrated bishops *in partibus infidelium*, as their president, Bishop Leyburne boldly remonstrated with him on this invasion of their rights. But James II. was resolved to exercise his royal prerogative, and the counsels of caution and moderation had no weight with him until it was too late. He regarded the ecclesiastical supremacy vested in the Crown as a weapon providentially left to him for undoing the work it had enabled his predecessors to do. Under Henry and Elizabeth it had been used to change the religion of England from Catholic to Protestant. He would employ it to effect the change from Protestant to Catholic. But he forgot that the days were passed wherein the monarch could act arbitrarily, and at his will set aside the laws of the nation without the consent of Parliament.

Religious Toleration proclaimed, 1687.— Accordingly, in 1687 a declaration appeared, granting religious liberty to all denominations. Although the king, it said, could not but desire that all his subjects were members of the Catholic Church, yet conscience was not to be enslaved, nor any one forced in matters of belief. During the last four reigns law after law had been passed to enforce conformity, and experience proved how vain was such legislation; therefore the bishops and clergy were to be maintained in the free exercise of their calling as by law established. The execution of the penal laws in matters ecclesiastical was to be suspended; assemblies for religious worship might be held without disturbance; religious tests of every kind were to be abolished.[1]

Trial of the Seven Bishops.— In consequence of this proclamation, Catholics could once more breathe freely; the different bodies of dissenters

---

[1] Attention may here be called to the fact that, even if James II. were somewhat imprudent in his method of action, his endeavour was merely to secure liberty of conscience for the Catholics, and in consequence of this endeavour, he was turned off the throne by Protestant bigotry. Even had he gone further, he would only have done very leniently what Henry VIII. and Elizabeth did very ruthlessly, that is, he would have forced on an unwilling people the religion of its ruler.

likewise received it with joy. Not so the members of the Establishment. The interference of the king in the appointments at Oxford already appeared to them a grievous wrong. The new measure aroused their alarm; they suspected that something more was in view than the emancipation of Catholics from the restrictions imposed on them. Accordingly, when in the following year an order was issued that the declaration should be read by the clergy in their respective churches in the time of divine service, on a given Sunday, the bishops openly defied the royal command. The document was, they asserted, founded on an illegal power of dispensing with the laws in cases contrary to the design in making them. The Protestant clergy supported their prelates; in only a few of the parish churches was the obnoxious declaration read. In this ill-advised contest with the Established Church in which he was now involved, the king acted with a want of prudence which spoilt the cause he upheld. The petition presented to him by the bishops he styled a standard of rebellion, and sent the seven prelates who had subscribed it to the Tower. They were tried and acquitted. The sympathy of the people was with them; they were considered to have won a victory for the constitutional liberties of England against absolute monarchy, for the freedom of religion from the papal yoke; and the tidings of their acquittal was hailed with shouts of triumph.

William III. and Mary, 1689.—Meanwhile, some intriguing politicians had invited William, the Prince of Orange, who was married to the king's elder daughter, to intervene with force of arms for the restoration of English liberty and the protection of the Protestant religion. The landing of a Dutch army gave the signal for a revolution. James II. abandoned the struggle in despair, and left the kingdom; William and Mary were acknowledged as joint sovereigns. Thus the year 1688 witnessed the transfer of the crown of England to the Protestant branch of the royal family, whereby the Catholic clergy and Catholic institutions were involved in fresh calamities.

CHAPTER XXIV.

TROUBLES OF THE EIGHTEENTH CENTURY.

Toleration for all but Catholics. Their Disabilities.—The two centuries which followed the revolution of 1688 may well be regarded as forming a distinct period in the history of the Catholic Church in England. All hope of the speedy conversion of the nation had vanished. The authorities had, it is true, learnt wisdom in one respect from what had gone before. They did not any longer shed upon the scaffold the blood of priests, and of those who harboured them. Publicly inflicted martyrdom was an occasion when Protestants heard and saw the most impressive of sermons, when Catholics had their courage renewed, and went away proud of their religion, when all nations were moved to sympathy with the victims of persecution. Imprisonment and fines were more effectual weapons, involving none of these drawbacks. They had been used freely from the beginning of Elizabeth's reign with fearful effect, and they were used still more freely on the weakened and broken remnant of English Catholics under the Prince of Orange and the first two sovereigns of the House of Hanover.

Toleration was supposed to have been imported with William III., but it was toleration for all except Catholics. In the first Parliament of this reign an Act was passed to exempt all Protestant dissenters from the Established Church from the penalties of the laws against them, and in it was a clause that "Papists and Popish recusants" were to receive no benefit by the Act. The same Parliament renewed the oath introduced by James I., to the effect that no foreign prince, prelate, or potentate had, or ought to have, any jurisdiction or authority, spiritual or ecclesiastical, within the realm. It also declared that any one refusing the oath, which denounced transubstantiation and other Catholic doctrines as superstitious and idolatrous, should be deemed a recusant convict, subject to all the punishments of the penal code. Other acts of the same session commanded "Papists and reputed Papists to remove from the cities of London and Westminster, and ten miles distance of the same"; to forego the use and possession of arms, and the possession of any horse above five pounds in value. Any two justices could authorize persons to search for arms or horses, and seize them for the king's use.

A still more malicious Act was passed in the eleventh and twelfth years of this reign. By this statute all priests or Catholic laymen convicted of keeping school, educating or boarding youth, and every bishop or priest convicted of saying mass or exercising his functions within the realm, were to suffer perpetual imprisonment, and the informer who apprehended them was to be rewarded with the sum of one hundred pounds. Furthermore, Catholics were made incapable of purchasing or inheriting lands; and the heirs of any estate were required, at the age of eighteen, to take the oaths of supremacy and allegiance, and when of age to take the test, on pain of the property passing to the nearest Protestant relative. Thus a premium was offered to children to become Protestants, for in that case they could apply to the Lord Chancellor for a maintenance out of their father's estate, and on his death the Protestant child became the heir, in preference to elder brothers who were Catholics, and in contravention of the terms of the father's will; while if all the children were Catholics, any Protestant kinsman could wrest the inheritance from them. These cruel enactments might well be called " for the further preventing the growth of Popery." To divest the landed gentry of their estates, and give them over to Protestants, was the most effectual means of exterminating the Catholic religion. There were very few priests in the country whose home was not in some gentleman's house. Hence the forfeiture or confiscation of an estate meant one place less where a priest could find shelter. It might well be expected that these two statutes, one of which inflicted perpetual imprisonment on a priest for no other offence than the mere fact of his presence in England, and the other which, by the destruction of the houses where he found refuge, rendered him homeless, would cause Catholicism to die a natural death in England. That they did not do so must have been partly due to the kind feelings of Protestant neighbours, as well as to the courage of the Catholic laity, without which the priests could not have exercised their self-sacrificing devotion on behalf of their persecuted flock. The laity suffered severe penalties with heroic constancy; but their numbers were thinned by the dying out of Catholic branches of their families, and in many cases by the loss of the faith for which they had suffered so much and so long.

Results on Catholics.—It is not to be wondered at that such legislation led many men to act against their conscience. Fathers, heads of families, nominally conformed and took the iniquitous oaths, thus preserving their property at the cost of their religion. At heart they remained true to the faith, being called schismatics by their fellow-Catholics, and hoping before death to be reconciled to the Church. In Elizabeth's time, the wife could continue to be a Catholic, without bringing pains and penalties on her conforming husband; but James I. struck at her also, by disabling every man whose wife was a convicted Popish recusant from holding any public office, and adjudging every married woman, three months after conviction for recusancy, to be committed to prison until she conform, unless her husband pay £10 a month, or yield up a third of his lands. Even a man's servants, and children above nine years old, must repair to the heretical worship once a month, to save him from penalties. The persistent pressure of one Act after another—from that in Elizabeth's reign, which forbade the Papist to go five miles from his home without a license, down to William and Mary's prohibition to keep a horse above £5 in value—with the uncertainty of what would come next, is the excuse, if any excuse is possible, for numerous apostasies. Exterior conformity to escape penalties made England Protestant. It is one of the saddest parts of this sad story to watch the disappearance of one Catholic family after another. All glory to the constancy of those who bore the galling pressure, in spite of the example of their neighbours who yielded to it.

Division of England into Catholic Districts.—The Catholics in England remained without episcopal government from the time that Dr. Smith, Vicar-Apostolic of England and Bishop of Chalcedon, was compelled to withdraw to France in 1629, until August, 1685, when Dr. Leyburne, as will be remembered, arrived in London after consecration in Rome. For two years he was sole Vicar-Apostolic; at the close of 1687, Pope Innocent XI., at the request of James II., divided England into four districts, to which bishops were appointed, the king assigning to each an income of £1,000 a year. Dr. Leyburne became Vicar-Apostolic of the London district; the three new bishops being consecrated in London by the Papal Nuncio. It was not in the power of the king to carry out his good intentions as to their maintenance, for scarcely twelve months later he had to fly from England. Bishops Leyburne and Giffard attempted to leave the country with him, but they were arrested and imprisoned, the former for two years, the latter for one. Dr. Ellis, a Benedictine, Bishop of the Western District, was detained for a time in Newgate; when released he left England, never to return. The fourth bishop had to leave York, but he was received and entertained till his death by a private gentleman. William III. did not insist on the banishment of the two bishops who were his prisoners. Dr. Leyburne was allowed to live quietly in London; on his death, Dr. Giffard was transferred from the Midland District to succeed him in that of London. Although harassed by continual dangers and alarms, obliged incessantly to change his lodgings—as often, he tells us, as fourteen times in one half-year—the good bishop lived through all his troubles until 1734, when he died at Hammersmith in the ninety-second year of his age.

Rising in Scotland.—The condition of Catholics was indeed then bad enough, but unfortunately circumstances led them to make it worse. In 1715 took place the well-known rising in Scotland and invasion of England, on behalf of the Stuart line. This movement was by no means distinctively Catholic, but many Catholics joined it out of a feeling of loyalty to the principle of hereditary succession. When the revolt was crushed, it was on the Catholics that the weight of the Hanoverian wrath chiefly fell. An Act was passed in 1722 which placed their property still more in the power of the Government. The land-tax was doubled for every reputed Papist, and in addition a tax of one hundred thousand pounds was levied upon the estates of the impoverished Catholics.

Further Oppression.—These severe laws, which deprived the Catholics of landed property, were daily put in execution, as the records of the times testify. In other respects also, Catholics were subjected to incessant vexations and contumely; no Catholic, it is said, who did not live in those days, can imagine the depression and humiliation under which the whole body laboured. The persecution of priests and bishops for the execution of their spiritual functions continued without intermission. Arrests were of frequent occurrence, thanks to the busy and pertinacious informer, eager to obtain the large reward promised to his successful researches. "The continual fear and alarm we are under is something worse than Newgate," said Bishop Giffard, who had spent some time in prison. A little later (1747) Bishop York, Coadjutor in the Western District, wrote to the Propaganda: "We are compelled to fly from house to house, and from city to city. I have been for eighteen months and more a fugitive from my ordinary residence, and as yet have no fixed abode." In 1733, Bishop Williams, O.P., Vicar-Apostolic of the Northern District, had been actually "obliged to fly to remote places, to escape prison and torture, on account of his having made a conversion which caused a great noise." It is related of Bishop Hornyold that while still a simple priest, being warned on one occasion that the constables were coming to seize him just as he was finishing mass, he had barely time to substitute for his flowing periwig the cap which a woman who was present hastily offered him, and wrap her large cloak over his vestments, before the officers of the law entered the apartment. Kneeling motionless in a corner, in an attitude of prayer, he contrived to escape observation.

Almost all priests passed under an alias, and assumed disguises. The untiring zeal, courage, and devotion displayed by both prelates and clergy in these evil times is beyond all praise. Whenever an obscure retreat could be found to shelter a poor audience, they were indefatigable in preaching the word and instructing the young. The tradition is that Bishop Challoner used to meet a number of Catholics on Sunday evening at a publichouse called "The Ship," near Lincoln's Inn Fields; and sitting there, with a pot of beer as a blind on a little table before him, he would preach to those who were present. The little table, marked with circles by the pewter pot, was preserved to our time. It is said the floor of the room was partly movable, so that people in two stories could hear the preacher at the same time.

Bishop Challoner.—Bishop Challoner and his friend, Alban Butler, were (we quote the words of Fr. Morris, S.J.) our greatest men in the wretched eighteenth century; and they did more than any of their contemporaries in preserving the faith amongst men of their own generation, and in promoting conversions to the Church. Challoner was sent to the English College at Douay in 1704, and left it in 1730. In the latter part of this period he was professor of dogmatic theology and prefect of studies. This time devoted to study and to teaching fitted him for the literary work that awaited him in England. Although he was most assiduous in the discharge of his sacred functions, making pastoral visits, administering the sacraments at all risks to the scattered members of his flock, in fulfilling all the laborious duties of a poor missionary, the list of his books would fill a page. They are remarkable in the first place for their painstaking accuracy, and next for a gentle, unassuming persuasiveness, that was due as much to the writer's piety as to his learning. His books were the saving of Catholics who needed support and instruction, and they were well adapted to break down the absurd prejudices of Protestants as to the doctrines that the Church really teaches. Alban Butler, his fellow-professor at Douay, was the more learned man of the two.

To him we are indebted for the "Lives of the Saints," a work which has not yet been, and is not likely to be, superseded; and also, conjointly with Challoner, for the "Memoirs of Missionary Priests," the admirable book that has saved our martyrs from oblivion.

Relief Bill, 1778.—Challoner had the happiness of seeing the first beginnings of the relaxation of the oppressive penal laws. In 1778 an address was presented to the Crown by the principal Catholic nobles and gentlemen, the consequence of which was that an Act of Parliament was passed in the same year "for relieving his Majesty's subjects professing the Popish religion from certain penalties and disabilities imposed on them by the legislation of the eleventh and twelfth years of King William III." This new Act imposed an oath of allegiance without any renunciation of Catholic doctrines; repealed the penalty of perpetual imprisonment on Popish priests and schoolmasters, and rendered Papists capable of buying and inheriting lands. It was known as Sir George Savile's Act; that gentleman in introducing the Bill described the penalties on Catholics as "disgraceful not only to religion, but to humanity." For this he was rewarded by the destruction of his house, during the riots to which the passing of the measure gave rise.

Gordon Riots, 1780.—More than a year elapsed before the outburst came, prompted by Protestant bigotry and the usual reckless love of destruction that animates a mob. Lord George Gordon, a fanatic, and president of the Protestant Association, drew up a petition to the House of Commons for the repeal of the small instalment of justice conceded to those whom he designated "the followers of Antichrist." At the head of an immense band of rioters he presented this petition to the House. After going through the usual stages it was rejected. Meanwhile the mob, estimated at from sixty to one hundred thousand men, paraded the streets with flags and bagpipes, plundering and burning one Catholic chapel after another, as well as the private houses of persons known to be Catholics, or friendly to Catholics. For nearly a week the metropolis was at the mercy of the rioters; every day witnessed some fresh act of violence. The prisons were broken open and destroyed, and the felons released; the Bank, the public offices, and the houses of the ministers were threatened. In some cases Protestant neighbours offered Catholics shelter, in others they were afraid to do so; and the fear lest his turn might come next, of being driven into the streets, homeless and penniless, involved every Catholic in the common misery. The Government seemed paralyzed, and it is to the credit of George III. that he should have been the first to take upon himself the responsibility of ordering that the rioters, if they refused to disperse, should be fired upon. The soldiers then attacked the mob in various directions; but not until some five hundred rioters had fallen was tranquillity restored, and the cry of "No Popery" hushed. The author of these calamities died in Newgate.

Bishop Challoner was roused from sleep on the night when the riot broke out, by the news of the attack upon the Sardinian ambassador's chapel, the first one that was demolished. It was with difficulty that he was induced to leave his house and betake himself to Finchley, to the country-house of Mr

William Mawhood, a leading man amongst London Catholics, who had a large place of business in Smithfield. On the following day both houses were visited by the rioters, who threatened to destroy them. The bishop spent an hour in prayer, while the coach was at the door which was waiting to convey him to a safer refuge. He then told the family that "he who dwells in the help of the Most High shall abide under the protection of the God of Heaven;" and he assured Mr. Mawhood that he was certain no harm would happen either to his country house or his town house. The bishop's prediction was exactly verified.

Had this destruction of property taken place some years before, Catholics would never have dreamed of hoping that restitution would be made to them for their losses, although the law provided that the county must make good the depredations caused by a riot. Now they were told that they had taken the oath of allegiance to the king, and could claim the protection of the laws, like all other subjects. Compensation was therefore made to them, as well as to those Protestants whose property had been destroyed by the mob.

The state of feeling among Catholics in consequence of this outbreak of violence was not altogether favourable to religion. The comparative immunity they enjoyed from the penal laws occasioned a relaxation of fervour. Instead of abandoning their interests as formerly to the care of Divine Providence, they turned their eyes to the Government for protection, and sought the favour of the great and powerful. As long as the laws remained on the statute-book their revival might happen at any time, and fear and dread of this led some to go too far in their desire to propitiate Protestants. Several sad instances of apostasy occurred among the peers, who purchased a seat in the House of Lords at the price of eternal salvation. Even in the ranks of the clergy some men were found who preferred a position of ease in the well-endowed Establishment, with freedom from oppressive restrictions, to the reward promised hereafter to the good and faithful servants of Christ.

The Committee of Five Laymen. Its Uncatholic Spirit.—But such individual instances of apostasy were not the worst symptom. A spirit of opposition to Rome, an attempt to diminish the Pope's authority and jurisdiction, manifested itself in a committee of five laymen, appointed for five years to promote the political interests of Catholics in England. This Committee began by asking for a change in the ecclesiastical government of the country, by the substitution of bishops in ordinary for vicars apostolic; the reason alleged being "that the frequent recurrence to Rome for dispensations and other ecclesiastical matters might cease." The change asked was, in itself, perfectly legitimate and very excellent: it was, in fact, a petition for the re-establishment of the hierarchy. The reason, however, which supplied the motive for the demand betrayed an un-Catholic spirit and also much ignorance: for bishops in ordinary frequently need faculties from the Holy See no less than vicars apostolic, in order to grant dispensations. Later on, when their number was extended, the Committee issued a circular, calling attention to the fact that "the government by vicars apostolic is by no means essential to our religion, and that it is not only contrary to the primitive practice of the Church, but is in direct opposition to the Statutes of *Præmunire* and Provisors." An appeal to the primitive from the present discipline of the Church is, as Canon Flanagan remarks, "the usual badge of schism, since it virtually denies that the Church of Christ is a living body, under a living head, the successor of St. Peter; the more so when the objectors shelter themselves behind statutes enacted by man to cramp the action and curtail the liberties of the Holy See."

A document was also drawn up by the Committee, called a Doctrinal Test, denying the false charges made against the Church, and setting forth the civil and religious principles of Catholics, in view of furthering the repeal of the laws so eagerly desired by them. This was to be signed and presented to Parliament; but the lay theologians had gone too far in their concessions through their desire to propitiate their enemies, and the opposition of the bishops saved their flock from committing themselves to this unauthorized "Test."

Somewhat later the Committee, to which some clerical members had been added, one of whom was Bishop Talbot, the London Vicar Apostolic (who however, did not sympathize with their aims), entered into further negotiations with the Government to obtain measures of relief. Unchecked by the presence of the bishop, who endeavoured to restrain them, the Committee prepared a "Declaration and Protestation," which was very largely signed both by clergy and laity throughout the country. It contained, however, many expressions that were theologically inexact, and tended to break down the distinction between Catholics and their Protestant fellow-subjects by adopting the epithet "Protesting Catholic Dissenters," the name of Papist being applied to those Catholics who should condemn their project. Of course the bishops would not sanction the declaration. Moreover, in spite of promises previously made that no new oath should be proposed, the Committee, to gratify their Protestant friends, attached to their Bill a form of oath which, amongst other things, declared that no foreign prince or prelate hath, or ought to have, "any spiritual authority, power, or jurisdiction whatsoever that can directly or indirectly affect or interfere with the independence, sovereignty, laws, or constitution of this kingdom, or with the civil or ecclesiastical government thereof, as by law established."

Unhappily the Committee would not submit to the censure of the bishops, and a painful controversy resulted, which continued for nearly two years. During this interval two bishops died, and an attempt was made to assert the right of the clergy and laity to elect their prelates without reference to Rome, one of the Committee stigmatizing the vicars apostolic as "foreign missionaries, who preside in virtue of an authority delegated by a foreign prelate who has no pretensions to exercise such an act of power." A schism might have ensued, had not the clergy almost universally, and the laity generally, supported the vicars apostolic, and recognized the appointments made by the Holy See. The bishops then issued an encyclical letter, renewing their former condemnation of the proposed oath, and exhorting Catholics to oppose it if it were introduced into Parliament. A violent protest was immediately issued by the Committee, declaring the encyclical to be arbitrary and unjust, and appealing from it to "other Catholic Churches, especially to the first of Catholic Churches, rightly informed."

The Toleration Act, 1791.—In June, 1791, the Bill which proposed relief to the "Protesting Catholic Dissenters" (as they termed themselves), and to no others, was read in Parliament. The result of the debate upon it was discomfiting to the Committee; Bishop Milner, the courageous opponent of the Committee, to whose efforts we principally owe the completeness of our present religious liberty, distributed a paper among the members of parliament, which pointed out that the name of "Protesting Catholic Dissenters" and the terms of the proposed oath were distasteful to the mass of Catholics, who did not accept the Committee as their representatives. The result was that the title "Protesting Catholic Dissenters" was struck out by the ministry, and the proposed oath discarded and replaced by the Irish oath of 1778. The Bill thus passed without a dissentient voice. It repealed the statutes of recusancy and various disabilities in favour of persons taking the oath, and extended toleration to the schools and religious worship of Catholics. The double land-tax was, moreover, never again exacted, although not until 1831 was an Act passed relieving Catholics from it.

By this Act of 1791 the oaths and declarations prescribed in the preceding reigns were no longer required of Catholics, and they were allowed to live in London. Catholic chapels were to be certified at quarter sessions, and only in chapels thus certified was religious worship to be performed. It was made unlawful to lock, bolt, or bar the doors during service, from some lurking fear, apparently, that Catholics, whose concealments and disguises in time of persecution had simply been the defence of the weak against the strong, were a secret society that plotted against their neighbours and the State. The priest had no permission to officiate until his name and description (the order, if any, to which he belonged) had been registered by the clerk of the peace; nor was he allowed to officiate at a funeral in any church or churchyard. This last prohibition has been done away with in recent times by the Burials Act, which allows any religious service to be held in churchyards in accordance with the religion professed in life by the person there buried.

A provision was inserted in this Toleration Act that no Catholic could be the master of any school or college at Oxford or Cambridge, or of any royal foundation or other endowed school. It was also made illegal to found Catholic schools and colleges, or establish any religious order or society of persons bound by monastic or religious vows.

About a year after this Act had been passed the Committee changed its name into "The Cisalpine Club," as a permanent protest against "certain encroachments of the Court of Rome on civil authority." The club was a source of trouble and division for nearly thirty years, but later on it became perfectly harmless, and was finally broken up.

CHAPTER XXV.

CATHOLIC EMANCIPATION.

Removal of Catholic Disabilities, 1829.—The passing of the Toleration Act of 1791 made, as we have seen, an important alteration in the status of Catholics. Much was, however, yet wanting before they could count themselves as placed on an equality with their Protestant fellow-subjects. The principal of their grievances were these:—they were still debarred by law from holding any position in the State or office under Government; they were excluded from Parliament, and even from the election franchise; Catholic soldiers and sailors were compelled to attend the service of the Church of England; property given for the purposes of education was liable to confiscation; Catholic marriages, although publicly solemnized in licensed chapels, were not regarded by the law as valid.

Opposition from George III. — Emancipation was not attained without a long and weary struggle. After the passing of the Bill of Union with Ireland (1800), the prime minister, Mr. Pitt, prepared to lay before Parliament a measure which would have raised Catholics and Dissenters to perfect equality of civil rights. He proposed to do away with all religious tests which were required for admission to parliament, the magistracy, the bar, municipal offices, or posts in the army, navy, or the service of the State. Political security was to be provided for by the imposition of an oath of fidelity and allegiance to the sovereign in the place of the sacramental tests, while the loyalty of the clergy was to be ensured by the grant of some provision for their support by the State. Before this scheme obtained the assent of the Cabinet, it was communicated to the king. "I count any man my personal enemy," his majesty angrily answered, "who should propose such a measure." It was represented to him that the political circumstances under which the laws it was proposed to abrogate originated, now no longer existed. Enactments arising from the conflicting power of hostile denominations, the apprehension of a Catholic queen as successor to the throne or a foreign pretender, a division in Europe between Catholic and Protestant powers, were no longer applicable to the present state of things. But argument and representations were lost on George III. He thought himself bound by his coronation oath to maintain the Tests; and his bigotry agreed too well with the religious hatred and political distrust of Catholics which still lingered among the mass of the people not to make his decision fatal to the Bill. The "No Popery" cry was still general, and petitions were numerously signed against any further concession to Catholics. An old woman, when asked to sign a petition of this nature, answered that it was useless, for the Scriptures said that the Romans should come and take away our place and nation;

Catholic Emancipation.

and it appears that better educated persons had the same fear that this would be the result of Catholic emancipation. But from time to time bills in favour of Catholics were laid before Parliament; and at length the Duke of Wellington gave way, and introduced a measure which, like that designed by Pitt, admitted Roman Catholics to Parliament, and to all but a few of the highest posts, civil or military, in the service of the Crown.

Dr. Milner's Determination.—Before this Bill was passed, an unfortunate difference arose among the English bishops. Three of the vicars apostolic were silent when it was proposed in Parliament to give the English Government a veto on the appointment of our bishops, and even, by granting them an endowment, to place our clergy under the control of the State. Bishop Poynter, a peace-loving man, willing to yield as far as possible, signed a resolution assenting to the proposition; Dr. Milner alone, supported by the Irish bishops, strenuously opposed it. Every effort was made to win him over by fair means or foul. On one occasion he was invited by the Duke of Buckingham to Stowe, where to his surprise he found himself beset after dinner with pressure of all kinds to obtain his signature. It was with difficulty that he stood his ground that night; at daybreak the next morning he sallied forth by a window, found his way to the stables and saddled his horse; then riding away down the avenue, he sang *In exitu Israel de Ægypto.*

The conduct of Dr. Milner in fighting the battle of the Church received the approval of the Holy See when in 1814 he went to Rome, to obtain the recall of a rescript which, during the absence of Pope Pius

VII., and without his authorization, had been sent by Mgr. Quarantotti, the Secretary of the Propaganda, to Bishop Poynter. This letter declared that Catholics might accept a Bill which had been drawn up in accordance with the resolution of the Catholic Board, and was of a most unsatisfactory nature. The decision of His Holiness in regard to the subjects of debate was given in the following year: 1. Three forms of an oath were given, any one of which was allowed to Catholics. 2. The examination by Government of documents from Rome was not to be tolerated. 3. The nomination to bishoprics should never be given to princes who are not Catholics.

Daniel O'Connell.—This utterance of the Holy See had the effect of putting an end to all discussions and controversies, and reunited the four vicars apostolic. Neither Bishop Milner nor Bishop Poynter, who had laboured each according to his lights for the emancipation of English Catholics, lived to see the measure passed which granted it. Another champion was destined to arise, and to overthrow, by the might of his powerful personality, the obstacles which had so long stood in the way. To Ireland belongs the glory of having carried Catholic Emancipation. In 1823 a Catholic Association was formed, which in 1828 secured the return of Daniel O'Connell for Clare—that is to say, he was elected for Clare, but the sacramental test still stood in the way of his taking his seat. Backed, however, by the strong determination of his fellow countrymen, he presented himself at the bar of the House of Commons, and demanded admission without taking the oath. The result was to force upon the Government the necessity of removing the Catholic disabilities; and in 1829 the Duke of Wellington and Sir Robert Peel, who had both previously been its determined opponents, brought in the Bill, which then passed successfully. By this Bill the oaths of supremacy and abjuration were abolished, and in place of them one was substituted promising to maintain the Protestant succession, and abjuring on the part of Catholic members of parliament any intention to subvert the present Church establishment as settled by law in the land. More recently this oath, only less objectionable than its predecessor, gave place to a simple oath of allegiance. Catholics were further forbidden by the Act to take the title of sees occupied by Protestant dignitaries; and as a concession to Protestant prejudice, provisions were inserted with the view of gradually extinguishing the Jesuits and the monastic orders of men. All who at this time belonged to this class were enjoined, under penalties, to register themselves, and in future the taking of religious vows by men was to be penal. This clause still remains a blot upon the statute-book, although after the lapse of sixty-five years it may now be considered obsolete.

Existing Disabilities.—Though Catholics have been permitted to leave money for the endowment of their worship or their education, masses for the repose of the soul of the deceased are still held to be superstitious and void. Under an Act passed in 1832, Catholics are placed on the same footing as Protestant Dissenters in respect of their schools, places of worship, education, and charities, the property held therewith and the persons employed therein. In 1860 another Act was passed to enable Catholics to take the benefit of the general law relating to charities, without, however, altering the law as regards superstitious uses or objects deemed against the policy of the law. The grievance of the marriage law has only been partially remedied. As under the old marriage acts Catholics could obtain civil validity for their marriages only by presenting themselves before the Protestant clergyman, it was lawful in conscience so to do, as he was thus to them not a minister of religion, but an official of the State. When the marriage law was altered for the benefit of nonconformists, it was made felony for the priest to celebrate marriage without the presence of a registrar, which presence is only legal in a duly registered building, unless the parties have previously contracted a civil marriage in the registrar's office in which case the ceremony may be afterwards performed by the priest. The expense this law necessitates—the registrar's fee—often induces the poor to be married in the Protestant church, where the ceremony is performed for a very trifling sum. This regulation may be ranked among our legal grievances, for which a remedy is still desired. Another invidious restriction is that when the offices in the State were thrown open to Catholics, exception was made of the Lord Chancellorships of England and Ireland, and the Lord Lieutenancy of Ireland. The Chancellorship of Ireland, however, is now open to Catholics.

The history of the Church in England may be considered as ended, in as far as its political position is concerned, from the time that the Catholic peers, availing themselves of the Emancipation Act, resumed the hereditary seats of their ancestors in the House of Lords. We must now go back a little, in order to treat of other things besides our relation to the State, and note how the events that happened upon the continent towards the close of the eighteenth century affected the religious life of Catholics in our own country.

Educational Institutions transferred to England.—It has been seen that at Douay College, as at St. Omers, Valladolid, Lisbon, and Rome, the descendants of those who had refused to break with the Holy Roman Church were educated for the priesthood for many generations; and, free from all contact with Protestantism, kept pure the Catholic traditions of their forefathers. The old secular college at Douay, founded by Dr., afterwards Cardinal, Allen, in 1568, amid the storms succeeding the Reformation, had done more to save England from the extinction of the faith through the loss of her clergy than all the other colleges together. It was in a most flourishing condition when it was destroyed by the French Revolution, and all its professors and students were imprisoned or scattered. The secular college of St. Omers, established in 1763, shared the same fate, as did likewise those conducted by the Benedictines at Douay and Dieulouard, and by the ex-Jesuits at Liège. The last-named establishment, founded in 1592 by Father Persons at St. Omers, had been driven thence by the Parliament of Paris in 1762 (the secular college above mentioned taking its place), and had migrated first to Bruges, and later, in 1773, on the suppression of the Society of Jesus, to Liège.

From the institutions thus expelled by the Revolution have descended most of the Catholic colleges now flourishing on English soil. The secular college of Douay is the parent of Ushaw, and—in conjunction with that at St. Omers—also of St. Edmund's, Old Hall, which claims an earlier progenitor in a boys' school, after various wanderings settled in the same place some thirty years previously. The Benedictines of Douay ultimately established their college at Downside, those of Dieulouard at Ampleforth; while the refugees from Liège, by the invitation of Mr. Thomas Weld, transplanted themselves to Stonyhurst, where the members of the restored Society still carry on the work of their predecessors at St. Omers.

Convents.—Not only were colleges and seminaries for priests transferred to England at the time of the French Revolution; many convents of English origin likewise took refuge in this country from the violence of the storm. In the days of persecution, under circumstances which would have justified, if any could do so, their attending solely to those essentials of their Christian profession which were daily becoming more difficult to secure, not a few ladies of rank desired to practise the counsels of perfection. This they could only do in exile, since on the accession of Elizabeth the English convents were all suppressed. Thus a considerable number of English convents came into existence on the continent in the seventeenth century. The first house founded for English religious women after the Reformation was the Benedictine monastery of the Assumption, founded at Brussels by Lady Mary Percy in 1598. This was also the first to reach England, when, on the outbreak of the Revolution, the communities were driven to seek shelter on our shores. It was established first at Winchester, and transferred thence in 1857 to East Bergholt in Suffolk. The Revolution also sent over to us several houses of the same order, and other houses of various orders founded in France or the Low Countries. The most ancient religious house of those founded in England since the Reformation is the Institute of our Blessed Lady at York, which has never moved from the place of its original foundation. It was founded by Mary Ward in 1642, and was long the only convent in this country.

Refugee French Priests in England.—Another signal service was rendered to the Catholic religion in England by the expulsion from France of the flower of the French clergy and laity. At one time we gave hospitality to above eight thousand priests, who came over between 1792 and 1799. There was a large voluntary subscription for their support, and this proving inadequate, the Government, rising superior to its prejudices, voted a considerable sum annually for their support, regarding the refugees as objects for the exercise of philanthropy. Seven hundred priests were lodged in the king's house at Winchester; some lived in community in various towns, the rest being scattered freely about the country. These exiled ecclesiastics were in a difficult position in this Protestant realm; they behaved with great prudence, and worked for their livelihood with the greatest diligence at a thousand incongruous occupations. Nothing that they could do was left untried, even to agricultural labour. Some, though comparatively few, obtained employment as teachers of French or of music; others found opportunity for the one congenial work of the ministry. In London and in other parts of the country, leaving out of account the chapels that were opened simply to enable them to say mass, many missions owe their existence to the apostolic zeal of the exiled French priests, who supported themselves mainly by teaching, and devoted their little earnings to establishing chapels.

Danger of Gallicanism.—When Pope Pius VII., in consequence of the concordat made with Napoleon in 1801, divided France into fresh dioceses, the banished prelates were called upon to resign their sees. The greater number at once acquiesced, and returned to their own country, together with a large majority of the refugee priests. A certain number, however, refused to comply; they even ventured to censure the action of the Pope, and to declare that he had exceeded his powers in creating a new hierarchy. The refusal to accept the new ecclesiastical arrangements in France, and to acknowledge the Church thus reconstructed as a true part of the Catholic Church, gained for this party the name of the *Petite Église;* and as their chief leader was the Abbé Blanchard, they were often called Blanchardists. How far Gallicanism went under these circumstances may be seen from the terms of the test imposed in 1818 by the vicars apostolic on all the French clergy resident in England as a condition for their exercise of the priesthood. It was found necessary to make them declare that Pope Pius VII., was " not a heretic or schismatic, or the author or abettor of schism." It was the more essential that these Gallican principles should be stamped out, because English Catholics were not entirely free from them. The spirit that called into existence the Cisalpine Club (so named as opposed to Transalpine or Ultramontane principles) was still energizing amongst us, leading men to minimize their Catholic position and tenets, and to concede the utmost to their antagonists without actual surrender of essentials, for the purpose of making themselves acceptable to a Protestant Government and legislature.

Good Results of the French "Emigrés."—There is little doubt that the presence in our midst of the *emigré* French clergy contributed greatly to overthrow anti-catholic prejudices in this country. The admiration entertained for their fortitude and fidelity led practical English people to think better of their religion. More certain still it is that a blessing came to the nation from the hospitality afforded them. Not only was the Sacrifice of Propitiation offered by thousands of priests on English soil, but the generosity that provided for the support of a large number of aliens, with whose country we were at war and who were themselves priests of a detested religion, has been abundantly repaid by Him whose priests they were. The Catholic Church was beginning gradually and slowly to emerge from obscurity, but the shadow of the penal laws had not yet passed away; and the fear of reawakening persecution made Catholics timid and cautious, anxious to shun publicity. Families used to go in a cart at night to hear mass, the priest dressed in a round frock to resemble a labouring man, as late as the close of the eighteenth century. In Dr. Milner's time, Catholics never spoke of hearing mass, but used the word *prayers* instead; a habit which was retained by most of the old priests down to a very late period, the same expression being employed in the old Directories. The exterior of the chapels, when these were more than upper rooms in houses, was purposely made similar in appearance to that of the surrounding buildings; in the country the approach was concealed more or less, and until the close of the last century there was generally on the watch a person who knew the congregation, and who would without ceremony exclude any one who awakened his suspicions. This precaution, which dated from the days, still well remembered, when priests were informed against, was often an unfortunate custom for strangers, to whom, as being unknown, admittance was refused.

"In those traditional days it was unusual for a priest to say mass every day. Benediction of the Blessed Sacrament was very rare. High mass was almost unknown. It was accounted frequent communion to go at the eight Indulgences. The first priest who appeared in black was blamed for exposing priests to danger of persecution. The Roman collar did not come into general use until it was prescribed at the first Provincial Synod in 1852. Dr. Milner had the only cope in his district, and his crozier, made like a fishing-rod with a crook at the end of it, served also to open gates as he rode. Chapels were very poor, with nothing but a holy-water stoup at the door, a poor altar and picture, and a tabernacle without a lamp; and the chapels were in back streets and out-of-the-way corners. The church at Moorfields, for which the Corporation of London gave the site in 1817, was one of the first to be seen in a prominent position."[1]

Close of the Century. Retirement of Catholics.—How completely Catholicism had

---

[1] We quote the words of Father John Morris, S.J., from whose *Catholic England in Modern Times*, this chapter is principally compiled.

passed out of the life of the nation, and even out of the knowledge of the average Englishman, has been described by Cardinal Newman in a striking passage of his sermon on "the Second Spring," preached at the First Provincial Council of Westminster: "No longer the Catholic Church in the country," he writes, "nay, no longer, I may say, a Catholic community, but a few adherents of the old religion moving silently and sorrowfully about, as memorials of what had been. 'The Roman Catholics' —not a sect, not even an interest, as men conceived of it—not a body, however small, representative of the great communion abroad, but a mere handful of individuals who might be counted like the pebbles and detritus of the great deluge, and who, forsooth, merely happened to retain a creed which, in its day, indeed, was the profession of a Church. Here a set of poor Irishmen, coming and going at harvest-time, or a colony of them lodged in a miserable quarter of the vast metropolis. There, perhaps, an elderly person, seen walking in the streets, grave and solitary and strange, though noble in bearing, and said to be of good family, and a Roman Catholic. An old-fashioned house, of gloomy appearance, closed in with high walls, with an iron gate and yews, and the report attaching to it that Roman Catholics lived there; but who they were, and what they did, or what was meant by calling them Roman Catholics, no one could tell, though it had an unpleasant sound, and told of form and superstition. And then, perhaps, as we went to and fro, looking with a boy's curious eyes through the great city, we might come to-day upon some Moravian chapel or Quaker's meeting-house, and to-morrow on some chapel of the

Roman Catholics, but nothing was to be gathered from it except that there were lights burning there, and some boys in white swinging censers; and what it all meant could only be learnt from books, from Protestant histories and sermons; and they did not report well of the Roman Catholics, but, on the contrary, deposed that they once had power and had abused it. And then, again, we might on one occasion hear it pointedly put out by some literary man, as the result of his careful investigation, and as a recondite point of information which few knew, that there was this difference between the Roman Catholics of England and the Roman Catholics of Ireland, that the latter had bishops and the former were governed by four officials, called vicars apostolic. Such was about the sort of knowledge possessed of Christians by the heathen of old time, who persecuted its adherents from the face of the earth, and then called them *gens lucifuga*, a people who shunned the light of day."

Amongst the Catholics of those days there was much substantial virtue and sterling merit to be found. The French exiles were greatly edified by what they saw in England: the piety of the laity, the zeal of the clergy. Theirs was the solid unostentatious religion that had been tried in the fire. Their fasting would put Christians in the present day to shame. From time immemorial the fasts observed in England were singularly severe; all Fridays throughout the year, excepting in Paschal time, and many vigils not kept at Rome, were fasting days.[1]

---

[1] These fasts were binding on English Catholics until Pius VII., in 1777, substituted the abstinence on the Wednesdays and Fridays of Advent, for the fasts on many vigils throughout the year. In 1781 the Friday fast, as distinguished from the abstinence, was abrogated.

They thought nothing of going long distances to Mass, and if they only went to the sacraments at somewhat wide intervals, they prepared themselves long beforehand with great care. Mixed marriages were almost unknown, and children were thoroughly instructed in their religion. As a rule there was little intimacy between Catholics and their Protestant neighbours, though there was friendliness and good feeling on both sides.

CHAPTER XXVI.

THE CATHOLIC REVIVAL.

Conversions. The Oxford Movement.—In consequence of the abolition of the penal laws, and the liberty granted to priests to celebrate divine worship in public and to preach, a great increase took place in the number of Catholics, both before the Act of 1829, and still more after it had been passed. It has been calculated that in 1814 there were about 160,000 Catholics, with 390 priests. Twenty-five years later the number of priests in the country was said to be over five hundred, whilst the total number of Catholics seems to have reached 400,000. The bishops reported to the Holy See that conversions were frequent, and that religion was beginning to flourish again. In one year (1837) Bishop Griffiths wrote that in his district (the London District) more than five hundred Protestants had been converted to the Catholic faith. In the north of England also the number of Catholics increased rapidly.

But the conversions that followed and were the fruit of the Oxford movement, were different in quantity and quality from what had gone before.

The Catholic Revival.

The accession of considerable numbers of persons of intelligence and education, men of influence and position, especially clergymen of the Church of England, marked an epoch in our history, and created hopes that time has not altogether weakened. It was the result of a spontaneous external movement—not the work of man, of some great preacher or zealous missionary, but the work of the Holy Spirit, begun and brought to completion in the hearts and minds of men.

The Oxford movement has been one of the strongest possible signs of God's merciful Providence in our regard. It began with a love of historic Christianity and a respect for the Fathers of the Church, which led to a belief in dogma, a trust in sacramental grace, preserved for us by apostolical succession and obedience to ecclesiastical authority— in one word, the Oxford movement rested on the visibility of the Church of God. But its initiators assumed that the visible Church was divided, that the infallible voice was hushed; that the Church of Rome was not to be regarded as the sole teacher and guardian of truth, invested with all the power Christ bequeathed to His Church. In 1841 John Henry Newman wrote the famous Tract XC., to prove that the Thirty-nine Articles might be subscribed by men who held all Roman doctrine; and somewhat later Mr. Ward published his "Ideal of a Christian Church." These writings represented steps in their progress towards the light. The authors soon felt they must go on further. Newman's reception took place in 1845; Ward, Oakeley, Dalgairns, Faber, and many others, were received the same year. The Anglican Church reeled "and still reels" (to quote Lord Beaconsfield's phrase) from the blow, and the growth of the movement, to which the name of Pusey was attached, though Newman was the real leader of it, was contemplated with unfeigned alarm.

The events of the following years did little to allay this feeling, and the Gorham decision, four years later, brought an influx of converts into the Catholic Church only less noteworthy than those of 1845. Among them was Henry Edward Manning, then Archdeacon of Chichester, but destined to become the second Archbishop of Westminster. Many of these converts were Anglican clergymen, a large proportion of them married men, who had to give up affluence and position for comparative poverty, or even real privation and hardship. Every such sacrifice has brought its blessing to the land, and has helped forward the great work of its conversion.

Dr. Wiseman, Vicar Apostolic of the London District, and afterwards Cardinal Archbishop of Westminster, thoroughly understood the Oxford movement, its tendencies and difficulties; and innumerable converts found a friend in him. A quarter of a century has passed since his death, and the Cardinal Archbishop of Westminster who succeeded him was himself a convert. Mr. Newman, after his conversion, was made by Pope Pius IX., first a doctor in divinity, then Superior of the Birmingham Oratory. One of the first acts of the present Head of Christendom, Leo XIII., on his accession to the papal throne, was to create him a Cardinal. His Holiness knew how to appreciate his high culture, deep devotion, and great services to the cause of religion. This, however, is anticipating.

Restoration of the Hierarchy, 1850.—In 1840 Pope Gregory XVI. created eight vicariates in England instead of four. This change proved to be but a preparation for one far more important, the re-establishment of the Hierarchy. The demand for this was of long standing. We have seen that in 1783 the Catholic Committee asked for it, "that the frequent recurrence to Rome might cease." In 1815 Bishop Poynter, in a very different spirit, urgently represented to the Holy See that the restoration of the hierarchy was much needed for the fuller development of Catholic life and work. All the vicars apostolic petitioned for it in 1845, and two years later two of their number went to Rome to press the request. So important a step, however, required much consideration, the course of which was also impeded by the political troubles at Rome in 1848. Hence it was not until September, 1850, that Pius IX. published his Brief erecting the archbishopric of Westminster with twelve suffragan sees. Dr. Wiseman, who had shortly before received a Cardinal's hat, was appointed to be the first Archbishop of Westminster, and at once issued a pastoral letter, announcing the redivision of Catholic England into dioceses, each having a bishop and a territorial title. "Catholic England," he wrote, "has been restored to its orbit in the ecclesiastical firmament, from which its light had long vanished."

Ecclesiastical Titles Act.—These tidings were received with a storm of anger by Protestant England. The English Parliament and Press for the moment lost their balance. *The Times* of October 14th characterized the step as "one of the grossest acts of folly and impertinence which the Court of Rome has ventured to commit since the Crown and people of England threw off its yoke." The Anglican hierarchy presented an address to the Queen, protesting against this attempt to subject our people to a tyranny from which they were freed at the Reformation. Effigies of the Pope and of Cardinal Wiseman were burnt in the towns. The sole legislative effect of this violent outburst of anti-Catholic public feeling was the futile Ecclesiastical Titles Act, which has since been repealed without having once been put into execution. The social effect was deeper, but the excitement died out after a time, and the country that received Cardinal Wiseman on his first arrival with outrage and insult, learnt to value and respect him. His successor, Henry Edward Manning, had no such hostility to live down, but advanced year by year in the appreciation and esteem of Englishmen.

Cardinal Manning's name will be imperishably connected with the education of the Catholic poor, the cause of temperance, and various social questions. By his lucid expositions and untiring energy he changed the face of things in regard to the Catholic poor schools, a work which has been admirably carried on by his successor. In the cause of temperance, by his crusade against the vice of drunkenness which has desolated so many English homes, he roused the conscience of many who had hardly realized the effects of that curse to hearth and home and hindrance to the spread of religion. In regard to social questions, Dr. Hedley, the Bishop of Newport and Menevia, felt justified in saying in his funeral eulogy that the Encyclical of Leo XIII. on " the Conditions of Labour " " owes something, beyond doubt, to the counsels of Cardinal Manning." The part which the Cardinal took at the Vatican Council in exposing the hollowness of the exceptions taken to the opportuneness of a definition on Papal Infallibility has also earned him the gratitude of Catholics.

Development of Catholic Life and Work.—As far as the Church in England is concerned, the re-establishment of the Hierarchy has been an unmixed good. To its action must be largely attributed the astonishing development of Catholic life and work during the half century which has succeeded. Two of the dioceses have since been divided, so that there are now fifteen sees in the ecclesiastical province; and the Apostolic Vicariate of Wales has been separated from the dioceses of Shrewsbury and Newport. Cathedral chapters exist in every diocese, and to these the Holy See has confided the choice of three names to be presented for the appointment of a new bishop when the see falls vacant. The ordinary canon law prevails in all ecclesiastical matters, subject only to such modification as special decrees of the Holy See may have sanctioned; and a body of appropriate local law has arisen from the enactments of our provincial and diocesan synods.

The immigration of the Irish into England—which dates back for its commencement to the Irish rising in 1798, and reached its height in 1846, when the famine in Ireland drove multitudes across the Channel—considerably affected the position of English Catholics, of the poorer classes principally. Without the Irish our numbers would have been smaller and our influence much less. We should also have had comparatively no power. When the

Irish immigration began, there were neither priests nor schools enough for them, and for this reason thousands have been lost to the Catholic faith. But the multiplication in late years of churches and schools, and much more of priests, has resulted in an increased number of children being educated in their religion and of adults practising it. England is not yet provided with enough priests and churches for the needs of her Catholic population, the number of which is said to amount, in England and Wales, to about a million and a half, but a vast change has in this respect passed over the face of the land. As statistics are of more value than vague assertion, it may be well to quote the figures given by Father Morris in proof of the advance of Catholicism since the erection of the Hierarchy in this country. The number of priests, 813 in 1850, has more than trebled itself; of churches, chapels, and stations, we have now 1,387, whereas in 1851 there were 586; of religious houses of men there are 220, against 17 forty years ago; the convents of women, which counted 53, now number 450, nearly nine times as many. Cardinal Manning, who estimated the number of the Catholics of his arch-diocese at 180,000, wrote in 1890 that during his episcopate thirty-three new missions and seventeen stations, making in all fifty new centres, have been founded; and to this increase of centres, not to an increase of population, he attributed the greater number of children attending the schools, and of Easter communicants. In the last twenty-five years the children in the elementary schools have doubled, and the Easter communions have increased by more than a thousand each year. The work of the Catholic School Committee, the Brook Green Training Institute, a college for male teachers, the training colleges of Mount Pleasant and Wandsworth for female teachers, the reformatory schools, &c., testify to the efforts now made for the Catholic education of the poor.

Seminaries.—Of the three principal seminaries for the training of the secular clergy, Ushaw and Old Hall are the second home, as has been shown, of the ancient colleges at Douay and St. Omers. St. Mary's College, Oscott, was founded by Bishop Milner as his episcopal college in 1808. It began with about forty-five boys, of whom a few were intended for the priesthood, and was partly secular and partly ecclesiastical until quite recently, when the seminary founded by Bishop Ullathorne at Olton was removed thither by Bishop Ilsley. Oscott is now exclusively an ecclesiastical seminary. It is unnecessary in this place to mention all the episcopal and other colleges now happily existing in England, and doubtless well known to the reader by name.

Religious Orders and Congregations.—Besides the Jesuit and Benedictine Fathers engaged in educational and missionary work in this country, of whose apostolical labours we have already spoken, several other ancient Orders have reappeared amongst us. There are now in England some sixty sons of St. Francis, divided among the Capuchins and the Observantine and Recollect branches of the Order. The Order of St. Dominic, too, has some important houses, with about forty fathers, in different parts of the kingdom. It will be remembered how in the Middle Ages the members of these Orders were instrumental in infusing new vigour and fervour into the spiritual life of our people at a period when the monasteries, for centuries the centres of missionary zeal, of piety, of learning, had lost their former prestige. The Order of Mount Carmel, which made its home in England when expelled from Palestine, has returned to our shores within the last thirty years, and is once more fulfilling the mission of its rule amongst us. The sons of St. Bernard have our only English abbey with a mitred abbot in the shadow of Charnwood Forest, where they pursue their penitential toils in perpetual silence and contemplation. The Carthusians, who were amongst the first to lay down their lives rather than be unfaithful to Rome, and who were finally driven out of England at the accession of Elizabeth, are now represented in this country once more. St. Hugh's at Parkminster, an offshoot of the Grande Chartreuse, enables us to realize what our old Carthusian cloisters were like. The Premonstratensians are in several places—Storrington, Manchester, Ambleside, as well as at the remarkable priory at Farnborough, erected by the Empress Eugenie as a resting-place for the bodies of her husband and her son. We have also Canons Regular of other Congregations, and two houses of Servites, one of the few religious orders that did not exist in England before the Reformation.

There are also the modern religious congregations to whom English Catholics are greatly indebted for the revival of religion in recent times, and who are the edification of all who witness their poverty and their labours. There are the Fathers of Charity, among whom Father Gentili will always be celebrated as having been the first to preach public missions or retreats in England, a work which he discharged with signal success. These Fathers have several houses in England, together with a school at Ratcliffe. Then there are the Redemptorists, who also devote themselves with great energy and success to the work of parochial missions. Their three houses are at Clapham, Bishop Eton, and Teignmouth, and their number is nearly forty. The Passionists, with their head-quarters at Highgate, have about as many fathers engaged in the English mission. Father Dominic, who died in the odour of sanctity, was a close follower of St. Paul of the Cross in his love for England; it was his privilege to receive the late Cardinal Newman into the Church. Another Passionist to whom we owe much was Father Ignatius Spencer, one of the most notable converts of the nineteenth century, who went about Europe preaching a crusade of prayer for the conversion of England, and laboured zealously for this end until his death in 1865. There are still several congregations left unnamed, amongst them some teaching congregations consisting of brothers only. Besides these, occupying an intermediate position between the religious orders and the secular clergy, are the Oblates of St. Charles at Bayswater, founded by Cardinal Manning, and the Oratorians. The Birmingham Oratory was founded by Cardinal Newman, who was its Superior until his death in 1890. The London Oratory had for many years as its Superior Father Faber, whose hymns and ascetical writings are familiar to all Catholics.

The transfer of the English communities of religious women from the continent to the land of their birth has been spoken of in the preceding chapter. One single community that existed before the Reformation has come down to our time. The Bridgettine nuns of Syon House, Isleworth, went into exile at the commencement of Elizabeth's reign, and, after wandering about in the Low Countries, settled down at Lisbon. Some years since they returned to England, and are now at Chudleigh. Besides the English houses of various orders which the Revolution compelled to seek refuge across the Channel, numerous communities of foreign origin have taken up their abode in our midst. Amongst these special mention must be made of the Good Shepherd, which began its most useful work in London some fifty years ago, and has prospered exceedingly of late years. The congregations of religious women who devote themselves to teaching, and to the care of the poor, have multiplied literally a hundredfold.

If Catholics owe this wide extension and development of the Church's external activity in England in recent times to the restoration of the Hierarchy, it is to the Oxford movement immediately preceding it that they are indebted for the renewed vigour of intellectual life after the stagnation of penal times. There was, it is true, formerly much exemplary piety and vigorous faith amongst them, but, owing to the persecution and oppression of centuries, little intellectual activity and breadth of view, their religion itself was of a silent, unenterprising kind. The new converts were eager to gain for the Church into whose fold they were received, learning and culture that was sorely needed; enlargement of view, a higher standard of mental attainments and general cultivation.

Beatification of the English Martyrs.—Yet more than to these neophytes is the revival of Catholic life in England due to others, many of whom it is the glory of our Universities to have trained; we mean the martyrs who suffered torture and death in defence of the prerogatives of the successors of St. Peter. Oxford in the time of Elizabeth has been called "the nursery of Jesuits," "a recruiting-ground whence year after year students passed over to the colleges abroad," to return as priests to their native land and devote their lives to the Catholic cause. Their labours on earth preserved the faith from extinction in England; their glorious confession has sown the seeds of a harvest that will appear in God's good time; their intercession in heaven has prevailed on behalf of the country that shed their blood, and caused it to be visited again by "the promise of spring."

Some of these brave martyrs Rome has recently raised to our altars. By decrees dated December 4 and 9, 1886, and May 13, 1895, the Holy See permitted us to venerate sixty-three of them publicly under the title of Blessed. Besides this there are 253 others, into the story of whose deaths it purposes to examine, and to whom, therefore, the Pope gives the title of Venerable Servants of God. The names of 316 have thus been held up for our veneration, almost all of whom died on the scaffold or the gibbet. The cases of forty-four others have been postponed for further consideration; they are chiefly those who died for their faith in prison.

In rendering to those of her sons who made the generous sacrifice of their lives in defence of the truth, the glory due to them, England must not overlook the thousands who preferred to suffer imprisonment, fines, exile, every kind of disabilities, to live in poverty and obscurity during the long night that lasted over two centuries, rather than renounce their allegiance to the See of Peter, and deny the doctrines held by their forefathers. The impious and cruel oaths invented by the parliaments of Charles II., and of William and Mary, had for their object not, as was alleged, to promote loyalty and civil order, but to insult and wound Catholics in their tenderest feelings. They were framed so as to constrain them, if possible, to abjure the beliefs and the devotions nearest to their heart, the Presence of our Lord in the Holy Sacrifice of the Mass, the worship of the immaculate Mother of God. " England is the only country," we quote the words of Cardinal, then Dr., Wiseman, "that has persisted in and renewed in every generation formal acts of apostacy, exacting from every sovereign in the name of the nation, and from all who aspired to office or dignity, specific declarations that they held Catholic truths to be superstitious and idolatrous. This national sin calls for contrary acts, as explicit and as formal, to remove its bad effects." The writer of these words, when he became the leader of England's established hierarchy, laboured most successfully in the work of reparation; he introduced more frequent celebrations of Holy Mass, more frequent Benediction of the Blessed Sacrament, the devotion of our Lady's Rosary and of the month of May.

England dedicated anew to the Mother of God and to St. Peter.—The result of Cardinal Wiseman's labours is seen in the formal and public reparation which it has been the privilege of his latest successor to make. The act of consecration whereby England was again dedicated to her ancient patrons, the holy Mother of God and the Prince of the Apostles, was almost the first act of the present archbishop, Cardinal Vaughan, whom Westminster received from the hands of the Pope in 1892.

On the Feast of St. Peter and St. Paul, 1893, pontifical high mass was celebrated in the church of the Oratorian Fathers, at which as many as possible of the bishops, and representatives of the clergy, regular and secular, and of the laity from all parts of the kingdom assisted. A sermon was preached on our Lady's Dowry, and an act of consecration to the Blessed Virgin was read aloud at this function. In the afternoon of the same day, pontifical vespers were sung, followed by a sermon on St. Peter, an act of consecration to the Prince of the Apostles, and a procession and *Te Deum*.

Invitations to Reunion.—In April, 1895, Leo XIII. addressed a letter to those " Englishmen who seek the Kingdom of Christ in the Unity of Faith "—a happy phrase whereby he sought to reach every English heart which mourns over the scandal of religious division now so conspicuous, though unknown before the Reformation. He reminded them of the affectionate solicitude for the souls of their ancestors displayed by the Popes who sent them their first apostles; and assured them that it has never ceased to fill the hearts of all who have sat in the chair of Peter, or to cause them to take whatever steps seemed feasible at the time to give effect to their good desires. He exhorted them not to be dismayed by difficulties, but to multiply their prayers to God, whose providence, when men undertake arduous work with a sincere and right intention, finds in the very greatness of the difficulty a bright illustration of its power.

The year 1896 witnessed two further efforts on the part of Leo XIII. to draw Anglicans back to the Catholic Church. On June 29, His Holiness issued an Encyclical (*Satis Cognitum*) on the Unity of the Church, the purport of which is that if ever Christendom is to be reunited, it will not be through federation based on a system of compromises or delusive explanations, but by a return of obedience to the Apostolic See. It reasserts as essential the doctrine of a Supremacy by Divine Right, as distinguished from a so-called Primacy of Honour. It also reasserts, as an indispensable condition for valid episcopal jurisdiction, that the Bishop shall be united by obedience and communion with the Roman Pontiff, so that Bishops who are separated from the Holy See, whether they have valid orders or not, are, so far as jurisdiction is concerned, no Bishops at all.[1]

Condemnation of Anglican Orders.—On September 18, this Encyclical was followed by a very important Bull on Anglican Orders (*Apostolicæ Curæ*). Certain High Anglicans had mooted the matter of Orders as one on which a decision from the Pope would be very acceptable; and a small knot of French writers had somewhat lost their way in dealing with this subject, which required an intimate knowledge of English affairs, such as is seldom possessed by foreigners. The first result of

[1] *Cf. Companion to the Encyclical Satis Cognitum*, by the Rev. Sydney F. Smith, S.J. (Catholic Truth Society, 1s.), for an excellent collection of answers to objections raised by Anglicans.

the matter being stirred was that evidence was drawn from the Archives at Rome to the effect that Anglican Orders had been thoroughly investigated, and emphatically condemned by Cardinal Pole, and that the result of the Cardinal's investigation had been confirmed by the Pope. Documents of the most unequivocal character were discovered by Dom Gasquet, O.S.B. This condemnation of Anglican Orders in the sixteenth century proceeded on the ground that the Form of Ordination, the essential portion of the rite, had been changed, and lost its value.

Nevertheless, a Commission was ordered by Leo XIII. to sit at Rome, and a most thorough examination of all the documents bearing on the question was instituted, which resulted in an unanimous condemnation of the validity of Anglican Orders. They had been conferred by a Form, which differed essentially from all known forms in the Catholic Church. In this new-fangled Form, invented by Cranmer, and unhappily acquiesced in by the English authorities, there is no designation of the Order to be conferred, either by express, or equivalent, mention of the order, or by allusion to the power of sacrifice, such as is conferred on priests in the Catholic Church. The "Form," it must be remembered, is not, in theological language, the whole rite, but that which, in close conjunction with the matter of the Sacrament, determines the matter to a special end. In the Sacrament of Holy Orders, the essential matter is, at least, imposition of hands; and the Form consists of a prayer designating the Order or its powers, thus determining the imposition to its special effect. All that could thus determine the "matter" had been eliminated by Cranmer, with the intention of doing away with the idea of a Sacrificial Priesthood in the sense in which those terms are understood in the Catholic Church. Consequently, even the use of those terms (which, however, do not occur in the new Form) ceased to have its previous significance. So that the ministry of the Church of England has been evacuated of the central power which belongs to the ministry of the Catholic Church.

This Bull, the result of a "Feria Quinta" Session (as it is called) of the Commission under the personal presidency of the Pope—*i.e.*, of a specially solemn session—has reaffirmed the judgement of previous Popes, and declared the matter to be irrevocably settled. A special value attaches to it also through its having given the reasons for the previous and present condemnations.

INDEX.

A

Abingdon, 101, 103
Adrian I., 89
  ,,   IV., 189
Agatho, St., 62, 71, 95
Aidan, St., 37, 66, 133
Alban, St., 5, 12
Alcuin, 79, 93, 129, 133, 140
Aldhelm, 74, 81, 129, 278
Aldred, St., 118, 122
Alexander II., 117, 148
  ,,   III., 122, 197, 199, 205, 208, 224
  ,,   IV., 240
Alfred, 91, 94, 96, 99, 103, 127, 278
Alien priories, 305, 308, 345
Ambleside, 503
Ampleforth, 488
Angles, 18, 59
Anglia, East, 117
Anglican Orders condemned, 510
Anglo-Saxons, 96, 124, 130, 266, 301
Anabaptists, 361
Annates, 327
Anne Boleyn, 319, 327, 330, 334, 341

Anselm, St., 160, 167, 177, 196, 226, 266
Antipopes, 148, 195, 301, 307
Arles, Council of, 7
Armada, 427
Articles (Six), 360, 364, 374
  ,,   (Thirty-nine), 368, 400, 409, 497
Arundel, Archbishop, 283, 293, 297
Augustine, St., 18, 77, 89, 98, 129, 133
Augustinians, 239

B

Babington Conspiracy, 426
Bacon, Friar, 230, 269, 445
Ball, John, 274
Bangor, 23, 25
Bardney Abbey, 95
Beads, 132
Bec, 149, 155, 159, 163, 175
Becket, St. Thomas, 186, 189, 203, 228, 236, 266, 296, 359
Bede, Venerable, 76, 133, 229, 278
Bede-roll, 142
Bergholt Monastery, 488
Benedict, St., 132
Benedict Biscop, St., 52, 62, 72, 76, 93, 129

Index.

Benedictines, 63, 181, 446, 488
Benefices, 256, 261, 289, 327
Bernicia, 32
Bible, see Scripture
Birinus, St., 38, 41, 75, 257
Bishops, Election of, 170, 216, 257
Black Death, 253, 274, 268, 303
Blois, see Henry
Boniface VIII., 248
,, St., 83, 86, 140
Bonner, Bishop, 364, 382, 395
Bridgettines, 505
British Bishops, 7, 16, 23

C

Caedmon, 73, 129, 137, 278
Calvin, 390
Calvinism, 368, 446
Cambridge, 229, 301, 323
Canterbury, 19, 20, 57, 59, 149, 150, 197, 217
Carmelites, 239, 446, 503
Carthusians, 213, 315, 338, 342, 349, 503
Catholicism, progress of, 502
Catherine of Aragon, 300, 318, 327, 375, 385
Celestine I., 10
,, III., 104
Chad, St., 44, 55, 57
Chancellor, 265, 306, 320, 324, 344, 382, 486
Chapels, 479, 491
Chaplains, 411
Charlemagne, 79, 93
Charles I., 441, 443, 447
,, II., 453, 456
,, V., 314, 371, 373, 394
Charter, see Magna Charta.
Charterhouse, 405
Chartreuse, 215
Chepstow, 10
Chicheley, 291, 294, 305, 308
Cisalpine Club, 480, 490, 499
Cistercians, 181, 185

Claudia, 3
Clement VII., 321, 328, 330, 337, 339
Clergy, Benefit of, 250, 305, 419
Columba, St., 16, 50, 53, 66
Columban, St., 16, 82
Committee of laymen, 476
Common Prayer, Book of, 364, 368, 397, 401, 405, 412
Commons, 274, 289, 347, 378, 397, 447, 484
Commonwealth, 449
Communion, 134, 136
Conquest, Norman, 121, 124, 130, 187, 218
Constitutions of Clarendon, 195, 206, 208
,, of Arundel, 297
Convocation, 272, 289, 324, 326, 332, 361, 397
Councils—
  Arles, 7
  Bari, 167
  Calcuith, 90
  Calne, 106
  Chalcedon, 58
  Clarendon, 195
  Clermont, 171
  Cloveshoe, 88, 124
  Constance, 137
  Constantinople, 171
  Hatfield, 62
  Hertford, 57
  Lateran, 171
  ,, 233
  Lyons, 241
  Nicæa, 51, 55
  Northampton, 196
  Oxford, 229
  Rheims, 185
  Rockingham, 163
  Westminster (1102), 173
  ,, (1125), 179
  ,, (1163), 194
  Whitby, 51
  Winchester, 105

Index. 515

Cnut, 111, 117, 119, 127
Cranmer, 269, 327, 329, 361, 364, 367, 374, 384
Cromwell, Thomas, 343, 348, 353, 359, 363
,, Oliver, 450, 453
Croyland, 95
Crusades, 210, 229, 233, 235
Curia, 267, 292
Customs, Royal, 173, 194
Cuthbert, St., 40, 63, 66, 93

D

Damascus, St., 9
Damianus, 4
Danes, 92, 94, 97, 103, 109, 111
Danegelt, 114, 193
Defender of the Faith, 317, 360
Deira, 18, 32, 73
Divorce, 58, 319, 323, 375
,, 313. *See* Catherine of Aragon.
Disabilities of Catholics, 466, 485
,, relief from, 473, 480, 483
Doles, 139
Dominicans, 231, 446, 503
Donatists, 7
Dorchester, 39, 41, 115, 150
Douay, 415, 487
Downside, 488
Dunstan, St., 99, 106, 111, 125, 136, 174
Durham, 114, 164, 306

E

Eadmar, 177
Easter, 22, 24, 26, 49, 51, 54, 58, 76
Ecclesiastical Titles Act, 499
Edmund, St. (King), 96, 100
,, of Canterbury, 231, 242, 259

Edward, St., the Confessor, 27, 65, 114, 119, 121, 123, 223, 509
,, I., 245, 247, 255
,, III., 252, 288, 290, 293, 345
,, VI., 362, 369, 371, 374, 385, 389, 391, 399, 402
Edwy, 100
Egbert (King), 55, 93
,, (Archbishop), 77, 79, 87, 133, 134, 136
Egwin, St., 80
Eleutherius, St., 3
Elgiva, 101
Elizabeth, Queen, 292, 329, 354, 387, 389, 391, 426, 430, 447, 462, 465
Elphege, St., 109, 150, 155
English Martyrs, 507
Erasmus, 311, 313, 324
Erastianism, 336
Ethelbert, St. (King), 19
Ethelred, 96, 109, 114, 117, 121, 129
Ethelwold, 102, 105
Ethelwulf, 94
Eucharist, 132
Eutychianism, 62
Evesham, 80, 130, 244
Eynsham, 231

F

Fathers of Charity, 504
Felix, St. (Bishop), 33
Finan, St., 49, 70
Fines, 175, 408, 413, 432, 438, 442, 465
Fires of London, 108, 452, 456
Fisher, Bishop, 313, 318, 333, 339, 385, 399
Fitzurse, 204
Flambard, 158, 162
Fountains Abbey, 181, 185
Franciscans, 231, 446, 503

French Emigrés, 491
Friesland, 16, 39, 60, 83
Fugatius, 4

G

Gardiner (Bishop), 362, 363, 376, 379, 382
Garnet (Father J.), 434
George, St., 294
George III., 474, 481
Gilds, 138, 301, 369
Glastonbury, 81, 99, 101, 128, 133, 154
Godwin, 116
Gordon Riots, 473
Gregory I., 17, 20, 24, 47, 50, 89, 125, 180
 ,, II., 83
 ,, VII., 174
 ,, IX., 233
 ,, XI., 271
 ,, XIII., 416
 ,, XVI., 499
Grey, Lady Jane, 372, 374
Grosseteste, 238
Guilds, see Gilds.
Gunpowder Plot, 433

H

Harold, 122, 229
Henry I., 169, 178, 180, 187, 196, 226, 354
 ,, II., 186, 189, 207, 213, 226
 ,, III., 27, 228, 234
 ,, IV., 283, 297, 304
 ,, V., 290, 297, 346
 ,, VI., 291, 293, 296
 ,, VII., 178, 303, 306, 308, 315
 ,, VII., 69, 72, 207, 286, 292, 299, 306, 312, 315, 318, 325, 332, 340, 351, 354, 357, 373, 376, 386, 397, 402, 459, 462
 ,, of Blois, 184

Hereford, St. Thomas of, 247
 ,, (See of), 118, 247, 403
Heresy, punishment of, 314, 380, 382, 388
Hierarchy, Restoration of the, 499
Homage, 170, 171, 176
Hooper, 369, 384
Hubert, Archbishop, 211
Hugh, St., 213
Humanists, 316

I

Images, 299, 360, 366
Ina, 75, 81, 91, 127, 133
Innocent II., 183, 185
 ,, III., 212, 219, 221, 227, 243
 ,, IV., 240, 242, 243, 261
 ,, XI., 469
Inquisition, 386
Interdict, 184, 205, 221
Investiture, 169, 179
Iona, 16, 47, 50, 133, 140

J

James I., 431, 436, 439, 441, 445, 447, 448, 466, 468
 ,, II., 456, 459, 461, 464, 469
Jarrow, 76, 93
Jesuits, 418, 427, 433, 436, 446, 454, 458, 461, 487, 503
John, St., of Beverley, 63, 65, 73, 77
John, King, 209, 215, 220, 228, 250, 255
Joseph of Arimathea, 2
Jubilee, 508
Julius II, 327, 330
 ,, III., 376, 378
Jurisdiction (spiritual), 174, 176, 179, 208, 243, 333, 338

K

King's Book, 361
Kitchin, 399, 402

L

Lanfranc, 149, 174, 196
Langton, 219, 226, 228, 231, 233, 249, 259
Latimer, 361, 374, 383
Latin Service, 133, 365, 366, 375
Laud, 443, 445, 447
Laurence (Archbishop), 26, 29
Legates, 89, 152, 165, 178, 185, 198, 208, 210, 223, 230, 234, 241, 244, 321, 356, 376, 386, 410, 445, 461
Lent, 136, 138
Leo IX., 122
,, X., 313, 317
,, XIII., 498, 508
Liberty of the Church, 192
,, Worship, 461
Lichfield (See), 44, 57, 89, 90
Lindisfarne, 37, 40, 42, 45, 68, 92, 140
Lincoln (See), 213, 299, 306, 320
Liturgy, 364, 375, 407
Lollards, 269, 279, 285, 359, 364, 382
Longchamps (Bishop), 210
London (See), 4, 27
,, (Fire of), 108
,, (Great Fire of), 452, 456
Lords (House of), 378, 397, 457, 486
Lucius, 3
Luther, 269, 286, 314, 317, 324
Lutterworth, 272, 277, 287

M

Magna Charta, 226, 249
Malmesbury Abbey, 102
Manning, Cardinal, 500
Margaret, Countess of Salisbury, 358
Marriage, 58, 318, 405, 481
,, *See* Catherine of Aragon
Martin, St., 9
Martin I., 62

Martin V., 291, 294
Martyrs (English), 338, 416, 419, 422, 435, 441, 457, 506
Mary, B. Virgin. 80, 108, 129, 131, 139, 204, 232, 251, 294, 297, 359, 507, 510
,, Month of, 508
,, Dowry of, 297, 509
,, *See* Rosary, Tewkesbury
,, (Queen of England), 319, 371, 373, 376, 378, 385, 387, 391, 393, 403, 404, 407, 412, 446
,, (Queen of Scots), 409, 412, 427, 432
Mass, 133, 134, 277, 335, 366, 373, 379, 382, 395, 407, 420, 466, 492
Mendicant Friars, 271, 308
Mercia, 34, 35, 39, 41, 55, 63, 87, 89, 90, 109
Milner (Bishop), 483, 492
Miracles, 23, 69, 114, 123, 130, 206 247, 452
Monasteries, 107, 147, 233, 252, 254, 353
,, Suppression of, 345
Monothelite, 62
More, B. Thomas, 311, 313, 314, 324, 340, 342, 385

N

Newman, Cardinal, 497, 504
Nicholas II., 118
,, IV., 247
Ninian, St., 8
Normans, 115, 122, 147, 202
Northumbria, 30, 33, 40, 51, 54, 55, 57, 63, 65, 68, 71, 76, 89, 92

O

Oath of Abjuration, 449
,, Allegiance, 439, 467
,, Supremacy, 333, 467

O'Connell, 484
Oblates, 505
Odo, 97, 101,,150
Olaf, St., 108
Oratory (Birmingham), 498, 505
,, (London), 505, 510
Ordeal, 152
Orders, Anglican, condemned, 510
Ornaments, 131, 295, 351, 360, 420, 451, 492
Oswald, St., 36, 39, 95
Oswy, 41
Oxford, 187, 229, 244, 269, 275, 308, 313, 315, 357, 412, 444, 461, 480, 506
,, Movement, 496, 505

P

Pallium, 21, 56, 87, 101, 116, 118, 151, 165, 166, 257, 384
Pandulph, 225
Parker, 400, 401, 412
Parliament, First Completed, 245
Paul, St., of the Cross, 504
Paul III, 339, 357
,, V., 439
Paulinus, St., 30, 32, 35, 133
Passionists, 504
Peckham, 246, 259, 293
Pelagian Heresy, 10
Penal Code, 436
,, Laws, 336, 439, 450, 457, 462, 467, 470
Penance, 135, 205
Penda, 39
Persons, Father, S.J., 418, 487
Peter, St., Patron of England, 294, 508
Peter's Pence, 91, 112, 118, 138, 173, 250
Peterborough, 95, 102
Pilgrimage, 87, 112, 121, 125, 207, 283
,, of Grace, 347

Pius IV., 409
,, V., 327, 408, 409
,, VII., 483, 490, 494
,, VIII., 129
,, IX., 498, 499
Pole (Cardinal), 357, 376, 378, 386, 388
Pontigny, 199, 236
Præmunire, 262, 287, 291, 293, 322, 325, 336, 338, 379, 395, 413, 477
Prayers for the Departed, 140, 143
Preachers, Poor, 277
Premonstratensians, 503
Provisors, Statute of, 261, 291
Pudens, 3

R

Recusants, 414, 429, 432, 440, 447, 451
Relics, 7, 122
Remigius, St., 150
Richard I., 208, 210, 215, 224
,, II., 283, 292, 297
,, of Canterbury, 206, 211, 215, 259
Ridley, 361, 364, 372, 384
Ripon (See), 63
,, Abbey, 65
Rochester (See), 162, 164
Rosary, 131, 251, 413, 508

S

Salisbury (Use), 155
Scapular, 239
School, Saxon, 91
Schools, 296, 302, 308, 369, 461, 466, 480, 502
Scotland, 179
Scripture, 229, 277, 311, 314, 360, 380
Sebert, 27
Seminaries, 416, 429, 431, 480, 487, 502
Simony, 118, 149

Sixtus III., 133
Soul-book, 142
Spiritualities, 224
Stephen, King, 181, 196
Stigand, 115, 116, 122, 149, 150
Stock, St. Simon, 239
Supremacy, Royal, 332, seq.
Sussex, 46
Sweyn, 108, 114
Swithun, St., 94, 125

T

Taxes, 193, 211, 234, 241, 245, 247, 264, 468, 479
Tertullian, 4
Tests, 477, 482
Tewkesbury, 452
Theobald, 185, 188, 189, 196, 200, 226
Theodore, St., 56, 58, 68, 94, 136, 145
Thomas, of York, 150
  ,, of Canterbury, see Becket
Thurstan, 183, 185
Tithes, 94, 235, 247, 251
Tonsure, 22, 54, 56
Toleration, Act of, 479, 481
Topcliffe, Pursuivant, 423
Tower of London, 285, 333, 338, 340, 374, 422, 434, 447, 463
Tract XC., 497
Transubstantiation, 360, 367
Tyburn, 340, 417, 424, 458
Tyndal, 287, 360

U

Uniformity, Act of, 397, 416
Universities, 187, 229, 289, 369, 397, 400, 480
Urban II., 163
  ,, V., 255
  ,, VIII., 441, 445

V

Vassalage, 222
Vicars Apostolic, 440, 460, 469, 477

W

Walsingham, 421, 427
  ,, Our Lady of, 298
Warham (Archbishop), 310, 324, 329
Wellington, Duke of, 485
Wells (See), 118
Wessex, 40, 46, 76
Westminster, 27, 120, 405, 466, 493
  ,, (See) 498
  ,, Abbey, 121, 245, 373
William I., 119, 123, 130, 146, 156
  ,, II., 157, 169, 171, 180, 196
  ,, III., 464, 468
  ,, of Wykeham, 264, 265, 296, 305, 308
Wiseman (Cardinal), 498, 500
Wulstan, St., 119, 228
Wyclif, 269, 286, 303, 359

Y

York (See of), 4, 14, 68, 90, 151, 359
  ,, (Minster), 32, 128, 133

www.ingramcontent.com/pod-product-compliance
Lightning Source LLC
Chambersburg PA
CBHW031942290426
44108CB00011B/640